I0814599

Atrocity

Atrocity

A Literary History

Bruce Robbins

STANFORD UNIVERSITY PRESS
Stanford, California

Stanford University Press
Stanford, California

Printed in the United States of America on acid-free, archival-quality paper

Library of Congress Cataloging-in-Publication Data
Names: Robbins, Bruce, author.
Title: Atrocity : a literary history / Bruce Robbins.
Description: Stanford : Stanford University Press, 2025. | Includes bibliographical references and index.
Identifiers: LCCN 2024037988 (print) | LCCN 2024037989 (ebook) | ISBN 9781503640559 (cloth) | ISBN 9781503641419 (ebook)
Subjects: LCSH: Violence in literature. | Atrocities in literature. | LCGFT: Literary criticism.
Classification: LCC PN56.V53 R63 2025 (print) | LCC PN56.V53 (ebook) | DDC 809.933552—dc23/eng/20240816
LC record available at https://lccn.loc.gov/2024037988
LC ebook record available at https://lccn.loc.gov/2024037989

Cover design: David Drummond
Cover image: David Drummond and Shutterstock

"Of the gods we hold the belief, and of men we know, that by a necessity of their nature wherever they have power they always rule. And so in our case since we neither enacted this law nor when it was enacted were the first to use it, but found it in existence and expect to leave it in existence for all time, so we make use of it, well aware that both you and others, if clothed with the same power as we are, would do the same thing."

The Athenians to the Melians, 415 BC, Thucydides,
History of the Peloponnesian War, book 5, chapter 105

"All I said is that we will do to you what you would do to us."

Brigade Commander Gutman to the Palestinian Dignitaries,
Lydda, July 1948

Contents

Preface

Mass violence against noncombatants did not always have a name. Once upon a time, it was more likely to be seen as a misfortune than an injustice. Like conquest, of which mass violence against noncombatants is a reliable feature, what we now call atrocity was not seen as inviting indignation. Often, like conquerors, it was hailed as heroic—the more dead, the more heroism. Something had to happen in order for mass violence to be paired with outrage. Minds had to change, and not just about the legitimacy of conquest. A lot of violence had to be meted out and suffered before a concept of atrocity could arise, not to speak of the possibility—in modern times, more than a possibility, though less than the rule—of writers accusing their own country of atrocities committed against the inhabitants of other countries.

When I was fishing for a title for this book, I tried out "The Invention of Atrocity" on some friends. One preferred "Manufacturing Atrocity." Another suggested "Fabricating Atrocity." These suggestions didn't dispel my unease about proposing a title phrase whose structure was so painfully unoriginal. A search of Google Scholar yielded over 7,000,000 hits for titles of the form "The Invention of X," one of them Gaurav Desai's essay "The Invention of Invention." Desai's essay came out in 1993. Discomfort with the formula goes back at least three decades, if not more. I surrendered. But the friendly counterproposals did help me clarify one thing about what I was trying to say, even if I eventually gave up on that title as uninspiring. As Desai observes, "the invention of" always refers both to making and to faking. In the minds of readers, it's the faking that most often seems paramount, no doubt because of the desire to credit the exposure of its constructedness as a critique of the object constructed. Desai gives the examples of primitive society, virginity, and tribalism. All of them are instances of fakery (that is, they are misleading), and all are demonstrably harmful in their effects. Among the first items that came up in my Google Scholar search were the inventions of development, the Mizrahim, monolingualism, kleptomania, and nature. In each of these cases, the assumption seems to be that we would be better off without the thing invented. That assumption holds even more dramatically for "fabricating" and "manufacturing," as in *Manufacturing Consent*, Noam Chomsky's coauthored 1988 protest against media manipulation.

The concept of atrocity does not belong in this company. It departs from recent critical habits in presenting an unembarrassed example of making that is not an example of faking. One argument of this book is that, though there are obvious grounds for skepticism, and though failing to embrace skepticism may make the argument seem unenlightened to the point of perversity, the invention of the concept was on the whole a good thing. The concept was manufactured, but its manufacture is not something to be regretted or rescinded. Before the term was invented, the terrible violence it registers was largely not registered, or was not thought of as terrible in the way we, or most of us, would now understand it to be. Although registering that violence has not resulted in all the actual benefits that might have been hoped for, and has resulted in some collateral damage, like inciting further violence and distracting from injustice that doesn't take openly violent forms, it is surely better for the human species that the concept now exists and the terribleness of the violence is widely acknowledged and deplored. Anyone coming to this book expecting the revelation of sinister powers conspiring to produce a piece of injurious distortion will therefore be disappointed. But even if that is the reaction, I hope the disappointment will serve as an opportunity to rethink what shape modern history has taken. If there was a prolonged period in which indignation at mass violence against noncombatants enjoyed no adequate or convenient mode of expression, it's not because noncombatants were not slaughtered on a large scale. Adding this old violence to the newer forms of violence with which we are more familiar does more than extend a modern name to an already-existing premodern thing. Expanding the temporal frame of moral judgment cannot help but have an effect on judgments in the present.

Indignation, an indispensable component of atrocity, is anger in the face of perceived unfairness. It is not just anger, that quintessential political emotion. Nor is it just the anger that follows the suffering of a harm, one's own or someone else's. Rather, indignation is the anger provoked by someone or something held to be wrong or unworthy. The sufferer is in the right. And the sufferer knows it. Their anger is righteous anger. Like dignity, which has the same root and originally belonged only to the nobility, indignation may include a sense of disdain. Hence the possibility of an unpleasant aftertaste. Disdain presumes a certain entitlement. Democracy, for all its imperfections, has increased the number of the entitled and made indignation as pervasive as it now is. (Not always for the better.) Since the period following World War II, a crucial period in the history of the concept of atrocity, dignity, presented now as a universal, has been central to the discourse of human rights. As a way of registering indignation at mass violence, the understanding that norms and solidarities have been violated, the concept of atrocity cannot be disentangled from the history of human rights and (not quite the same thing) the history of humanitarianism. But my subject here is literary representations of atrocity, and there is thus a certain tension, I hope a productive one, between what the discourse of human rights has to say about atrocity and what other sorts of texts do, foremost among them literary texts. A tension, and also an overlap. Dignity and indignation are among the raw materials out of which narratives are fashioned, and changes in how those materials are allocated seems sure to have narrative effects. The hypothesis presents itself that accounts of atrocity will follow a trajectory of literary democratization, though (as I will show) it's not the trajectory that might have been expected.

Indignation had a moment, in the second decade of the twenty-first century, when it became the central organizing principle of anti-austerity protesters, first in Spain in 2011, then in Greece and elsewhere, including Occupy Wall Street. As an organizing principle, indignation proved both powerful and imprecise, the imprecision allowing it to gather up (like populism) potentially incompatible kinds of outrage, including in this instance those of the proto-fascist right—perhaps too many to maintain its political integrity. (In this sense it resembles anger.) I do not try to run away from that imprecision, which also characterizes responses to atrocity. But my intention is not so much to delimit or defend it as to give indignation about violence a literary history, and a much longer history. My working assumption is that even something as apparently natural and inevitable as a sense of victimhood had to be born, and that its birth (or fashioning) required some of that sense of entitlement or self-worth that comes of what we have learned to call agency. The victims are not always better seen as the vanquished. They did not always arm themselves with agency and go into battle with their victimizers. But Nietzsche, who has taught many of us to despise passive suffering, is right at least that passive suffering is not enough to make history. Suffering alone was never enough to make history do anything but repeat. It's not enough to look for even when one looks into the very heart of atrocity.

One objection I anticipate is that war will always produce what we now call atrocities, so the real problem is not atrocities but war. War *is* the atrocity. The antimilitarism of the Vietnam War generation that I carry in my personal baggage does not lead to the conclusion that to reject atrocity is meaningless because what must be rejected is war itself. I never felt I had the right to rebuke the Vietnamese for their resistance to their American invaders. Ditto, more recently, for Ukrainians resisting the Russians and Palestinians resisting the Israelis. Violence is always terrible, but sometimes flagrant injustice in the absence of violence is worse. Atrocity, as the most terrible violence, remains therefore something to be set apart.[1] Another objection to be anticipated is that, the world being in the state it's in, to celebrate the invention of a concept that has had so little effect on the state of the world is in bad taste, or a symptom of moral laziness or complacency. The desire to avoid moral complacency at all costs is itself a symptom of our times, in my view, and one that obscures the true complexity of our times, which contain such moral achievements as the naming of atrocity, atrocity as a cause of collective shame. If such a thing has indeed been achieved, by whatever twisted means, it ought to have a recognized place in our history, including the history of literature. Ethnocentrism being as pervasive and as violence-producing as it has been, the concept certainly also deserves a place in the history of cosmopolitanism. The overlap between these two histories does not cover the whole moral history of humankind, but the premise here will be, from the perspective of the full archive of atrocity stories old and new, that history will look different.

This book can be thought of, then, as an experiment in cosmopolitan literary history. Definitions of cosmopolitanism are notoriously fuzzy. At one end of the spectrum is a big-tent version that celebrates as cosmopolitan any and all traces of transnational or transethnic hybridity. A chillier, less populated pole demands the prioritizing of the welfare of all members of the species equally, whether they are known and loved or distant strangers. Another definition, closer to the latter but not identical with it, is the ability to take critical distance from one's own culture—not in general, but in a moment of urgency when one's own culture has (for example) committed violence against the members of another, most likely in wartime, and when the pressure to fall into line will therefore be most intense. This understanding of cosmopolitanism, universalizing but also situated, has been somewhat neglected in the critical discourse, but it will be assumed here. This book takes special interest in representations of atrocity that have been committed by one's own people—what I will refer to, with legalistic awkwardness, as national self-indictments. The premise is that these self-indictments are valuable both from a moral and from an aesthetic point of view even if, as will be apparent, there are never enough of them and such examples as exist are often somewhat unsatisfying. However limited in number and quality, they offer a stopgap answer to the objection to the atrocity story genre that George Orwell records in his diary for June 11, 1942. The Germans have massacred all the male inhabitants of the Czech town of Lidice, sent the women to concentration camps, sent the children to be "reeducated," razed the village to the ground and changed its name.[2] They have done this because the population of Lidice had harbored the assassins of a high Nazi official, Reinhard Heydrich, who as it turns out (Orwell could not know this at the time) had also been a leading architect of the "final solution" for Europe's Jews and thus deserved assassination even more than other, run-of-the-mill Nazis. The announcement comes via the BBC, but it also comes from the Germans themselves, who are obviously not afraid to publicize what they have done. Publicizing it, they assume, will discourage resistance elsewhere. "It does not particularly surprise me that people do this kind of thing," Orwell tells his diary, "nor even that they announce that they are doing them. What does impress me, however, is that other people's reaction to such happenings is governed solely by the political fashion of the moment."[3] What surprises Orwell is that the news of an act of disproportionate and indiscriminate violence aimed at civilians does not give rise to instinctive, universal horror and indignation. Instead, he says, people react according to their preexisting political loyalties. Political loyalties are so strong that they cannot be overridden even by an atrocity as atrocious as the destruction of a whole village, most of the inhabitants of which could not have had anything whatsoever to do with the killing of Heydrich, however justified we may judge that killing to have been. Simple human decency, confronted by the simple facts, seems unable to suspend partisanship. To Orwell, this failure comes as an especially unpleasant revelation. He wanted very badly to believe in the power of the bare facts. He based his own politics—socialist politics, as is often forgotten—as well as his strategies for getting his politics across to the unconverted on the assumption that human decency, once put in clear, forceful possession of the facts, is capable of overriding differences of allegiance, whatever their basis, and coming to an independent, fair-minded conclusion.

If this is the argument that Orwell was preparing, the slaughter at Lidice does not seem an ideal example of it, and that is perhaps why he did not put the event to direct use in an essay. Could there really have been, as Orwell grumpily suggests, people around him in England in mid-1942 who were ready to "write off all horror stories as 'propaganda'" (387), including horror stories about the *Nazis*? That seems unlikely.[4] Orwell would surely have done better to cite some of the earlier atrocities that he lists on the next page of his diary. They are arranged in two columns, the first titled "Believed by the Right," the second "Believed by the Left." In the first column are, for example, atrocities attributed to Sinn Fein and the Bolsheviks; in the second, atrocities attributed to the Black and Tans in Ireland, the Americans in Nicaragua, and the British in India (387). The ones Orwell knew best were from British rule in India, where he had served (in Burma) as a military policeman, and from the Spanish Civil War, where he fought for the Left and where each side did indeed point to the atrocities committed by the other while ignoring or justifying those its own partisans had perpetrated. He himself had taken sides, and he seemed to want to continue taking sides. And yet the logic of atrocity as he saw it pushed against side-taking—that is, against politics. By politics, Orwell means taking sides and doggedly sticking to your own side no matter what. And that in turn means, he suggests, that your side, whichever side it may be, is finally not worth sticking to. Political adhesiveness allows for no space outside itself. And that space seems unworthy of adhesion—if not morally uninhabitable, then unspeakable, placing a burden on speech that no principled speaker will want to tolerate.[5] This book does not pretend that atrocity is always a reliable guide to political side-taking, but in documenting a history of side-taking that refuses to be contented with national loyalty, it brings us a step closer to a politics that is worth the commitment, or what has come to be called a cosmopolitics.

Cosmopolitanism is also relevant here because of its unresolved business with deep time—that is, with the scale of geological, archaeological, and environmental temporality that notoriously makes the concerns of modernity (a highly contested concept that will be at issue below) look different, and perhaps slighter. Cosmopolitanism in its most familiar guise is spatial and normative. As such, it entails putting the welfare of those outside the borders of your nation on the same moral plane as the welfare of your fellow citizens. In recent years, as the term has made room for plural, limited, adjectivally qualified forms of cosmopolitanism, there has also been a shift from spatial toward temporal cosmopolitanism: an expansion of its timescale to make room for the more distant past, including the distant past of distant places. And like the pluralizing of cosmopolitanism, which has been one of my own projects for twenty years now—I mean the shift from one ethical cosmopolitanism to many anthropological cosmopolitanisms, defined not by an overriding fidelity to the good of humanity but by multiple and overlapping commitments to different social collectivities—this inclusion of a more distant past creates problems for anyone who wants to see cosmopolitanism as exerting normative pressure on us: pressure to behave differently, to throw our loyalties into question. The tension between deep time and ethical judgment is not susceptible to any easy resolution, but it's an animating framework for the readings and reflections that follow. An expanded past would include the acknowledged greatness of historical actions, cultural traditions, and literary canons. But it would also include a great many atrocity stories, and the question of how to look at them if we aren't prepared either to judge them by the moral standards of the present or to give up on judging them at all.

There are good reasons for simply looking away from atrocity stories. They seem to promise a quick moral-political fix, a shortcut to clarity on unfamiliar and perhaps disorienting terrain, but they cannot always deliver on that promise, at least not quickly. They are often untrustworthy. The emperor Nero, who supposedly fiddled while Rome burned, is accused by classical authors of perpetrating an impressive amount of torture and murder. "Modern scholars have determined," however, "that many of the tropes used to characterize his depravities bear a remarkable similarity to literary accounts of mythical events." One authority adds that much supposed testimony against Nero is "based on literary techniques that were taught in Roman rhetorical schools."[6] (For what it's worth, violins weren't invented until the sixteenth century, and it appears that Nero wasn't in Rome when the fire broke out.) Stories of the deaths of martyrs, once a hugely popular atrocity-based genre, are often demonstrably untrue. According to historian Candida Moss, "for the first two hundred and fifty years of the Christian era there are only six martyrdom accounts that can be treated as reliable" (16).[7] Even when atrocity stories do turn out to be reliable, they can make one wonder why one is reading them. To prevent future atrocities? Martyrology does not lend itself to a promising program of atrocity prevention. When Agrippa d'Aubigné writes about the St. Bartholomew's Day massacre of 1572 in *Les Tragiques*, he suggests that the Protestants who were killed are martyrs who gained eternal life while their Catholic murderers lost their souls. That suggestion makes violent death sound like a not unreasonable bargain.[8] It invites the counterintuitive but perhaps theologically tenable idea that when your killers put you to the sword, they were actually doing you a favor. If this is how you find meaning in violence, the intuitive modern option—to admit that mass violence cannot be made sense of—is going to look attractive, and humanity's relentless drive to make sense, whatever the cost, is going to look like an obstacle to be overcome. Stop making sense—it's a version of today's common sense to which atrocity seems to offer a great deal of support.

Like the idea that your suffering is God's punishment for your sins (a popular refrain among the English victims of Native American violence in colonial New England), the martyrdom story exemplifies the redemptive view of violence that Etienne Balibar very properly warns his readers to avoid.[9] It makes violence seem too easily justifiable. (Not that it never can be). Even in their more modern, more secular form, atrocity stories also often neglect systemic, impersonal injustice in favor of actions for which particular persons can be held accountable, the accountability then serving as a sort of rite of exorcism or illusory redemption. For the purposes of political decision-making—to take a familiar American example, the decision to bomb or not to bomb—it is never sufficient to know that there are very bad people out there doing very bad things. There are, and the things done are often *very* bad, but your intervention against the perpetrators of atrocity may make things much worse. Examples are easy to come by. In some cases, as has often been said, it might be better to treat the bad actors, even very bad actors, as something less than absolute monsters. If they are seen as monsters, and impermeable to reason of any kind, the possibility is of course foreclosed that they might become acceptable participants in a negotiated settlement that might end up leaving fewer corpses on the ground. As humanitarians have often observed, holding perpetrators to account and preventing future atrocities are different goals, though they can overlap, and even a piece of humanistic scholarship concerned with accountability for the past has got to keep an eye on the telos of fewer future atrocities.

Atrocity doesn't help you understand everything. Suffering is not always a result of physical violence. Neither is injustice itself. From the perspective of justice, the claim that atrocity makes on our attention, while peremptory, should never be seen as an *exclusive* claim. On the other hand, as we will see, finding ingenious ways to indicate that it is *not* an exclusive claim, and doing so in the very act of faithfully transcribing the horror, is one unexpected virtue of the best literary accounts of atrocity, a discovery that makes the assembling of those accounts seem worth the effort.

That's not the end of arguments against the project of assembling an atrocity archive. What is such an archive good for? An account of the *literature*, of how atrocities have been described, of the sense people have made of them, is a different thing than a chronicle of atrocities themselves. For one thing, it makes for a slimmer and more selective volume. Yes, even in the most violence-prone regions of the world, it's by descriptions, not by direct experience, that most people tend to encounter atrocities. That gives a certain significance to the descriptions. When they are encountered, however, the descriptions tend to be mere slivers of larger texts that are mainly about something else. They also tend to be propagandistic and sensational.[10] Too small and marginal an archive, suspicion of the motives for the telling, and suspicion of the reductiveness of the tale told: three more things to worry about.

One final source of qualms, perhaps the most compelling, is the proposition that, as Siep Stuurman writes in *The Invention of Humanity,* "ethnocentrism . . . is ubiquitous" (11). Not all atrocities target ethnic, racial, or religious outsiders. But when they do, as is frequently the case, ethnocentrism prevents the violence from being understood as blameworthy. If it is indeed everywhere, or has been until quite recently, ethnocentrism puts a severe limit on both the quantity and the quality of the available materials out of which a literary history of atrocity could be composed. If, in the writings that humanity has seen fit to preserve, the alien "has mostly been presented as savage, barbarian, irrational, inscrutable, uncivilized, irreligious, heathen, idolatrous, nonwhite, colored, primitive, backward, traditional, premodern—and the list goes on" (3), the description of the killing of large numbers of aliens, internal or external, will not have seemed morally scandalous, and reading such descriptions is not likely to issue in an instructive or gratifying reading experience, at least to modern eyes.[11] It is not rare in adventure tales of the imperial period (a period that may not be over) for the protagonist to slay hordes of racialized others, the anonymous expendable zombies of yesteryear. But this genre does not satisfy modern expectations of readability, and for my purposes those expectations will be decisive. What this project demands are literary texts of a certain quality which invite some degree of readerly reflection. The premise that ethnocentrism was both ubiquitous and essential to atrocity (a premise at which we will take a closer look) would imply that such texts will not be abundant. As it happens, they are less abundant than one might have liked. Great writing about atrocities committed by one's own countrymen, like Leo Tolstoy's account of the Russian conquest of the Caucasus in *Hadji Murat* or Ishikawa Tatsuzo's account of atrocities committed by the Japanese army against Chinese civilians in the 1930s, are exceptions. Even the most virtuous, like Bartolomé de las Casas's descriptions of Spanish atrocities in the Americas, tend to be predictable and repetitive. In Las Casas and elsewhere, what might seem to be arrestingly original details turn out to be borrowed from classical sources, themselves borrowed from earlier sources.[12] Taking off from the extraordinary horror of the event, describers of atrocity are often quick to declare ordinary language incapable of capturing that horror, or the evildoers responsible for it. Gladstone's "Bulgarian Horrors" pamphlet (protesting Ottoman atrocities committed in 1876) speaks in this mode of "crimes and outrages, so vast in scale as to exceed all modern example, and so unutterably vile as well as fierce in character, that it passes the power of heart to conceive, and of tongue and pen adequately to describe them."[13] What the inexpressibility trope lacks in descriptiveness it makes up in power to provoke the passions, passions which would frequently have to be described as racist. (In Gladstone's case, they were.) But once the moment for taking indignant action has passed, a writer's announcement of failure to do justice to their subject cannot compensate; what remains is a writerly failure, if an understandable one. Will I put prose like this on my syllabus? Probably not. No one can feel good about imposing more than a taste of it on impressionable minds.

Writing like Gladstone's is, however, good to think with. One might even have to admit that it represents moral progress. It recognizes atrocity as a moral scandal about which something should be done and can be done. For much of the West's cultural history, it's unclear whether either of those premises would have pertained. But Gladstone's moral outrage will itself outrage modern readers. Humanitarian principles emerge (good), but they are applied so unevenly, so blatantly in the interests of the great powers (bad), that it would be misleading in the extreme, morally or politically, to speak of a step forward. Where atrocity is concerned, can one *ever* speak of a step forward? It's with that question foremost in mind that this book addresses itself to atrocity's literary archive, the putative line between modern and premodern treatments of mass violence, and a few distinctive modern renderings.

The Allied bombing of the German cities during World War II, in which hundreds of thousands of civilians were killed, is seen by some and not by others as an atrocity. The same can be said of the Israeli bombing of Gaza which began (the latest episode, that is) in October of 2023, after the Hamas attack of October 7, and continued as I was finishing the revisions to this manuscript. There is no mystery as to why the accusatory label "atrocity," like the stronger label "genocide," has been resisted by those whose collectivity stands accused. There is some mystery, on the other hand, swirling around the historical fact that, in certain times and places, it has become possible for the people of country X to accuse themselves of committing an atrocity against the people of country Y. How could something so seemingly unlikely have come to pass? Is it registered in the literary record? Assuming it is, is self-indictment of violence against foreigners and noncombatants solely a modern phenomenon, a product of the modern discourse of human rights? Does the same hold for the concept of atrocity itself? Is indictment too crude a measure of what literature can do with atrocity, or what needs to be done? Along with a kind of stunned bafflement that human beings continue to do such things to each other, these are the questions that have animated this book.

Introduction

The Air Raid on Halberstadt on 8 April 1945

In the spring of 2016, preparing to teach a summer seminar on world literature, I lay down on the living room sofa to read a recently published book by the German writer, filmmaker, philosopher, and TV producer Alexander Kluge. The book was called *Air Raid*. At least, *Air Raid* was the title on the cover. Inside, there was a longer title: *The Air Raid on Halberstadt on 8 April 1945*.[1] As I read about the American bombing of the small German city of Halberstadt, the city where the thirteen-year-old Kluge and his parents hid in the cellar of their house while bombs exploded across their neighborhood, a small but uncomfortable thought tickled the edge of my consciousness. April 8, 1945. Halberstadt. It seemed unlikely, but hadn't I seen those words somewhere before? I got up from the sofa and went into my office. On the wall, beneath a framed photo of my father's plane, taken in the air over Germany in the last months of World War II and sent to me after my father died by his buddy and wing man, there is a list of his missions. There it was, on a yellowed piece of paper that I kept meaning to put under glass, in my father's own handwriting. April 8, 1945. Halberstadt. The mission was number 14 on the list, between Bayreuth on April 5 and Oranienburg on the April 10. While a barely adolescent Alexander was somewhere below, unknown and unknowable to him, my father, Captain Eugene Rabinowitz, pilot and squadron commander, just eight years older, was in the air over Halberstadt, leading the B-17s of his squadron to their target, the bomb bay doors opening.

Some months later, I managed to meet Alexander Kluge. I got a notice from the Goethe Institute that he would be doing a book tour in the New York area, and I wrote back asking if they could give me his email address. My father, I said, had bombed him. I thought this excuse had a good chance of working. It didn't. Still, the organizers said they had forwarded him my message. The result, after exchanges with assistants, was that a few weeks later we met for an hour in the lobby of a hotel in Chelsea. The lobby was modern, narrow, noisy, drafty, not the ideal spot for a significant encounter. One or two young people who seemed to be traveling in Kluge's party passed by from time to time, trying not to look as if they were protecting him from whatever threat I might pose—maybe only the threat of taking up too much time. I knew he had to prepare for an event that night. But Kluge himself smiled kindly, seeming totally untroubled by the time I was taking out of his schedule. I didn't apologize to him for what my father had done, and whatever he expected, it obviously wasn't an apology. The men in those planes, he told me, were like workers in factories. Workers in factories do not decide what is produced by their factories. He had said the same thing in the book. And why not repeat what was in the book, since what he had written there was clearly the outcome of careful thought? In the book he had decided, for example, not to describe his own firsthand experience of the bombing. I assumed he didn't want the gut-level sympathy that a first-person narrative would have pretty much guaranteed he would get. Who could refuse it? Over 2,000 of his neighbors died around him that day, their homes and shelters smashed and incinerated, and for absolutely nothing. The goal of bringing the war to a speedy conclusion could not possibly justify the destruction. Yes, there were munitions factories in the area, but they were well outside of town, while the bombers deliberately and successfully targeted the city center. US ground forces were only a day or two away. That morning in the hotel lobby, however, Kluge didn't seem interested in reexamining the evidence in what I was not thinking of as my father's case. Instead, he mentioned the awful situation at that moment in Aleppo, and then Max Horkheimer's gratitude to the US, in the 1960s, for rescuing him from the Nazis, despite what the US was doing at that moment in Vietnam. The conversation jumped from period to period. He put some emphasis on a pogrom against the Jews in Prague in the seventeenth century. His point, not that he seemed eager to make one, might have been to remind me of what the Nazis had done to my fellow Jews. Or it might have been to suggest that these old outrages had to be remembered even if they seemed to take something away from the intensity of feeling about more recent outrages. It occurred to me that he might be wanting to relativize modern violence in general, even violence so bad that there seems nothing left to say about it. Given the passage of time, does any atrocity *stay* a moral absolute? Is any atrocity exempt from time's relativizing power, which as it passes drags us further and further away from the reactions we would have had, would have *had* to have, in the moment itself? Moral sentiments that would otherwise appear firm, inevitable, eternal seem to drown and dissolve in the depths of time.

Edmund Burke noted this logic in a haunting letter to a friend written during the French Revolution: "It is possible that many estates about you were obtained by arms, that is, by violence: . . . but it is *old violence*; and that which might be wrong in the beginning, is consecrated by time, and becomes lawful."[2] If the unsettling effect of time on moral judgment is not morally unspeakable, it is certainly hard to speak about without some fear of getting morally lost. The fear of getting morally lost among the world's many atrocities, coupled with a certain temptation to get lost, is among the motives behind the writing of this book.

Later, when I thought about how Kluge had juggled with time in the book's description of the bombing, jumping backwards from the explosions, fires, and falling buildings to a past that, had it been otherwise, might have left Halberstadt intact, yet not forgetting that for the inhabitants of Halberstadt it was already much too late, it started to make sense that his conversation, in that hotel lobby, also skipped around and went back so far. At one point it bounced all the way back to the violence that *Homo sapiens* had committed against the Neanderthals. Then it bounced forward to the divorce of Kluge's parents. The divorce of his parents had to be counted as another reason, I suppose he was saying, to help explain how bad he had felt after the bombing. A banal, everyday reason for emotional trouble that he might have presented, instead, as grandly traumatic, a way of synching his childhood up with world history. If there was a larger history of the world that his family and my family could synch up to, the moral seemed to go, it would have to include seemingly disparate materials, some of them widely distanced in time and space, resistant to any one linear narrative.

The idea for this book was not born out of my conversation with Kluge. I was reading *Air Raid* on the sofa because I was already hooked, no doubt in large part for personal reasons. I had decided that there are more atrocities out there than get acknowledged as such, that a great deal of what passes as history, including and perhaps especially literary history, is history whitewashed of violence, even violence noteworthy for the very high price paid in human lives. But I had also acknowledged that I had doubts about my own apparent convictions. The conversation with Kluge had a certain complicating effect on the indignation that initially fueled the project. It made me wonder, among other things, whether history, with its aspiration to coherent narrative, was the most accurate name for what I was trying to do. It cast some doubt on my professional habit (which other humanists may recognize) of taking quiet credit for the preservation of historical memories, some of them distant and unpleasant, that society would prefer to forget. Our conversation was richly enigmatic, and not, I think, just because Kluge was avoiding the event itself, the obvious subject of our shared concern. Yes, there was a certain delicacy in the apparent randomness of the topics he touched on, but I felt sure that his delicacy was not the whole story. Kluge's accumulation of seeming irrelevancies had an aesthetic force, as if it were calculated to display the bombing in an uncommon light. From a certain angle, I could imagine that the montage of times and places was a way of enacting a structure of feeling about the bombing, and perhaps also about atrocity in general, that was not easy to describe and that he perhaps could not have arrived at by any more direct route. Inspired by *The Air Raid on Halberstadt on 8 April 1945*, this book too tries to pick its way through the blood-spattered confusion of world history without either taking the high road or losing all sense of going somewhere.

My personal interest in the Allied bombing of the German cities had already worked its way into my scholarly writing. In 1999, I had used aerial photographs of Europe taken from my father's B-17 after the war to illustrate my book *Feeling Global: Internationalism in Distress*, and I had begun that book by remembering how my first perceptions of the world outside the US were associated with my childhood habit of going down to the basement and picking through those photographs, stored in wooden artillery shell boxes. The boxes were inscribed in black with German words that turned out to mean, "This Side Up. Handle with Care." (Literally, "Don't Throw.") Those same boxes, stacked in a neat but staggered pile of three, now form the do-it-yourself end-table next to the sofa where I opened *The Air Raid on Halberstadt on 8 April 1945* on that spring day, almost exactly seventy years after the bombing.

In 2007 I had also included a page or two about my father's Army Air Corps service in an essay I was invited to write for a collection, edited by two legal scholars, devoted to forgiveness, mercy, and clemency. I accepted their invitation because, although I had never thought much about forgiveness and at the time had no plans to, I had thought a lot about blame, the other side of it. On the surface at least, my subject in that essay was not my father and how I felt about what he did in the war. The subject was a work of literary criticism by a great novelist, recently deceased: W. G. Sebald's book *Luftkrieg und Literatur*, or "Air War and Literature" (published in English, a bit misleadingly, as *On the Natural History of Destruction*). That book takes Sebald's fellow German writers to task for their silence about the Allied bombardment of the German cities, a bombardment in which, as he reminds us, some 500,000 to 600,000 civilians were killed.[3] On the few occasions when they wrote about the bombing, Sebald said, they wrote about it badly. They had failed in a literary version of their civic duty.

I was glad that Sebald had written his book, but I was also a bit irritated that he seemed to be blaming his fellow German writers for *not* blaming the Allies, or for being silent because they blamed themselves rather than the Allies. Sebald spends no pages at all on what seemed to most observers the most plausible reason why the Germans did not blame the Allies: because most Germans (though not the residual Nazis, nor the rest of the German Right) thought that they, the Germans, had started the war, and had pioneered the bombing of civilians, and in a sense were therefore reaping what they had sown. Of course, blame was not really Sebald's focus. What Sebald wanted was for German writers to *make sense* of the bombing. Blame was only one way of making sense, and not necessarily the preferred one. Sebald gave several reasons for why the Germans had not been able to make sense of it. Maybe the bombing felt incomprehensible to them because it really *was* incomprehensible. As a target, Halberstadt, for example, made no sense. Bombing it would not bring the end of the war any closer. All those deaths, all that suffering accomplished nothing. How do you tell a reasonable-sounding story about an event that is so unreasonable? Sebald was also channeling the German-Jewish critic Walter Benjamin on the cultural effects of advanced military technology. In an essay called "The Storyteller," Benjamin had noticed that soldiers returning from World War I no longer had stories to share, as travelers returning home almost always carry with them.[4] Being shelled by distant, invisible artillery, he suggested, had altered the experience of warfare. More precisely, it had stopped war from *becoming* an experience in the strong sense, like a face-to-face duel, which is to say an event of which personal sense could be made. Turning the passage of time into meaningful, sharable experience was what storytelling had always tried to do. But the terrible impersonality of killing and being killed at a distance had cut down on everyone's capacity to tell meaning-laden stories. You could talk about what it felt like to be bombed or shelled—many people had, of course, and at least some of what they reported about their thoughts, feelings, and sensations has come to count as literature. Still, there was a higher or more important kind of sense-making by means of narrative that bombing seemed to obstruct or even rule out. Like Benjamin, Sebald was not very clear about what that higher kind of literary sense-making might look like.

In reflecting on "Air War and Literature," I decided that unlike Sebald I had no bone to pick with the common sense of the German majority, who preferred to blame themselves. Blaming has a bad rap, of course, but it doesn't follow that *self*-blame should also be considered a bad idea. Politically, that would be counterproductive. Didn't Americans stand to learn from the Germans, as Susan Neiman proposes, about their own collective responsibilities for violence their country has committed?[5] After September 11, 2001, American common sense had not on the whole decided, as the majority of Germans had, that the attack on us, horrible as it was, was in part a result of our own policies, including violence we had been perpetrating or at least abetting for years in the Middle East. The 9/11 attack might be indefensible, but it was not incomprehensible.[6] So why hadn't Sebald seen something so obvious? He may have insisted that the bombing of the German cities was incomprehensible, even at the cost of looking away from possible if partial explanations, because he didn't want to be tempted to justify or forgive those who perpetrated it. But whether that was his motive or not, the effect of his commitment to incomprehensibility would be the same: it would *always* be impossible for him to find any literature about the atrocity that he could value positively. Good writing about atrocity, whatever it might be (one preoccupation of the pages to come) was a contradiction in terms. Literature exists to try to make sense, if only (sometimes) by bringing readers up against the apparent limits of sense-making. If Sebald had been presented with a literature of the bombing—and perhaps he had—by his chosen criteria he could not have recognized it *as* literature, or as good literature. In his eyes, a true portrait of the bombing would have to declare it incomprehensible. Committed as he was to the idea that the bombing *had* no meaning, Sebald could only draw one conclusion: any writing that did deal with the bombing in a literary fashion could only be, for him, bad writing, full of coherence and reassurance, each of them illusory. That was not what America needed in the wake of 9/11. And to me, teaching as I do in a department of literature, it also laid out a professional challenge: where was the literature that was *good* in the specific sense I now, suddenly, cared about?[7] When and how and why had writers started to be able to do justice (whatever justice might mean) to *other* atrocities, the many atrocities of which the historical record is so very, very full?

The Global Frame of Moral Judgment

What I had wanted to do in the essay on Sebald, aside from offering sage counsel about American responsibility in the aftermath of 9/11, was to suggest that, as far as atrocity was concerned, there was something wrong with the human rights consensus. As a description of contemporary common sense, what the human rights consensus meant to me was a willingness to extract civilian suffering from its historical (national, causal) contexts, from all narratives of provocation, collective responsibility, just retaliation, what goes around comes around. The event should be looked at in itself, for itself, in the instant in which it occurred, with no reference to anything but that instant. In eliminating context from their descriptions, forensic or human rights–based accounts of atrocity make it easier to hold the perpetrators accountable. Here is an example from Amnesty International: "Witnesses of such killings of relatives and neighbors, and FDN personnel who have deserted the force, have described in detailed testimonies made available to Amnesty International execution-style killings, in which captives were bound, tortured, and their throats slit by FDN forces. . . . The number of captives tortured and put to death by FDN forces since 1981 is impossible to determine, but it is believed they total several hundred."[8] The effort here is to give the facts and nothing but the facts, careful not to claim anything that cannot be impartially verified. This account is free of the controversies that would inevitably arise from any reference to the whys and wherefores behind the violence—for example, the fact that the setting is Nicaragua. The result is impersonal and dispassionate. This ought to be understood as a moral advance. Without it, we would not have been able to see the Allied bombing of the German cities as a war crime or an atrocity. It can't be wrong to stop identifying German civilians sufficiently with the Nazis, or even as Germans, to begin thinking that everyone can and must be detached from their national belonging, at least for this purpose, and that they must be treated instead as individuals. Each human rights violation, according to the human rights consensus, must be looked at alone, without regard for mitigating circumstances, guilty histories, yesterday's provocative actions by today's suffering victims, comparisons of any sort.

The human rights consensus is hard to argue with. Who wants to argue that things were better in the days of vendetta when one family member could be murdered for what some other family member had done generations earlier? (Not that vendetta belongs entirely to the olden days: consider the house demolitions routinely practiced by Israel against the families of Palestinians accused of acts of resistance.)

And yet the consensus also suits Americans because of other things we tend to believe, or not believe, that are more questionable. As has often been remarked, grossly but not inaccurately, individualism has a large place in the national ideology of the United States. And (another way of saying the same thing, but with regard to how we live in time), so does presentism. That is, we Americans tend not to believe that anything that came before our birth or will come after our death can really be considered part of us, a matter of our own responsibility. Responsibility is individual for us in a way that squeezes the amount of time we believe we inhabit. This means we tend to reject reparations for past wrongs like slavery. We resist even historical apologies, which involve only symbolism and do not call for expenditures that would have to come out of someone's budget. The critic Walter Michaels puts this in a memorable phrase: for Americans today to apologize to the Native American victims of genocide or the African American victims of slavery, he said, would mean "apologizing for something you didn't do to people to whom you didn't do it (in fact, to people to whom it wasn't done)."[9] Michaels is saying that African Americans today do not belong to the same collectivity as those who used to be slaves (hence slavery was not done to *them*, only to their ancestors). And white Americans today do not belong to the same collectivity or community that once enslaved African Americans (hence "we" didn't do it). "We" exist inside our own skin, and nowhere outside it, and only for as long as that skin (here assumed to be white) covers an individual body that walks the earth alone. We exist in the present, and only in the present. Nothing could be farther from the reasoning that I assume lay behind Kluge's attitude in that hotel lobby: yes, he seemed to be saying, I was a child of thirteen at the time, but for better or worse I belonged and belong to the country that pioneered the bombing of nonmilitary targets, a country that has a less than spotless record on the treatment of civilian populations. In one way or another, that belonging cannot help but affect how I think and conduct myself now.

In writing about Sebald, I felt comfortable arguing for a tighter sense of collective responsibility than the human rights consensus allows for, and this despite the fact that the argument led me into a paradox. I was on record as an advocate for cosmopolitanism, which aims at a less nationalistic, more self-critical view of ourselves, our country, and the violence that country has both suffered and inflicted. But getting to this cosmopolitanism would require a stronger rather than a weaker sense of national belonging. In order to be more cosmopolitan, Americans would first have to feel that the history that led up to America's actions was their own history, a history for which they were collectively responsible, a history that was part of who they are right now. In order to become more cosmopolitan, we would have to become, at least in this negative sense, more patriotic. We would have to have a stronger sense of belonging in time—belonging to the larger, violence-laden history of which American history is itself a part. We would need a usable past, one might say, but a past to which we would probably prefer not to belong, and whose putative uses, therefore, remain somewhat questionable.

I liked this argument enough, paradox and all, to include the essay in my book *Perpetual War: Cosmopolitanism from the Viewpoint of Violence* (2012). After the meeting with Kluge, however, I began to feel it needed rethinking. If the human rights consensus truly *was* a consensus, Americans today would be assuming that the American bombing of German civilians in World War II was in fact an atrocity. That does not seem to be the case. One might even suggest, with Nikil Saval, that in order to do so, the US would first have to undergo the kind of bombing that it meted out elsewhere. In a remembrance of the 1968 My Lai massacre on its fiftieth anniversary, Saval notes that "national self-indictment would not be arrived at. America, of all countries, was not one that could excoriate itself. Nuremburg was instructive. Only after prolonged bombing of its civilian areas could Germany, in a state of submission, be held to account" (26).[10] Perhaps the human rights perspective has not had as formative an influence on American common sense as I thought. And perhaps I should be more enthusiastic, then, about the prospect of it becoming *more* influential. Didn't I want the bombing to count as an atrocity? The idea struck me that perhaps I had resisted the human rights view of atrocity, which would answer that question with an immediate and unequivocal yes, in part because it would have implied that my father was guilty, or guiltier—guilty as an individual, a perpetrator. It was not an attractive perhaps. The question was starting to seem unavoidable: How guilty did I think he was? If the Allied bombing of Germany was a test of cosmopolitanism that the American public had failed, maybe I had failed it myself. Was I sure that if it had been me and not my father, I would have behaved any differently than he did? Would I have been happier if he had blamed himself instead of telling me, as he was no doubt told by his superiors, that his targets were exclusively industrial, not residential? Self-blame is still a form of blame. Finding someone to blame for an atrocity cannot be the only way to prevent the atrocity from falling into the black hole of sublime, amoral senselessness, thereby threatening to drag the rest of human history down with it. Or can it?

For some years now—the writing was interrupted by the pandemic, as well as by trials and tribulations internal to the subject—the elevator pitch for this project has been the following: When and how and where did it become possible for writers to accuse their own country or collectivity of atrocities committed against the inhabitants of some other country or collectivity? It's a question, I said, that no one seems to have asked. It may not be the most important question to pose about the shape of world history, for those who think history has a shape, or about how far world history has been shaped by large structural forces rather than rendered shapeless by local contingencies of violence—a question posed in Gopal Balakrishnan's *Antagonistics*.[11] From the perspective of what is to be done, there are more important questions. But still, I insisted, isn't it a question to which you would want to know the answer? Isn't this a chapter in the moral history of humankind that, however unkind the results to humankind's self-image, you would want to see filled in—and that, once filled in, would have at least some impact on your sense of world history as a whole and how you fit into it?

It is one thing (I would go on if not stopped) to bewail violence committed against me and mine. That's to be expected. It is probably universal, even if it must be qualified somewhat by the understandable reticence of some groups (actually quite a few) to speak openly about their vulnerability, their suffering, their humiliation. It is something very different, however, for me to make an accusation against my own kind, against the group to which I belong, and to make that accusation not because of general misbehavior or because my collectivity is not living up to my high expectations for it (that too is to be expected) but because of conduct toward some other group. The first seems a natural expression of belonging. The second seems likely to be seen as disloyalty, even treason. To accuse the group to which you belong of violence against another group looks like a major moral pivot—evidence perhaps of a new mode of belonging, and thus also of a new mode of moral thinking. Assuming it can be shown to have a significant presence in imaginative literature, it would also seem to count as a significant moment in literary history. For those who are tracking the history of cosmopolitanism, it could hardly help but show up there as well. Cosmopolitanism in a more than trivial sense arguably only begins with critical distance from one's homeland, the sort of critical distance for which the would-be cosmopolitan might have to pay a price. Putting the two trajectories together, this project becomes, as I said, an experiment in cosmopolitan literary history.

At this point the elevator pitch passes beyond the normal duration of an elevator ride. It also passes beyond the areas of knowledge in which I have any pretension to expertise. I was trained in modern English-language literature. My knowledge of the literature of earlier periods and other places and languages, knowledge that seems highly desirable if conclusions are going to be drawn at a properly cosmopolitan scale, is at best amateurish and impressionistic. My only excuse for taking on so large a topic is that, though others are far more qualified (I think for example of Alexander Beecroft, David Damrosch, and Martin Puchner), no one else seems to be doing it. Why not? One possible explanation is that the topic of massive, indiscriminate violence is not an alluring one for most people who study literature. We literature scholars have other, less grisly subjects that literature makes available to us and that we'd prefer to reflect upon. Another explanation is the tendency, among those literary people who can't stop themselves from contemplating violence, to think of the present as, in Lawrence L. Langer's words, "the age of atrocity." This seemingly innocent description makes the atrocities of past ages less interesting.[12] It is reasonable enough to assume, after what we know about the Holocaust, that the mass bloodshed of the twentieth century is unique to and definitive of the age, whether in kind or in degree. It is widely assumed not just that violence has not declined (that it *has* declined is Steven Pinker's claim in *The Better Angels of Our Nature*), but that from the viewpoint of violence, ours is the darkest of dark ages, unprecedented in its coldly calculated and technologically efficient bloodletting.[13] Whether this historical self-image counts as humility or arrogance, it's appealing for reasons to which Pinker is not attentive: it refuses a self-satisfaction (about the social effects of the profit motive, carceral democracy, arms sales, drone strikes) that, where collective violence is concerned, seems especially inexcusable. There is of course also a timeless and irrefutable motive for ramping up the critique of your own time and giving more of a pass to prior periods. By definition, yours is always the time you are best able to do something about. Your criticism is more likely to have some effect if you are critical of your own era than if you are critical of someone else's, especially an era long gone by. If where you hope you are heading is toward some version of social improvement, being critical of the past can look like spinning your wheels. Still, negative exceptionalism about the present is an unreliable guide to how we have arrived at this particular present, however degenerate it may be. And we need guides that are as reliable as possible.

At the global scale, negative exceptionalism obviously owes a great deal to the history of colonialism, which makes modernity special but gets no mention in Pinker's copious index. Colonialism in Africa and Asia, which was largely overthrown in the mid-twentieth century, was responsible for innumerable atrocities during its five-hundred-year reign. Do we still need to be told this? Well, Pinker does, and he is not alone. As Priyamvada Gopal writes, "national self-congratulation" on the supposed capacity of the colonial powers to achieve "reform without violence" (3) remains the mainstream view in much of the West. In revisionist historians of colonialism like Niall Ferguson, "massacres, violence, slavery, and famine [are] acknowledged as passing unfortunate occurrences rather than as constitutive dimensions of imperialism" (vii).[14] European civilization, seen through its treatment of non-Europeans, can look the very opposite of civilized, indeed like barbarism, implacable and incomprehensible. Add to this the ongoing legacy of settler colonialism in the Pacific and the Americas, the lingering systemic inequality between Global North and Global South, the proxy violence in the Global South that has continued after the achievement of national independence, and the persistence of anti-Black racism in the United States, among other bits of evidence, and it's no surprise that this perception has remained fresh, bolstering the sense that what Edward Said called Orientalism is a kind of original sin of the West. It would seem to follow that a willingness to condone uninhibited violence against supposed civilizational Others is all you need to know about the origin of atrocity. For better or worse, however, the origin of atrocity must be sought farther back than European colonialism—that's the immediate takeaway of temporal cosmopolitanism, or deep time. Going farther back complicates the picture, and the complications are more and more salient. The term *colonialism* has recently been revivified by the international movement of Indigenous people. It now refers to colonizing that was carried out by non-Europeans as well as by Europeans. It refers to colonizing that was carried out in premodern as well as in modern, capitalist times. As a result, it is not merely possible but necessary to allow discussions of atrocity to spread out beyond the modern Orientalist paradigm. Consider one example among many. When the army of the emergent Vietnamese empire moved south in the 1470s, conquering the supposed "barbarians" of Cham, now self-described as the Indigenous people of Vietnam and Cambodia, one of the cities they attacked, in the year 1479, was called Bon Man. The report back to headquarters afterwards reads in part: the army "burnt their capital, took their garrisons, and burnt their granaries. Before this [attack], Bon Man had 90,000 households; in this operation almost all of them starved or were killed and only 2,000 people remain."[15] Later, the Vietnamese name for the areas of neighboring Cambodia was the "pacified west." Can this episode be meaningfully distinguished from what the Spanish began doing twenty years later in Latin America or from the annals of Western colonialism and American "pacification"? I can't read it without wondering whether a new literary history of the world will discover a Vietnamese contemporary of Bartolomé de las Casas, a writer and perhaps even a witness who recounted what his people were doing and declared, in words that invite further commentary, that it was something like an atrocity. If humankind can be said to have a moral history, such moments would help compose it. The Cham people, who attend the annual meetings of the United Nations Permanent Forum on Indigenous Issues, are reminding the world that their history needs to be part of it.

Paying attention to empires built by non-Europeans before the modern era and to the atrocities they entailed is now part of what it means, or should mean, to avoid Eurocentrism. It is now a part of the humanist's job description, indisputable if not yet universally practiced. The same holds for the premodern conquests carried out by Europeans, which cannot be attributed to capitalism. (It may be helpful to know that Karl Marx, in his last years, devoted considerable energy to researching these precapitalist topics.) Humanists can't be put off by the fear that such research may look like bad faith or like a distraction from more urgent matters. The same is true for the endeavor of recalling European voices who accused Europe of violence against non-Europeans. Self-scrutiny is a virtue on which the West has prided itself, often by hinting that other regions of the world are less well-endowed with it. Assembling a sort of self-criticism scrapbook, which is what sections of this book may look like to ill-disposed readers, can seem to entail avoiding the civilizational self-analysis that the West so badly needs and instead falling back into vulgar self-congratulation. This fear is not unreasonable; I can only beg the reader to suspend it, at least provisionally.[16] My intention is not to set up, against overwhelming Western affirmation of colonial bloodletting, a minoritarian but symbolically potent archive of people of miraculous good conscience who can be applauded for defying mainstream prejudices that allowed the atrocities we perpetrated to pass almost unnoticed. I want to fill in a picture in which more atrocities were perpetrated and passed unnoticed and to explain, as far as possible, when and where and how they came to *be* noticed. One of my commitments is to explanation, and that goes for the good guys as well as the bad guys—who (as is often the case where atrocity is concerned) were sometimes the same people. The challenge will be to recapture for explanation territory that has too often been ceded, however reluctantly, to the inexplicable and the sacred.

From another angle, this shift in perspective can also be derived from the disconcerting proposition I took Kluge to be hinting at: as time goes by (that innocent, mystifying phrase!), recent violence, including colonial violence, comes to look different. It's not just the fact of earlier violence, for example precolonial violence perpetrated on non-Europeans by other non-Europeans. It's also time itself. How much time has gone by? What effect has the passage of time had on moral judgment? Like all books, but perhaps more anxiously, this book relies on a judgment of timing, and on the timing of judgment. Once upon a time, the habit in the West was of course to talk of the pyramids of skulls produced by the human sacrifices of the Aztecs and so on, as if it was *only* in exotic places (including the past) that atrocities were perpetrated. Then, following the social movements of the 1960s, that cultural arrogance flipped. There was a Western self-chastening. The human sacrifices were quietly shelved and their place in the conversation was taken by Hiroshima and Auschwitz. A step in the right direction, for sure, but perhaps (in the twenty-first century, at any rate) a step too far. Even given the imbalances of power and the huge disparities in harm inflicted, there is room in the conversation for all these atrocities, and there is arguably a need for them. I assume the point has come when a deep- or deeper-time argument no longer smells so much like an evasion of European responsibility. Self-chastening may satisfy a deep moral craving in the West, but it's not satisfactory as history, and (so I would argue) certainly not this far into the twenty-first century. If the response to atrocity is indeed time-sensitive, it has come to matter more than it recently did that the Aztecs who were conquered by the Spaniards in the sixteenth century were, and knew themselves to be, conquerors of other Indigenous peoples, conquerors whose complaint against their Spanish conquerors could therefore not be against conquest as such. When and how and why did it become possible for someone to be against conquest as such, no matter who committed it? If you want to understand the history of atrocity, you have to be curious about that sort of question. The this-is-the-worst-of-times assumption, which stands in the way of such questions, seems to bubble up every time the subject of violence is mentioned.

As it does for example in Adriana Cavarero's *Horrorism: Naming Contemporary Violence* (2007).[17] In Homer, Cavarero writes, physical violence is reciprocal: it "presents itself in the form of what, in the first decades of the nineteenth century, Clausewitz could still label 'nothing but a duel on a larger scale' . . . Reciprocity, making each one a body open to wounding by the other, is in fact a fundamental principle" (11). This changes radically, Cavarero says, in modern times. Suddenly noncombatants are factored in. "The First World War was not just one of many wars that, from Homer's day to ours, have covered the planet with blood. It inaugurated a model of total war, perfected in the 1939–1945 conflict and characterized by 'the placing of civilians on the same level as military personnel, and the propensity to exterminate them without hesitation.' The traditional, even heroic conception that defined it as 'a duel on a larger scale' was definitively abolished" (60). The large-scale killing of defenseless civilians and prisoners of war may indeed be definitive of atrocity—it's no more imprecise than most definitions. But it is something of a shock (and dramatically contrary to the historical record) to see it taken here as definitive of *modern* warfare, as if no such thing habitually occurred in warfare before the modern age. Whatever befell the inhabitants of a besieged city, in the many centuries full of sieges that preceded modernity, when the besiegers knocked down or poured over the city's walls, it was not analogous to a duel. Things did not generally go well for the local civilians. When you hear antiquated terms like sacking and pillaging, nothing very precise may come to mind. In search of greater imaginative precision, you could try out the current vocabulary of rape, theft, and murder. But you would then have to imagine rape, theft, and murder on a colossal, unheard-of scale. And you would have to imagine that rape, theft, and murder were collective and systemic. The besieging army had been promised a reward for its risks and its labors. One way or the other, it *would* be rewarded. I leave it to the reader to estimate the number of victorious sieges that fill the textbooks of world history. Then (although quantification obviously has its limits) multiply that number by the price in blood and bodily violation paid by the civilian inhabitants in each case. The total, taken as a proportion of the world's population at the time, will stand up very well by comparison with modern atrocities.

Definitions

The modern concept of the atrocity exists only because it expresses a discontent with the normality of plunder, sexual assault, and the butchery of noncombatants. Whatever it felt like to be on the receiving end of these practices, conceptually speaking this discontent did not always exist. Today something has changed; these practices are now frowned upon. Frowning upon the plunder, sexual assault, and butchery of noncombatants does not mean eliminating them or even, contra Pinker, necessarily diminishing them to any appreciable extent. (Which is not to say that this conceptual work has had no practical effect at all.) Nevertheless, the articulation of modern discontent must count as a real historical occurrence on a par with whatever counts as an occurrence in the worlds of literature and culture. Something culturally and literarily important had to happen in order for the concept of the atrocity to come into being. The word itself is not new. *Atrocity*, in Latin *atrocitas*, comes from *atrox*, for "fierce" or "cruel." Excessive cruelty has never gone unnoticed, and when it is noticed it has mainly been disapproved of. But on the whole the disapproval has applied only to cruelty suffered by those who were members of one's own nation or race; it has not applied to outsiders. And there have also been severe limits on the term's application when the victim of the cruelty was not the warrior with whom another warrior was dueling but unarmed civilians. It is hard to see how undoing those limits, a breakthrough which brought us the concept of atrocity in the modern expansive sense, could fail to be narrated as a positive step, as part of a progressive history, even if the discourses of human rights and humanitarianism, which did so much to break down those limits, are now viewed with skepticism, some of it justified.

I note that to describe atrocity as the mass killing of defenseless civilians and prisoners of war, as I just did, is, inconveniently, to admit that my elevator pitch had to be revised on the fly. The elevator pitch put the accent on the overcoming of ethnocentrism. The original premise was that, once upon a time, there were no moral restraints on violence directed at those who did not belong to one's own group, and that at some point that changed; qualms were expressed, constraints were formulated. The literary history it promised was therefore cosmopolitan. The same does not hold for a history that starts with violence directed at noncombatants rather than ethnic and racial others. It's unclear whether there was ever a time when women and children were not recognized as in some way distinct from armed soldiers, which is to say as defenseless and unthreatening, even if their distinctness did them little good. (Relevant here is Philippe Ariès's controversial argument in *Centuries of Childhood* that before early modernity Europeans were unsentimental about their children, many of whom did not survive to reach adulthood.) The distinctness of women and children was acknowledged in military thinking long before the wider concept of the noncombatant (a concept that of course includes adult males) came into existence; the *Oxford English Dictionary* dates the term from 1811. Scruples against the killing of noncombatants would seem to require a different trajectory than scruples against the killing of ethnic or racial others. And to the extent that the two stories intersect, the result could only be a more complex history.

My interest here lies largely with the victimhood of noncombatants and ethnic and racial others, but definitions of atrocity do not necessarily rely on either social classification. It would be ludicrous to assume that there is atrocity *only* when the victims are noncombatants, as if the moment people took up arms to defend themselves against conquest and massacre, they could no longer be considered victims. But there are perhaps reasons for not following Enzo Traverso in his preference for "vanquished," which assumes agency, over "victims," which does not.[18] Not everyone who suffered was fighting back, or fighting at all. In *The Atrocity Paradigm* (2002), philosopher Claudia Card takes atrocity as the paradigm of evil. She defines "evils" as "foreseeable intolerable harms produced by culpable wrongdoing" (3).[19] No specific categories of victimhood are mentioned. The key seems to be the combination of great suffering with clear culpability. Scale is essential both to the intensity of the suffering and to the number of victims. Individual murders don't qualify as atrocities. The insistence on culpability means that catastrophes and natural disasters also don't qualify. Atrocities must have human perpetrators; they must be intentional. (*How* intentional, however, is an interesting question—a question raised for example by commentators on Hannah Arendt's "banality of evil" thesis about Eichmann, which stressed the element of bureaucratic routine at the expense of active anti-Semitic intentionality.[20]) Further precision on this point seems unnecessary and might be counterproductive, but the definitional elements on which Card hesitates between her first and her second book on the subject are worth a moment of reflection. In *The Atrocity Paradigm* (2002) she says atrocities are "*uncontroversially* evil" (9, italics mine).[21] In *Confronting Evils: Terrorism, Torture, Genocide* (2010), she backs off from this adverb, as George Orwell did in the diaries he kept during World War II. "Responses to atrocity," she writes, "are a continuing source of controversy within and without congress halls and university walls" (3).[22] The *desire* for atrocities to be uncontroversial is a crucial aspect of the topic, as it is for Orwell. As both Orwell and Card are well aware, however, this desire is rarely satisfied. Lieutenant William Calley, who led the massacre at My Lai on March 16, 1968, in which some 350 to 500 unarmed Vietnamese civilians were killed and who was found personally responsible for the death of twenty-two of them, was punished by only three and a half years of imprisonment, served as house arrest. At that time, a great deal of the American public did not think he merited anything more severe, and many would probably say the same if asked again. And in the fifteen years of the Vietnam War, as Marilyn Young observes, "only one bad thing, My Lai, was accorded the label 'atrocity'" (243).[23] Controversy about atrocity seems endless: whether a given event counts, where the responsibility for it lies, and even whether it happened at all.

Not all of Card's definitional nuances seem to require commentary—for example, a differentiation between the adjectives intolerable, unforgivable and inexcusable. More intriguing are adjectives she doesn't call on, though others do, like excessive, unnecessary, and indiscriminate. Card is perhaps right to ignore them, given their implication that a calculated, instrumental, or somehow *proportionate* violence ought not to count. Every time the term *disproportionate* is used, as it was in response to the Israeli bombing of Gaza in the fall of 2023, there is of course implied reference to a violence that would be proportionate, or allotted rationally in relation to the provocation. Proportionality and excess are the major themes of Michel Foucault's discussion of how the term was used before the French Revolution.[24] But Foucault is entirely concerned with atrocity as "characteristic of the some of the great crimes" (56). He sees the magnitude of the crime reflected in the magnitude of the sovereign's punishment of the crime. He does not consider the possibility that, perhaps as a result of the subsequent "humanizing" tendencies about which he is so pointedly unenthusiastic, the term might come to be applied (as it has been) to the sovereign's own actions and used to focus on something more reprehensible than excess. In the meantime, the question of whether atrocity can or should be considered rational is something of a conundrum. As a first move, calling atrocity irrational seems unavoidable. Yet what would be the price of excluding rationality completely? The more constitutive irrationality is judged to be, the less likely it is that atrocity will seem to invite historical explanation. Equally significant is the question of rarity. In Card's reconsideration, she presents atrocities as less "extraordinary," which is to say more common, than she had first argued. She directs the reader's attention to "collectively perpetrated evils" (4) as opposed to evils for which individuals can he held accountable, and to the accumulation of what she calls "lesser wrongs," like "deep and pervasive inequalities" (7). This is a very proper and necessary recognition that the atrocity paradigm has a problem, as does this book, with *conditions* of injustice, conditions that may be more common and may not take the form of singular violent events.

Another conclusion to be drawn from these definitional elements is a seemingly self-evident point, but one that still needs to be made: atrocity must be distinguished from violence as such. It would be a serious mistake to count all violence as atrocity. Violence might well be ubiquitous, but atrocity is not. Thinkers like Etienne Balibar and David Simpson, who have pushed hard on the antithesis between violence and civility, have determined sadly that a civility completely purged of violence will always be unobtainable.[25] This proposition was already implied in the historical account of civility developed by Norbert Elias: "When a monopoly of force is formed, pacified social spaces are created which are normally free from acts of violence" (235).[26] Spaces that are free from acts of violence only arise, in other words, when force has been monopolized by early modern monarchy. In that process violence is displaced, not eradicated. Still, this does not quite mean that civility is an illusion, or simply "violence in disguise" (1). There is a difference, as Simpson argues, between microaggressions and macroaggressions, and that difference is not negligible. The "relatively minor aggressions" involved in, say, the exclusions that no civility (or literature) can avoid, "are (unless exploited by other interests) framed by a general performance of reflective detachment that inhibits acts of irreversible violence" (185). "Irreversible" is not one of the adjectives Card attaches to her definition of atrocity, but the point still holds: the worst kinds of violence, however defined, can in theory still be contained or diminished even if all violence cannot of course be eradicated—which implies that a history of atrocity is at least worth attempting. Such a history would not be possible if there were no differentiation between more violence and less violence.

As with racism, one of the prime causes of atrocity, this differentiation is not a premise that everyone will grant. Does history show lesser and greater degrees of racism? Does it show lesser and greater degrees of violence? Not everyone will be willing to entertain the idea that the answer may be yes. Resistance to the historicizing of atrocity is the common effect of a surprising variety of plausible logics. On the one hand, the unspeakable awfulness of massacres puts them in or near the category of the sublime, as if challenging and even incapacitating the categories on which we ordinarily rely to make such sense of life as we can. They defy comprehensibility itself. "Thought stood still," Susan Neiman writes of Auschwitz, "for the tools of civilization seemed as helpless in coping with the event as they were in preventing it" (256). On the other hand, there is the idea, rearticulated at the highest period of imperialism by its most fervent champions, that the struggle to conquer or be conquered is eternal, and in modern times only the scale has changed: "The struggle of races and of peoples has from now on the whole globe as its theatre; each advances toward the conquest of unoccupied territories."[27] Violent conquest is the only game there is; anyone who says otherwise is a hypocrite. The choice between eating and being eaten does not lend itself to a connected history, but only to chronicle: a list of horrible but singular events that repeat and repeat, going nowhere. Who these days is not a debunker of Hegel? And who, therefore, can claim to sit at a safe distance from what Hegel called (seeking to refute it, in full knowledge of what he was up against) history as a "slaughter-bench": people routinely butchered like cattle, day by day and week by week, with as little notice as a supermarket gives to the death of the animals whose meat it displays. It is an open question whether the rise of vegetarianism, spurred in part by environmental considerations, has made a dent in this powerful paradigm, taking over from the abolition of slavery as a key example of moral progress.[28] However carefully the case for a history that includes *moral* progress is separated off from a case for *actual* progress, it remains vulnerable to the charge that, by offering explanation, it also offers comfort where, in the eyes of many, comfort can only be illusory. Think of Roberto Bolaño's shunning of the narrative comforts of the murder mystery when he deals with the Ciudad Juarez femicides in *2666*. Each corpse is discovered as if it were the beginning of a detective story. Then, instead of the police following up on clues, instead of the gradual emergence of a detective story with its promise of clarification, exposure, perhaps even punishment, the reader gets only another corpse. And then another corpse. And then another. The pattern repeats until the reader is ready to throw the book across the room. Individual news items are gathered together to form a collective atrocity that might otherwise have escaped naming and even notice. What is striking in *2666*, as in the montage-like form Kluge chose for *Air Raid*, is that, while letting the chaos in, it doesn't keep explanation out. These are two examples of what I think of as good atrocity writing.

What *explanation* means itself needs to be elucidated, of course. It is what historian Caroline Elkins promises in *Legacy of Violence: A History of the British Empire* (2022).[29] After listing some of the kinds of violence for which the British Empire was responsible—"corporal punishments, deportations, detentions without trial, forced migrations, killings, sexual assaults, tortures, and accompanying psychological terror, humiliation, and loss" (28)—Elkins goes on: "I'm seeking to explain why and how Britain enacted these measures." Explaining is doing the historian's job. But observe how she explains her explanation. "Violence was not just the British Empire's midwife; it was endemic to the structures and systems of British rule. It was not just as an occasional means to liberal imperialism's end; it was a means *and an end* for as long as the British Empire remained alive. Without it, Britain could not have maintained its sovereign claims to its colonies" (23, italics mine). The italicized words illustrate how hard it is, entering the gravitational field of extreme violence, to maintain a reasonable level of explanation rather than dipping into moralizing or mysticism. It is different to propose, on the one hand, that violence was "endemic to the structures and systems of British rule," as Elkins proposes in the first sentence, and to propose that violence was not just a means to an end, but, as she says in the second sentence, an end in itself. Was imperial violence endemic? No doubt. Was it a means to the ends of extracting resources and maintaining imperial rule? Of course. But violence as an end in itself? What would that imply about the people who ordered it and carried out? The idea is certainly not unfamiliar—it is close to what some have said about Auschwitz. But the effort to explain atrocity does not commit the historian to entering a bidding war over the inexplicable monstrosity of the perpetrators or the kind and quantity of suffering they caused. It does not go without saying that the agents of British imperialism, as racist as many of them undoubtedly were, can be raised to the dark sublimity of motive attributed, rightly or wrongly, to the Nazis.

Terrible as British imperialism was, its historians don't have to play for such high stakes, at risk of losing their plausibility. There is no need to neglect the real if relative differences of scale and result between the Empire's "structures and systems" and those of the extermination camps. I say this while trying to keep in mind Arno Mayer's very proper insistence that Auschwitz cannot be understood without reference to the Nazi war of conquest and the attempt in the camps to mobilize resources for eastern conquest and resettlement, whatever the human cost.[30] Rationality had a place in the great irrationality of the Shoah. Even Las Casas, who frequently presents the cruelty of the Spanish conquerors as so excessive as to be incomprehensible, pauses to note that, as time went on and the Spanish goals shifted from plunder to control of labor, there was some calculated moderating of the violence: "Now they have sheathed their swords and no longer murder the natives on sight, they have gotten into the habit of killing them slowly with hard labour" (129). It's the same principle one can see at work, for those few prisoners who like Primo Levi did not go straight into the gas chambers of Auschwitz, in Levi's *If This Is a Man*.

This blurring of explanatory factors in Elkins's account is all the more striking because the comprehensive name she gives to the empire's structures and systems is not fascism but liberalism. Liberalism is in many respects a worthy target, but it doesn't explain what Elkins wants it to. It is no defense of liberalism to recall that it was not alone, ideologically speaking, in supporting imperialism. Christianity and militarism, for example, played a role, both of them often illiberal in the extreme. It seems at least as plausible to think of imperial violence as the mark of liberalism's gross if predictable self-betrayal. As Elkins herself observes, the extraction of resources by means of coercion only enters "center stage of our story when ordinary colonial laws and policing could not control labor unrest in the empire" (27). The rule of ordinary law: that's a rough account of what liberalism stands for. The idea that liberalism was driven to violate its own laws and contradict itself over the extraction of resources and the control of labor is perfectly consistent with its history in other times and places. That would seem the better explanation. But Elkins expresses discomfort with this alternative, which strikes her as too materialist. And then she takes her impatience with materialist explanation further. The violence, she says, "was inherent to liberalism. It resided in liberalism's reformism, its claims to modernity, its promises of freedom, and its notion of the law—exactly the opposite places where one normally associates violence" (27). Modernity is liberalism, she suggests, and liberalism *is* violence.

In discussions of atrocity, skepticism about (liberal) modernity's supposed moral blessings appears to have become the default setting. Those who do not go in for the sublime-incomprehensibility option, with its refusal of any historical trajectory, including the refusal of a provisional endpoint in something called modernity, are most likely tempted by the idea that while liberal modernity or modern liberalism is a historical reality, it is as essentially violent as Elkins says it is. Like some of the more generically uninteresting atrocity stories themselves, both of these alternatives might be described as excessively moralized. I mean by this that they are not truly historical: more interested in not shirking moral responsibility than in examining where moral responsibility should in fairness be allocated. But my effort to address them can wait for a consultation with the relevant texts. My own skepticism about the liberal discourses of human rights and humanitarianism, to which I alluded above, is less programmatic. My biggest problem, as mentioned, lies with their allergy to the contextualizing of atrocity and their corresponding reluctance (another way of saying the same thing) to balance moral indignation, which tries to stay eternally fresh, with historical explanation, which has no choice but to risk the relativizing of judgments. It is this reluctance that I was trying to underline in Elkins's otherwise valuable account of imperial violence. To these grounds for ambivalence, I add that the discourses of human rights and humanitarianism sometimes seem intent on displaying a sensitivity to suffering that is so relentlessly expansive that it escalates itself out of existence. As Ann V. Murphy observes, "A lack of recognition is seen as the gravest sort of violence . . . while at the same time, recognition itself is said to constitute a kind of violence in its own right" (5).[31] That's the assumption when liberal sentimentality is held to be merely a form of self-pleasuring, when the indignant witness to atrocity is held to be guilty of *enjoying* that atrocity. As James Dawes puts it in a discussion of the Rwandan genocide, "We are culpable, and it feels good to be culpable. It assures us that we are good people, because we are the kind of people who feel bad about these sorts of things" (21).[32] Take this one step further, as the sensibility of humanitarianism and human rights does not always discourage, and we become the kind of people who feel that, if we do something to prevent or punish or even merely investigate atrocity, we are as bad as the perpetrators of atrocity: "We must intervene, yet our intervention looks and feels much like injuring" (213).

When Card notes the need to frame responses to atrocity that are "honorable," the implication is that it is possible to respond to atrocity in a way that *is* honorable. This seems to me correct. It does not help our understanding of atrocity to pretend that all responses to atrocity are themselves necessarily dishonorable, and indeed just as bad as that to which they are responding. Yes, terrible things have been done in the name of humanitarian intervention and the so-called responsibility to protect.[33] But why make any effort to escape violence, let alone prevent it, if the apparent opposite of atrocity is condemned to be another atrocity? And how can you acknowledge that any effort to circumvent or diminish atrocity has ever succeeded even to the slightest degree—an acknowledgment that any genuinely differentiated history would require? To the extent that they encourage a hypersensitivity to suffering and the tirelessly accusatory finger that is the other side of that hypersensitivity, human rights and humanitarianism, the major players in any account of moral progress, in fact rule out any history of atrocity that would acknowledge moral progress. A progressive moral history would not have to be and indeed should not be teleological; it would merely have to recognize spaces provisionally emptied of atrocity in the past as well as some degree of herd immunity against the infectiousness both of atrocity itself and of its insidious legitimations after the fact.

This is a work of literary and cultural history. My theme is not, like a political scientist's, the action to be taken: who should act in the presence of atrocity, and when, and how. It is representations of atrocity after the fact, often long after the fact. Literary representations count as actions of a sort, of course. Describing violence always involves taking a position, and if it's a position that's critical of one's own military, it can certainly have consequences for the describer, as was the case for Tatsuzo Ishikawa's fictionalized account of ongoing Japanese atrocities against Chinese civilians in the late 1930s. (Ishikawa was arrested by the Japanese authorities—see below.) Still, even Ishikawa's novel, courageous as it was, is less consequential than the sort of action that the humanitarian militarists are proposing. It will not be obvious to everyone that, on a subject of such gravity, literature deserves to be listened to at all, or whether judgments of literary value really matter when the question at hand is accountability for massacres. If the relevant criterion of literary value is the avoidance of melodrama, as suggested in the brief history of atrocity writing offered by the volume *The New Killing Fields*, then the archive of qualified writings may end up being limited almost to the vanishing point. If the criterion is forensic verisimilitude, then writers will lose points if they rely, as they often do, on established tropes. It does not raise Las Casas in the estimation of modern readers to hear that some of his stories, like the one about "the Spaniard who stopped the mouths of the prisoners he was torturing with wooden bungs so as not to disturb his commander's siesta," were lifted wholesale from classical authors as (in Anthony Pagden's words) "part of a recognizable rhetorical strategy for arousing wonder in the reader" (xxxi).[34] And yet there can be no literary history of atrocity that does not pay attention to rhetorical strategies. Borrowings from earlier authors are not restricted to premodern or early-modern authors. A flagrant and fascinating example is prolepsis: specifically, the reverential bow offered to the famous opening sentence of Gabriel García Márquez's *One Hundred Years of Solitude* ("Many years later, as he faced the firing squad . . .") when atrocity is described by subsequent authors like Salman Rushdie, Orhan Pamuk, Haruki Murakami, and Kamila Shamsie, among others. Like Kluge's *Air Raid*, prolepsis forces the witness of atrocity to occupy at least one spot in time when the atrocity is *not* occurring. By its Homeric tradition, the future prolepsis evokes is also associated with fate, a premodern answer to the question of whether anyone is to blame for violence. Whether or not it avoids melodramatic binaries, this literary technique complicates questions of blame, just as the technology of aerial bombardment does. Assuming that there is no account of atrocity without some account of the blame for it, we can also assume that good writing about atrocity will do just that—will complicate blame, taking it beyond the simple binary of evil perpetrator and innocent victim, without doing away with blame altogether. Hence the discussion in chapter 5 of Kurt Vonnegut's *Slaughterhouse-Five* (1969), a novel about the mass killing of civilians from the air, a novel that marks one point of departure for the history of national self-accusation, and as it happens also a novel that makes a serious effort to blame no one.

Edward Thompson and Howard Zinn

That said, this book contains more than its fair share of admirable figures. Edward Thompson, father of New Left historian E. P. Thompson, was a Methodist missionary in India who abandoned his missionary work and became a notable critic of British colonialism. *The Other Side of the Medal*, published in 1925, was a scathing critique of British treatment of the Indian "Mutiny" of 1857, which Thompson argues had been hysterically partisan and inaccurate in the journalism of the time, with the falsehoods and the one-sidedness carrying over into the period's supposedly more objective historians. Thompson's book gave especially indignant attention to the atrocities committed by the British against Indian civilians, atrocities that, as it suggests, were a response both to the violence of the Mutiny itself and to the propagandistic, violence-inspiring misreporting of it. *The Other Side of the Medal* is a classic piece of atrocity writing, the genre which the present volume aspires to join. And yet it is possible to conclude that its project was misguided from the start, as is the genre. An Indian reviewer of Thompson's book pointed out that the atrocities Thompson discussed were "as nothing to the long-drawn out agonies of a whole nation of 247 million people, exposed daily to starvation, disease, ignorance and life-long misery."[35] As Sumit Sarkar comments in a 1989 afterword, "The focus on British atrocities as the root cause of Indian discontent is itself deeply limiting" (88).

The point could apply to any writing about atrocities. Atrocities are sensational. They bleed and they lead; they get more than their fair share of clicks. But they are relatively rare events, and (as indicated by Card) they are also arguably unrepresentative of the general conditions of life and the large-scale processes that determine any particular society and its discontents at that particular moment in time. It's very possible that *any* society is capable of committing atrocities as bad as those committed by the British in India if sufficiently provoked (as the British were) by stories, true or false, about horrors inflicted by the enemy on women and children.[36] It would be satisfying to think that what becomes visible in an extraordinary moment of horror is that moment's deep truth. (That extreme violence *is* the deep truth of any given moment is a familiar proposition to which we will have to return.) But it's possible that what is revealed is not the key to anything, but only a monstrousness that, given the right circumstances, is always lurking, always a potentiality, and always ready to embarrass the politically committed when those responsible come from the side to which they have given their loyalty. If what you want to understand is the horror of British colonialism, shouldn't you look elsewhere, as the reviewer of Thompson's book delicately suggests?

It's an important warning. One reason for persisting in this project nonetheless emerges from Sarkar's afterword. At some point Thompson seems to have gotten a bit tired of his missionary work in small Indian towns, Sarkar says, but it was not that fatigue that turned his life and opinions around. What happened was the Amritsar massacre on April 13, 1919. British troops fired into an unarmed crowd of Indian demonstrators at Jallianwallabagh, killing at least several hundred of them and wounding many more. Suddenly the atrocity-filled moment of 1857 came alive for Thompson, and with it much else about the colonial regime of which he knew he was a part. "The real transition," Sarkar writes, "began with Jallianwallabagh" (94). For better or worse—in this case, for better—that is the point about atrocity stories. They are events which, rightly or wrongly, make for real-life (and real *life*) transitions, as the atrocity at Jallianwallabagh did for Thompson and as other atrocities (the Holocaust, Hiroshima) have done for others.

It would perhaps be too much to claim that the same can be said about literary representations of atrocity, though more people are likely to encounter representations than are likely to experience atrocity personally, so that the literary archive might well have equal or even greater range.

At the risk of playing up exceptions at the expense of the rule—a risk that I will try not to run more often than necessary—I take another example of someone whose life was turned around by an atrocity. The biographer of historian Howard Zinn, famous author of the best-selling *A People's History of the United States* (1980), tells an anecdote from Zinn's military service at the end of World War II when Zinn, like my father, was flying B-17s.[37] (He was a bombardier.) "Two weeks before the European war came to a close—which everyone knew was imminent—Howard's squadron was ordered to bomb Royan, a beautiful French resort town (one of Picasso's favorite spots) far from the front, where several thousand German soldiers were encamped, awaiting surrender. Howard and the other crew members were offhandedly told that they wouldn't be carrying their usual load of 2,500-pound demolition bombs but instead thirty 100-pound canisters of 'jellied gasoline.' Howard realized only long after the war that the canisters were in fact napalm." The bombing "killed or maimed most of the German soldiers, caused severe damage to the town, and wiped out more than a thousand civilians. The Allied brass was delighted that it had managed to test its latest weapon before a peace treaty could inconveniently remove the opportunity" (15).[38]

It would be an exaggeration to say that Zinn had a personal experience of the atrocity. "The B-17s were flying so high that they were able to remain oblivious to the destruction their bombs were causing below. Howard was thereby spared any close-up of the war's horrors, of the screams and atrocities, of the dead children, the torn bodies, the glazed survivors wandering in search of family members" (14–15).[39] It was only a visit to Royan twenty years later, coupled with the sudden and painful consciousness of napalm that came with American involvement in Vietnam, also twenty years later, that turned the raid into an experience in the strong sense of the word, made it into an episode in a meaningful continuum.[40] When he returned to Royan, he learned that there was "widespread looting of Royan homes by French soldiers after 'liberation' " (269). The looting of French homes by French soldiers: like Rushdie's prolepsis, this realigns the antagonisms out of which atrocity is made, the antagonisms, which are obviously not simply national, of which the historian must make sense. Thus consolidated by time in the archives, the experience helped define the kind of large-scale history that Zinn would write, especially the book that made him a household name.

Although its subject is a national history, in *A People's History of the United States* Zinn's judgment of the Allied bombings must be described as cosmopolitan rather than national: "There was a mass base of support for what became the heaviest bombardment of civilians ever undertaken in any war: the aerial attacks on German and Japanese cities. One might argue that this popular support made it a 'people's war.' But if 'people's war' means a war of people against attack, a defensive war—if it means a war fought for humane reasons instead of for the privileges of an elite, a war against the few, not the many—then the tactics of all-out aerial assault against the populations of Germany and Japan destroy that notion" (412).[41] How do you write a people's history of a nation when the people in question support the aerial bombardment of another people? The narrower history of atrocity only makes that conundrum more difficult. Moralizing on behalf of the victims doesn't seem a satisfactory methodology. Can there be such a thing as a people's history of atrocity when atrocity, by its overwhelmingly violent nature, does not allow for the kind of popular agency that Zinn scrupulously records elsewhere? Can there be a people's history of atrocity when atrocity, the most extreme expression of injustice, can't confidently claim to guide the reader either to the everyday experience of injustice or to its deepest truth, which may not after all be its darkest truth? And what about blaming? Can writing about atrocity do without it? "Atrocities in modern warfare need not be deliberate on the part of the fliers or their superiors," Zinn writes; "they are the inevitable result of warfare itself. This fact does not exculpate the bombardiers; it implicates the political leaders who make the wars in which bombardiers fly, and all the rest of us who tolerate those political leaders" (260). Here blame is not judged to be irrelevant, but it is split in a complicated way between those who dropped the bombs, the political leaders who gave the orders, and "all the rest of us who tolerate those political leaders." If you are examining the description of a particular atrocity, that would be a lot to ask. What are the proper criteria, then, by which such a description ought to be evaluated? What would make it better or worse?

A People's History of the United States starts with Christopher Columbus. Columbus, arriving in the New World, takes some of the natives captive and demands to know where the gold is (1). Most of his captives end up dead. The founding story is thus an atrocity story. What's the moral of this paradigmatic-sounding anecdote? "My point is not that we must, in telling history, accuse, judge, condemn Columbus *in absentia*. It is too late for that. It would be a useless scholarly exercise in morality" (8). To the author of a book on literary representations of atrocity, the prospect of offering no more than "a useless scholarly exercise in morality" feels very real and very unpleasant. One would like to ask: Does the morality have to be dropped? *Can* it be dropped? What if anything would make such an exercise useful?

Zinn does not answer these questions directly, but what he says is suggestive: "The easy acceptance of atrocities as a deplorable but necessary price to pay for progress . . . that is still with us. One reason these atrocities are still with us is that we have learned to bury them in a mass of other facts, as radioactive wastes are buried in containers in the earth. We have learned to give them exactly the same proportion of attention that teachers and writers often give them in the most respectable of classrooms and textbooks" (8–9). We must unlearn, Zinn says, this "learned sense of moral proportion." But the upshot of his argument would seem to be that we cannot do without some sense of moral proportion, if only a sense of moral proportion with which we have not yet gotten well enough acquainted. No, we should not tell ourselves and our children, in Zinn's words, "yes, mass murder took place, but it's not that important" (8). "Not that important" cannot be the point. Mass murder is important. Less clear is: What kind of importance does it have?

One

Violence Was Like the Weather

In the late 1970s, the editors of the journal *New Left Review* conducted a series of interviews with Raymond Williams, subsequently collected in the volume *Politics and Letters*. One interview cast doubt on the great realist novels of the 1840s, which Williams admired for setting a new standard for a searching and comprehensive vision of social injustice. "In that decade," the interviewers say, "there occurred a cataclysmic event, far more dramatic than anything that happened in England, a very short geographical distance away, whose consequences were directly governed by the established order of the English state. That was of course the famine in Ireland—a disaster without comparison in Europe. Yet if we consult the two maps of either the official ideology of the period or the recorded subjective experience of its novels, neither of them extended to include this catastrophe right on their doorstep, causally connected to socio-political processes in England."[1] If more than a million deaths during the Irish famine, fatalities that were arguably caused in large part by English government policy, do not show up at all in the period's greatest novels, what does this say about the capacity of those novels to register the deep reality of its time? And if this incapacity holds true for catastrophic events "right on their doorstep," how much truer is it for more distant colonies like India, where atrocities were permitted and committed by the imperial system, even more directly and shamelessly? The *New Left Review* interviewers were asking their readers to imagine that even the English literature of the nineteenth century that is most respected today for its strenuous and unprecedented realism was unable to "do" atrocity when the atrocity was committed by their own country. There is much evidence in favor of this proposition. According to Google Ngram, usage of the word *atrocity* spikes around the French Revolution and remains much higher for *all* of the nineteenth century than it is for *any* of the twentieth century or after. Why? The most plausible reason is that in the nineteenth century, the term is a righteous accusation; it is aimed exclusively at the trespasses of others. Its righteousness has not yet been much troubled, as it would be in the wake of the Holocaust, the dropping of the atom bomb, and the movements of national liberation in Europe's colonies, which arguably shook Europe out of its pre-Copernican complacency. In the twenty-first century the word *atrocity* is still used a great deal, often too loosely, but its usage is more uneasy. It is restrained to some degree by an awareness that the accusation has been pointed back at the speaker's own collectivity, and for good cause.

If the movements of national liberation, the Holocaust, and the dropping of the atomic bomb were indeed among the primary sources of a new cosmopolitan sensibility, it follows that until recently there could only have been few self-indictments of atrocity. Ethnocentrism being as overwhelming as we know it to be, the relevant archive could only be meager; examples would be largely restricted to the mid-twentieth century and after. With a few exceptions, the bulk of the literature of imperial Europe and its settler colonial implantations would have to be judged incompetent to perform what has come to seem an important moral duty, perhaps even the duty that is definitive of cosmopolitanism: denouncing violence meted out by one's own people to foreigners. This would not be good news for humanists charged with upholding the value of the cultural heritage, or for someone trying to give atrocity a literary history.

A stronger version of this hypothesis would propose news that is even worse. The point here would be not just that for most of our cultural history self-indictment of atrocity has been close to impossible, but that there has been no room in it even for the *concept* of atrocity. The crucial element in that concept is not the scale of the killing, but an indignant response to it. Indignation derives from dignity; it presupposes a sense of worth or entitlement in the victim, a sense that is violated by violence. Without that sense of violation, there can of course be anger, mourning, a desire for revenge, and so on, but there cannot be the element of protest that the concept requires. In *The Better Angels of Our Nature: Why Violence Has Declined,* Steven Pinker argues that protest against violence is not natural or given. It comes into being only when the causes of violence can be reconceived as human and social, not religious or supernatural.[2] Initially it is seen as a misfortune. It is only later, in modernity, that it comes to be seen as an injustice. In ancient Greece, violence seemed unavoidable, and it was therefore attributed to fate or the will of the gods. (Pinker does not ask, as he might, whether violence seemed unavoidable because of the superstition or, as seems plausible, because Greek society's dependence on plunder *made* it unavoidable, and thus made the superstition unavoidable as well.) "Homer and his characters . . . deplored the waste of war, but they accepted it as an inescapable fact of life, like the weather—something that everyone talked about but no one could do anything about. . . . Rather than framing the scourge of warfare as a human problem for humans to solve, they concocted a fantasy of hotheaded gods and attributed their own tragedies to the gods' jealousies and follies" (5–6). The same holds, Pinker says, for the Bible's divinely ordained ethnic cleansing of the Midianites by the Israelites. In most of the culture that has been preserved up to one of several possible dawns of modernity, the successful exercise of violence might well be seen as tragic rather than triumphant, but like the weather it was something that humans could not imagine themselves understanding or controlling, let alone living without. In order for people to imagine themselves understanding and controlling violence, explanations that referred to fate and the will of God had to begin to sound as lame as "everything happens for a reason" sounds today.[3] Today, according to Pinker's metanarrative, violence has at last become something that humans feel they can at least potentially understand and, again at least potentially, can do something to prevent or inhibit. This conclusion is uplifting (perhaps too much so) for those whose main concern is the present, but it does even more damage to the cultural value of the past that we humanists make it our business to preserve and protect.

On the Politics of the Passage of Time

Setting aside for the moment the specifics of Pinker's history, I want to address a more general point: a backhanded defense of the value of the cultural past that works by rejecting *any* history, Pinker's or anyone else's, that locates the emergence of the concept of atrocity in a transition from the premodern to the modern era. Readers of Bruno Latour's *We Have Never Been Modern* will already be skeptical of Pinker's premise that modernity marks a significant moral as well as epistemological turning. Readers of Hayden White's "The Value of Narrativity in the Representation of Reality" will most likely have nodded at the Kantian-existential proposition that reality does not come in narrative form and that narrative, or history, is something we impose on a reality that in itself is formless, a chaos of random particulars. Atrocities, which are the most terrible things that humans can do to each other, give a special force to this perspective by stretching to the breaking point any and all beliefs in historical coherence. From this angle, the properly humble thing to do with accounts of atrocity is simply to list them, thereby respecting the singularity of each event and allowing it to speak to the present directly. The list is the chosen genre of Matthew White's *The Great Big Book of Horrible Things: The Definitive Chronicle of History's 100 Worst Atrocities* (2012).[4] An amateur historian and self-styled atrocitologist, White calls his book a chronicle. (His namesake Hayden might have preferred to classify it as annals, which refuse both narrative resolution and the organization of events around a center). White gives history's 100 worst atrocities in chronological order. His list begins with the wars between the Athenians and the Persians and ends with civil war in the Congo, 1998–2002. After the chronological listing, the book ranks the atrocities by the number of victims. (World War II, which for White subsumes the Holocaust, comes in first, ahead of Genghis Khan and Mao Zedong, who are tied for second place. Alexander the Great comes in at only number 70, with 500,000 dead, 250,000 of them civilians.) Both the numerical ranking and the chronological listing are set off against what White is repudiating: historical interpretation. For White, the irrefutable premise that controversy about atrocity can never be definitively abolished segues into the more questionable corollary that it would be foolish to try to interpret atrocity at all. White scorns those who track atrocities "back to some distant root cause and declare *that* to be the most horrible thing people ever did" (xv). This is not just true of *root* causes; he is equally scornful of historical causality as such. "So many threads of causality feed into any individual event that you can usually find a way to connect any two things you want" (xv). This is not as impassioned as declaring the project of understanding atrocity an obscenity, as Claude Lanzmann does, but it too rules out historical analysis as a profaning of the sacred. White's numerical ranking and chronological listing are also funny, detached as they are both from the interpreter's subjectivity and from the feelings of indignation, empathy, and shame that accounts of wanton slaughter might otherwise evoke.[5] The humor has a certain charm; it reflects White's cheery, hospitable promise that he will keep his appeals to readerly sentiment to a minimum. One of his subtitles is "Nobody Expects the Spanish Inquisition." Finding the right tone or angle of detachment when the subject is as viscerally gripping as atrocity is not a false problem, and humor is a defensible solution to it. (The first line of Zadie Smith's atrocity story "The Embassy of Cambodia" is "Who would expect the Embassy of Cambodia? Nobody.") Whatever solution one alights on, however, one would seem obliged to incorporate in some fashion the impulse to stop such things from happening. As far as that project is concerned, White has curbed his enthusiasm. If monstrous, melodramatic villains give you a burning desire to do something, he conveys the opposite message; he makes the very idea of doing something about atrocities seem misguided, even idiotic. As a collection of disconnected events, the list is comical in part because it is random, shapeless, incongruous, meaningless. A list has no through-line. It doesn't add up to anything. In this way it suggests that humanity's collective history, too, doesn't add up to anything—that the whole, even more than the parts, is random and meaningless.[6] And the same holds for any political action that might be taken in an effort to redirect that history. Try to intervene, and you would just make a fool of yourself.

White does not state explicitly that there is nothing to be done about atrocity. But that is the implication when he includes, as the first of his "three biggest lessons I learned while working on this list," the lesson that "chaos is deadlier than tyranny" (xvii). It follows that disruptive action taken against tyranny will be worse (measured in the currency of lives lost) than the tyranny itself. Action is thus counterproductive. Order, however unjust, is better than chaos. Justice is better left unpursued. The section on "The Three Kingdoms of China" (which ranks twenty-fifth, with thirty-four million casualties, though it also extends over almost a full century) opens with a paradigmatic sentence: "As the Han dynasty grew more corrupt, peasant revolts unleashed chaos" (53). Dynasties, kingdoms, and empires, however corrupt, represent order rather than chaos; hence they are preferable to peasant revolts even if their corruption is the cause of those revolts. And since (this is what White assumes) the peasant revolts in no way diminish the quantity of injustice or suffering in the world, for the peasants themselves or for anyone else, since they have no cumulative effect on subsequent social organization or on the number of future fatalities—to repeat, history imagined as a list is a list of *disconnected* events—there is nothing redemptive in the disorder unleashed by the downtrodden. White attaches the same lesson to the fall of the Roman Empire. Those concerned with atrocity should not rejoice at the overthrow of this prototypical imperialist power, for "the empire created real peace across a huge area for hundreds of years" (71).

Atrocity generates outrage, and outrage threatens to unsettle a status quo that, however imperfect, is better than the probably violent disorder that would follow if the outrage were to be expressed in action. That is the logic of White's compendium, and it is one logic from which I imagine some resistance to the project of this book will come. Burke's line about old violence, quoted above, puts that resistance concisely: "That which might be wrong in the beginning, is consecrated by time, and becomes lawful."[7] Here lawfulness means forgetting injustice, if only regretfully, rather than trying to rectify it. What the passage of time does is take the illicit benefits obtained by force of arms and legitimize them. Of course, Burke first reminds his reader that the benefits *were* illicit. On the one hand, he brings old acts of violence back to life, and does so without forcing anyone to watch the bloody acts of expropriation as if they were happening now—just what he did with British atrocities in India during the impeachment trial of Warren Hastings, and with sensational success. (I note in passing that this makes Burke a conspicuous counterexample to the hypothesis laid out above: in his examination of the misconduct of the East India Company, accusing his countrymen of atrocities committed against foreigners was exactly what he did.) On the other hand, with regard to property, he counsels the pragmatic wisdom of letting time decide in its quiet way that the scandal is yesterday's news, that the original injustice is no longer actionable.

Though Burke deserves credit for his ambivalence, many of his liberal followers have simplified his point, putting the emphasis on the pragmatic "let bygones be bygones" wisdom alone. They are not entirely wrong. Moral obligations *do* age. The passage of time *does* make a moral difference. The many, many deaths for which Alexander the Great was responsible are no longer grounds for criminal liability or reparative claims. Still, those many deaths (each of them once as real as more recent ones) do have to be talked about. And if so, *how* should they be talked about? How seriously they are taken will depend in part on how much time has passed, how discontinuous past atrocities are with the dilemmas facing the earth's current inhabitants. Discontinuity always seems to sound like the right answer. But it is a question, not an answer, and it depends in turn on what we imagine the passage of time has been filled by. In order to get a literary history of atrocity off the ground, attention must be paid to unspoken assumptions about the *content* of time, assumptions that may be both as instinctively persuasive and as counterproductive as Burke's. Does time work only to dissolve the clarity of moral judgments? Ta-Nehisi Coates has amended Martin Luther King Jr. by saying that the arc of the moral universe bends not toward justice but toward chaos. But chaos is no less an assumption than justice.

We cannot "wind the tape back to the injustice," legal theorist Jeremy Waldron writes, ventriloquizing Burke, "and make the world as though the injustice had never happened." Waldron continues: "The reparationist enterprise fails to take proper account of the fact that the people, entities, and circumstances in relation to which justice must now be done have changed radically from the peoples, entities, and circumstances in relation to which the violations were historically committed. Some of those changes are a result of the historic injustice. But . . . that does not mean they can be ignored or reversed. We must come to terms with each other here and now, irrespective of how we all got here."[8] In other words, let's not bicker about who killed whom.[9] Waldron's liberal cosmopolitanism wants to discourage any disturbing of the peace in the name of long-past injustices or acts of violence, especially where defending the peace means defending property rights. Humanist scholarship, whose mandate does not extend to adjudicating rival property claims or redistributing resources, is nonetheless a reparationist enterprise in its own sphere, and perhaps even beyond that sphere. How and what we remember inclines us to make up our minds about what does and doesn't need repair, how bad the need is, and eventually what is to be done. Along the way, it offers options of what history we think we belong to. This job can't be done well—this is the key point—unless it takes account both of old injustices and of the radical changes that, as Waldron rightly says, have intervened in the meantime. So we need to know what those changes are, and how radical.[10] The liberal position focuses on one kind of change. With time, victims and perpetrators have dispersed and disappeared, leaving behind only unaffiliated individuals. At best, those referred to as perpetrators today can be linked to the crime only as putative members of collectivities to which they can plausibly deny they belong.[11] What the passage of time does to collectivities is scatter them. What time does to an original act of injustice is disperse it, so that punishment and restitution could only target individuals who were not there at the time and cannot be properly held responsible for it. But solitary, unaffiliated individuals are not time's only product. If it seems intuitively that they are, this is an ideological effect whose liberal and neoliberal sources are not difficult to guess. Among the other products of time are norms and solidarities. Norms and solidarities bring people together. One of time's effects is the extension of solidarities. This is a less normative way of describing the rise of democracy. But let's not assume too much. Let's assume only that the effect of time's passage is not necessarily to split solidarities apart, generating an array of unaffiliated individuals, and let's assume that when solidarities do expand, they have an inhibiting effect on violence against those who are now newly included. It may not be much, but it's not chaos.

This needs to be said because, where atrocity is concerned, liberal common sense is compulsively drawn to chaos—perhaps more so, for liberalism's more careful champions, than to progress. According to David Rieff's book *In Praise of Forgetting: Historical Memory and Its Ironies* (2016), the effort to commemorate old violence, which is to say the effort to resurrect the motives, interests, and passions that accompanied atrocity, is the likely cause of further atrocity.[12] For Rieff, the power of time to erase violence is very real, and we should be grateful for it. In this sense, time is on our side. He writes: "The farther one goes back in time, say to the battles of the Chu-Han War in China (206–202 BCE) or to the Battle of Salamis between the Athenians and the Persians (480 BCE), the more questionable any moral justification for commemorating such events becomes" (17). There is a practical reason for forgetting old violence: "Far too often collective historical memory as understood and deployed by communities, peoples, and nations—which, again, is always selective, more often than not self-serving, and historically anything but unimpeachable—has led to war rather than peace, to rancor and resentment (which increasingly appears to be the defining emotion of our age) rather than reconciliation, and to the determination to exact revenge rather than commit to the hard work of forgiveness" (38–39). Forgiveness is hard work, yes, but for Rieff it is what will happen anyway, without any expenditure of effort at all. All you have to do is omit the commemorations and let time do its thing. Who needs to forgive if you have already forgotten, or know that ultimately you will forget? And when you do forget, what you will be left with is chaos, or what Rieff calls "the ultimate meaninglessness of history" (3–4). "Even if we radically narrow the frame," he writes, "excluding not only evolutionary or geological time but also the approximately 192,000 years that elapsed between the emergence in Africa 200,000 years ago of anatomically modern *Homo sapiens* and the advent of proto-writing (usually ideograms) in the sixth millennium before the Common Era . . . there still can be no reprieve from the reality that sooner or later every human accomplishment, like every human being, will be forgotten" (5). The conclusion is clear. If everything will ultimately be forgotten, then everything is ultimately meaningless.

In the long run, as the reader will have heard, we are all dead. But what does it mean in the short run to say that we are all dead in the long run? It amounts to deciding that, all things considered, things as they are are not so bad. Marking himself off from the pious sentimentality of those who always and everywhere call for remembrance, a sentimentality that he presents as dangerous, Rieff comes across as both pragmatic and tough-minded. Morally speaking, however, his argument seems not tough but remarkably soft. If I know that the meaning of an action I take today will come to depend on an infinite and totally unpredictable set of future consequences, will be manhandled by inhabitants of the future whose unpredictable perspectives I will not be there to appeal, and most likely will be of no interest at all to the future one way or the other, the power of time being what it is, then I can safely act now—for example, by committing acts of violence—without worrying about the meaning of what I am doing. Morally speaking, to be ignored and forgotten is to be protected from judgment, which is as close as makes no difference to being forgiven in advance. Everything is therefore permitted.

Rieff's argument can of course be said to obey a moral impulse. The suggestion is that, morally speaking, what we want is to prevent future violence, and forgetting about past violence is the best way to accomplish that. It's Burke's thought again, a thought applied specifically to atrocity in White's *Great Big Book of Horrible Things*: no theory of atrocity should be promulgated, for any theory would be likely to blame someone and, by generating or augmenting resentment, make another atrocity more likely. The status quo, however imperfect, should be treated as legitimate and defended against disturbances, for order is better than disorder, even or especially when disorder presents itself in the form of appeals for a higher version of justice. There is obviously some merit in this argument. How far you are willing to go with it will depend on how worth defending you hold the status quo to be and whether you can imagine efforts to improve it that are less atrocity-prone than the history that produced it. In short, it will depend on your understanding of history. To see history as something that cannot be understood—as meaningless by definition because everything will eventually be forgotten and the sun will eventually go out and life on earth will cease—is to short circuit an interpretive possibility that seems worth keeping in play.

Rieff is correct that historical meaningfulness is dangerous. Holding perpetrators to account will look to the victims' side like an invitation to long-delayed vengeance. But it's by no means certain that holding perpetrators to account is the only thing representations of atrocity do, whether literary or not, or even the main thing they do. Some would wish that they did more of it. In any event, there are modes and variants of blaming. In "Morally Blaming Whole Populations," Peter A. French coins the term "non-moral blaming," linking it to what J. L. Austin called "behabitive blaming."[13] Austin's examples, which include scolding, rebuking, and chiding, involve adopting a critical attitude without trying to hold the addressee responsible.[14] The addressee benefits from a familial intimacy, an assurance that the relation cannot be endangered by what is said, a permanence. Characteristic objects of behabitive blaming are, remarkably, children and the weather. Children and the weather, which seem so different from each other, come up with some frequency in these pages. The weather should have been better. I'm to blame that my child became a thief, though I'm not legally guilty. French suggests that behabitive or non-moral blaming may be the appropriate mode for collective war crimes like those of the US in Vietnam. "The American people" is not the same as "all Americans" (283). And "what is true of 'the American people' need not be, and actually often is not true of each and every American" (283).[15] If it is true that the bombing of civilian targets from the air, like the bombing of Halberstadt on April 8, 1945, calls for a different moral calculus than, say, the rape and murder that we observe in the first scene of Johann Grimmelshausen's novel *Simplicissimus* (discussed in chapter 2), a first step toward defining it is positing that, while blaming cannot be replaced by forgiving and forgetting, other modes of blaming exist. Specifying them would be the work of a moral philosopher. Tracing their development would be the work of a historian. The subset of literary history would necessarily pay attention to what literature has done with atrocity that is more subtle than merely registering the fact that it happened and blaming the perpetrators. But the relevant modern history, including literary history, would also have to include the obscure and unprecedented combination of empowerment and disempowerment involved in belonging to a nation-state. The nation-state, like the family, is something to which you cannot easily choose not to belong, though it can choose to reject you. It's the point that Hannah Arendt made in "The Right to Have Rights" when, acknowledging her own surprise, she turned back to Edmund Burke. About this, she says, Burke was correct: the stateless, like Arendt herself, know that human rights are indeed meaningless unless those who need them belong to a political community that is prepared to back them up.[16] The state has in its capacity to make those rights meaningful. Steven Pinker follows Norbert Elias in suggesting that the epochal shift in the conceptualization of violence (for Pinker, not merely a reconceptualization but an actual diminishment of violence) tracks the rise of the modern state, which "uses a monopoly of force to protect its citizens from one another" (680).[17]

Pinker's Whiggish misfortune-to-injustice narrative, crowned by a triumphant overcoming of premodern fatalism, invites immediate suspicion on its modern end. Kurt Vonnegut's novel *Slaughterhouse-Five* does what Williams's interviewers say the social realist novels of the 1840s cannot do. It charges Vonnegut's own society with committing an atrocity against the citizens of another nation: the firebombing of Dresden. The novel is one of the twentieth century's early and notable instances of atrocity self-indictment. And yet its single most cited phrase, "so it goes," suggests that fatalism has by no means disappeared from Vietnam-era America. Clearly the story is more complicated than Pinker makes it seem.

Old Violence

And on the premodern end? Pinker suggests that even scruples about violence will be impossible, let alone full-blown self-accusation. What young readers will take from exposure to the Great Books would certainly include a taste for sexual assault and large-scale bloodletting. For what it's worth, there is a great deal of evidence that this has indeed been the content of elite education. Over the centuries many aspiring killers have gratefully acknowledged the inspiration of the Bible and the classics. On his campaigns, where the casualties ultimately numbered in the hundreds of thousands, Alexander the Great slept with a copy of the *Iliad* under his pillow.

Pinker's summary of Numbers 31 in the Hebrew Bible goes like this: "As the Israelites proceed toward the promised land, they meet up with the Midianites. Following orders from God, they slay the males, burn their city, plunder the livestock, and take the women and children captive. When they return to Moses, he is enraged because they have spared the women, some of whom have led the Israelites to worship rival gods. So he tells his soldiers to complete the genocide and to reward themselves with nubile sex slaves they may rape at their pleasure" (7–8). This account of atrocity richly deserves the publicity Pinker gives it. If class discussion of Numbers 31 were to be mandatory, a move that local groups asserting parental rights over the curriculum could perhaps be tricked into accepting (after all, it's the Bible), the educational experience would be truly instructive. And yet the text invites some further nuance of the sort that doesn't seem to interest Pinker. Teachers trained in the Great Books might draw attention, for one thing, to the cause of Moses's rage. Moses is angry because the returning warriors seem to have taken for granted that women and children should *not* normally fall victim to genocide. It's true that their scruples, immediately countermanded, do not save any lives. It's also true that no scruples at all are expressed about the rape of captive women. Yet there the scruples are. They are one step of the two steps in a very short, two-step story. How to explain the hesitation to make a complete job of the ethnic cleansing if in that period violence could only be attributed to fate or the will of God? The initial assumption by the Israelites that Midianite women and children were not on the kill list casts doubt on the assumption that premodern writings were necessarily and totally indifferent to the killing of noncombatants, even foreign noncombatants—that they were obliged to see atrocity as fate, hence not really to see it at all.[18]

More reflection might also have gone into the fact that the Biblical text allots disproportionate space to enumerating the cattle, sheep, asses, and other booty taken from the massacred Midianites. The battle with the Midianites is over by verse 8. Verses 9–18 deal with the issue of what to do with the captives. The bulk of the book, verses 25–54, enumerates the booty and lays out with great care how it should be divided: who gets what livestock, and how many of each. (As one might expect, captured women and animals are subject to the same mode of utilitarian calculation.[19]) The Bible seems to be taking into account the possibility that some people would get more than they feel they deserve, and others less, and that, as in the *Iliad*, the results of this apportionment would be angrily divisive. More important, however, is the fact that the apparent necessity represented by the will of God can also be translated into material interest, material interest as it is conceived by a particular kind of nomadic society and as it is therefore also embodied in that society's moral norms.[20] Classroom discussion could certainly focus on the way ideological assumptions (for example, the assumption that the killing of foreigners is not a moral problem) are fitted to patterns of social organization (stealing livestock from foreigners is one important way in which our society survives and prospers). Homework assignment: Is this relevant to the contemporary United States? Homer notices that Achilles was famous for his accomplishments both as a warrior and as a thief of livestock. A society that did not rely on stealing animals might well have a different understanding of moral necessity. The hypothesis thus arises that the moral history of atrocity will have something to do with the extent to which the prevailing type of society is in the habit of depending on violence to secure or increase its material prosperity.

According to the *Oxford English Dictionary* the word *noncombatant* did not emerge until the early nineteenth century, but the concept clearly did not have to wait so long. In his account of how a mass slaughter by his soldiers followed the Roman conquest of Avaricum, Julius Caesar in *The Gallic War* says that his men "were so severely provoked" by the fighting they had been through "that they spared neither the elderly, nor the women, nor even the little children" (159).[21] By granting them an "even," Caesar makes it clear that he does not take for granted the slaughter of "the little children." He seems to have felt that scruples about the murder of the elderly, women, and little children had at least to be addressed even if, as in the Bible, those scruples had no consequences. It seems empirically verifiable, and not merely an assertion of dogmatic humanism, that there has always been at least some degree of revulsion against the killing of children, women, and old people, however weak and embryonic that revulsion might be, and that some sign of this revulsion or distaste could be found in a variety of premodern places.[22] So the trajectory of indignant representations of atrocity does not go from not-there to there. Like most histories, what we think of as invention or discovery is actually a matter of relative quantity and quality, of scale and proportion. It also seems worth noting how the "even the little children" passage starts. "Not one of our men gave a thought to booty. They were so severely provoked by the massacre at Cenabum and the effort they had put into the siege that they spared neither the elderly, nor the women, nor even the little children." To say that on this occasion the men did not give a thought to booty is to say that the norm in such cases was, of course, for the men to think very much of booty. And that would have had consequences for the civilians who stood between them and their taken-for-granted reward. The forcible dispossession of civilians was the name of the game. The first line of Matthew White's chapter on the Gallic War (number 61 on his list of atrocities, with 700,000 dead) goes like this: "The surest way to please the voters of Rome was to bring back plenty of loot from foreign conquests and distribute it liberally throughout the city" (37).[23] White may resist a general theory of atrocity, but he does some persuasive explaining of Caesar's atrocity-filled rise to power. To judge from the example, a large number of dead and raped civilians would have been the norm.

This is from Josephus's *The Jewish War*, written in Greek in the years following the destruction of the Second Temple in 70 CE. "The rebels were by now powerless to protect the building, and the whole area was a scene of carnage or rout. Most of the victims were ordinary citizens, unarmed and defenseless, slaughtered wherever they were found. Corpses piled up round the altar, as blood cascaded down the sanctuary steps and the bodies of those killed on the upper level slithered to the bottom" (326, section 259). Josephus pauses to express "deep mourning for the loss of this marvelous building" (326, section 267), and then he returns to the task at hand: "As the temple burned anything found was looted and anyone caught was killed. The slaughter was massive—no pity shown for age, no regard for rank: children, old men, laymen, priests were killed indiscriminately, and war extended its grip to encompass people of every class and condition, no matter whether they were begging for mercy or trying to resist" (327, section 271). It is unsurprising that Josephus pays as much attention as he does to civilian casualties among the Israelites. Until a year or two before, he had been an Israelite general fighting in the anti-Roman rebellion, and although he had gone over to the Romans, he had a certain extra empathy for the suffering of what had been his people. Divided loyalties, as in cases of civil war, are one obvious solution to the mystery (perhaps not a mystery at all) of how ethnocentrism could sometimes be overcome and a misfortune could be translated into an injustice.[24]

If a prize were to be awarded for literary history's first self-indictment of atrocity, one strong contender would certainly be Thucydides, whose *History of the Peloponnesian War* was the model Josephus was trying to imitate. Thucydides gives an account (it's not a full action-packed narrative, like Josephus's) of the 415 BCE ethnic cleansing of the island of Melos by his fellow Athenians. Melos wanted to remain neutral; the representatives of Athens answered that this was not permissible. After a lengthy dialogue between the two sets of emissaries, there was fighting, which goes undescribed. Athens wins. Thucydides tells us that all the Melian men who have not already been killed are put to death, and the women and children are sold into slavery. The island is then resettled by Athenians. As so often, it's unclear how far this neutral-sounding account of mass killing took a position or, if so, whether that position was critical enough to stand out against the mainstream opinion around it. Classical scholars have suggested that critique of the Melian massacre was also expressed, more obliquely, by Euripides's play the *Trojan Women*, which was also produced in 415. (Some readers might even follow Simone Weil in counting the *Iliad* as deploring the waste of life that the poem makes seem so inevitable.) Should the Melian dialogue even count as an accusation? Thucydides's account was too impartial-sounding for the taste of some of his fellow Athenians; he was suspected of harboring secret pro-Spartan sympathies. But elsewhere in his history he was much harder on the Thracians, whom he sees as a separate race, for their sack of Mycalessus: the Thracians "rushed into Mycalessus, looting homes and temples and killing all the people they came across, one after another, sparing neither old nor young. They even killed women and children, even beasts of burden, every living thing they saw. For when they are on a rampage, the Thracian race is the most murderous, on a level with the worst barbarians . . . They even burst into the boys school—the biggest in the town—that the boys had just entered, and hacked them all to pieces" (285).[25] As Kristofer J. Petersen-Overton comments, "The passing of more than two millennia has done nothing to soften the horror of this account" (16).[26] Yet as Petersen-Overton does not say, this account is more the rule than the exception both in its horror and in the fact that it is the Other who is accused of that horror. What is special about Melos is that if it can indeed be considered an accusation, it is unquestionably a *self*-accusation.

Logically speaking, it can only be an accusation if the accused were free to behave otherwise. That is what comparison with Mycalessus establishes. On Melos, unlike at Mycalessus, the women and children were not killed, but were merely sold into slavery. (I pause briefly to imagine how much is left unsaid in that "merely.") To kill or not to kill: on that issue, at least, Thucydides knew that the Athenians enjoyed some freedom of choice. To go back to Pinker's indispensable phrase, they knew the violence they committed was not like the weather because, having issued similarly genocidal orders against the inhabitants of Mytilini, on that occasion they had changed their minds and countermanded those orders. So atrocity was not necessity.[27]

On the other hand, no reference is made to a principle of justice that would be violated by ethnic cleansing. The Athenians say to the Melians, "of the gods we hold the belief, and of men we know, that by a necessity of their nature wherever they have power they always rule. And so in our case since we neither enacted this law nor when it was enacted were the first to use it, but found it in existence and expect to leave it in existence for all time, so we make use of it, well aware that both you and others, if clothed with the same power as we are, would do the same thing" (book 5, chapter 105, 166–69).[28] The Melians answer, of course. But their answer goes off to other matters. They do not reply that, if they had the power, they would *not* do the same thing. This missed opportunity suggests that when they refer to "justice," as they do more than once, they are not referring to any moral principle that would stop them from using their power, if they had it—that would restrain violence against, say, rebellious colonies or city-states refusing to submit to colonial power. This void in the dialogue suggests that no such principle existed.

If indeed there was no such principle, even if there is reason to believe that were the shoe on the other foot, the Melians would have killed and enslaved the Athenians, it does not follow that what the Athenians did was legitimate or that moral objections to other enterprises of ethnic cleansing vanish. First of all, who are the "they" who are imagined doing the same thing? Clearly "they" do not include the children. Secondly, moral objections may have no basis in a universal human decency—clearly they do not—but they do have a history. But before getting to the consequences of that history, precarious though it may, let us assure ourselves that a major shift in attitudes toward violence has indeed occurred. That shift can be illustrated by contrasting Nahuatl and Spanish accounts of the destruction of Tenochtitlan in 1521. Several Nahuatl texts, assembled and translated in the ten years following the fall of Tenochtitlan, describe the surprise slaughter of the unarmed celebrants of the Fiesta of Toxcatl at the hands of the invading Spaniards. One account of the atrocity, preserved in the *Codex Florentino*, goes as follows: "They attacked all the celebrants, stabbing them, spearing them, striking them with their swords. They attacked some of them from behind, and these fell instantly to the ground with their entrails hanging out. Others they beheaded: they struck off their heads, or split their heads to pieces. They struck others in the shoulders, and their arms were torn from their bodies. They wounded some in the thigh and some in the calf. They slashed others in the abdomen, and their entrails all spilled to the ground." (76).[29] The passage is surprisingly attentive to where the blows landed, though the diversity of body parts had no impact on the end result, which like the exposure of entrails that should remain unexposed was repetitive. Otherwise, what is most conspicuous in this passage is the absence of any explicit condemnation of the attackers. Later in the texts there will be eloquent expressions of mourning for those who were killed and for the civilization that was destroyed, but there is still little or no accusation. No one says, as a modern person might say, that this is an immoral war of aggression. Terms like *good* and *evil*, *guilty* and *innocent* do not appear. The Aztecs do not call what was done to them an atrocity.

To what can this lack of condemnation be attributed? To nothing more mysterious, it would seem, than the fact that the Aztecs too were violent aggressors. J. Jorge Klor de Alva, in the foreword to the English translation of *Broken Spears* (in the Spanish original, "visions of the vanquished"), observes that "in the sixteenth century texts . . . the Spaniards are rarely judged in moral terms, and Cortés is only sporadically considered a villain. It seems to have been commonly understood that the Spaniards did what any other group would have done or would have been expected to do if the opportunity had existed" (xxi).[30] If we moderns object that the sixteenth century lets the Spanish off too easily, that objection can serve as a useful reminder that, in other matters as well, we might want to grant more respect to our modern value judgments rather than assuming that the judgments of other times and places should be taken as authoritative. In historical context, however—and the impulse to factor in historical context is one of modernity's legacies—what Klor de Alva says makes perfect sense.[31] The Aztecs had built an empire. It would have been remarkable had they accused the Spanish of violating a moral norm that they themselves did not recognize, a norm that would have precluded them from the aggression that allowed that empire to be built.[32] Plunder, in the normalized form of tribute, was as much a part of their society as of any other empire. Another Nahuatl text, the so-called *Codex Mendoza*, chronicles the conquests of each Aztec ruler from 1325 to

1521 and includes lists of the tribute that resulted from each conquest. Moctezuma, it tells us, "made incessant demands for tribute" from the peoples he had subjugated.[33] Tribute entailed subjugation, and subjugation entailed violence.

Bartolomé de Las Casas, who is sometimes claimed as the first modern writer to accuse his countrymen of atrocity, describes the same event, and does so during the same years. (From hearsay, not from direct observation.) But Las Casas writes from a very different perspective—a perspective that, unlike the Aztec version, assumes it *was* an atrocity. Like the Aztecs, Las Casas emphasizes "rank and station," the fact that the victims were "the noblest of the citizens" (50).[34] He draws his Spanish readers into his own abhorrence of the massacre by reminding them of things that they and the victims have in common, like their own tradition of respect for high birth and their own custom of remembering their history in song. The killing, he says, "caused horror, anguish and bitterness throughout the land; the whole nation was plunged into mourning and, until the end of time, or at least as long as a few of these people survive, they will not cease to tell and re-tell, in their *areitos* and dances, just as we do at home in Spain with our ballads, this sad story of a massacre which wiped out their entire nobility, beloved and respected by them for generations and generations" (50–51). Summing up, however, he uses a distinctively modern vocabulary. He speaks of "this barbaric and unprecedented outrage, perpetrated against innocent individuals who had done nothing whatever to deserve such cruelty" (51). The victims were innocent; they had done nothing to deserve their suffering. The perpetrators were guilty. To Las Casas this massacre is not a misfortune, but an injustice.

The language of injustice helps Las Casas justify the historical fact that, after this provocation, the natives "took up arms and attacked" (51). He insists that "they had every right to, given the attacks we have described that had been made on them; a reasonable and fair-minded man will say that theirs was a defensive action and a just one" (51–52). His argument is largely persuasive to modern Western ears, and that fact says something important about the transformations of moral sensibility that modernity has wrought. For that matter, Las Casas's case already got some purchase in the Spain of the mid-sixteenth century. He was instrumental in getting a law passed to protect the Indigenous people. (It didn't.) But what Las Casas says has nothing in common with the lexicon of the Aztecs whose cause he is trying so hard to represent. To the Aztecs themselves, the decision to attack was no doubt strategic, a judgment of the new situation on the ground, and also emotional. There is no evidence in the existing texts, however, that it marked a moral turning point. To them, the Spanish destruction of Tenochtitlan seems to have been not an injustice but a terrible misfortune, like an earthquake. In that sense, these antithetical views of the violence, Indigenous and European, fall squarely within Pinker's narrative of violence as tracing a passage from representations of misfortune to representations of injustice—from premodern violence, seen as fate or the will of the gods, hence beyond moral judgment, to modern violence, seen as caused by humans, comprehensible to humans, at least theoretically preventable by humans, hence open to moral condemnation.[35]

Again, the break is far from absolute. The identification of atrocity with fate or the will of God does not disappear in Las Casas's time. One of the many atrocity stories Las Casas tells in his *Short Account of the Destruction of the Indies* recounts the Spanish pursuit and capture of a king of Hispaniola, who had gone into hiding after the rape of his wife.[36] The Spanish attack the local leader who was protecting him, and the story concludes as follows: "The carnage was terrible and, eventually, they tracked down the fugitive, took him prisoner, put him in chains and shackles and bundled him on to a ship bound for Castile, only for him to perish, along with many Spaniards, when the ship was lost at sea. A fortune in gold sank beneath the waves that day, among the cargo being the Great Nugget, as big as a loaf of bread and weighing three thousand six hundred *castilians*. In this way God passed judgment on the great iniquities committed by the Spanish" (20). The oddity of this narrative about God passing judgment is underlined on the next page when its structure is repeated. Another Indigenous king, Caonabó, is captured by trickery and put on board another Spanish ship, and the same thing happens: "The Almighty determined not to allow this act of duplicity and injustice to pass unnoticed and, that night, sent a violent storm in which all six of the ships, still in the harbor and on the very point of setting sail, sank with the loss of all hands. Caonabó, shackled and chained as he was, perished along with them" (21). What to do with the fact that Las Casas continues to see these shipwrecks as God's judgment on the Spanish, and does so even though in both cases the victims include the Indigenous prisoners? It might seem that, if He wanted, God would be clever enough to devise a way of punishing the Spanish without also sacrificing the captured Indigenous people along with them. This line of thinking does not trouble Las Casas. Nor does he enter into theological argument on this point with his fellow Spaniards, who as he notes see their victories over the Indigenous people as also expressing God's will. The Spanish "proclaim and record for posterity their conviction that the 'victories' they continue to enjoy over local populations, by dint of massacring them, comes from God . . . and take care to give paeans of praise to the Lord and to recognize the part He has played in their success" (70).[37]

Continuities like this between atrocity's supposedly distinct premodern and modern representations raise interesting questions about the before as well as the after. How fatalistic *was* premodern fatalism? One Nahua poem ends, unsurprisingly, by asking the Nahua god whether he is "weary of your servants? / Are you angry with your servants, / O Giver of Life?" (149).[38] What did it mean for a non-European voice to ascribe mass violence to a divine source—for example, when the Narragansetts who were burning Providence in the midst of King Philip's War told Roger Williams "that God was [with] them and Had forsaken us for they had so prospered in Killing and Burning us far beyond What we did against them" or when they taunted the English victims of the killing and burning, "Where is your O God?" (120, 105).[39] It had clearly occurred to the Narragansetts, as it has occurred to others since, that one might address a god in the presence of injustice and not get back a satisfactory answer, or not get back any answer at all. Where *is* your O God? Is there even an interlocutor on the other end of the dialogue, with its so very evocative vocative? No question could be more modern. If there is a line dividing premodern from modern conceptions of atrocity, it is not an unbroken one.

It may be, then, that Pinker is underestimating the force, complexity, and ambiguity of premodern thinking about violence. He is clearly right, on the other hand, that with regard to its attitude to atrocity, modernity has indeed witnessed a significant change, as Las Casas's account of the massacre at Tenochtitlan decisively indicates. The case can be confirmed by following the history of the word *conquest*. In premodern Europe, according to Yves Winter, conquest was not only not condemned; it was celebrated. If anthropologists have discovered a society inside or outside Europe in which conquerors were not hailed as heroes, I would beg to be informed about it. Hero-hailing seems universal, and it also seems natural enough given that in Europe at least, conquering a given territory conferred the legal and moral right of dominion over that territory and all of its inhabitants. Winter pays special attention to the long continuity of this right both in Spain and in England. "Until the early 16th century, the English Crown exercised its authority on the basis of the right of conquest." In the seventeenth century, the Whigs "contested the *fact* of the Norman Conquest" but for the most part "did not challenge the *right* of conquest."[40] It was the Levellers, representing the left-wing of Cromwell's forces and eventually an opposition to Cromwell himself, who argued that "the king's law is tyrannical precisely because it has its origins in conquest in violence." For "the first time in European political discourse," conquest thus "becomes the basis for claims not only in favor but also against political authority." Las Casas, Winter points out, refused to describe what the Spanish were doing in the Americas as a conquest because in the eyes of his readers, even the most well-disposed, to do so would have made the atrocities seem legitimate. It would have given them "*a legal and moral claim, . . .* a legal *title to rule.*" That was the logic of established thought across Europe: "The conquerors—whether it was the Norman conquerors of Sicily or the crusaders in the eastern Mediterranean—*derived their political rights and authority directly and explicitly from the fact of conquest.*" It was not until the period of the Enlightenment, Winter goes on, that conquest begins to be disavowed, gradually and only partially. By the middle of the twentieth century, however, the illegitimacy of conquest is pretty well established. Participating in the dispossession of a peaceful Palestinian village in 1948, the soldier-protagonist of S. Yizhar's *Khirbet Khizeh* asks himself, "Wasn't it our right?" And he gets an immediate answer from within himself: "My guts cried out. Colonizers, they shouted. Lies, my guts shouted. Khirbet Khizeh is not ours. The Spandau gun never gave us any rights" (109).[41]

The disavowal of the right of conquest has of course never been complete. Its incompleteness can be savored in the fact that so much of the world declined to condemn the Russian invasion of Ukraine in 2022, or in the realist/nihilist assumption (which can also be seen as distinctively modern) that there is no alternative to an unending struggle to conquer or be conquered—that this is simply what life *is*. It's perhaps worth noting how consonant this sophisticated modern realism/nihilism is with the views of Adolf Eichmann, which came to light only after his execution and the controversy over Hannah Arendt's "banality of evil" thesis. "For Eichmann and his fellows, genuine thinking is racial thinking. He held every people to be engaged in the struggle for world domination; he believed this to be a law of nature, in which the drive for self-preservation is stronger than any other force, especially 'so-called moral drives'" (332).[42] If the drive to conquest is omnipresent and eternal and is only camouflaged by liberal moralizing, then the modern disavowal of conquest is not so much incomplete as hypocritical. (I return to this idea in the Epilogue.) The beyond-good-and-evil, morality-as-hypocrisy position has considerable purchase on educated common sense. Still, the forswearing of conquest seems to have been successful enough to allow atrocity to be discriminated from the unending flow of misfortunes, which is to say identified as something that can and should be discouraged. If so—I repeat myself—why would this not count as a moral accomplishment, if only a small and unsatisfying one?

Conquest and the Crusades

It is unwise, of course, to generalize about premodern accounts of atrocity on the basis of a handful of instances, some of them no doubt questionably translated or otherwise unreliable. Still, for anyone who is curious about whether humanity possesses something that can be called a moral history, it's hard to see another course of action, and it would seem intellectually irresponsible to give up on the question of whether anything significant has changed out of fear of generalization. Meanwhile, there remains a separate question about *how to evaluate* the contrasting accounts. To put this crudely: Are we sure that the modern ones are morally and aesthetically superior? Those who are allergic to modern moralizing might for example prefer the earlier descriptions. Consider some exemplary premodern moments. For the Arab historian Imad ad-Din, describing the battle between Saladin's army and the Crusaders at Tiberias, there is no question who the good guys are. The stakes of the battle are "monotheism at war with Trinitarianism, the way of righteousness looking down upon error, faith opposing polytheism" (131).[43] Saladin's victory is thus a victory of good over evil. But the gruesomeness of the description is not governed by this moral division. "I passed by them and saw the limbs of the fallen cast naked on the field of battle, scattered in pieces over the site of the encounter, lacerated and disjointed, with heads cracked open, throats split, spines broken, necks shattered, feet in pieces, noses mutilated, extremities torn off, members dismembered, parts shredded, eyes gouged out, stomachs disemboweled, hair colored with blood" (135). The list of body parts has much in common with the parataxis of the Nahuatl texts. It extends for another twelve lines, each body part matched up with injuries specific to it. As it goes on, it becomes more a virtuoso display of rhetorical skill than a visualization of corpses. And it is also remarkable for what it leaves out. It says nothing about which side the owners of these body parts belonged to. The description is of the fall of the city of Tiberias, which has been besieged, and the fall of a city ordinarily meant the death of many noncombatants, yet the text says nothing about whether the corpses are those of noncombatants or of soldiers. That distinction doesn't seem to register. Like the Nahuatl account of the massacre at Tenochtitlan, the scene of carnage is rhythmically full to overflowing, but the moral significance one might have expected from the killing, the connection between the injuries suffered and the issues at stake, is a powerful absence.

Perhaps surprisingly, some Christian accounts of the violence meted out by the Crusaders to the infidels follow much the same rhetorical pattern. Discussing the

Christian capture of Jerusalem in July 1099, during the First Crusade, Geraldine Heng quotes a famous eyewitness account as follows:

> Some of the pagans were mercifully beheaded, others pierced by arrows plunged from towers, and yet others, tortured for a long time, were burned to death in searing flames. Piles of heads, hands, and feet lay in the houses and streets, and indeed there was a running to and fro of men and knights over the corpses. . . . Shall we relate what took place there? If we told you, you would not believe us. So it is sufficient to relate that in the Temple of Solomon and the portico crusaders rode in blood to the knees and bridles of their horses. (358)

Again, there is no question about which side the witness is on. "In my opinion," Raymond d'Aguiliers writes, "this was poetic justice" (*Historia* 127–28).[44] As Heng comments, such scenes offer something less than justice as justice might be construed today: "The eyewitness chroniclers are awed at the magnitude and particulars of crusader carnage, but they register little concern at the bloodletting, let alone horror, outrage, or condemnation. Like the abhorrent digital content put online today by the ideologues of the so-called Islamic State, the words and images of the chroniclers are released without remorse and with an air of satisfaction" (358). Heng's implication is that the crusaders were, as we might expect, helpless prey to a ubiquitous ethnocentrism, and it seems plausible to assume that this Scripture-based indifference to the bloodletting of the Other is representative of the period. Magnitude and particulars, yes; remorse, absolutely not. The nonforensic tradition in premodern atrocity description relies heavily on the citing of prior literary authority and on the will of God, the two overlapping in their shared deference to Holy Scripture: "When the army of the First Crusade conquered Jerusalem in 1099," Robert Irwin writes of the same event, "a slaughter of the Muslim and Jewish inhabitants took place, and contemporary chroniclers reported that when the Christian knights rode through the Temple area of the city, the blood of the slaughtered rose to the level of their stirrups. This was not documentary reportage. The aim was rather to present the conquest of the city as a fulfillment of Revelation 14:20: 'And the winepress was trodden without the city, and blood came out of the winepress, even unto the horse bridles'" (28).[45] In this period, the aim was not to describe what you had seen with your own eyes or offer testimony that would stand up in court. Even in supposed descriptions, repeating remembered images and phrases from Holy Writ was held to strengthen the writing, not detract from its verisimilitude.

And yet—the qualification seems crucial—the magnitude and the particulars of the violence are capable of overwhelming even the "air of satisfaction" that Christian observers display after a Christian victory. One might say they are capable of overwhelming Orientalism itself. And this evasion of the sway of Orientalism, however momentary, makes the premodern account of atrocity literarily interesting—more so than many of the modern texts that will later follow it. In context, it is logical enough. When life without violence was nearly inconceivable—when plunder was a nearly ubiquitous principle of social organization, when peasants systematically had their "surplus" agricultural product extracted by force, or the threat of force—there was a certain grudging respect for the amoral, world-shaping exercise of violence, and this respect, which seems to have been transcultural, had the potential to undercut racist or otherwise dogmatic loyalty to one's own religion or civilization. Violence relativized even religion itself. No one should be astonished, then, to discover, in and around accounts of atrocity, a certain veneration for supposed civilizational enemies who had notable accomplishments in the military domain. Why else were Saladin and Tamarlane (the latter is ninth on Matthew White's list of agents of the world's bloodiest atrocities, with seventeen million dead) so admired even by the Christians they defeated in battle?[46] As we have noted, conquest had not yet come to register as a violation of any declared legal or moral principle.[47] For better or worse, the heroism of the conquerors could therefore threaten to break free from a society's other judgments of value, including religious ones. An amoral admiration for successful violence also meant that defeat could be a learning experience. According to Pinker, the premodern world was incapable of imagining "crimes against humanity" because the victims of those crimes retreated into silence. "Survivors of earlier genocides had treated them as humiliating defeats and felt that talking about them would only rub in history's harsh verdict" (335)[48]. But another option was available. The defeated could decide that yes, violence was the will of the gods, but they had been worshipping the wrong gods. According to Klor de Alva, the "visions of the vanquished" tell a sorrowful story in which the Aztecs' gods, whom they believed invincible, turned out to be (as they saw things) too weak to defend their civilization.[49] Defeat in battle might not entail disbelief, but it made disbelief possible, along with the option of a turn to other gods. It's not quite a secularization of violence, but it's a step in that direction.

The logic by which violence can undermine us-and-them divisions and the beliefs that prop them up offers a useful way of explaining what we see in Imad ad-Din, and what we see again in other Arab witnesses. The same event—the conquest of Jerusalem by the Crusaders—is described by the Arab historian Ibn Al-Athir as follows: "The population was put to the sword by the Franks, who pillaged the area for a week." Here the Christians are ruthless killers. Yet the next sentence strikes a different note: "A band of Muslims barricaded themselves into the Oratory of David and fought on for several days. They were granted their lives in return for surrendering. The Franks honored their word, and the group left by night for Ascalon" (11).[50] Here credit is given to the Christians for keeping their word—keeping their word to pagans whom they might have enjoyed deceiving as well as slaughtering. And this generosity is all the more remarkable because of what immediately follows: "In the Masjid al-Aqsa the Franks slaughtered more than 70,000 people, among them a large number of Imams and Muslim scholars, devout and ascetic men who had left their homelands to live lives of pious seclusion in the Holy Place" (11). Also noticeable here is the attention and detail given to the booty, which (as in Las Casas) permits a sort of neutral admiration for the scale of the morally deplorable Christian accomplishment. "The Franks stripped the Dome of the Rock of more than forty silver candelabra, each of them weighing 3,600 drams, and a great silver lamp weighing forty-four Syrian pounds, as well as a hundred and fifty smaller silver candelabra and more than twenty gold ones, and a great deal more booty" (11). Al-Athir allows to those who have escaped the task of summing up "the sufferings of the Muslims in that Holy City: the men killed, the women and children taken prisoner, the homes pillaged" (11). Looking for causes of the Frankish victory, he blames "the discord between the Muslim princes" rather than any Christian merits, and he ends his account with a stirring poetic call to arms. When the Franks are mentioned, Al-Athir adds "God damn them!" (18). Yet he is more interested in squabbles over their own spoils between different Muslim factions (19–20). It is Muslims, in his account, who resort to trickery, like dressing soldiers in the clothing of the enemy (20). The least one can say is that he does not aim all his ire at the victorious Christians, let alone treat them as barbarians. One might expect that an account of violence suffered would sound wholly different from an account of violence inflicted. But al-Athir's account of Muslim defeat does not differ markedly from ad-Din's account of Muslim victory. It's not that partisanship is missing—it is clearly assumed—but the writing is not imbued with, organized around, or dragged down by side-taking. Sentence for sentence, there are no good guys or bad guys.

Once alerted to blurred lines like these between premodern and modern, one discovers further blurring in even unlikelier places. Torquato Tasso's verse epic, *Jerusalem Delivered* (1581), which goes back to the same events, is a predictable celebration of Crusader violence against the Muslims. It is also, in deference to the sixteenth-century moment of the poem's composition, a celebration of equally bloody violence against the Protestants of the Reformation who from a Catholic perspective had divided Christendom. As David Quint observes, "The epic thus depicts a double crusade against the infidel outside the Church, against disunity and potential heresy within" (215).[51] Critics since the nineteenth century have tried to rescue it from the burden of "the poem's objectionable ideology" (213). And yet in canto 19, at the moment when the Christian army finally takes Jerusalem, what we get is what we would now call an atrocity—mass violence that, although visited upon the "guilty," is also "sorrowful," "cruel," and "pitiful."[52] "The victors' wrath is passing beyond bounds and spreading through the city upon the guilty people. Now who would ever be able fully to draw on his pages the sorrowful portrait of the captured city, or in his speech prove equal to the cruel and pitiful spectacle?" (Nash translation).[53] "Sorrowful"—*dolente* in the original—sticks out; it's perhaps enough of an affront to Tasso's presumed point that another translator gives "glorious" instead. In the context of this book, it is worth adding that the Italian for "cruel" is *atroce*. "These are the Christian armies, in a programmatically Virgilian poem," Christian Thorne notes, "except they are conducting themselves in a manner that violates both Christian morality and the Virgilian code, since 'anger'—furor—is what Virgil flags early on as the opposite of Aeneas's piety. *Furor* is . . . the engine of disorder that it is the project of Augustan imperialism to overcome." What is crucial here is how contested the project of imperialism is, and with it the violence against noncombatants that imperial conquest cannot do without.

> The town was now one general massacre,
> heaps and mountains of corpses. Here were spread
> the wounded over the lifeless men, and there
> the sick were buried beneath unburied dead—
> and the wailing mothers with their streaming hair
> pressed to their breasts their babies as they fled,
> and the predator was full of theft and spoil,
> dragging girls by the hair to rape, defile—
>
> (Esolen translation, 19.30)

It's easy to forget that all this, including the rape as well as the predatory quest for booty, is the work of the Christians, not the Muslims, and is transmitted to readers by an advocate of the Christian cause. In the very midst of full-blast Crusader ideology, the passage gestures toward a self-accusation of atrocity, and this despite the fact that the poem goes on to propose that all the bloodshed was, after all, God's justice.[54] And then, having stated that this is God's justice, the poem continues to vacillate. The civilian population of Jerusalem crowds into the ancient Temple, their last refuge against the rampaging Christians. Rinaldo batters down the gate and the Christians swarm in, making "of the great house that was the house of God / a bitter slaughter, bloody, miserable." The self-critique seems unmistakable. And then, without a pause, we get "O justice of heaven! the more delayed, / the heavier on that wicked race you fall! / From the depths of your providence you made / sternness and wrath awake in the merciful, and the blasphemous pagan washed in his blood's rain / the very temple he had made profane" (19.38). Massacre, which had been categorized as "passing beyond bounds," here becomes a sign of divine justice, even an expiation. "But if that's the case," Thorne goes on to ask, "why praise Rinaldo along the way for not killing civilians?"

A volume called *The New Killing Fields*, edited by Nicolaus Mills and Kira Brenner, argues in favor of humanitarian intervention to prevent atrocity. Intervention is a policy which no one who has paid attention to recent atrocities can afford to rule out entirely, though its proponents are not always suspicious enough of the agents called upon to do the intervening. The book also sketches a potential literary history of atrocity. In doing so, it lays out potential criteria for distinguishing better from worse atrocity writing. "Since the end of the nineteenth century," Mills writes in his introduction, "a small but distinct group of writers, linked primarily by their willingness to bear witness, has developed a language of slaughter that in its descriptive simplicity and freedom from easy moralizing, portrays the mass suffering it describes unblinkingly, while simultaneously making the point that the governments and individuals have the power—if they will only use it—to stop this mass suffering" (6–7).[55] It's not obvious that "freedom from easy moralizing" ought to count as the decisive criterion of quality writing about atrocity. But if it does, then the premodern and early modern accounts of the Crusades cited above would have to be credited with just this freedom, a freedom Mills sees as distinctively modern. Mills cites Hemingway's *A Farewell to Arms* as exemplary of the avoidance of melodrama. But the Nahuatl texts too might seem to anticipate Fredric Henry's modern or modernist embarrassment about recourse to words like "sacred, glorious, and sacrifice and the expression in vain" to refer to the battlefields of World War I (9–10).[56] The Indigenous texts notice treachery on the part of the Spaniards, who suddenly attacked unarmed men celebrating a festival, but that observation falls well short of moral condemnation, and it is also diluted by a strong trace of self-accusation: If they tricked us, isn't this partly our own fault for allowing ourselves to be tricked? Why were we so trusting?[57] Al-Athir on the other hand praises the Christians for *not* being treacherous. In neither case is the encounter framed in terms of vice and virtue. The Aztecs call out the Spanish greed for gold, which they find laughable, but like Hemingway they seem allergic to the exalted vocabulary of national or religious identification that would make some higher sense of what has befallen them. Like Hemingway, they prefer to dwell on the literal facts of what was done and suffered, adding nothing. If good writing about atrocity is writing that avoids melodrama, even to the point of refusing to say that what has occurred is indeed an atrocity, here is a passage connecting modern and premodern moral landscapes.

Two

Plunder

Historicizing Atrocity

Grimmelshausen's Farmyard

The *Oxford English Dictionary*'s first mention of *plunder*, from 1643, goes like this: "Abhorre all violence, plunder, rapine and disorders in souldiers." A note adds that the German verb *plündern* was much used during the same period, the period of the Thirty Years' War (1618–1648). Something seems to have been happening in those rowdy years that set an old style of misconduct in a newly critical light. The suggestion is that, implausible as it might seem, the abhorrence of plunder was a new thing.

According to the OED, in the seventeenth century the word *plunder* sometimes referred to the theft of household goods. It didn't always refer to booty seized from an enemy. Before the emergence of the modern nation-state, there would have been little incentive to distinguish between the robbing of enemies and the robbing of fellow nationals. Nor were soldiers easily distinguished from those they plundered. In the Thirty Years' War, most of the troops did not wear uniforms. They were hired mercenaries, and they did their violent work while wearing their everyday clothes. They were not directly accountable to the state, and they did not always expect to be supplied by it. As often as not they were expected to live off the land. Living off the land—that is, taking what you needed from those who lived *on* that land—helps explain the high proportion of civilian to military casualties in the Thirty Years' War:

an extraordinary twenty dead civilians for every dead soldier. Compare that with the proportion in World War II, a war in which civilians were deliberately targeted; there were not twenty but only *two* dead civilians for every dead soldier.[1]

The custom of living off the land helps explain the opening scene of Johann Grimmelshausen's classic novel *Simplicissimus* (1668), which is set in the Germany of the Thirty Years' War. In that scene, a visit to the family farm by some disorderly soldiers bent on plunder, violence, and rapine leaves our hero an orphan and sends him out into the world to seek his fortune. "The first thing the troopers did was stable their horses. Then each went about his own particular task, though they all resulted in slaughter and destruction. Some set about a general butchering, boiling, and roasting, so that it looked as if they were going to hold a banquet" (25).[2] Here Grimmelshausen recalls the slaughter-bench origins of the word *massacre* by withholding, briefly, the knowledge of whether it is animals or people that are being butchered.[3] Then the phrase "as if they were going to hold a banquet" confirms that it is not a banquet, meaning it is not animals alone that are being butchered.

> Shameful to report, they handed out such rough treatment to our maid in the stall that she was unable to come out. Our farmhand they gave a drink they called Swedish ale: they bound him and laid him on the ground with a stick holding open his mouth into which they poured a milking pail full of slurry from the dung heap. By this means they forced him to lead a party to a place where they captured more men and beasts, which they brought back to our farm. Among them were my Da, my Ma, and our Ursula. (26)

After thus ingeniously obtaining information on the whereabouts of further booty and further victims, the soldiers proceed to rape and torture the remaining female members of the household, an episode that is no less disturbing for going undescribed. "What they did to the women, maidservants, and girls they had captured I cannot say, as the soldiers did not let me watch them. What I do know is that I heard constant pitiful cries coming from all corners of the farmhouse and I guess my Ma and our Ursula fared no better than all the rest" (27). In a display of his signature simplicity, Simplicius implies he would have *liked* to see more: "The soldiers did not *let* me watch them" (27, my italics). But he is smart enough to run. Within a page, he has escaped alone to the forest, where he "could hear both the cries of the tortured peasants and the song of the nightingales" (28).

To what literary history might this brief representation of atrocity belong? If history means something more than one damn thing after another, it cannot be taken for granted that an episode like this belongs to *any* history. Wherever you choose to look, there has been one damn atrocity after another. For those willing to listen, when has the song of the nightingales not been mingled with the cries of the tortured peasants? The chronicle of human brutality is very long and very repetitive. One searches in vain for a beginning, and it certainly has not yet come to an end. Given the sheer quantity of suffering and the geographical and historical range of the raids, sieges, sackings, and other acts of aggression that would demand to be attended to, it would seem foolhardy to speculate that any narrative can be constructed that would be adequate to its contents, whatever adequate might mean. And yet, on reflection, one possible storyline can perhaps be extrapolated from the novel's opening scene. What is heard in the farmyard is not, strictly speaking, the voice of atrocity's victims. We know this because some fifteen pages after fleeing, having found temporary refuge with a hermit, Simplicius leaves the forest again. Arriving in a village, he finds it "in flames, for a party of troopers had just plundered it, killed some of the peasants and driven off the rest, apart from a few they had taken captive, among them the pastor himself" (46). He hears news of a counterattack by angry peasants in which six soldiers have been captured, made to stand in a row and shot with one bullet. The peasants cut off the ears and nose of the last in line, whom the bullet had not touched, "though not before forcing him to lick—if the reader will forgive me for mentioning it—the arses of five of them" (49). Soon after, some of these same peasants are captured in their turn by other soldiers and themselves tortured, with persistence and imagination, for another two pages.

Simplicius is a peasant boy whose family has been murdered in front of him, but he does not seem to feel very distressed by the suffering of other peasants. Nor does he seem to enjoy even momentarily the peasants' vengeance, which one might have thought he would welcome as payback. He does not express the abhorrence for his parents' killers that a modern reader would almost certainly feel. He does not appear to be conscious of himself as a victim. And if he somehow falls short of speaking in the voice of self-conscious victimhood, one would be curious to know when and why that voice does emerge in its fullness. The moment at which victimhood *would* express itself in a direct and unambiguous fashion, which seems so strangely missing here, presents itself as a landmark around which a hypothetical history of atrocity might be organized. Whatever has happened to violence itself since the seventeenth century, there is no doubt that consciousness of it, and in particular published indignation at the violent victimization of foreigners and noncombatants, has risen precipitously. Since the end of World War II and the victory of the anti-colonial movements, scenes of the butchery of civilians have become familiar, even a relatively routine marker of the novelist's moral seriousness. The massacre of the banana plantation workers in García Márquez's *One Hundred Years of Solitude* (1967) has probably inspired more subsequent writers than any other single scene (think again of the Amritsar Massacre of 1919 as depicted in Salman Rushdie's *Midnight's Children* [1981]), but modern literature is rich in other examples. Attention is now being paid to atrocity, and when it is, abhorrence is expressed. This acknowledgment of victimization is not proof that a benevolent providence has been guiding literature in a humanitarian direction, but it is not negligible either, and seeing it as a noteworthy event helps frame further questions that might not otherwise be asked, questions both literary and moral. How did we get to this point? Was there a blockage that had to be overcome in order for writers to express what Grimmelshausen leaves imperfectly expressed—in order for atrocity to speak its piece in fiction, or speak at all? Is the overcoming of that blockage a distinguishing accomplishment of modern literature, or is atrocity also recognized for what we now take it to be in texts that predate modernity? If mass violence against noncombatants was not always a moral scandal, when and why and how did become one? And finally, is the making of a moral scandal the story's happy ending, or is it the source of still more nagging questions about literature's moral mandate in a space-time of bewildering global violence? If answers to these questions are to be had, it would be good to have them.

Rather than treating the absence of abhorrence (or indignation, or victimhood) as an event to be historicized, as I'm proposing, it would be possible, following a certain modernizing practice, to psychologize Simplicius, taking his nonreaction as a symptom of childhood trauma such as any child anywhere might experience it. Students might prefer to take this relatability route. His failure to identify as a victim might also be attributed to the novel's distinctive literariness, which operates in the mode of picaresque satire. The Candide-like simplicity of the narrator's voice, which has been cited as a possible influence on Voltaire, usefully holds the narrative open to both religious dogmas that clashed in the Thirty Years' War, Catholic and Protestant, thereby enabling the novel to achieve its extraordinary comic-epic comprehensiveness. At the same time, his innocence is not merely a formal convenience; it also allows him, and the narrative, to float above any partisan mobilization, thereby beckoning toward the ideological option of an as-yet unavailable religious neutrality. On this more ideological reading, the atrocity representation in *Simplicissimus,* which takes an unmistakable and even unforgettable step toward the condemnation of violence against noncombatants, could be located within the history of secularism, one of the key components of modernity.

Pinker's application of the narrative of modernization-as-secularization has some purchase on *Simplicissimus,* at least as far as it goes. Grimmelshausen is clearly aware of the prevailing will-of-God theory of violence. He brings it up, and he ridicules it exuberantly. His parents were murdered, Simplicius tells us, because God wanted to teach them, and him, a lesson. "My story demands that I set down for posterity the cruel atrocities that were committed from time to time in our German wars since, as my own example demonstrates, all such evils are visited upon us by the Almighty out of His great love towards us and for our own good. How else would I have learnt that there is a God in Heaven if the soldiers had not destroyed my Da's house, thus forcing me out into the world where I met other people from whom I learnt so many things?" The novel maintains this satirical note, ending the paragraph with "the Almighty took pity on my innocence": "Although He had a thousand means of achieving this, it was doubtless deliberate that the one He chose also punished my Da and my Ma, as a warning to others for the ungodly way they had brought me up" (25).

The secularization hypothesis also accords with Grimmelshausen's refusal to take sides in the religious wars. He himself converted to Catholicism, but he has Simplicius tell the pastor, "I am neither Papist nor Protestant. I simply believe what is contained in the Twelve Articles of the Christian Faith and I refuse to commit myself to any side until one or the other can furnish convincing proof that it is the one true religion" (262). He does not announce the religion of the soldiers who torture and kill the farm's inhabitants. There are signs, like the "Swedish ale," strongly suggesting that the disorderly soldiers who enter his family's farmyard are Swedish Protestants, as was the army that violently interrupted Grimmelshausen's own childhood and forced his family to flee for their lives. It can be understood by equally inconclusive signs (like the pastor) that the local peasants are probably Protestants, as was Grimmelshausen's family.[4] But the irony of a probably Protestant army raping and killing probably Protestant peasants goes unremarked. Armies lived off the land, and Grimmelshausen suggests that it didn't matter very much whose army it was, Catholic or Protestant, or whose land they were living off.[5] Plunder is tolerantly nondenominational.

Simplicissimus is less supportive, however, of Pinker's assumption that secularization would banish superstition and fatalism. Like his author, Simplicius will be captured by the Catholic forces and will become a soldier fighting at different times on both the Catholic and the Protestant sides. We do not see him do in anyone else's farmyard what the disorderly soldiers do in his, but it is not inconceivable that he could have, or might have been obliged to. How much choice would he have in the matter? The maid, before losing the power of speech, tells him, "Run away, lad, or the troopers will take you with them" (27). If one is trying to sketch out a larger history of representations of atrocity into which Grimmelshausen's scene might be fitted, the absence of choice seems worth pausing on. It's a necessary supplement to superstitions about fate and the will of God. The decisive concept here would not be superstition, which is to say more or less enlightened epistemology, but something closer to social disempowerment.

Historically speaking, peasants as a collectivity have been decisively and perhaps uniquely disempowered. In *The Moral Economy of the Peasant* (1976), James C. Scott quotes R. H. Tawney's metaphor for the rural population as "a man standing permanently up to the neck in water, so that even a ripple might drown him" (vii).[6] Households whose agricultural production was geared more to subsistence than to the market were often indignant at grasping landlords and tax collectors, but they did not routinely enjoy the freedom to see themselves in the light of other possible ways of living or to imagine joining together with others to renegotiate their conditions of war and peace. What Marx and Engels meant by the notorious phrase "the idiocy of rural life" in *The Communist Manifesto* was not below-average scores on an intelligence test but an exclusive concern with private interests (the German *Idiotismus* recalls the original Greek for privacy) at the expense of public and political ones.[7] Ironically, producing the goods of the earth that armies could then forcefully expropriate hindered the political self-conception that might have allowed peasants to defend themselves, whether from exorbitant rents and taxes or from disorderly soldiers.[8] Fatalism does not require superstition. All it requires is knowing that you are relatively defenseless and that, as a peasant, you may even one day find yourself, due to overpowering circumstances, forced into joining those who are victimizing other peasants. As one of Grimmelshausen's translators puts it, this is a world "where the individual is subject to forces beyond his control."[9] In such a world, peasants knew that they might well end up not only having the fruits of their land seized, but also seizing the fruits of land cultivated by other peasants, with consequences like those we see in Grimmelshausen. To phrase this in modern terms, no one could be sure they would *not* become a perpetrator. To say this is not to echo Sunday sermons about how we are all sinful creatures. It is to offer a materialist gloss on atrocity as well as on the social background of that theology.

Critics who are suspicious of dividing lines between the modern and the premodern—they are among the readers I am most interested to engage, concerned as I am in this book to propose a multiperiod argument on a theme that crosses that divide—may be tempted to see *Simplicissimus* not as a secularizing step forward but on the contrary, thanks to the protagonist's amoral innocence, as a repository of premodern practical wisdom, and in that sense as our contemporary in a positive, anti-melodramatic sense. As Catherine Nichols and Marina Benjamin write in "The Good Guy/Bad Guy Myth," premodern myth and folktale did not, as often imagined, depend on these taken-for-granted moral distinctions: "Stories from an oral tradition never have anything like a modern good guy or bad guy in them, despite their reputation for being moralizing."[10] Outside official dogma, premodern evil is often not measured by any moral principle; it is only situational. Evil is that which opposes you, whomever and whatever you happen to be. This anti-moralistic, anti-universalistic vision can seem refreshing and indeed, to some, more truly secular than the projected endpoint of secularization, which is unabashedly universalistic. Yet it has its obvious downside. It is hard not to believe that anti-moralism is an effect of long-term disempowerment. It is hard not to believe that it perpetuates or at any rate fails to challenge that disempowerment. Premodern populism—apart from its value as a correction of stereotypes, that is what the Nichols/Benjamin position amounts to—would make the freedom to abhor coherently difficult to imagine, and thus also the possibility of acting together with others on your shared abhorrence and indignation. In rejecting the presentism of moral norms, it chooses to ignore plunder. It rules out in advance, perhaps in cynical resignation, the sort of redistribution of power that would be necessary to keep disorderly soldiers out of the farmyard.

Along with the narrative of increasing secularization, another framework into which the Grimmelshausen scene might be inserted is the narrative of increasing cosmopolitanism, as mentioned above, understood as the overcoming of a primal ethnocentrism. (Pinker refers to both secularization and cosmopolitanism as causes of the modern decline of violence.) If, as Stuurman says, in the writings that humanity in its wisdom has seen fit to preserve, the alien "has mostly been presented as savage, barbarian, irrational, inscrutable, uncivilized, irreligious, heathen, idolatrous, nonwhite, colored, primitive, backward, traditional, premodern—and the list goes on" (3), it cannot be a surprise that foreigners have frequently been the victims of massacre. And it cannot be a surprise that such massacres did not normally register as morally scandalous, or register at all.[11] Ethnocentrism would count both as a cause of atrocity and, at least as important for the purposes of literary history, as a reason why until recently atrocity did not become a more salient part of the literary record. That record is unambiguous: in this department modernity has brought major changes. "Genocide was not a moral problem for the ancient world," Michael Freeman writes in the entry for "Genocide" in the *Dictionary of Ethics, Theology and*

Society.[12] In *The Gallic War,* Julius Caesar is not embarrassed to mention the genocidal violence he orders. When David Johnston notes, in his magisterial history of the concept of justice, that "commitments to freedom and equality" are "nowhere to be seen" in the domestic laws of the ancient world, he doesn't even bother to ask about foreign policy—about the possible existence of rules restricting violence against members of other groups, tribes, nations.[13] For "our" treatment of "others," there apparently were no restrictions. And if not, to repeat, then massacres of those others would not be much noticed. Hugo Grotius (1583–1645), who helped negotiate the end of the Thirty Years' War, declared holy war unacceptable (a major moral accomplishment), but he had nothing to say about violence against non-Christians. That was not unacceptable.

On the other hand, one lesson that can be learned from Matthew White's *Great Big Book of Horrible Things*, the useful list of history's one hundred worst atrocities referred to above, is that racial and religious otherness, which might seem the single most obvious, indispensable, and decisive cause of atrocity, is in fact only optional. In *The Gallic War,* Julius Caesar does not take advantage of the opportunity to present the Gauls as barbarians deserving of nothing better than extermination. He writes that his opposite number, the Gaulish leader Vercingertorix, "used harsh punishments to bring waverers into line. For the more serious offences, death was inflicted by burning and all kinds of torture, while for lesser faults the offender's ears were cut off or one of his eyes was gouged out" (146).[14] True enough, but not evidence that Vercingertorix was thought to be ontologically distinct from the civilized Romans. As Josephine Quinn observes, the same punishments were meted out by the Romans to their fellow Romans, and everyone knew it. "The truth is that [Caesar] didn't need to justify slaughter and slavery; in Rome, as in Gaul, human rights were non-existent, life was cheap, and its worth was often reckoned in a brutally utilitarian fashion."[15] More generally, she concludes, "Caesar does not dehumanize the Gauls; in fact he presents their individual causes and their desire for liberty as rational, even sympathetic" (6, online). Much the same holds for Josephus in *The Jewish War.* Josephus does bestow different cultural characteristics on the Jews and the Romans, but (unsurprisingly, given that he had been an Israelite general before going over to the Romans) he does not Orientalize the Jews.[16] He can justify their massacre without help from Orientalism. Grimmelshausen too does atrocity without heavy reliance on the non-Germanness of the perpetrators. If the rampaging soldiers in the farmyard are indeed foreigners, as they seem to be, he doesn't underline that fact or allow it to make any obvious difference.

One alternative to the cosmopolitan or anti-ethnocentrism narrative is to follow the booty. The recently resuscitated term *racial capitalism* serves as a reminder that, in many instances if not of course everywhere, racialization has aided in the extraction, transfer, and accumulation of material resources. In an argument that seeks to cover, however sketchily, as much of the temporal range of world literature as its author's limited knowledge makes possible, there are obvious limits to what the concept of capitalism can explain, whether qualified as racial or not. Violence did not begin with modernity. Plunder is older than capitalism. If it is a historically broader concept, it is also a vaguer one. Perhaps because of its vagueness, it's a word that tends not to show up in the indexes of books of world history even when there is a great deal of plunder recorded in those histories. It's not in the index of C. A. Bayly's *The Birth of the Modern World, 1780–1914* (2004) or David Christian's *Maps of Time: An Introduction to Big History* (2004). It's not in the index of Stephen Howe's *Empire: A Very Short Introduction* (2002) or Anthony Pagden's *Peoples and Empires* (2001) or Jane Burbank and Frederick Turner's *Empires in World History* (2010). Perhaps indexers and the authors they serve assume it to be like the weather, too universal and too uncontrollable to explain anything in particular. And yet even attention to otherness, which explains a lot, needs to be supplemented by attention to plunder, which on inspection reveals its own historical curve.

Consider Friedrich Schiller's celebrated account of the 1631 destruction of Magdeburg in *The History of the Thirty Years' War.* In that siege, 20,000 inhabitants of Magdeburg died out of a population of 25,000. The city's bürgermeister, one of the few survivors, described the scene as follows: "Then was there naught but beating and burning, plundering, torture, and murder. Most especially was every one of the enemy bent on securing much booty."[17] Grimmelshausen would have seen Magdeburg's ruins when he was involved in another siege of the city five years later. Unlike Grimmelshausen, Schiller was looking back on the destruction from a considerable distance, and that may be why first-person observation is less salient in his history than formulaic borrowings from classical sources: "the living crawling from under the dead . . . infants still suckling the breasts of their lifeless mothers" (218). Unlike Grimmelshausen again, Schiller takes pains to place maximum responsibility for the bloodbath on foreigners—but also on the common soldiers, as opposed to the officers. Here the city has just fallen: "Even a more humane general would in vain have recommended mercy to such soldiers, but Tilly never made the attempt. Left by their general's silence masters of the lives of all the citizens, the soldiery broke into the houses to satiate their most brutal appetites. The prayers of innocence excited some compassion in the hearts of the Germans, but none in the rude breasts of Pappenheim's Walloons. Scarcely had the savage cruelty commenced, when the other gates were thrown open, and the cavalry, with the fearful hordes of Croats, poured in upon the devoted inhabitants" (64).

The distribution of blame for the atrocity follows a clear pattern. Tilly, the general of the Catholic army, is at the top of the social pyramid and is almost ignored in the blaming. He is silent, apparently indifferent to the fate of Magdeburg's citizens, but he does not actively wish them harm. Much more relevant are the common soldiers, with their "brutal appetites." No mention is made of whether the common soldiers are Germans (as many were) or foreigners. Finally and most damningly, Schiller gets to the foreigners. The German attackers (he does recognize that Germans were among the attackers) feel "some compassion," but not so the non-Germans: Walloons and Croats. Those who are not fellow nationals are monsters of pure cruelty. "The Croats amused themselves with throwing children into the flames; Pappenheim's Walloons with stabbing infants at their mother's breast" (64).

According to Schiller's officer-class theory, the prime cause of the violence is the "brutal appetites" of the common soldiers. One mention of that class-based theory is not enough: "Some officers of the League, horror-struck at this dreadful scene, ventured to remind Tilly that he had it in his power to stop the carnage. 'Return in an hour,' was his answer; 'I will see what I can do; the soldier must have some reward for his danger and toils'" (64). Schiller is strongly committed to his class. But his commitment to his nation is just as strong. It is only "the League," made up of Germans fighting on the Catholic side, who are "horror-struck." The general, who is Dutch, displays no such feelings. Schiller shows some loyalty to him by failing to observe, at the general's expense, that the "rich booty" the troops find in the cellars was also promised to them, like the violence and rapine, as "some reward" for their "danger and toils." On the contrary, the general is credited as the one who "put a stop to the plunder" (64). Schiller does everything in his authorial power to deflect blame from his fellow Germans while also deflecting as much as possible from the officer class, irrespective of nationality, and placing it on the common soldiers.

Nationalism serves the useful function of distracting from discontent about inequalities within the given nation, like the inequality between landowners and peasants or between soldiers and their officers. That inequality—of resources, but also of accountability—is more likely to be visible from below. From a peasant perspective what "the army" *means*, in Teodor Shanin's words, is "young peasants in uniform, armed and officered by men different from themselves."[18] With access to this perspective, those of peasant origin, like Grimmelshausen, had some cushion against the nationalism that so emphatically inflects Schiller's account of Magdeburg. On the other hand, looking at atrocity from the viewpoint of social hierarchy also ought to protect against the too-easy assumption that the modern nation-state, tainted as it is by nationalism, must be understood as the prime agent of plunder and thus the chief source of modern violence.

The commonplace that hovers over every mention of the Thirty Years' War is the Treaty of Westphalia and the birth of the system founded on the modern European nation-state. In the liberal mainstream, the birth of the modern nation-state system is widely understood as the end of the bloody wars of religion, as a flawed but noble ancestor of the United Nations and the European Union, as a significant step on the road to world peace. Outside the liberal mainstream, it is widely understood as the inauguration of a period of discrimination against national minorities and outright aggression against other European nationalities and colonized non-Europeans. The strength of the case for this latter view does not completely erase the former, but it does disrupt the narrative of modernity as a steady progress toward cosmopolitanism. Neither of these views, however, is quite adequate to the scene in Grimmelshausen's farmyard or to the unsteady but nonetheless progressive narrative to which it arguably belongs.

Even within the liberal mainstream, progressive narratives are having a hard time of it. Climate change has given a push to the counternarrative of modernity-as-decline. Another plausible alternative, as mentioned above, is no narrative at all. Given the sheer quantity of violence on both sides of the modern/premodern divide, it can be tempting to fall back on Hegel's slaughter-bench vision of history in which violence is so terrible and so ubiquitous as to make any the proposition of any meaningful historical narrative of the whole a nonstarter. The default position for educated common sense today might well assume, along the same lines, the gratuitousness of violence, hence the randomness of the history of violence, and thus, by extension, the randomness of history as such, given how much violence history contains. This is roughly the judgment that Jean Franco extracts from Primo Levi's *The Drowned and the Saved*. The Nazi years "were characterized by widespread useless violence, as an end in itself . . . occasionally having a purpose, yet always redundant, always disproportionate to the purpose itself" (105–6, Franco 13).[19] Franco generalizes the uselessness of violence, hence its meaninglessness, both in Latin America (her subject) and in the rest of the world. Yet she is not quite satisfied with that generalization. In *Cruel Modernity* (2013), Franco is more drawn to a narrative in which violence is not random at all, but an effect of the modern European nation-state, which has been a unique and unprecedented disaster, and not just for Latin America. This linear narrative of decline—not after all a refusal either of narrative or of linearity—merges the state, modernity, and violence into a single toxic agent. Franco asks: "Why, in Latin America, did the pressures of modernization and the lure of modernity lead states to kill?" (2) Although her argument includes "rogue groups" as well as "armies [and] governments," the key agent of atrocity for Franco is the government, which is to say the state, and the cause that lies behind the bad behavior of the state is modernity, of which in any case the state is usually understood as representative. Franco's examples of mass violence begin with the openly racist Dominican massacre of Haitians in 1937, for which the responsibility lies on the American-supported General Trujillo. Her examples end with the murder of hundreds of working-class women in Ciudad Juárez, as documented in Roberto Bolaño's novel *2666*. The first is clearly state-sponsored, though racism, of course, has a much deeper history. In the second, the state just as clearly has *some* responsibility, but perhaps (full clarity has not yet been achieved) more for its complicity with the drug cartels and its failure to bring the guilty to justice. The obvious role played in the Ciudad Juárez killings by misogyny, which like racism of course existed before modernity, puts in relief Franco's own uncertainty about how large a causal role can in fact be attributed to modernity or to the modern state. On the one hand, she links Spanish racism to the recent peninsular project of nation-formation by reconquest and quotes Enrique Dussel's claim that "the Spanish conquest of the Americas was an event that inaugurated modernity" (5). On the other hand, she cites Freud on "mankind's aggressive tendencies" (3) and links the Ciudad Juárez murders to "archaic codes" (21). Taking the examples together, it might seem that the "modernity" of her title is after all less a causal agent, sufficient to account for the violence occurring on its watch, than a chronological frame which encompasses a great deal of cruelty without offering the promised explanation of it or, more precisely, without laying that cruelty at the state's door.

The sponsorship of internecine warfare abroad and the perpetuation of racialized incarceration at home testify to the fact that the modern state has not done away with armed robbery as a way of doing business. Exploitation has never entirely superseded expropriation.[20] The system still cannot seem to do without violence even if the need for extra violence to make it work implies that it is after all not, in the strongest sense of the word, a system. Yet with the advent of the modern state, something has in fact changed, and changed in a way that sets limits on physical coercion. As Nancy Fraser argues, a certain percentage of the population, including a sizable proportion of formerly colonized and presently racialized people, have now won at least minimal political rights.[21] As possessors of political rights, they have largely moved from targets of expropriation to targets of exploitation. Although this is not a happy ending, it is a nonnegligible achievement. It affords them certain new possibilities of self-defensive action. It does not protect them from the nonviolent looting that we call exploitation, but it lowers their risk of falling victim to violent expropriation, hence to participation in scenes like the one in Grimmelshausen's farmyard.

This achievement tends to be neglected by scholars who are trying to avoid Eurocentric complacency, especially about such supposed European accomplishments as the extension of democracy. One case in point is Jane Burbank and Fredrick Cooper's book *Empires in World History: Power and the Politics of Difference*. Burbank and Cooper are trying to escape, as they say, from "the usual—and we think misleading—shorthands and signposts: a transition from empire to nation-state, a distinction between premodern and modern states, a focus on Europe and the west as uniquely powerful agents of change, for good or for evil" (xi).[22] In order to avoid flattering the institutions and values of European modernity, especially the nation-state, they make a moral case for a premodern alternative, the empire: "The nation-state tends to homogenize those within inside its borders and exclude those who do not belong, while the empire reaches outward and draws, usually coercively, peoples whose difference is made explicit under its rule. The concept of empire presumes that different peoples within the polity will be governed differently" (8). What is distinctive about empire, in other words, is that it accepts diversity as its very substance, not as an anomaly that must be rejected, and it therefore finds ways of managing that diversity. Unfortunately, to put the focus on diversity is to take the focus off violence. Burbank and Cooper are perfectly conscious, as we see in the passage above, that empires, which have no pretense of offering democratic rights, cannot be made or sustained without violence. "Empires, of course, hardly represented a spontaneous embrace of diversity. Violence and day-to-day coercion," they recognize, "were fundamental to how empires were built and how they operated" (2). But that is not where their emphasis falls. "As successful empires turned their conquests into profit, they had to manage their unlike populations, in the process producing a variety of ways to both exploit and rule" (2). Yes, there is both exploitation and coercion, but the real point is successful management of difference. Burbank and Cooper don't appear to concede that nation-states, however much violence they may be guilty of, are not *forced* to use violence by their very principle of being. Empires are. Is it irrelevant that, though the modern nation-state excludes, by their own admission it need not exploit, enslave, or massacre those it excludes? Is it irrelevant that the existence of political rights, which do not interest them, offers at least some protection against atrocity?

Like the pure voice of victimhood, political rights go unrepresented in Grimmelshausen's farmyard. When the soldiers ride in, there is no 9-1-1 number to call. The institutions of the modern state are nowhere to be seen. And yet one might say that, like the religious neutrality made possible by the modern state and prefigured in Simplicius's narrative simplicity, the hypothetical existence of political rights can be extrapolated from that scene. No one would dispute that, focused as it is on the period of the Thirty Years' War, *Simplicissimus* straddles the transition between a world of empires (here, the Hapsburg empire) and a world of modern nation-states. Even if it makes no immediate difference whose army is passing through, it does matter, collectively and in the long run, which social unit the peasants and their descendants will find themselves inhabiting. A modern state would offer the potential, at least, for political representation. States often and perhaps always have violent origins—violence is more or less ensured by the state's need to assert sovereignty over a given territory, if not by its need to tear itself free of the empire that had previously ruled that territory. It also follows, unfortunately, from the impulse to ground sovereignty on a wishful ethnic or religious homogeneity. Still, as I have said, atrocity is not necessary to the state's continued functioning, once founded, as it is for entities like empires that base their prosperity on the acquisition of new territories and the subjugation of new populations.[23] In its dedicatory letter to Louis XIII, Grotius's *De jure belli ac pacis* (The Rights of War and Peace) declares that though Louis's kingdom is huge, "it is kingdom greater than that kingdom, that you do not covet other kingdoms . . . nor disturb the old boundaries."[24] For all their history of coveting other kingdoms and disturbing old boundaries, states are not *defined* by bloody expansiveness; their everyday operations do not depend on conquest and tribute. The hypothesis presents itself, then, that the middle of the seventeenth century, when the system of modern nation-states was just being consolidated, registers a swerve in atrocity's representations, an increase in the tendency to recognize atrocity and (another way of saying the same thing) to register abhorrence of it *because it has become conceivable that, unlike the weather, something could be done about it.*[25] What could be done about it was the founding of the modern nation-state. Plunder is eternal; what is new, and what makes the abhorrence of plunder newly conceivable, is the rise of a secular authority that could be appealed to, whether confidently or not, whether effectively or not, as a bulwark against plunder.

For Grimmelshausen, religion has lost its authority to legitimate violence, leaving only the naked illegitimacy of looting. The new, alternative authority that was to replace it has not yet quite arrived. The state, with its new assertion of a monopoly on the legitimate exercise of physical force, as argued by Norbert Elias, remains just below the horizon, not yet visible.[26] Still, perhaps it is close enough so that the reader might imagine Grimmelshausen gesturing to get its attention. David Graeber and David Wengrow, who dispute almost everything Pinker says about violence and the need for the state to curb it—they call him "our quintessential modern Hobbesian" (13)—somewhat surprisingly do not dispute the proposition that premodern rulers did not rule a state in this sense. If the rulers made such claims at all, "their claims to a monopoly on coercive force held about the same status as their claims to control the tides or the weather" (360).[27] Graeber and Wengrow unexpectedly agree with Pinker than in the premodern period "coercive force" *was* like the weather—that before Grimmelshausen's disorderly soldiers make their appearance, no appeal to the state could yet be made against them. The question of modernity is whether anything changed in this situation. The Peace of Westphalia that ended the Thirty Years' War and consolidated the modern system of nation-states did not, of course, put an end to scenes of atrocity. But as Elias suggested, the emergence of the modern nation-state did add the promise that disorderly soldiers seeking provisions and causing mayhem might be restrained, and would at least have to worry about their potential accountability. The rising authority of the state, entirely absent as it is from the episode itself, perhaps explains why Grimmelshausen feels empowered to mock the conventional wisdom about violence: that the murder of his family expresses the mysterious will of a benevolent God. The mockery required a countervailing power to God, and such a power was indeed rising. At least theoretically, the power of the state would be delegated to speak for the otherwise helpless, now at least somewhat more empowered as rights-bearing citizens. The narrative of the secularization of violence converges here with a narrative of democratic empowerment. The hypothesis is that some degree of empowerment is necessary in order for the peasant victims of atrocity to begin to name atrocity, to express abhorrence, and to accuse its perpetrators, rather than resign themselves to their fate—the complex fate of possibly inflicting (as soldiers) as well as suffering atrocity. The modern state holds out even for peasants, who were certainly not the first to be represented by it, the image of a toehold on power, hence the incipient capacity to name what they are being made to endure.

To sum up: if there is room for a history in which representations of atrocity are not random and chaotic but trace a certain curve, that curve cannot be measured solely by its deviations from superstition or ethnocentrism. Without losing sight of either, the would-be historian of atrocity has to insist on attention to those forms of social organization that were more or less likely to demand plunder. Going back to Pinker, one might say that if violence once seemed unavoidable, it was both because the world was awash in superstition and ethnocentrism, and because the dominant mode of social organization made plunder seem unavoidable. Change the mode of social organization, and you do something about the mass violence. What had to become imaginable was not just a world with less otherness or fatalism, but a world that diminished the fatal demand for plunder as a go-to mode of enrichment or survival.

Can Atrocity Be Theorized?

I have been proposing a theory that links representations of atrocity to modern class structure, the rise of the modern state, and the possibility of organizing society without reliance on plunder, again a feature of modernity even where it remains merely potential. One obstacle that I will have to overcome in order to be persuasive on this point is the sense that, in the presence of mass violence, theorizing of any sort is misplaced. I suspect that this sense is widely shared—indeed, that among the educated it might pass as *common* sense. The Holocaust is not the only site of atrocity that is understood to repel explanation. As a work that self-consciously addresses itself to common sense, I return to White's *Great Big Book of Horrible Things*, which forcefully rejects all theorizing. For White, it's not just that controversy about atrocity will never be resolved. It *should* not be resolved, even roughly and provisionally. Any attempt to settle on a theory or meaning would assign responsibility, thus aligning the interpreter with a possible agent of violence. This alignment would make it more likely that the interpretation would contribute, down the line, to unleashing chaos. As I've said, chaos is White's worst-case scenario; it leads to more atrocities than injustice does. Better, then, to acknowledge incomprehensible randomness. Refuse to pursue any line of causal explanation, and you may achieve an attitude of humorous detachment from the horrible spectacle, like White's own. At any rate, you will not be complicit in creating new atrocities.

Nevertheless, it is rewarding to read White's book against the grain, looking for things that he himself observes but hesitates to arrange in causal threads and patterns of meaning. Immediately before the section on Caesar's Gallic War and its motivation in booty comes the Third Mithridatic War, the Roman campaign against the Black Sea kingdom of Pontus, with 400,000 dead. That war ended when Lucullus alienated his soldiers by "being stingy with his loot" (36).[28] The First Punic War, against Carthage, is also said to have begun with local mercenaries "raiding some of their neighbors for loot" (13). Loot drops out of the picture, strangely, when White does Alexander the Great, but it reappears again and again in other vignettes. About Timur, or Tamarlane, or Tamburlaine the Great, he says, "The most confusing thing about Timur's biography is that he simply attacked every which way, with no specific long-term plan other than conquest. Part of this was economic. Loot sustained armies in those days, so obviously he had to find a steady supply of rich enemies to rob" (147). The authority of the leader depended on his ability to distribute loot to his followers. Loot "sustained armies in those days"—it was an independent and overriding principle of social organization, perhaps more revealing than coherent plans of conquest.[29]

The Vikings do not figure in White's index, and perhaps for good reason. Gareth Williams, in his contribution to the 2008 survey *The Viking World*, notes that the popular image of "the Viking warrior, brutal and terrifying, raping and pillaging, burning monasteries, committing a variety of atrocities and demanding Danegeld . . . has been increasingly downplayed since the 1960s and 1970s, as scholars have rightly pointed out that there were many other important aspects to Scandinavian society in the Viking Age, and that only a small proportion of the population were warriors, while also noting that, since the surviving historical accounts were written by the Vikings' Christian victims, they may give an exaggerated picture of both the impact and the barbarity of raids by the pagan Vikings" (193).[30] On the motivation behind the famous Viking raids, Williams dismisses the idea that they "represented a pagan political/ religious response to the aggressive Frankish Christian mission against the Saxons and the Danes"—in other words, that the other side started it. He returns eventually to what seems self-evident: the proposition that the raids were motivated "by a desire to gain wealth abroad" (193). This proposition does not go unqualified, but it is qualified only by the reflection that others did it too: "Raiding in order to plunder portable wealth is typical of warfare between the petty kingdoms of pre-Viking Britain and Ireland, and survived long after across medieval Europe . . . Similarly, taking tribute seems to have been a central part of the relationship between greater and lesser kings in early medieval Britain." He offers Charlemagne as an example of rule "largely carried out on the basis of a combination of raids against neighboring kingdoms in pursuit of conquest where this was feasible, tribute where long-term dominance could be established that fell short of full conquest, and plunder when Charlemagne had the resources to raid but not to establish lasting domination. This provides a useful paradigm for much of early medieval warfare, and the Vikings are only unusual in that their expeditions were often led by 'private' warlords rather than by national leaders" (196).

It seems plausible that "the Vikings were not markedly more atrocious than others," as this summary of the extant scholarship concludes, because at that time "campaigns based around the combination of plunder and tribute were not unusual" (196).[31] A norm of atrocity is what one would expect if the economic existence of that sort of society at that time *depended* on violence. And the principle holds for a substantial number of times and places. "A great deal of the world's history is the history of empires," Stephen Howe writes. "Indeed, it could be said that *all* history is imperial—or colonial—history, if one takes a broad enough definition and goes far enough back" (1).[32] What the representatives of Athens told the representatives of Melos before the forces of the Athenian empire wiped out the island's entire male population and sold the women and children into slavery, according to Thucydides, was roughly the same: Athens can't afford to look weak in the eyes of the colonies from which it extracts tribute. Without the ability to coerce the payment of tribute, it would no longer be an empire. In the era of empires, a very prolonged era, violence for the accumulation of wealth was not merely a social fact, but one of its society's defining principles, essential to its functioning, reproduction, identity.

There is of course an incipient theory of atrocity here, looming fuzzily behind an account of atrocity that does not go in much for theory. The same holds for Anthony Pagden's account of the destruction of Persepolis by the army of Alexander the Great in the winter of 331–330 BCE: "Until now Alexander had been relatively constrained in his handling of defeated populations. But his men were growing restless, eager to lay their hands on some of the booty they had been promised. Persepolis was turned over to the victorious army. The houses of the nobility were looted, the men slaughtered, and the women enslaved" (9).[33] Pagden is noticeably gentle with Alexander. He says that Persepolis "was turned over" to Alexander's army; we don't watch Alexander give the order to sack the city. What Pagden tells us is that Alexander has been "relatively constrained in his handling of defeated populations."[34] But was it ever within Alexander's power to constrain the slaughter of this defeated population? He had promised his men the booty, meaning the population's possessions, perhaps including free utilization of the female inhabitants as the soldiers wished. Sooner or later the booty would have to be turned over as well, and the inhabitants would pay. It was a system.

And because it was a system, it often went unremarked. As Josephine Quinn notes, Julius Caesar says nothing in *The Gallic War* about "the vast personal profits that [he] made in Gaul—enough to pay off his accumulated electoral debts, reward his officers and men, and fund a series of vanity building projects in the heart of Rome that kept the absent general at the center of attention during the 50s" (No, his contemporaries did not see this degree of self-enrichment or the loyalty it bought him as merely standard practice: "The poet Catullus, writing in Rome, says that one of Caesar's corrupt officers 'has all the riches that used to belong to remotest Britain and Hairy Gaul.'"[35] But if it was remarked, it was not rebuked, let alone penalized. When it was proposed that Caesar be extradited to the Germans after an especially bloody massacre, the objection was not to the massacre itself or to the stolen riches, but only to the breaking of a truce. As I've said, the ordinary workings of the system shine unmistakably through when Caesar offers as extraordinary, in his account of how a mass slaughter followed the Roman conquest of Avaricum, the *absence* of the usual force that motivated his men: "Not one of our men gave a thought to booty" (159).[36] The rule to which this is an exception is the promise of loot, which keeps the soldiers willing to take and risk lives, and the result is therefore always a wholesale slaughter of the civilian population, either as a necessary step toward the seizure of their possessions or as an enjoyable accompaniment to it and a respite from actual fighting with an armed enemy. In mentioning the enemy's earlier misconduct and the energy his troops had made to conquer them, Caesar is addressing hypothetical scruples about the murder of civilians. He seems to have felt he had to. And yet, as the editor of Caesar's *Gallic War* puts it, "the legionary expected profit to come from successful campaigns" (xx).[37] Profit derived from plunder was the norm, as was, therefore, the killing of civilians. According to A. C. Grayling, "the very first effort to say anything about restraint in war" is Sun Tzu's *The Art of War,* written in the sixth century BCE. "Sun Tzu advises maintaining the moral of troops by allowing them booty."[38]

Josephus might be enlisted into the select company of writers who, going further than a passing mention of dead children, have laid the full blame for atrocities against defenseless civilians on their own side.[39] This is how Josephus was read, in the sixteenth century, by Las Casas. It is arguably a rose-tinted reading. But there is no mystery about why Josephus might have had mixed feelings as he beheld the destruction of Jerusalem in 70 CE. He was not only born a Jew; until a few years earlier, he had been an Israelite general, actively involved in the revolt against the Romans. Ambivalence might be expected from someone who (as he tells the story) was offered a choice, after a defeat in battle, between going over to the Romans and instant death. Still, his scruples are not what is most striking about his account of the burning of the Second Temple, the slaughter of Jerusalem's last defenders, who had taken refuge in it, and the mass killings of what were not yet called noncombatants. Like Pagden, Josephus wants to protect the high-born leader who might be accused of atrocity. The potential for accusation that hangs over his narrative is more evidence that scruples exist, even if those scruples are ineffective. And like Pagden, he is tempted to pass much of the responsibility off onto the men on the ground. Yet what can't be missed is the logic of plunder that again links the men back to their leader.

Titus, the Roman commander, decides at first to spare the temple: he "would never burn down a monument of such splendor; its loss would damage the Romans, just as its preservation would retain a jewel of the empire" (324).[40] But "other causation was at work." Under the heading of causes Josephus mentions God, and then the Jews themselves, who inconveniently refuse to surrender. Finally he mentions a single Roman soldier who, "without waiting for orders and oblivious to the horror of what he was doing" (325), throws a burning stick of wood into the sanctuary. A messenger runs to tell Titus, who was "resting in his tent," that the sanctuary is on fire. "Caesar [Titus] shouted and gestured to the combatants to put out the fire, but his voice was drowned out by the greater din filling their ears, and his hand signals went unnoticed by men concentrating on the fight or the satisfaction of their own rage. When the legions poured in, no persuasion or threat could stop their intent—passion alone was their commander" (325–26). Here the spectacle is of a humane, rational commander trying in vain to save the temple and stop his less rational men, who are crazed by blood lust. The men "pretended not even to hear Caesar's orders" (326). Titus continues "to make personal appeals to his troops in an effort to persuade them put out the fire" (326). By this point there has already been a considerable slaughter of civilians: "Most of the victims were ordinary citizens, unarmed and defenseless, slaughtered wherever they were found" (326). The Roman troops continue to ignore their leader's appeals. What are their motives? Josephus says that "any respect for Caesar or fear of the officer ordering them back was eclipsed by the men's fury, their detestation of the Jews, and a lust for battle yet more consuming than either. And a further incentive for many was the expectation of loot" (326). "And so, though it was none of Caesar's wish, the temple was fired" (326).

As a motive behind the slaughter of civilians and the destruction of the temple, the "expectation of loot," added as if as an afterthought, clearly makes Josephus uncomfortable—almost as uncomfortable as it would be for him to have to lay the guilt on Titus, his patron and the son of the emperor. Yet the coupling of loot and the killing of noncombatants seems irrepressible. "As the temple burned anything found was looted and anyone caught was killed. The slaughter was massive—no pity shown for age, no regard for rank: children, old men, laymen, priests were killed indiscriminately, and war extended its grip to encompass people of every class and condition, no matter they were begging for mercy or trying to resist" (327). When it is all over, the troops "with huge shouts of acclamation hailed Titus as *Imperator*." And without a pause Josephus then adds, as if suggesting the reason for the acclamation: "All the soldiers have amassed so much loot that throughout Syria the trading price of gold fell to half of its former value" (330–31).

Would the commander have been so acclaimed if there had not been so much amassing of loot? The loot was the fulfillment of the promise that Titus, like any other Roman general, had implicitly or explicitly made to those who fought his campaigns. The slaughter of civilians was not an accident, but a logically necessary fulfillment of that contract. The acclamation Titus receives is his reward for carrying through on his promise. The underlying theory is pretty clear: atrocity was a product of societies that were organized around plunder and, at least in many cases, that depended on plunder not just for their prosperity and identity but also to cement relations between commanders and soldiers, political leaders (like Caesar) and their base. The killing of civilians was not random or negligent, but systemic.

This is not to say that plunder is always and everywhere a satisfactory explanation for atrocity, or even the best explanation available. The plunder theory—the theory that literary representations of atrocity track those modes of social organization that depended either more or less on plunder—was already displaying its limits in Alexander Kluge's account of the bombing of Halberstadt.[41] The B-17s flew in, destroyed the city, and then flew home without the crews landing. There was no hunting for valuables in the ruins. If the crews were seeking plunder, they did not choose the most effective means of acquiring it. As Kluge himself suggests in his comico-philosophical way, the advent of aerial bombardment changes the principle of war itself, and this precisely because it takes plunder out of the equation. The modern cavalry, Kluge writes, revived "what had motivated early tree-climbers in the history of the species to find the nourishing amnion eggs of large dinosaurs, to bite the shell open from the side or from below and either to place their own brood inside or suck them dry. It is quite clear that this root of strategic interest, booty, does not apply in the case of bomber crews, since they put something into the town that is their target, will never take anything away from it, 'in order, even in the most abstract sense, to suck something out'" (38). This is a bit of an overstatement. It presents bombing as unnatural, but it does so by naturalizing the quest for booty. The two are not so perfectly opposed. In an abstract sense, it's arguable that modern industrialized aggressors do suck something out of their victims. Still, modern warfare being both as expensive and as destructive as it is, one might have to argue at a *very* abstract level in order to make the argument stick. When his armies invaded Russia, Napoleon, who is credited with the line about an army marching on its stomach, certainly did not stop his men from what is euphemistically called foraging. But he was also quite interested in the scientific preservation of food—the immediate ancestor of canning—which is to say in a modern method of waging war that would be less likely to depend on taking provisions by force from the local inhabitants. Even if looting keeps happening, as of course it does, it becomes something more like an incidental vice, not the principle of warfare that it had been. Martin Van Creveld's classic history of military logistics, *Supplying War*, dates the end of what it calls "the tyranny of plunder," which "from time immemorial" had been "the rule rather than the exception" (7), to Napoleon's campaign against Austria in 1805.[42]

In the meantime (this seems to be Kluge's real point), aerial bombardment reinforces the intuitive sense that modern atrocity, like bombing from the air, is absurd, diverging as it does from the rationality of direct self-interest which governs the booty-seeking of tree-climbers and boots-on-the-ground soldiers, on foot or on horseback.[43] Absurdity, seen as the preferable alternative to any theory of violence as instrumental, is the explicit takeaway of Vonnegut's *Slaughterhouse-Five*. As noted above, the slogan Vonnegut invents for a modern fatalism, "So it goes," is the perfect accompaniment to the slogan he borrows from Primo Levi's memoir of Auschwitz: "There is no why."

The go-to argument for those, like Jean Franco, who deny that there is any material explanation for modern atrocity, even a partial one, is the Holocaust. (Franco cites Primo Levi in support of the idea that violence is not utilitarian). At the same time, there is just as strong and just as obvious a counterargument available to the opposite side: colonialism. Considering the economic benefits that accrued to the colonial powers and the no-holds-barred violence that colonial extractivism entailed, motiveless malignity seems an unlikely paradigm for atrocity. And keeping one's eye on atrocity's self-interested motives guarantees that attention will also fall on the emergence and development of misgivings about atrocity, however feeble and unsatisfying those misgivings may be.

Perversities of Democracy

The unequal distribution of power does not apply only to victims and perpetrators; it's also a fact of domestic social organization. In both contexts, it introduces into the history of violence a causal factor that must be kept distinct from the rising individualism, secularism, and cosmopolitanism adduced by liberal champions of progress. If there has been progress in terms of the more equal distribution of power, which is different, its name would be democracy. To be more precise, it would be substantive as opposed to merely formal democracy. That's a harder case to make. The difficulty of assuring oneself of progress in this area might help explain why fatalism has remained so persistent. Still, a critical consciousness of atrocity would hardly be possible if all the power were on one side and none on the other. If such consciousness has indeed arisen, we would have to suppose that there has also been some redistribution of power, however irregular. Historian David Bell sees progress in the denunciation and restriction of violence as real, but nonlinear. Pre-Enlightenment warfare, he says, generated more plentiful atrocities than much of the fighting that came afterwards: "Soldiers routinely massacred the inhabitants of towns they had captured, and the overall population statistics tell a story unmatched in their grimness until the days of Stalin and Hitler" (45).[44] Bell is impressed with the "increasingly important attempts" made in eighteenth-century Europe "to establish legal limits on war making—and thus formally to outlaw atrocities" (46). Before they were interrupted by the massive civilian deaths of the Napoleonic period (1791–1815) that are his primary subject, Bell declares that those efforts made an appreciable difference to the general level of violence. Of course, there were notable eighteenth-century atrocities. "Nevertheless," Bell writes, "—and distasteful as it may be to weight atrocities against each other—it is still the case that such horrors took place less frequently, less systematically, and on a smaller scale than during the age of religious wars—especially in Western Europe" (48). In an effort to explain this trajectory, Bell plots violence in relation to class. This is an explanatory effort that seems worth pursuing further, although (or because) it promises to complicate the trajectory. On the one hand, as Elias argued, the diminishment of violence in the modern period had much to do with the decline of the aristocracy. Aristocratic elites (in Bell's words) "saw war as a natural, unavoidable part of human existence" (48). The shift in power toward a centralized monarchy and away from aristocrats who identified themselves with the use of weaponry undermined the assumption that violence was like the weather. On the other hand, class solidarity (among fellow aristocrats) could also be, as Bell adds, a motive for limiting the "scope and damage" of violence. That function is illustrated, in the late medieval period, by one of the most famous episodes in the early history of transnational protest against the killing of the defenseless. After the Battle of Agincourt in 1415, English nobles complained about the slaughter of French prisoners of war, all of them fellow nobles, though the killing was ordered by the English king. This counts as a moment of national self-accusation. The key to national self-accusation of atrocity was not, however, the emergence of individualism, secularism, cosmopolitanism, or any other component of a universalistic humanitarianism. The protest was articulated in the name of class solidarity. The rules of chivalry protected members of the nobility, whatever their nationality. They were of course held to be irrelevant to commoners, who could be killed with impunity. Eventually, in the epoch of human rights, commoners would be judged to possess the "dignity" that in 1415 was held to be the exclusive possession of the nobility.[45] They too could then become indignant.

The awkward self-consciousness of a declining military-identified aristocracy was not the only cause of the emergence, extension, and consolidation of anti-violence scruples in the early modern period. It seems clear that some came from below as well as from above. According to Jill Lepore, the English massacre perpetrated in 1676 at the Great Swamp, a fortified Narragansett settlement that had been vacated by most adult Narragansett males, "violated several English codes of just conduct during warfare, not least among them the rule that 'to cut off a few nocent, wee are not to cut off multitudes of Innocents, such as are Weomen and Children (as in sieges, and other depopulations) of whom the one is to be spared for sex, the other for want of age'" (88).[46] Lepore's source for the assertion that in 1676 some "codes of just conduct during warfare" in fact existed is not those who carried out the massacre at the Great Swamp—the English killers do not see themselves as violating any codes—but rather a distant participant in the English Revolution. The words Lepore quotes come from Anthony Ascham's "A Discourse wherein is examined, what is particularly lawfull during the confusions and revolutions of government," which was published in London in 1648. Ascham, who was assassinated by Royalists two years later, seems to be giving voice to the social ferment of that decade, which made it possible for revolutionaries, if not for the mainstream, to question both the murder of noncombatants and the conquest of foreign territory. One year later, in 1649, the Levellers, who were slated to invade Ireland with Cromwell, circulated a pamphlet with the mild title of "Certain Queries Propounded to the Consideration of such as were intended of the Service of Ireland." The pamphlet posed questions, as Peter

Linebaugh and Marcus Rediker note, that were "far from mild: 'Whether Julius Caesar, Alexander the Great, William Duke of Normandie, or anie other the great Conquerors of the world, were anie other than so manie great and lawless thieves?'" (120). Another leaflet "questioned the right of Englishmen 'to deprive a people of the land God and nature has given them and impose laws without their consent'" (121).[47] Class consciousness did not prevent the terrible atrocities that would be committed by Cromwell's troops in Ireland, but its anti-colonial force still demands a place in record.

As does the testimony of the Dutch merchant and explorer David Pietersz de Vries in the same decade. Pietersz de Vries tried to stop a massacre of Lenape people by his fellow Dutchmen in February of 1643 in what came to be called Kieft's War. Remarkably, he seems to have managed to forget that he was a Christian facing heathens who as such were undeserving of human sympathy. This does not make him a saint. In counseling the governor of New Amsterdam against making the raid, he seems to have considered very practically that, as a farmer and tradesman, he and others were likely to suffer from Lenape vengeance. (As indeed he did; his farm was burned to the ground, and he left the area forever.) Perhaps commercial practicality was all that was required. Still, for him as for other pre- and early modern writers, a moral norm clearly existed that ought to have protected small children. What he saw, he says, looking across the Hudson River to what is now New Jersey from the ramparts of what was then Fort Amsterdam, was chopped-up babies:

> Infants . . . torn from their mother's breasts, and hacked to pieces in the presence of their parents, and the pieces thrown into the fire and in the water, and other sucklings, being bound to small boards, were cut, stuck and pierced, and miserably massacred in a manner to move a heart of stone. Some were thrown into the river, and when the fathers and mothers endeavored to save them, the soldiers would not let them come on land but made both parents and children drown—children from five to six years of age, and also some old and decrepit persons. (169–70)[48]

The conclusion he draws from this "deed of Roman valour, in murdering so many in their sleep" (169) is a national self-indictment: "This is indeed a disgrace to our nation" (170).

As forensic testimony what Pietersz de Vries offers is not extremely convincing. Anyone who has stood in lower Manhattan and surveyed the distant Jersey shoreline will know how much detail it was and was not possible to obtain from that vantage point, even with a telescope (none is mentioned), and even allowing for the fact that in 1643 there would have been less noise and light pollution. Would an observer so located have been able to affirm with confidence, for example, that the children drowned were "from five to six years of age"? The observation would be hard to replicate. It seems more plausible that Pietersz de Vries's indignation is feeding on both hearsay from the soldiers and on a set of literary tropes and conventions going back to Las Casas, a century earlier, and to a lesser extent to classical authors like Josephus. In Las Casas's *Short Account of the Destruction of the Indies* (1542), which was especially popular in its many Dutch translations, no doubt because the Dutch were then fighting for their independence from Catholic Spain, he would have found an infant formula, so to speak: "They grabbed suckling infants by the feet and, ripping them from their mothers' breasts, dashed them headlong against the rocks" (15).[49] The formula is both secondhand and melodramatic. If the victims are infants, figures of unblemished innocence, the perpetrators become figures of unsurpassable malignity. It invites the reader to take on a certain self-defensive callousness, and even to edge toward the godforsaken domain of dead baby jokes. "What's the difference between a baby and an onion? No one cries when you chop up the baby." Imperfect and abusable as the formula is, however, it is out of such components that a concept of atrocity as moral scandal little by little comes to be composed.

The unsatisfying hodgepodge of elements that goes into its composition can be illustrated by looking more closely at both Las Casas and, two centuries later, Edmund Burke. Both made history, in the strongest possible sense, when they testified to atrocities committed by their European compatriots against non-Europeans. Burke devoted fifteen years of his life to exposing the often violent misdeeds for which the East India Company was responsible on Warren Hastings's watch. He became famous for his colorful and passionate accounts of atrocities. Many observers were moved by his accounts; many were immediately skeptical. But the color and passion come through even in the retellings of skeptics like Nicholas Dirks, who speaks of Burke's "extravagant use" of "supposed atrocities" in his speeches (110–11).

> Burke described the use of public floggings to obtain the revenue demand, sometimes the flogging of a man's children in front of him . . . "Virgins," Burke went on, "whose fathers kept them from the sight of the sun, were dragged into the public Court, that Court which was the natural refuge against all wrong, all oppression, and all iniquity. There in the presence of day, in the public Court, vainly invoking its justice, while their shrieks were

> mingled with the cries and groans of an indignant people, these virgins were cruelly violated by the basest and wickedest of mankind." Now he had his audience virtually aghast, and he continued: "It did not end there. The wives of the people of the country only differed in this, that they lost their honour in the bottom of the most cruel dungeons . . . But they were dragged out, naked and exposed to the public view, and scourged before all the people . . . they put the nipples of the women between the sharp edges of split bamboo and tore them from their bodies." (420–21)[50]

Las Casas devoted his entire lifetime to exposing the brutality of his fellow Spaniards in the Caribbean. His reputation, unlike Burke's, depends exclusively on his accounts of the atrocities they committed. Along with the account of the fall of Tenochtitlan already cited, a small sample should be adequate:

> They forced their way into native settlements, slaughtering everyone they found there, including small children, old men, pregnant women, and even women who had just given birth. They hacked them to pieces, slicing open their bellies with their swords as though they were so many sheep herded into a pen. They even laid wagers on whether they could manage to slice a man in two at a stroke, or cut an individual's head from his body, or disembowel him with a single blow of their axes. They grabbed suckling infants by the feet and, ripping them from their mothers' breasts, dashed them headlong against the rocks. (15)[51]

It might seem that violence like this would always and everywhere have generated much the same abhorrence we observe in Las Casas and Burke. But as we have seen, the literary record does not support this assumption. Abhorrence, indignation, and victimhood were not totally unheard of, but neither were they supported by clear, transparent principles. Those principles had to be invented. How and why, then, did Las Casas and Burke manage to disapprove so suddenly and strongly of the cruelties inflicted by their fellow Europeans on non-Europeans? It was not because either Las Casas or Burke rejected colonialism. Nor, as students will quickly notice, can it have been because they considered non-European pagans the moral equals of Christian Europeans; equality was more than they were willing to claim for the victims. They were not imitating great writers of antiquity who had denounced violence against foreigners. None of these propositions holds up to scrutiny. Why then? The Agincourt example suggests an answer. Las Casas and Burke shared a class-based disapproval of plunder. They also shared an understanding of the state as an agency that could be appealed to against that plunder.[52]

If it is no longer fashionable to see Las Casas and Burke as miracles of moral and literary greatness, standing alone and apart from everything that Europe was saying about and doing to non-Europeans, it is because these facts have been noticed, though from different angles. It is well known that, for all the severity of his critique of Spanish violence in the Americas, Las Casas had supporters back in Spain; he was not censored even during the Inquisition; his complaints took the form of a bureaucratic report and won him an audience with his king. It got legislation passed to curb the violence, even if the Spanish settlers, like other settlers before and since, proceeded to ignore it. (As Andrew Jackson, spokesman for another set of settlers, may or may not have said when Chief Justice Marshall ruled in favor of the Indians whose lands had been stolen: "John Marshall has made his decision, now let him enforce it.") Burke was a member of Parliament who spoke the language of the law and had sufficient authority to force his somewhat reluctant colleagues to sit through seven years of impeachment proceedings against Warren Hastings. It is no secret that neither was a radical democrat; both respected traditional authority. Seen as part of a hypothetical history of atrocity, however, these facts arrange themselves somewhat differently. In order for atrocities like these to be condemned, plunder had to be condemned. And in order for plunder to be condemned, there had to be a new sort of objection to it. What was new—there were Roman precedents, but it was new enough—was an objection to plunder's democratizing effects: its subversive effects on the hierarchical society that was doing the plundering. Both Burke and Las Casas were strongly motivated to make this objection. Both were believers in natural social hierarchy. From the viewpoint of their own societies (though not of course from the viewpoint of the societies being plundered), plunder was a force that spread money around to the unworthy, thereby undercutting hierarchies of birth. The threat of democratic leveling was new. As was the idea that the authority of the state might be on their side in their appeal against self-enriching plunder.[53]

Sara Suleri makes Burke's appeal to authority a centerpiece of her critique of him. She speaks of "Burke's essentially conservative impulse and his concomitant desire to protect the idea of authority rather than to expose the abuses of power" (46).[54] But the same point could be made in more neutral terms—and Suleri herself does so. The focus, for Burke, is "the bitter contest between the language of the merchant and the language of the state" (24). Hastings is "the epitome of an 'arbitrary power'" (47). "Eliminate Hastings, argues Burke, and colonial power will return to the law of accountability" (47).[55] With an exception made for Burke's failure to reject colonial power as such, the argument could even be made in frankly positive terms: "Empire was to be no longer the province of unprincipled pirates, but rather an affair of state answerable to the nation" (125). My own phrasing would not be so positive: the authority of the state could be appealed to against plunder because plunder, the unprincipled greed of pirates and merchants, was subverting the hierarchical social structure on which the state's authority was based.

Nicholas Dirks observes that Burke's overblown descriptions of atrocity "seemed calculated to mobilize the paternalism of men and the sentiment and sensibility of women . . . India itself was cast as feminine, in a way that dramatized its exoticism and difference, and rendered into the object of Britain's protective, and patriarchal, benevolence" (112).[56] It's a fair point. But it doesn't answer the question of what was novel in Burke's account of atrocity—novel enough to sponsor a dramatic and unparalleled intervention on behalf of a colonized people. The abuse of women was certainly not new, nor was the casting of men in the role of rescuers of damsels in distress. Whatever questions might be raised about Burke's own sexuality (Isaac Kramnick argues that Burke was rather too interested in the unrepressed sexuality of other men, to which he attributed their misdeeds in India), that too would have been familiar enough.[57] The plundering of a conquered country both for the enrichment of the conquering country and for the personal enrichment of the conquerors and administrators was, of course, anything but new. What was arguably original was the effect of that plunder on someone, like Burke, who identified passionately with the blue-blooded owners of the great estates. Those landowners had put him in office, but his feelings for them were also personal. As a result, he was especially well placed to deplore the new money that was pouring into England from South Asia. That money was stolen from the Indians, yes, but it was also open to censure because it allowed upstarts to rise suddenly to wealth and influence within a transformed and perhaps vulgarized English society. To Burke, as Kramnick puts it, Warren Hastings stood "against property, rank, and dignity" (133). He and his men "personified the bourgeois spirit" (130). Their sole motives were "avarice" and the "extraction of wealth" (130). They "were ambitious upstarts restlessly tampering with the traditional order of power and status" (130). Plunder was enriching the unworthy, empowering the parvenus.[58] Las Casas was also a believer in natural hierarchy, and his defense of the Indigenous peoples of the Americas against his fellow Spaniards is again a case against greedy, upwardly mobile upstarts (that is, not people of good standing in existing society) whose stolen riches were destroying the natural (that is, hierarchical) fabric of society at home as well as abroad.[59] The point could not be made more clearly: "The reason the Christians have murdered on such a vast scale and killed anyone and everyone in their way," Las Casas goes on, "is purely and simply greed. They have set out to line their pockets with gold and to amass private fortunes as quickly as possible so that they can then assume a status quite at odds with that into which they were born" (13).[60]

Common sense would propose that democratization, which bestows dignity on the victims of atrocity, makes victims more likely to be represented. And common sense would not be totally wrong. But atrocity also becomes visible—visible, that is, as a moral scandal and not a mere misfortune—because democratization itself is seen as a scandal. In a society committed to the belief that hierarchy is natural and proper, democratization translates as a threat to social order even when it takes the form of social climbing, and those who have been plundered and perhaps murdered abroad appear on the moral radar of their conquerors because the riches stolen from them enable upstarts with no breeding to make pretensions of superiority at home. In other words, atrocity becomes visible not from below, but from above. This story is not moral comfort food.

History has other examples of class solidarity overriding national solidarity and thus giving birth to atrocity protest. Another Great Book in which this logic appears is the epic poem *La Araucana*, which came out in three volumes between 1569 and 1590, by the Spanish aristocrat Alonso de Ercilla. The poem deals with the long struggle of the Spanish to subdue the Mapuche people of Chile, whom they called Araucanians. A soldier as well as a poet, and a participant in the Spanish campaign for two years, Ercilla called the Mapuche barbarians, yet he also praised their courage and ferocity as warriors, and indeed in the poem's 1569 prologue felt he had to defend "his inclination toward the Indian enemy," as David Quint puts it (159).[61] His praise, obviously distinct from the they-are-submissive-and-ready-for-conversion case made for the Indigenous peoples of the Americas by Las Casas, mattered in the debate raging over Spanish colonialism at home; it served to refute Sepúlveda's influential "picture of craven Indians submitting without much struggle to Spanish arms," hence as a people who "deserved to be conquered" (171). In this sense, Ercilla was intervening against the Spanish colonists, who thought the Indians were theirs "by right of conquest," and in favor of the Spanish monarchy, which was trying to "break down the local privileges and power of the settlers" (172). In Quint's words, "Ercilla identifies with the power and interests of the king over those of the colonists," and this "often carried with it a more sympathetic, protective attitude toward the Indians whom the colonists were charged with mistreating" (172). It would make no sense to idealize the self-interest of the monarchy where Indigenous people were concerned, but factoring in the divergence of interest between monarchy and colonists offers a more nuanced perspective than the usual deference to racism's black-and-white absolutes. If it was all racism all the time, it would be next to impossible to understand the dialectical twists by which Europeans did in fact come, if too little and too late, to accuse their own people of atrocity. Those twists take us back to class.

Although Ercilla, like Las Casas, judged the state worth appealing to against the colonists, he had also been formed as an aristocrat and a warrior, and he wrote as a man of his class. That class was in the process of losing a prolonged struggle with the centralized monarchy, which was undermining the aristocracy's authority and even seeking to demilitarize it. (As mentioned, this is the story told from the decline-of-violence angle by Norbert Elias, among others.) As Quint astutely observes, Ercilla's identification with the Mapuche cannot be understood without reference to his divided allegiances: on the one hand to the monarchy, on the other to his own class's warrior ethic. "There is a kind of nostalgia in Ercilla's attribution to the fiercely independent and unyielding Chilean Indians of the values and attitudes that were being relinquished—not without a struggle and various atavistic revivals—by *his own* aristocratic class . . . No small part of Ercilla's sympathy for the defeated, but obstinate, Araucanians stems from his projection upon them of the ideology clung to by a European aristocracy itself in the process of historical defeat" (174–75).

In canto 32, when Ercilla describes the Spanish massacre of the Mapuche at the fort of Cañete, what stands out is the absence of any reference to justice, let alone any line distinguishing civilization from barbarism. "Everlasting God! What utter havoc, carnage, and devastation there was, what a battering among those wretched men, blindly rushing forward in their deception, expecting to deceive! Who could describe the grievous injuries, the tremendous, terrifying artillery, the sudden, turbulent storm of shots all fired at once? / Some were pierced clean through, others had their heads and arms taken off or were pounded into shapelessness, and many were punctured by pikes: limbs without bodies, bodies dismembered, with chunks of flesh raining down far and wide, livers and intestines, broken bones, palpating entrails, heaving lungs" (414–15).[62] There can be no individual heroism in such a scene, for there are no individuals. The Spanish killers go unnamed, and the victims, also unnamed, become unnameable, broken down as they are into interchangeable body parts.

By a very narrow definition, this is not an atrocity. No noncombatants were involved; all of those killed were warriors attacking the Spanish fort.[63] The killing is so one-sided because the Mapuche have been lured into a trap, convinced by a deceitful Spaniard that the defenders would all be asleep. They pour through the gate, which has been left open on purpose, and they are ambushed and slaughtered. Stylistically, we are in the same zone of massacre description as in the accounts of the Crusades mentioned above. But the judgment of the violence has changed, and changed radically. Ercilla describes this slaughter, perpetrated by his own side, as "partly justified but entirely regrettable." Why regrettable? For practical reasons: because "the spilling of so much blood [has] utterly destroyed the hoped-for benefits of this land" (414). But also for reasons of honor. Ercilla will not say that his fellow Spaniards have behaved dishonorably, but that is the implication when he gives the voice of honor not to the Spaniards but to the Mapuche captains, who have disdained to participate in their own side's trickery. Those captains therefore escaped the massacre, and Ercilla explains: "Since [their] general had resorted to a fraudulent tactic they all condemned, no noteworthy captain or cacique was present, believing it vile and cowardly to attack an unprepared enemy and saying a victory achieved by such ignoble means deserved neither glory nor praise . . . They considered it shameful to defeat unarmed, unclothed men, the peril of war being that which makes it honorable, and dishonorable those who win without it" (417). All of this could have been said by the Spanish about their own dishonorable victory. What Ercilla says himself, summing up the event, is unambiguous. He accuses the Spanish perpetrators of the massacre of exceeding "the laws and limits of war, in their invasions and conquests committing enormities and cruelties such as were never seen before" (canto 32, lines 3–5; Quint 176). Victory itself proves nothing about which side is just.

It's in this way that qualms about atrocity enter humanity's repertoire: by means of an undeserving authority, here that of the aristocratic warrior ethic. Moral progress enters by the back door. We have seen much the same dynamic at work in Las Casas and Burke: an appeal to the power of the state (a state that was no less violent than the colonizers against whom they are appealing), but also identification with social hierarchy out of fear (at least somewhat justified) that fortunes made by the colonizers at the expense of non-Europeans would turn into a leveling, chaotic force back home in Europe. The social and political authorities appealed to are not morally pure. Yet the dialectical effects of these flawed national self-critiques extend far beyond the expression of statism or aristocratic solidarity. In Ercilla's case, his larger target is breaking the equation of successful violence with fate or the will of God. His opinion, he says, contradicts that of the common voice: "The common voice persuades me to the contrary that ultimately in the law of the world and of fortune everything is just and licit for the victor" (176). It's not just that he is not persuaded. It's also that violent victories should be attributed only to "fortune," or chance, not to God or to justice.[64] Atrocity is now naked, unprotected from contestation like his own.

As Quint argues, Lucan's *Pharsalia* is an important classical antecedent for Ercilla, part of a countertradition which, if not fully anti-imperial, certainly distinguished itself from the epic genre of imperialist apologetics and thus opened the door to the deploring, if not quite the naming, of atrocity. And with these texts in mind, one can perhaps see another side to Thucydides's unenthusiastic if not quite accusatory account of the ethnic cleansing of Melos. According to Josiah Ober in "The Rules of War in Ancient Greece," violence between Greek city-states was not like the weather. Norms restricting the use of violence existed, though they did not extend to the treatment of non-Greeks.[65] The basis of those norms was class solidarity—a kind of middle-class solidarity. Asking "in whose interest the rules of war were developed and maintained," Ober answers: the hoplites (57), or those adult free males who "could afford the appropriate arms and armor" as well as the time for military service (58).

> During the archaic and early classical periods, the Greek way of war, which placed the heavy infantry in the center of the action, supported and reinforced the privileged social position of the hoplite class vis-à-vis the very rich and the poor. Because their arms determined the outcome of military encounters, the hoplite class occupied a clearly defined middle ground between the small elite of leisured aristocrats and the majority of males who were unable to afford hoplite equipment. Although it is dangerously anachronistic to speak of a self-conscious Greek "middle class," the hoplites, as a well-defined social group, staked out a broad and central position in polis society. (59)

This was true in a large number of Greek city-states, Ober goes on. In all of them the hoplites were protected, at least to some extent, by the rules or norms limiting the conduct of war—for example, rules banning the strategy of encouraging uprisings by the poor in the enemy's territory. It was these protocols that broke down in the Peloponnesian War, Ober argues, and the massacre of the Melians is an example of the breakdown. The reason they broke down in Athens was that Athens was more democratic. In Athens, the privileged position of the hoplites was undercut both by a blurring of the lines between them and poorer citizens and, not coincidentally, by the rising importance of the Athenian navy, which was manned by those poorer citizens: "As the navy's role became increasingly decisive for Athens' position in the Greek world, the poorer citizens took a correspondingly larger role in the governance of the state . . . The mass of ordinary citizens, rather than the hoplite class, now defined Athens' political and military center of gravity. As a result, Athens' social structure was no longer fundamentally dependent on a continued adherence to the hoplite ideology—nor to the rules of war that sustained that ideology" (64–65). Again, as for the Spanish in the Americas and the British in India, a certain democratic opening at the heart of imperial society makes atrocity more visible while also making it more likely that atrocities will happen.

Three

Self-Scrutiny in the Era of High Imperialism

"But the service rules are 'ard"

When Raymond Williams's interviewers pressed him about writerly neglect of the Irish Famine, the mid-nineteenth century fiction that was on the table provided him with no ammunition with which to fire back. If the subject is European violence against Europe's colonial subjects and what you are looking for is European self-scrutiny, the period of high imperialism does not promise rich pickings. As mentioned above, usage of the term *atrocity* skyrocketed after the French Revolution, reaching levels in the nineteenth century that it has never attained again. In that period, it would seem, there were no inhibitions on it. The term was unreservedly self-righteous; it was only Others who committed such acts; "we" were free to label "them." From the twentieth century on, so the logic would go, speakers have been somewhat more inhibited, knowing as they have good reason to know that atrocity is something of which they themselves might be accused. Charles Dickens was one of the more enlightened writers of his time, but he does not seem to have acquired that knowledge. Atrocities were indeed committed against English civilians during the 1857 Mutiny, and they filled him with a rage so unthinking that it could not be penetrated by any idea of why or what was being done in revenge to entirely innocent Indian civilians. What he did with the topic in "On the Perils of Certain English Prisoners," co-written with Wilkie Collins, is, unlike the rest of his writings, very close to unreadable today. On his first sight of a native inhabitant of the Caribbean island to which the threat to innocent civilians has been displaced, the narrator, a winningly humble Englishman of the working class, says, "I never did like Natives, except in the form of oysters." He restrains himself from kicking his native interlocutor, then regrets his self-restraint.[1] Eventually the violent treachery of the natives toward their hostages is exposed and revenge is taken.

But "The Perils of Certain English Prisoners" does feature something that still might intrigue today's readers. The tale's crude narrative of native barbarity and English virtue is complicated by a divide *within* English virtue—more precisely, by the protagonist's working-class identity, which obstructs the expected transit in the ending from a heroic rescue to the fulfillment of the rescuer's desire. The sour taste of its nonfulfillment signals that the imperialist nation is divided, and imperialist violence cannot make the divisions—which, as we have seen, are one source of the critique of atrocity—go away. Internal division doesn't do so much in Rudyard Kipling's poem "Loot," published in *Barrack-Room Ballads* in 1892, but it does interfere noticeably with the enthusiasm for imperialist violence. The poem's one problem with that violence is how to assure that the perpetrators are properly motivated to carry it out. The motive of racism against the victims of the violence, though much in evidence, seems to be insufficient. But the poem has a solution, and the solution is in the title: "Bloomin' loot" is "the thing to make the boys git up an' shoot!"[2] The second stanza includes the N-word, and uses it about the general classification of those to be shot and looted, so I will content myself with citing only the first:

If you've ever stole a pheasant-egg be'ind the keeper's back,
 If you've ever snigged the washin' from the line,
If you've ever crammed a gander in your bloomin' 'aversack,
 You will understand this little song o' mine.
But the service rules are 'ard, an' from such we are debarred,
 For the same with English morals does not suit.
  (*Cornet*: Toot! toot!)
W'y, they call a man a robber if 'e stuffs 'is marchin' clobber
 With the —
  (*Chorus*) Loo! loo! Lulu! lulu! Loo! loo! Loot! loot! loot!
 Ow the loot!
 Bloomin' loot!
That's the thing to make the boys git up an' shoot!

It's the same with dogs an' men,
If you'd make 'em come again
Clap 'em forward with a Loo! loo! Lulu! Loot!
(*ff*) Whoopee! Tear 'im, puppy! Loo! loo! Lulu! Loot! loot! loot!

In the midst of all this festive whoopee-making, it is easy to miss the fact that Kipling's speaker is on the defensive. Whether he is ventriloquizing common soldiers or delivering a pep talk to them in what he imagines is their language, his ballad posits the existence of an antagonist. That antagonist is not the people of color who the speaker will later complain are off limits to plunder, even after they've been killed. It is the "service rules" that put them off limits, that debar soldiers from looting. It's the "English morals" that England has presumably written into its army's service rules. More abstractly, Kipling's enemy is the modern British state, understood to disapprove of looting by those whom it has asked (or required) to serve it. In the name of the common man, Kipling disapproves of the state because the state condemns plunder. There is reason to doubt that the rules against plunder were ever effectively enforced. But even without the slightest threat of enforcement, the ethic written into the "service rules" has made something happen. Its existence is registered in the anxiety underlying Kipling's merry ballad. This is a sign, however faint, of a moral trajectory.

In the background of Kipling's poem, the state looms darkly as an active agent, inhibiting some of the violence it occasions even as it sends its soldiers out to seek occasions for further violence. The fact that the state can now be imagined as a force working to prevent or restrain atrocity is as notable as the fact that the state can now mobilize popular self-righteousness in order to generate new sites and occasions of aggression. That intersection between the state and atrocity, a distinctive feature of atrocity in the nineteenth century, has a good side as well as a bad side. The ambiguity is also visible in Gladstone's 1876 pamphlet on the so-called Bulgarian Horrors. On the positive side, Gladstone's pamphlet is evidence that the nineteenth century has taken a measurable step away from the fatalism that had always, to one degree or another, held back a full recognition of atrocity.[3] Massacres had just been carried out by the Ottoman authorities and their local paramilitary allies against Bulgarian nationalists, who were in revolt, and against Bulgarian civilians, who as so often were merely in the wrong place at the wrong time. The news was sensational, and thanks to the new technology of the telegraph and newly cheap newspapers it traveled swiftly. So did Gladstone's condemnation of the indifference and inaction of

Disraeli's Tory government, which was willing to look the other way not just because looking the other way was established procedure in such cases, but also because the government felt it needed the support of the Ottomans against the expansionism of Russia. Gladstone called on Disraeli to intervene. Public opinion, horrified by the atrocity stories, was on the side of intervention, at least initially. Riding a wave of democratic sentiment that pushed hard against the political elite's careful realpolitik, morality showed itself as an independent force in foreign affairs. Action to punish and perhaps prevent atrocity had been proposed, and it had been proposed by one of the most powerful figures in the world's most powerful nation. Violence was no longer like the weather. This is the very opposite of equating violence with fate.

It was now conceivable that something could be done about atrocity. But this was a mixed blessing. Had events not taken an unforeseeable turn (Russia abruptly declared war on the Ottoman Empire), the action that might well have been carried out was the one Gladstone proposed: the shelling of the coastal cities by ships of the Royal Navy. Even the false promise of so-called precision-guided artillery lay far in the future. Inhabitants of those cities unlucky enough to be in the wrong place at the wrong time would again have been blown up.[4] In 1882, when Gladstone had become prime minister, this is the policy that was in fact carried out in Alexandria. The official intention was to ensure the safety of the locals, who in fact were not in any danger. The actual intention, according to Wilfrid Blunt, who tried very hard to dissuade Gladstone from sending in the navy, was to protect British and European trade interests. It is estimated that 30 percent of the artillery shells aimed at Egyptian forts went awry and hit civilian targets.[5] In Bulgaria, there is no doubt that the recognition of an atrocity would again have led to an atrocity. Blundering righteous retaliation like this, the dark side of separating violence off from fate, could also be seen as a return of the dismal violence-as-fate equation: try as you might to eradicate mass violence, you will end up succumbing to it. The threat of righteousness out of control is inseparable from the century's emergent humanitarianism and its recognition of atrocity. A hundred and fifty years later, the threat has been realized again and again, and anyone who speaks the word *atrocity* is morally obliged to remember the punitive, often misdirected violence with which hearers may be tempted to respond. If atrocity is increasingly open to human agency, the variety of forms that agency can take is an ambiguity from which it cannot free itself.

The same can be said of the openness of atrocity to social explanation. Much depends on how the given atrocity is explained. Fate can easily be confused with causality as such, that is, with determination, which as Raymond Williams points out is not necessarily deterministic.[6] (As in: I am *determined* to do something about that.) Some determinants are more heavily fateful than others. When he sets himself to explain the atrocities he wants to chastise, Gladstone doesn't point to the moral variable of greed, like Burke and Las Casas; instead, he points to the supposed invariable of race. He attributes the perpetrators' indescribable evil not to Islam, or what he calls "Mohametanism," but to "the Turkish race." The Turks, he writes, are "the one great anti-human specimen of humanity," and their commitment to bloodshed rather than law is visible in the fact that their "guide of this life" is "a relentless fatalism"[7] It is good that Gladstone thinks the atrocities can be explained. But he cannot pull his explanation free from fate, or fatalism—the fatalism in which "we" of course don't believe, but "they" unfortunately do.

Ethnocentric othering is one form in which the violence-as-fate formula persists, secularized, into the nineteenth century. As suggested above, class division is another. Among the most-quoted lines of Alfred Tennyson's "The Charge of the Light Brigade" (1854) is "Theirs not to reason why / Theirs but to do and die." Though these words are arguably not about an atrocity (the victims are neither noncombatants nor foreigners), they do recoil from reasoning why about mass violence. Later observers have not always surrendered to this nineteenth-century fatalism. Cecil Woodham-Smith did not hesitate to entitle her classic history of the Battle of Balaklava *The Reason Why*, and her book does indeed offer a reason why.[8] In Woodham-Smith's interpretation, "the fatal mismanagement of the affair" was caused by the "sworn enmity" (so the back cover phrases it) between two aristocratic officers, Lord Cardigan and Lord Lucan, each with a strong sense of what was owed him by virtue of his rank. More abstractly, the reason why is military glory, a dream that had somehow "survived" into the modern era although it was "not a dream for the common man" (9) and the modern era is supposedly the era of the common man. For the historian of this era, it matters that the glory-seeking blunderers were not common men but officers and aristocrats. For Tennyson, this is less clear. Tennyson had his poem distributed in pamphlet form among common soldiers in the Crimea, and he no doubt thought it would reinforce their heroic determination to obey their officers' orders even when, in the eyes of reason, those orders would seem idiotic, criminally negligent, and excessively motivated by rivalry with fellow officers. But it would not be quite accurate to conclude that Tennyson is counseling the Light Brigade not to reason why. The fact that the Light Brigade thought they had a duty to do and die, or at least behaved as if they did, coupled with the fact that Tennyson seems to praise them for it, suggests that not reasoning why also belongs to the duties of those who receive orders. But it must be noted, in fairness to Tennyson, that the possessive "theirs" could also suggest that not reasoning why, like doing and dying, belonged to them in a different sense of belonging: that it was theirs as their unhappy destiny, imposed on them by their rank and their orders, rather than theirs as their moral duty to obey those orders. That would make Tennyson less of a militarist. Whether what is involved here is duty or destiny, however, it is implicit that those who are doing and dying are following orders. In other words, not reasoning why is not a universal, either as duty or as fate; the frame in which it shows to best advantage is sociological, not theological. The injunction against reasoning why exists, a century before Primo Levi heard "there is no why here" in Auschwitz, as an identification of fate with social hierarchy.[9]

The familiar forms of nineteenth-century fatalism about atrocity sometimes merge into one another. Sir Charles Trevelyan, the administrator who failed to provide the victims of the Irish Famine with resources he had at his disposal, said publicly that he was reluctant to intervene in the workings of "all-wise Providence." He is also said to have written, privately, that the calamity was sent by God to teach the Irish a lesson.[10] In Trevelyan, the will of God, still understood as a legitimate means of explanation, has been reinvigorated by its merger with laissez-faire liberalism and liberalism's secular embodiment of fate, the all-wise market. But race cannot be counted out. Would Trevelyan have been so blithe in his inaction if those starving had not been Irish, which is to say conventionally racialized? It's very possible that he would not. Between 1846 and 1857, when he was in charge of famine relief in Scotland, Trevelyan declared that despite his commitment to the wisdom of the market, he could not allow people to starve. Perhaps he had learned a lesson from Ireland, where he did allow people to starve. Perhaps things looked different when he contemplated starvation in Scotland, where the starving were fellow race-neutral Protestants.[11]

As his interviewers suggested to Williams, the failure of the nineteenth century's greatest English writers to register England's responsibility for Irish suffering in the 1840s—indeed, their near-absolute silence on the very subject of the Famine—leaves a gaping hole in the record of social realism. The scale of what is missing can be gauged by comparing the number of novels devoted to the atrocities of the so-called Indian Mutiny of 1857. In his exhaustive study of this archive, Christopher Herbert notes that there were "*fifty or sixty* novels in which the Mutiny was reenacted in the nineteenth century" (3).[12] The emphatic italics are in the original. The word *atrocity* comes more readily to the lips when the accused belong to a different race. Although that was not the case for the Terror in France, the racialized disproportion is unmistakable in the century that followed, a period of ramped-up imperial militarism. No one needs to be reminded about the nineteenth century's characteristic translations of race into fatality. As Bernard Porter notes in *Critics of Empire*, there is "a strong streak of fatalism" even in the "enlightened and progressive" ideas of the Fabian socialists.[13] George Bernard Shaw writes to Henry Hyndman in 1900 that "the partition of the greater part of the globe . . . is, as a matter of fact that must be faced, approvingly or deplorably, now only a question of time" (115–16).[14] Fatalism, which for Pinker is the default setting for violence in the time of Alexander or Tamburlaine, has clearly survived its secularization without losing its authority—including the authority needed to dim the memory of atrocity in the past and obscure it in the present. Consider how Tamburlaine, infamous perpetrator of mass atrocity, pops up again in *Middlemarch* during Dorothea's visit to Rome:

> "I have been making a sketch of Marlowe's Tamburlaine Driving the Conquered Kings in his Chariot . . . I take Tamburlaine in his chariot for the tremendous course of the world's physical history lashing on the harnassed dynasties. In my opinion, that is a good mythical interpretation." Will here looked at Mr Casaubon, who received this offhand treatment of symbolism very uneasily, and bowed with a neutral air.
>
> "The sketch must be very grand, if it conveys so much," said Dorothea. "I should need some explanation even of the meaning you give. Do you intend Tamburlaine to represent earthquakes and volcanoes?"
>
> "O yes," said Will, laughing, "and migrations of races and clearings of forests—and America and the steam-engine. Everything you can imagine!"
>
> "What a difficult kind of shorthand!" said Dorothea, smiling towards her husband. "It would require all your knowledge to be able to read it."
>
> Mr Casaubon blinked furtively at Will. He had a suspicion that he was being laughed at. (book 2, chapter 22, 148)[15]

Casaubon is being laughed at, as well as deceived—Ladislaw is distracting him from a covert attempt to sketch the beauty of his wife—but he cannot be the only reader who finds something suspicious in Will's account of Tamburlaine. Can the world-class violence Tamburlaine committed be identified with "the tremendous course of the world's physical history"? That is, can it be morally neutralized by being assimilated to the West's increasing mastery of the physical world? Dorothea is not wrong to ask whether the intentionality of violence belongs in the same narrative with the victims of "earthquakes and volcanoes," which are not man-made, and if so whether that proximity would disable the moral judgment of violence. If it did, modernization would become a version of divine providence, which is beyond the judgment of mortals. As for "migrations of races and clearings of forests," they might seem to stand in, though phrased as innocuously as possible, for colonialism, which might then look like the modern West's imitation, in "America" and beyond it, of the long-past conquests of Tamburlaine. The list ends with "the steam-engine," or technological progress again—the exemplary agent of an impersonal modernizing fate for which presumably no one can be held morally responsible. Lurking behind this light-hearted banter is a shadow plot in which fate is now modernization, which cannot be refused, and atrocity is both evoked and whitewashed: and yet of course the entire scene is indeed banter, and we cannot tell whether this is because the violence, though it was terrible, is now superannuated, and common sense does not require that it be vividly remembered.[16]

Self-Scrutiny

In *Oh What a Slaughter*, his playlist of top atrocities committed by whites in the American West, Larry McMurtry sums up the century's secularization of fate in one line: "The whites had better equipment, and always prevailed" (127).[17] Atrocity was either justified or rendered invisible by belief in the moral and technological superiority of the intruding civilization, a belief which (however sympathetic the intruders might be to their victims) condemned Indigenous peoples to inevitable extinction, whether violent and immediate or not. And yet even in a settler colonial context, this is clearly not the whole story. "The Myth of the Vanishing Indian" is recognized as a myth by no lesser institution than the White House Historical Association, which acknowledges (contrary to what is suggested by some of the White House's decorative art) that Native Americans have of course survived the country's genocidal efforts. (As has the myth that they have not survived.) In the general confusion, it's not surprising that the story of how, how far, and why such beliefs have changed remains less gripping than the myth itself, and less familiar. How and when did phrases like "the survival of the fittest" and "manifest destiny" pick up their moldy, antiquated smell? What made it possible for the "myth" to be labeled as such, even in such a prominent site? Evidence that atrocity was not always dismissed as inevitability, even in its immediate aftermath, has not found its own narrative—perhaps for cogent reasons. But it needs to be better known that, however partial and unsatisfying the results, some moral transvaluation of values was already happening and that it had an effect on representations of atrocity. Here I turn to nineteenth-century self-scrutiny.

Data about the nineteenth century's hyperabundant usage of the term *atrocity* seems to point in an obvious direction, but it can be interpreted in more than one way. Although the term was obviously pervasive and no doubt largely self-righteous, Herbert's study of British responses to the uprising of 1857 makes it clear that a certain number of citations came from "the debunking of the atrocity stories," not from the tellers of those stories themselves. The project of debunking, Herbert says, was pursued "by a long string of high-profile writers during the war and afterward, and not at all in 'muted' terms, either" (15).[18] According to Herbert, the work of exposure and demystification began almost immediately. The Mutiny war hero T. Henry Kavanagh, writing in an 1860 memoir of the fighting, singled out for denunciation the original colonizers of India who "plundered and oppressed [Indians] to retire to sumptuous homes in England" as well as the "atrocities" committed by soldiers around him (12). (Kavanagh's reaction to the "sumptuous homes in England" should recall the argument about Las Casas and Burke above). "The falsity of the atrocity tales was perfectly well known," Herbert continues, "by the time that Sir George Trevelyan, in his 1865 study of Cawnpore . . . denounced those 'prurient and 'ghastly fictions' which, he declared, 'it is our misfortune that we once believed, and our shame if we ever stoop to repeat' " (15). British reaction to the so-called Mutiny is often taken as definitive evidence of a solid edifice of racist hysteria in which, at least where violence was concerned, there were no cracks whatsoever. Patrick Brantlinger writes in "The Well at Cawnpore: Literary Representations of the Indian Mutiny of 1857," "Victorian writing about the Mutiny expresses in concentrated form the racist ideology that Edward Said calls Orientalism, the hegemonic discourse of imperialist domination which applies specifically to the Near and Far East" (199).[19] If this discourse were as hegemonic as Brantlinger says, it would be hard to explain how William Howard Russell, after touring the scenes of atrocity and counteratrocity, could put so much of the blame on *British* racism: "The fact is, I fear the favourites of heaven—the civilizers of the world—*la race blanche* of my friend the doctor, are naturally the most intolerant in the world. They will forgive no man who has a coloured stratum." (51).[20] Russell does not question that the British, finding themselves in charge in India, have the responsibility to govern. He is not anti-imperialist. He merely says that "our antipathies and 'natural' dislikes produce the most deplorable results in alienating from us the affections of the people among whom our lot is cast for the time" (52). Thus he finds the "rebellion" of the Indians entirely natural and understandable. Russell was not a marginal voice. He was foreign correspondent for the *London Times.* His Indian diary, which is full of indignation at the British revenge murders of random Indian civilians, was a best-seller.

Clearly it was not impossible to explain atrocity in the nineteenth century except by reference to racist stereotypes. On July 27, 1857, a few short weeks after news of the Mutiny arrived in Britain, Prime Minister Benjamin Disraeli gave a three-hour speech in the House of Commons in which he dismissed the greased cartridge explanation (that is, an explanation based on trivial grievances within the army, or what some were calling superstition) and pointed instead at the British themselves and their extractive, structurally disrespectful mode of governance. The British rulers of India, he said, had dispossessed the native princes, disturbed traditional arrangements for the inheritance of property, and tampered with the local religions. In short, as Herbert puts it, Disraeli analyzed the Mutiny as a reaction of the people themselves to "the whole conduct of British rule" (9).

Wilfrid Blunt, the former diplomat who tried so hard to stop the bombardment of Alexandria in 1881 that began British rule over Egypt, has sometimes been dismissed as an eccentric. But he was extremely well connected, and he clearly thought that a great deal of British opinion was on his side. As British warships were maneuvering in the harbor of Alexandria, Blunt wrote in his diary: "Strangely enough, I am in high spirits. My idea is that this bombardment and bloodshed, however it terminates, will produce a revulsion in public feeling here and stop further proceedings. Nobody really wants war or annexation, except the financiers. And these would soon go to the wall if the public spoke" (367).[21] Foreign affairs being as complicated as they were, many hooks existed on which popular anti-militarist feelings might be hung. Blunt continued, "Gladstone was being persuaded to apply the astonishing remedy for unruly Egyptian Nationalism of bringing in on it the 'unspeakable Turk,' the 'Bashi-bazouk,' fresh from his 'Bulgarian atrocities,' and the 'man of sin' himself, Sultan Abdul Hamid." (294). The intervention Gladstone was clamoring for was not just against an Egyptian nationalist uprising, but in defense of the Turks, who were not popular—and in large part thanks to Gladstone himself.[22] As always, in Britain stories of atrocities in which the victims were British circulated more rapidly.[23] But Blunt was not entirely wrong about British public opinion.

Assuming that ethnocentrism today is no longer absolutely hegemonic (a safe assumption—otherwise how could Said's *Orientalism* have become a contemporary classic?), a narrative is needed that would account for when and how its rule came to be challenged. As the cases of Las Casas and Burke have already shown, such a narrative could not follow a steadily rising arc of moral illumination. The nineteenth century's intensification of imperialist racism stands out shamefully, as Jennifer Pitts has shown, in contrast with the previous century, when European criticism of imperialism was not anomalous but more or less normal, if never an expression of majority opinion.[24] Voltaire's *Candide* (perhaps influenced by Grimmelshausen) and Swift's "A Modest Proposal" exemplify the oblique but stirring recognition of atrocity made possible within the genre of satire—a recognition, to repeat, of atrocity as a moral scandal, a recognition that assumed its actors were free to act otherwise. Edmund Burke did not treat the conduct of the East India Company as an instrument of imperial destiny. More important than Burke's example is the fact that Burke could drag so many of the nation's leaders and so much of its public opinion into the impeachment trial of the East India Company's head, a trial that went on for seven years and was rife with accounts of atrocity committed against Indians by the company's agents. If the possibilities for Europeans to protest violence against non-Europeans tend to close down in the next century, as Pitts argues, the least one has to recognize is that they had once been more open, and the agents and agencies that held them open can't be erased from the history.

Although the anti-fatalistic legacy of the Enlightenment is weakened in the century that follows, it does not disappear from representations of mass violence, such as they are. Pause a moment to consider Samuel Bamford's account of the 1819 Peterloo Massacre. Peterloo did not involve violence against non-Europeans, so it can't count as an example of national self-indictment, but it does offer an interesting contrast with the simplicity of other-directed accusation. In Manchester cavalry charged into a large, peaceful demonstration on behalf of parliamentary reform, killing some (the exact number remains controversial) and wounding hundreds. The event invited severe denunciation even from those who were not in solidarity with the protesters; after all, the perpetrators had inflicted agony on an unarmed crowd. It says something about the common sense of the period that Bamford, who found himself in front of the charging horses, could avoid the seemingly unavoidable melodrama.[25] Bamford writes: "On the cavalry drawing up they were received with a shout of goodwill, as I understood it" (206). Noteworthy here is "as I understood it," which raises the awkward possibility that he did not understand it correctly and that the shout meant the cavalry felt themselves provoked. The gesture toward understanding the subjectivity of the perpetrators is slight, but it is there. "They shouted again, waving their sabres over their heads; and then, slackening rein, and striking spur into their steeds, they dashed forward and began cutting the people" (206). Provocation would not wipe away the blame for the injuries that are about to be described, many of them grievous, but it does make a difference. Bamford continues in a style of dry military history. The crowd stands fast, making a "compact mass" that the cavalry cannot easily penetrate. There is a quick pivot to the human side of the story, as the cavalry use their sabres to "hew a way through the naked held-up hands and defenceless heads; and then chopped limbs and wound-gaping skulls were seen" (207). The crowd breaks, tries to run, appeals for mercy. "Women, white-vested maids, and tender youths, were indiscriminately sabred or trampled, and we have reason for believing that few were the instances in which that forbearance was vouchsafed which they so earnestly implored" (208). Bamford is saying that the horsemen were merciless, but he says it with such elegant obliqueness as to distract from the victims' bloody injuries.[26] He also pauses to note that, with the special constables and artillery that had been gathered, "force for a thorough massacre was ready, had it been wanted" (209). This is a way of saying that, horrible was it was, what happened was *not* a "thorough massacre." He also finds an almost comical way of declaring that he himself was neither exemplary victim nor chivalrous defender of the still more defenseless.

> For my own part, I had the good fortune to escape without injury, though it was more than I expected . . . In my retreat a well-dressed woman dropped on her knees a little on my left: I put out my hand to pluck her up, but she missed it, and I left her. I could not stop; and God knows what became of her. Two of the yeomanry were next in our way, and I expected a broken head, having laurel in my hat, but one was striking on one side, and the other on the other, and at that moment I stepped betwixt them and escaped. (208)

How can Bamford manage to refuse melodrama even when he himself is directly in harm's way? It seems worth speculating that his membership in a movement, the paradigmatic nineteenth-century movement for democratic reform, makes a rhetorical difference. As a political figure, he is trying to rally his side, and at the same time he is trying to win wider sympathy for that side among those who are not members; perhaps he is even trying to address his opponents. He speaks as though his opponents can in fact be spoken to, and just might be induced to listen. In other words, Bamford's voice sounds as if the movement toward democracy, having developed, has achieved some purchase on mainstream opinion, some degree of or potential for empowerment.[27] Empowerment, even as a mere prospect, allows him to take some distance from the equation of violence with fate. From that angle, his unmelodramatic style of speech could be read as testimony that democratization, even very incomplete democratization, has had an impact on accounts of atrocity. From Grimmelshausen on, that is after all what one might have expected. In an analysis of nineteenth-century melodrama, Christine Gledhill and Linda Williams connect the form to Britain's aristocratic regime and aristocratic ideology. That regime was in the process of transition, however, and so therefore was melodrama. "The displacement of rank as a dramatic source of moral authority reoriented the focus of tragedy from the idea of fate and heroic endurance toward 'poetic justice,' a new ideal consonant with Protestant morality, based in private, individual conscience, demanding virtue be rewarded and misdeeds punished" (xi).[28] Fate, like tragedy, expressed, roughly speaking, the worldview of feudal hierarchy, which of course had persisted, if to a diminished degree. It must be distinguished from poetic justice, which came from below and depended on actions, not on birth. Characteristic nineteenth-century forms of narrative, even providential forms that were contiguous with melodrama, marked a step away from fatalism. The culture has changed. There has been a change in moral common sense. To consider yourself the master of your fate is always to be in the grip of illusion, and yet collective mastery, however limited and piecemeal, is both the goal of democracy and to some extent its accomplishment.

Atrocity becomes more visible when conquest becomes more questionable. Common sense, helped along by capitalism's enticing promise that violent conquest can be replaced by nonviolent commerce, was moving beyond the hailing of conquering heroes, even where the conquered were non-Europeans. Capitalism's pledge did not have to be fulfilled in order to have an effect. Contempt for conquest is assumed in Jeremy Bentham's pamphlet, "Emancipate Your Colonies! Addressed to the National Convention of France."[29] "Conquer, you are still but running the race of vulgar ambition: Emancipate: you strike out a new path to glory. Conquer, it is by your armies. Emancipate, the conquest is your own, and made over yourselves. To give freedom at the expence of others, is but conquest in disguise: to rise superior to conquerors, the sacrifice must be your own." Critical responses to the events of 1857 in India detached themselves further from the once-unquestioned virtue of conquest. Alexander Duff, a missionary and author of *The Indian Rebellion: Its Causes and Results* (1858), put the rebellion's "causes" into his subtitle when the Mutiny had barely ended, and he gave as one of those causes the natural resentment of the conquerors by the conquered: "The mere fact of a forcible conquest, together with the systematic restraint and all-pervading regularity of our rule . . . were enough to awaken and perpetuate feelings of exasperation and intensest hate."[30] To recognize resentment of the conquerors is not to defend the atrocities committed by the Indians. Nor is it to denounce the atrocities committed in response to them by the British. But as an act of contextualization, it invites critical attention to both of those stronger, better-defined options. A moral common sense that is getting into the habit of contextualizing, and even contextualizing context-repellent atrocity, is emancipating itself at least somewhat from fate.

On the Persistence and Denial of Fatalism: *Hadji Murat*

One of the answers Williams might have given when he was interrogated about the absence of atrocity from nineteenth-century fiction that was supposed to tell the deep truth about the social reality of its time was Tolstoy's novella *Hadji Murat*. Tolstoy's final work of fiction, *Hadji Murat* is set during the mid-nineteenth-century Russian conquests of the East in which Tolstoy himself participated as a young man and which so neatly mirror the genocide of the Native Americans that the US was carrying out in the same years in the American West. At one point it informs us of the destruction of an Indigenous village in the Caucasus in what would now be called Chechnya. It does not actually describe that destruction. Tolstoy shows the military excursion through the eyes of a Russian soldier, and the Russian's mind is elsewhere, preoccupied with themes that could not be more conventional for men of his social class: women and gambling. For him it is an unremarkable day, so though we are told afterwards that the village has been destroyed, the reader does not see it happen; the Russian sees nothing remarkable: "War presented itself to him only in the sense that he subjected himself to danger, the possibility of death, and in so doing earned both decorations and the respect both of his comrades here and his friends in Russia. . . . The mountaineers [he does not call them Chechens] presented themselves to him only as skilled horsemen against whom one had to defend oneself" (83).[31] There is literally not a single word of description of what we will soon be told was indeed an atrocity. Given this failure of Russian consciousness, the narrator must step in and somewhat intrusively make a connection on the next page that no one within the novel's world is there to make:

> The village sacked in the raid was the very one in which Hadji Murat had spent the night before he went over to the Russians . . . On returning to his village, Sado [at whose house we have seen Hadji Murat greeted hospitably in the first scene] found his hut ruined: the roof had fallen in, the door and pillars of the gallery had been burnt, and the interior had been defiled. His son,

> the handsome boy with the shining eyes who had looked at Hadji Murat in rapture, was carried dead to the mosque on a horse covered with a felt cloak. He had been bayoneted in the back. (84)

The sentence about the child bayoneted in the back does not end the paragraph. The prose flows onward without pausing. It's as if, from a Russian point of view, the death of an unthreatening Chechen child (he is bayoneted in the back, presumably while running away) is not forceful enough, ethically or emotionally, to justify a hesitation, even a very brief hesitation, to absorb the gravity of what has been done. And even perhaps as if, from a Chechen point of view, this is just what is to be expected from the Russians, just more of the same. In "The Raid," his first attempt to describe the destruction of the same Chechen village, written decades earlier, Tolstoy does not give a Chechen perspective, but he allows one of the soldiers to *suspect* that violence is being committed against a Chechen child.[32] That soldier registers some discomfort—and then he is reassured, having discovered that what he has been hearing is not the sound of a child, but the sound of an animal being slaughtered for the soldiers' lunch. In *Hadji Murat*, on the other hand, Tolstoy allows not even the slightest suspicion of Russian discomfort. And by ruling out any morally critical observer among the soldiers, he widens his denunciation to Russian imperial violence as a totality. It's not surprising that he could not get the novella published in his country in his lifetime, at least in full. On reflection, it seems surprising that he left this record at all.

On second thought, denunciation is probably too crude a term to describe the rhetorical operation that *Hadji Murat* performs on Russian imperialism. For that matter, so is contextualization, though contextualization at least suggests a willingness to register morally compromising nuance. Nuances that might get lost in a rhetorical framework of attack and defense come to the surface in Tolstoy's treatment of Avdeyev, a Russian soldier who drops out of the novella early on, well before the destruction of the Chechen village. Avdeyev is shot in a minor skirmish with the Chechens and hours later dies of his wound. This is not an atrocity, though the scene is violent and it is quite important to Avdeyev, if not important to the plot. Like Simplicius, a fellow peasant, Avdeyev does not seize the opportunity to consider himself as a victim. In the face of his own violent death, Avdeyev has no complaints. He displays a tranquil and even cheerful resignation—a resignation that Tolstoy, at some risk of political self-contradiction, seems to find attractive. As he is dying, Avdeyev does not draw attention to his pain or fear; instead, he asks a comrade whether he has found his lost pipe. Questioned by the doctor about the wheals on his back, "the scars of his punishment for spending money on drink" (36), he has nothing to say against the whipping—unlike his author, whose short story "After the Ball" is an unforgettable indictment of corporal punishment in the Russian military. Avdeyev relegates his suffering to an irrelevant past; " 'That's old stuff, Your Honour,' croaked Avdeyev" (36). He appears surprised when he feels his death approaching, but he dies in full consciousness of what is happening to him, and Tolstoy seems to admire this just as he admires it, at the end of the novella, in Hadji Murat himself. For Tolstoy, fatalism seems to be a source of dignity. And yet the dignity of accepting one's fate is not Tolstoy's last word on the subject. After Avdeyev's death, Tolstoy uses a prolepsis to extend his death, and his life, into the future and into ordinary life far from the front lines. The posthumous prolepsis gifts him a story that, as an extremely minor character of no significance to the plot, he would not otherwise enjoy. Here, as elsewhere, prolepsis functions as a supplement; it provides some of the extra historical understanding that would be necessary in order for Avdeyev to see his fate in some relation to justice—in this case, to see himself as a victim, though from the viewpoint of the Chechens he would no doubt be a perpetrator even if he dies before his unit commits the novella's one particularized atrocity. As I have said, it's the fate of the common soldier to be both perpetrator and victim. There is no way to avoid this moral confusion except to empower the peasants, protecting them from choices that are not really choices at all.

After Avdeyev dies, and after his death has been shrouded in the usual official falsehoods by the communiqué that reports it, the narrative suddenly switches to the family he has left behind. "On that very day when Petrukha Avdeyev was dying in the hospital in Vozdvizhenskaya, his aged father, the wife of the brother in whose place he had become a soldier, and the daughter of his elder brother, a young girl of marriageable age, were threshing oats on a frosty threshing floor" (38). We are told how early the father began the work, when he finally wakes up the others to join him at work, how much snow has fallen, and how well they work together—with the exception of the older brother, who arrives late, doesn't work as hard, and is pestered by his father about his laziness. The work is then interrupted by the news that they have been summoned by "the master" to deliver bricks. His father thinks of the injustice of Avdeyev being compelled to go off as a soldier—the injustice *to him*, the father, that is, since he has lost a useful pair of hands, but not (not quite) the injustice to Avdeyev himself. "The old man was sorry for him, but there was nothing for it. Soldiering was like death. A soldier was out on his own, and there was no point thinking about him and torturing your soul. Only from time to time did the old man reminisce about him, like today, to irritate his elder son" (40). The father's thoughts gingerly approach the injustice by which his younger son has been shipped off to war, but he backs away from it. Theirs is not to reason why. Soldiering is like death. There is "nothing for it"—nothing to be done about it. This is fatalism, more precisely the fatalism of those with very few choices. It helps explain Avdeyev's own fatalism. No connection is made between the system that demands that the family contribute a son to the army and the system that demands that the family break off its threshing to carry bricks for the master. The voice of necessity is not interrogated. Mentioning the hard-working younger son so as to irritate the lazy elder son may be a way of registering that the threshing of the oats does have to be done, so he has no time to spare on matters he cannot change. And it may be no more than everyday family squabbling. Tolstoy does not choose between the more political and the less political reading. Still, the old man agrees to add a ruble to his wife's news-filled letter to their son at the front.

And then we get the prolepsis: "But Petrukha was not destined to receive either this news about his wife leaving home, or the ruble, or his mother's final words. This letter and the money came back with the news that Petrukha had been killed in the war" (41). Here, as so often, the prolepsis that disrupts the narrative sequence refers to destiny. But what does destiny mean here? It is certainly not the tragic inevitability of a war that has to be fought in the interests of the noncombatants back home. The section ends with the thoughts of the soldier's wife, who has left home and who "in the depths of her soul was pleased at Pyotr's death. She was pregnant again by the shop assistant she lived with" (42). This benefit of the war to her cannot be what its planners in Moscow had in mind. But it is the reaction of Avdeyev's mother that best sums up the pages appended to Avdeyev's death. "When the old woman received this news she lamented while she had the time, and then she got on with her work" (41). For her, destiny is work, and more work. As her son has no time for complaint, so she has little time for lamentation. Both see their lives as ruled by necessity. (If this were a novel rather than a novella, it would have to be more taken up with feelings; the center of those feelings would be Butler and his officer comrades, who don't work the way Avdeyev's family works, and who don't see that an atrocity has been committed. Atrocity would not be central and perhaps would not be narrated at all.) Tolstoy is suggesting that Avdeyev's family would need a different understanding of history in order to see themselves as free agents and therefore as victims of human agency. Or perhaps they would need to enjoy a different material relation to history in order to have a different understanding of it.

Still, Tolstoy takes the trouble to insinuate that, even for those most burdened by necessity, freedom of choice is not irrelevant. Avdeyev did not have to go to war in place of his elder brother; the decision to go expressed his personal generosity. And the qualification becomes significant when one steps back to consider what the novella has to say, finally, about the Russian conquest of the Caucasus, in which Avdeyev was choosing to participate, and the atrocities it could hardly avoid bringing with it. If the Russians were destined to conquer the East, as Americans consider that it was their Manifest Destiny to conquer the West, could Tolstoy be accusing the Russian government of committing an atrocity? In that case, accusation would be immaterial. Necessity nullifies accusation. And whether because fatalism persists through the nineteenth and twentieth centuries or because in any period accusing your nation presents undiagnosed difficulties, it is a thing to be noticed that Tolstoy softens his national self-accusation. At the moment when it is his own nation that must be blamed, he too plays with the possibility that atrocity is fate, hence that the model of blaming is misguided. The last scene in the novella is Hadji Murat's death scene, taken out of chronological order and memorable among other reasons because it is imbued with Tolstoy's vitalism. The text's final words repeat the analogy between that death and "the crushed thistle in the middle of the ploughed-up field" (125) that brought Hadji Murat's story to mind, as the narrator tells us in the text's first pages. In those first pages, the ploughed-up field is described at length: "The ploughing had been done well, and nowhere across the field could there be seen a single plant or a single blade of grass—everything was black" (4). The sight leads the narrator to make a general reflection: "What a destructive, cruel being man is, how many different living creatures and plants has he annihilated to sustain his own life" (4). This reflection then attaches to the sight of a thistle, broken by the ploughing, yet somehow full of vitality, "standing nevertheless. It was as if it had had a piece of its body torn off, its innards turned inside out, its arm torn away, its eyes poked out. But it remains standing and does not surrender to man, who has destroyed all its brethren around it" (4). The meaning of this parable for "a story from long ago in the Caucasus" (4) seems clear: Tolstoy admires the noble Chechens who refused to surrender to their Russian conquerors, but he generalizes the Russian conquerors as "man," not as a territorially expanding nation, and he generalizes man's relation to nature, though cruel, as the necessary work of ploughing, which is to say agriculture, without which the species could not feed itself. From this perspective, the conquest of the Indigenous peoples of the Caucasus might be described as tragic, but it would also be described as necessary. Tolstoy's position would echo that of James Fenimore Cooper on the vanishing Indians. The way of life of the Native Americans was fated to be replaced by modern technology and modern civilization, and the atrocities that accompanied its disappearance, while tragic, are therefore not a moral scandal.

Remarkably, this reading is not authoritative. The novella begins when the narrator picks another, different thistle, a beautiful crimson thistle called a "Tatar." This time he finds the thistle not in a ploughed-up field but in a ditch. This time the destruction of the flower is very much his own free choice. He wants to add it to a bunch of flowers he has already picked. "I took it into my head to pick this thistle and put it in the middle of the bunch." The destructive effects are much the same: "When I finally plucked the flower off, the stem was already quite ragged, and the flower no longer seemed so fresh and pretty either . . . I felt regret at having needlessly ruined a flower which had been fine in its place, and I threw it away." The admiration that follows is much the same. " 'How vigorously it defended, and how dearly it sold its life' " (3). As applied to the Indigenous peoples of the Caucasus, the moral of this version of the parable is totally different. Their conquest (and the atrocity that attends it) may again be tragic, but it is not necessary. It does not spring from the nature of man or from the species' need to feed itself. It was a choice, like the picking of a flower to make a bouquet. There was nothing fated about it. And this rejection of the idea of fate is consistent with the details that follow. The army's scorched-earth policy, which results in the raid on the Chechen village and the killing of the fifteen-year-old boy, no doubt among other victims who go unmentioned, is decided on by Tsar Nicholas for the most personal and arbitrary of motives. We are told when and how the tsar decided on that scorched-earth policy, as we are told when and how Tolstoy decided to pick the flower.

There are few texts like *Hadji Murat* in the nineteenth century, or any other century. But there is some evidence of self-scrutiny even in the society that was squeezing the Indigenous peoples of the American West even as Russia was symmetrically squeezing its Indigenous peoples in the East. I will not address the question of how far genocidal violence against Indigenous peoples was a matter of official government decisions in the US, as it was in Tsarist Russia, and how far it was a result of land hunger among white settlers, with the government trotting obediently along behind to secure their safety and property rights. Presumably it was a toxic mixture of both. That said, it must also be said that, as Larry McMurtry insists in *Oh What a Slaughter*, disapproval of violence against Native Americans did find expression in high places. "General Ulysses S. Grant himself called Sand Creek 'murder,' and he later said the same about the killings at Camp Grant. This may not seem like much, but it was important. Grant was a well-respected man" (21).[33] In 1871, when the Camp Grant massacre occurred, Grant was not just well-respected; he was president. The fact "that civilized human judgment finally rejects massacre" may not be "a hopeful sign" (22), as McMurtry writes, but it is a sign that white American opinion was not perfectly unanimous. Self-scrutiny was not unheard of. This needs to be said, however exceptional it was, because of the temptation of cultural relativism: If no one at that time could think any differently, how can we judge their actions by our own standards? And it needs to be said because of the lazy but not unreasonable assumption that if there were any cracks in the solid wall of nineteenth-century racism, such fractures as let some light through came only from the non-European victims of European violence. That is the argument Priyamvada Gopal makes in *Insurgent Empire: Anticolonialism and the Making of British Dissent*.[34] Focusing on 1857 and the following years, Gopal argues that it was only anti-colonial violence that spurred the British to reconsider their own conduct. Anti-colonial violence did indeed have this effect, but as I argued about Las Casas and Burke, dissent also had internal or domestic causes. The same can be said of Wilfrid Blunt, one of Gopal's main characters, and a worthy one. It makes sense that as a Conservative landowner and a horse-breeder, Blunt would dislike the policies of Whigs like Gladstone, whom he saw as shamelessly supporting commercial interests at the expense of national ones. It makes sense that, as a patriot, he might also recognize patriotism when he encountered it outside Europe, as when Urabi led a patriotic movement to replace Egypt's Turkish rulers. It makes sense that, as a member of the country gentry setting himself again against the Whigs, he might feel some affinity with Urabi, the country's first national-level leader who came out of the fellah or peasant class. None of these factors is adequate in itself; others who had them obviously did not come to Blunt's radical conclusions, perhaps even those who like Blunt had studied Arabic and had a taste of French rule in Algeria before coming to Egypt. These supporting factors don't eliminate the personal credit Blunt deserves for the positions he came to hold or the tenacity with which he propagated them in Egypt, in England, and in Ireland (where he was imprisoned for his activism on behalf of Home Rule). But ascribing agency to the victims—turning the victims into agents—can become a piety that distracts from the facts on the ground. Gopal's claim that anti-colonial thought and action were primarily responsible for the self-scrutiny of those colonizers who did indeed take a critical distance from their country's violence scratches a moral itch. But it also accords suspiciously well with the unreliable response of atrocity survivors. An elderly Chinese woman interviewed for the documentary "In the Name of the Emperor," about the Rape of Nanjing by Japanese forces in December 1937 and January 1938, offers a reason why her family survived the machine-gunning of civilians, while so many others didn't. The reason she gives is that she and her family didn't run, they crawled. It's not impossible that she is right. But in the light of so many other testimonies, one would want to add the possibility that their survival was the result of dumb luck.

The historian Karl Jacoby, who gathered testimony from the Apache (or Nnēē) survivors of the 1871 Camp Grant massacre, suggests that "it must have been experienced in real time as a sudden, unexpected intrusion, disrupting not only the People's existence but also the ceremonies that guided their spiritual life" (245).[35] His stress on massacre as disruption of spiritual ceremonies will perhaps also remind readers of the Nahuatl account of the 1521 massacre at Tenochtitlan. But the accounts Jacoby quotes also put a certain emphasis on what we would now call the women's agency. For example, this by M-ba-lse-slā ("Coyote, Two Dead Ones Lying There"):

> During the night a big bunch of Mexicans and Papagoes had got up on these ridges, and surrounded the camp completely. The Mexicans and Papagoes . . . fired on them while they were still dancing. They killed a lot of people this way. They all scattered . . . I ran into an arroyo. I had my bow and arrows, and I pointed at them as if I was going to shoot. This scared some Mexicans and Papagoes back, who were after me. I ran on, trying to get away, but four of them followed me, but they did not kill me or hit me. In those days we Apaches could run fast. (246)

There can be no doubt of narrator's intention to give her people as much credit as the situation will bear. And it is in this spirit that the survival narrative continues.

> I ran in behind some rocks, below an overhanging bluff finally, and hid there. They shot at me, but could not hit me those four enemies. They four were afraid to come close. I shot arrows at them. Finally they ran away, and left me. (246)

Again as with Tenochtitlan, notable here is the absence of a discourse of victimhood or the moral condemnation that would accompany it. Here as there, it seems likely that no such moral point would occur to people for whom raiding was as much their own practice as that of their enemies. The fact that the majority of the victims were women and children, for example, goes unmentioned.

In their parlays with the representatives of the government, the surviving Apaches insisted that what they cared about most now was getting back the twenty-nine children who had been seized and, as it turns out, sold into slavery in Mexico.

The issue got much attention in the US press, but that didn't help; the stolen children were never recovered. Apache trust in the American government is heartbreaking. It was not entirely misplaced. As mentioned above, President Ulysses S. Grant termed the massacre "murder, purely" (121).[36] But he was far away. The Arizona press was "flamboyantly pro-massacre" (121). "But the uproar in the East was just as passionate, and did not subside. To the great outrage of the citizens of Tucson a trial was finally held and 148 raiders were indicted" (122). This was, truly and literally, a self-national indictment of atrocity. Grant sent a special investigator. The result was farcical: "The jury took only nineteen minutes to acquit the defendants" (122). And yet it matters that, as McMurtry puts it, "The atrocities were aired in open court" (122).

Victimhood can't be claimed without a corresponding sacrifice of agency. And here, as with the Aztecs of Tenochtitlan, agency included perpetrating violence of one's own, and not merely in response to the violence of others. It is perhaps no surprise, then, that certain Native American writers and historians of Native American experience have renounced an identity first and foremost defined by their suffering of the colonialism of the whites and have instead embraced their capacity to inflict violence on others. In his book about the Utes of the Southwest, *Violence over the Land: Indians and Empires in the Early American West* (2006), historian Ned Blackhawk describes his argument as follows: "Ute adaptation in the face of imperial expansion is . . . neither celebrated nor glorified. Utes responded in kind to the shifting relations of violence sweeping throughout their homelands, redirecting colonial violence against their neighbors, Spanish and Indian alike. Carrying violence to more distant peoples in New Mexico's expanding hinterlands, Utes attempted to monopolize the trade routes in and out of the colony while besieging neighboring groups, particularly those without horses" (6).[37] Ute alliances with the Spanish, he says,

> carried high and deadly costs for Ute neighbors, particularly non-equestrian Paiute and Shoshone groups in the southern Great Basin, whose communities were raided for slaves by Utes, New Mexicans, and later Americans. Like their neighboring Indian and Spanish rivals, Utes remade themselves in response to the region's cycles of violence, and did so at the expense of others, as violence and Indian slavery became woven into the fabric of everyday life throughout the early West . . . *In short*, before their sustained appearance in written records, Great Basin Indians endured the disruptive hold of colonialism's expansive reach, brought to them first by other Indian people. (7, emphasis mine)

The phrase "in short" that I have italicized tries in the end to restore the firstness of colonialism, as if it were the sole and unique origin of the violence even if (as the sentence finishes) the violence was "brought to" the basin by other Indians. But the passage clearly flirts with an omission of origin stories, for example by making the subject of the action, if not the grammatical subject, "the *region's* cycle of violence." If the violence belongs to the region, it is not colonialism's violence to the same degree, or Europe's; at any rate Europeans no longer possess a monopoly on it. The passage makes it hard to resist asking the question of whether there were such inequalities of violence and domination between Indian tribes before the arrival of the Europeans and of horses.

Blackhawk's aim is to get Indians into the historical record. Getting them into the record often means admitting they have committed acts that, if committed today, would not pass moral muster. Such acts are front and center in the 2008 book *The Comanche Empire* by the Finnish historian Pekka Hämälainen.[38] Along with systematic and deliberate campaigns of slaughter and robbery directed as much at other tribes as at Spanish officials and settlers, these acts include the active participation of Comanches in the eighteenth-century slave trade and, as part of that trade, the public rape of captive women so as to encourage the Spanish colonial authorities to continue buying the women back. Here the presumption of innocent victimhood has disappeared completely. As Hämälainen sees them, the Comanches were colonizers themselves. Hämälainen's introduction, entitled "Reversed Colonialism," begins as follows: "This book is about an American empire that, according to conventional historians, did not exist. It tells the familiar tale of expansion, resistance, conquest, and loss, but with a reversal of historical roles: it is a story in which Indians expand, dictate, and prosper, and Europeans colonists resist, retreat, and struggle to survive" (1). It's clear from his abundant footnotes, which cite the work of Blackhawk among others, that he is far from the only scholar to be interested in what he calls "indigenous imperialism." If this phrase has become sayable, then we would seem to be at an interesting moment both in how we view colonialism and in how we view the US.[39]

Hämälainen is proud of the Comanches, but you couldn't exactly say that he takes their side. Focusing on their ability over more than a century to expand in territory and population, exploiting (it's his word) both the Spanish and the other Indian tribes around them, creating and controlling trade routes, quashing or subduing competition, and generally doing a great deal of what colonizers do—this is not a way of helping the Comanches formulate legal demands for restitution. On the contrary, it's a powerful example of moral relativism about empire. Or perhaps the better phrase would be moral neutrality. It's almost refreshing, but it's also frightening, that this telling of the story offers so little sympathy for colonialism's Native American victims. The victims are apparently dismissed as losers. Could those who are slower to adapt or less adept at it really have expected anything better? On what grounds could the winners be condemned? The single largest key to the Comanches' success as colonizers, as Hämälainen sees it, is their ability to adapt to their environment, especially their natural environment (in brief: exploiting changes in climate and the new technology of the horse to move from the mountains to the plains and from a mixed lifestyle of hunting and gathering to sole dependence on hunting and the acquisition of surplus by trading and raiding). To stress environmental and evolutionary adaptation is to take a morally neutral stance toward the Comanche expansion—but also (why not?) toward expansion in general. On what grounds could the same excuse be denied to the imperialism of the Europeans? Given Hämälainen's methodological (or undialectical) materialism, moral judgment does not seem a relevant option in discussions of any form or moment of colonialism, modern or premodern. What matter whether you cross the plains on horses or cross the ocean on ships? In any historical period or circumstance, it is equally natural to try to exploit the advantages you have been given by your geography and your technology. So-called Big History, as in David Christian's *Maps of Time*, applies the same questions to every human society from the prehistorical through the premodern to the postmodern.[40] This is one form—an eco-evolutionary form—that the new cosmopolitanism in time has taken. As the time frame widens, indignation drops out of the nineteenth-century confrontations of Indigenous and white settlers, and the possibility of a moral history of atrocity disappears.

Barbarism and Temporality: The Indigenous Peoples of *Cloud Atlas*

A postapocalyptic sequence from David Mitchell's 2004 novel *Cloud Atlas* re-stages, in a far-distant future, a familiar nineteenth-century scene from American Westerns: hooting Indians on horseback gallop in circles around a lonely wooden stockade on the prairie and blue-coated soldiers plummet from the ramparts, pierced by arrows. There is screaming and confusion. Suddenly the attackers are inside the walls. Innocent civilians are being murdered. Civilization is in danger from barbarism.

Mitchell does not identify the arrow-shooting attackers racially. Their name is the Kona; the setting is Hawaii, not the American West. Their weaponry is not a giveaway. Crossbows could belong to any one of various historical collectivities, European or Asian. It is perhaps unsurprising that, so far into the planet's future, what we see before us can no longer be attributed to European settler colonialism, whose violence in places like Hawaii and the American West does a lot to explain the reciprocal violence by its victims in paradigmatic scenes like the besieged stockade on the American prairie. The surprise is that Mitchell offers no explanation at all. Despite the advantages of historical hindsight, which would have much to say about the whys and wherefores of atrocity at the frontier, Mitchell does nothing to understand or humanize the perpetrators. Like the Native Americans in the least enlightened of cowboy-and-Indian narratives, his Kona slaughter and enslave without compunction or even apparent motive. What we see before us are pure, inscrutable Others. They are the antithesis of what their victims call civilization.[41] In other words, they are what used to be called barbarians. It comes as a bit of a shock to realize that in Mitchell's otherwise very sophisticated text, one can no longer rely on the by now seemingly commonsensical idea that the feared barbarians outside the city gates were "a kind of solution" for those inside, to quote Cavafy's poem. Or, as we might also say, the "barbarian" is an ideological construct, a refusal of analytic thought.[42] For Mitchell, the barbarian is not a construct. Barbarians really *are* barbarians, without explanations, qualifications, or ironic quotation marks.

The assumption that barbarians are indeed barbarians, and that nothing more needs to be said about their acts of violence, also helps explain why Mitchell makes the novel's first and last sections revolve around a historically verified atrocity: the genocide of the Moriori by the Maori in December 1835 on the Chatham Islands, near New Zealand. Jared Diamond offers an account in *Guns, Germs, and Steel: The Fates of Human Societies*:

> Groups of Maori began to walk through Moriori settlements, announcing that the Moriori were now their slaves, and killing those who objected. An organized resistance by the Moriori could still then have defeated the Maori, who were outnumbered two to one. However, the Moriori had a tradition of resolving disputes peacefully. They decided in a council meeting to offer peace, friendship, and a division of resources. Before the Moriori could deliver that offer, the Maori attacked en masse. Over the course of the next few days, they killed hundreds of Moriori, cooked and ate many of the bodies, and enslaved all the others, killing most of them too over the next few years as suited their whim . . . A Maori conqueror explained, 'We took posses-

> sion . . . in accordance with our customs and we caught all the people. Not one escaped. Some ran away from us, these we killed, and others we killed—but what of that? It was in accordance with our custom." (53–54).[43]

In their history of the Chatham Islands, Michael King and Robin Morrison write that it was the Maori themselves who translated "in accordance with our custom" into "by right of conquest" (91), adding that this right was confirmed by the courts: "In 1868 and 1870 sittings of the Native Land Court settled ownership claims throughout the Chathams (the vast bulk of the islands being awarded to Te Ati Awa [that is, a section of the Maori]), by right of conquest."[44]

Cloud Atlas offers itself as cosmopolitan both in its temporal scope, which reaches in stages from the early nineteenth century to a far-distant future, and in its geography, which is as seriously invested in the Pacific Islands, East Asia, and North America as in Mitchell's native England and its European neighbors. The question it poses with a certain force for the emergent field of world literature, and for educated common sense in general, is whether there has been any adequate translation of that newly expanded vision in space and time into the realm of morals. In giving such prominence to the massacre of the Moriori by the Maori, Mitchell seems to be saying, among other things, that the days of the colonizer/colonized paradigm, which in its crude form attributes all historically significant evil to the Global North, are over.[45] He is careful to add extenuating circumstances. As he tells the story, the European settlers are complicit in the ethnic cleansing; they helped the Maori make the journey to the Chatham Islands. But most of the blame for the violence falls on the Maori, an Indigenous people who are of course better known as victims of colonialism, not as colonizers themselves. One Indigenous people conquers, massacres, and enslaves another Indigenous people. Mitchell is emphatic about it: Europeans have no monopoly on barbarism. Perhaps this too is now educated common sense. The proposition that there is no nationality or race or region that does have a monopoly on genocidal violence does not seem to have struck Mitchell's readers as audacious, though the fact that it is embedded in science fiction, which habitually imagines a denationalized, deracialized future, may have somewhat blunted the provocation. If human history is considered as a whole and if the line between the premodern and the modern has been dissolved once and for all, perhaps this human rights–style leveling has become, or is becoming, a generally accepted truth about the world.

Mitchell is conscious of the danger of depoliticizing his newly broad-brush history, and he takes measures to avoid it. In every period, he suggests, there are those who fight back against the violence that surrounds them, who are untainted by it, try to live outside it, or simply fall victim to it.[46] Mitchell's Moriori are the purest possible example of the innocent: they are extreme pacifists, and thus they are absolutely defenseless victims. It's as if the abstract category of the noncombatant could be embodied in a whole social collectivity. In the beginning is atrocity—and again at the end. Atrocity defines our single great collective story. For what it's worth, it seems likely that Mitchell's idealized version of the Moriori is factually untrue. Diamond tells the story in terms of environmental factors that in his view prevented the Moriori from making a living by agriculture, as they had before splitting off from the Maori, and thus put them at a fatal disadvantage. Other sources on Chatham Islands history suggest that in terms of warlikeness the Moriori were not initially much different from the Maori at all. One hypothesis is that once they were conquered, they created a myth of their eternally peace-loving nature as a back-formation to help justify their subordination. One way or the other, the fairy tale idea that once upon a time there was a tribe of pacifists, now exterminated but somehow also managing to persist, at least in the form of an individual here and there, seems an implausible organizing principle for world history. As is the counterpart that neatly balances it. What Mitchell says about the Maori—that they are barbaric—differs in no way from what the unenlightened European colonists arriving in New Zealand said about them. Mitchell clearly does not want to forgive European colonialism on the grounds that those it colonized were no less barbaric than they were, but that implication hangs darkly over the novel, echoing the commonplaces of the period of high imperialism, and morally speaking it does not sound like a step forward.

Mitchell is not inconsistent here; the novel follows Nietzsche in its skepticism that any such a thing as a step forward has even existed or indeed could exist. Its most obvious Nietzschean is its villain Dr. Goose, but Goose is a thief and murderer who, unlike Nietzsche, embraces progress with enthusiasm, thus contaminating the idea. Goose cheerfully justifies European colonialism:

> "Our weaponry was not dropped onto our laps one morning. It is not manna from Sinai's skies. Since Agincourt, the White man was refined & evolved the gunpowder sciences until our modern armies may field muskets by the tens of thousands! 'Aha!' you will ask, yes. 'But why us Aryans? Why not the Unipeds of Ur or the Mandrakes of Mauritius? Because, Preacher, of all the world's races, our love—or rather our rapacity—for treasure, gold, spices, and dominion, oh, most of all, sweet dominion, is the keenest, the hungriest,

> the most unscrupulous! This rapacity, yes, powers our Progress; for ends infernal or divine I know not. Nor do you know, sir. Nor do I overly care. I feel only gratitude that my Maker has cast me on the winning side." (489)

Nietzsche's parable of the lambs and the birds of prey in *On the Genealogy of Morals* comes out of Goose's mouth as follows: "Why tinker with the plain truth that we hurry the darker races to their graves in order to take their land & its riches? Wolves don't sit in their caves, concocting crapulous theories of race to justify devouring a flock of sheep!" (509). By all means, let the conquering continue; let's just not pretend there is anything moral about it. This is obviously not Mitchell's position, and yet there is considerable evidence that in this novel Mitchell is of the devil's (that is, the Nietzschean) party without wanting to say so. Nietzsche is the favorite philosopher of the composer Ayrs, whose masterwork-in-progress is to be entitled "Eternal Recurrence."[47] Nietzsche inspires Frobisher to put his faith in art, not in history, and his reason is that history merely repeats: "'Another war is always coming, Robert. They are never properly extinguished. What sparks wars? The will to power, the backbone of human nature. The threat of violence, the fear of violence, or actual violence is the instrument of this dreadful will. You can see the will to power in bedrooms, kitchens, factories, unions, and the borders of states. Listen to this and remember it. The nation-state is merely human nature inflated to monstrous proportions. QED, nations are entities whose laws are written entirely by violence. Thus it ever was, so ever shall it be" (444).[48]

Mitchell strays from his Nietzschean disbelief in progress long enough to deliver (on the last page) the pious and official moral that it is not too late to change our ways. Slavery, he suggests, is everywhere, and faced with it, or faced with whichever equivalent your period throws at you, your duty is to be an abolitionist, even if everything you do is a mere drop in the ocean. In every section, characters struggle against some form of tyranny, and their struggles make the novel seem committed to the metanarrative of emancipation. Yet why should you make the emancipatory effort if the name of the game is Nietzsche's eternal repetition of the same?[49] Here Mitchell's Nietzsche makes common cause with his Maori. According to the anthropologist Marshall Sahlins, the Maori see events not as "unique or new" but as part of "the received order of structure" In Sahlins's words, "the Maori world unfurls as an eternal return, the recurrent manifestation of the same experiences" (57–59). For Sahlins's Maori as for Mitchell's Nietzsche, eternal return is the rule, and historical progress is a vicious illusion.

Mitchell cleverly arranges for the story of each period to be overheard by someone in the next period who is then inspired by it. But the inspiration is always random. Although the chapters of *Cloud Atlas* are interlocking, in no way are they incremental. There is no place, for example, for the novel to acknowledge that the right of conquest, embraced on the Chatham Islands by Europeans and non-Europeans alike, was later renounced. That is the upshot, though neither conquest nor aggression is mentioned explicitly, of United Nations instruments defending self-determination and territorial integrity, instruments formulated and endorsed by former colonies as well as by former colonizers. (By way of example, no nation other than Turkey has recognized the independence of Northern Cyprus, a state set up by Turkey after invading and occupying the area.) Novels can't be held accountable for everything they fail to mention, but in the case of *Cloud Atlas*, a novel centered on atrocity, the programmatic exclusion of any historical constraint on violence does real damage. Mitchell makes development from period to period—the kind of development that has put *barbarian* between scare quotes—a nonstarter. In every period, the moral dilemmas are more or less identical: real civilization versus real barbarism. In going morally fractal in this way, the novel arguably *regresses* from our contemporary moral common sense—most obviously, from our achieved disbelief that the world can be so divided, or that the term *barbarism* can be attached to any nation or race.[50] Alas, the novel also seems representative of an emergent common sense that sees violence, in Hegel's slaughter-bench model, as random, repetitive, and unavoidable.

If Mitchell is purveying a vision of eternal return, the pacifism of the Moriori is a particularly bad choice. Like vegetarianism, pacifism supports the opposite argument. It is not a belief system that was there at the beginning. It is an empirically verifiable product of modern history.[51] Though it has philosophical roots in India, China, and Congo (not in classical Greece, interestingly), it was only in modern times that pacifism ceased to be a marginal phenomenon restricted to the domain of thought and developed into a relatively organized series of protests and movements. It was in the nineteenth century that the first recognizably pacifist organizations were established; the word was not coined until 1901. The factors involved are clearly modern ones: Enlightenment thinking as it converged, for example, with evangelical resistance to slavery. In the eighteenth century and after, the Quakers. In the nineteenth century, the US invasion of Mexico and Thoreau. The unprecedentedly large conscripted armies of the Napoleonic Wars. Tolstoy and his influence on the nonviolent mass movements of Mahatma Gandhi and Martin Luther King Jr. Resistance outside and inside Europe to the intensification of European colonialism.

"If the twentieth century brought the steady advance of war and war-related human enterprises," Barbara Ehrenreich concludes in her *Blood Rites: Origins and History of the Passions of War*, "it also brought the beginnings of organized human resistance to war . . . This represents an enormous human achievement" (239).[52] The fact that Mitchell allows the Maori to stand for an eternal and inexplicable barbarism is especially ironic in that the Maori themselves, responding to the violent seizure of their land, developed a pacifist philosophy of their own, and did so in the 1870s and 1880s, only a few short decades after the genocide of the Moriori.[53]

Four

Contextualizing and Decontextualizing in the Twentieth Century

Modernity and Inter-imperiality

As Dierk Walter argues, the convenient belief that "savages" and "heathens" did not regulate warfare in any way had to be invented by their imperial opponents. "The Europeans disregarded or flouted existing regional sets of rules designed to contain the conduct of war within certain limits, taking its unfamiliarity as proof of total lawlessness and consequently obeying no rules themselves, either the local ones or their own European regulations" (159).[1] Scholars have revealed numerous examples among the Indigenous peoples of North America. "According to their ways of war," Roxanne Dunbar-Ortiz writes of the Pequots, "when relations between groups broke down and conflict came, warfare was highly ritualized, with quests for individual glory, resulting in few deaths" (63).[2] "There is considerable evidence," Jill Lepore writes, "that Algonquian standards included a distinction between concepts roughly equivalent to *jus ad bellum* and *jus in bello*. Narragansetts who fought with the English in the Pequot War, for instance, agreed with the waging of the war in the first place, but then refused to participate in acts they found unacceptable to their notions of just conduct" (116).[3] In short, the totally unscrupulous "before" in Steven Pinker's narrative, in which what we now call atrocity was like the weather, turns out under inspection to be as illusory as any other state of nature. Still, the idealized antithesis—premodern culture as making atrocity impossible—is just as illusory. Whatever the norms that regulated violence within a given society, it cannot be assumed that there was ever, anywhere, an adequate level of normative discouragement regarding violence against outsiders, including women and children. In her *Political Violence in Ancient India*, Upinder Singh focuses on the development of an explicit "nonviolence school" in Indian thought in the sixth and fifth centuries BCE (25–26), the influential story of Ashoka's transformation from an exceptionally violent man into a pious Buddhist king, and the *Mahabharata*'s brooding over "the burdens, dilemmas, and inherent violence of kingship" (91).[4] As Singh says of ancient India and even of Ashoka, scruples about the exercise of violence tend to be relaxed or forgotten in border zones, especially where so-called forest people are concerned.[5] But forest people and border zones are precisely the issue in cases of what has to be called colonialism, modern or ancient. Ancient colonialism, like modern colonialism, was fertile ground for atrocity, as was the recently prominent subset of colonial aggression aimed at Indigenous peoples, an aggression practiced both by Europeans and (much less noticed, but no less real) by non-Europeans, many of them victims of colonial violence themselves. What the Indian constitution recognizes as "tribals and scheduled castes," now a political movement of their own and collaborating actively with the Indigenous peoples of other countries, have had many relevant tales to tell.

Discussion of those tales has come to seem mandatory, not elective. Humanists, however determined they may be to take a proper critical distance from the modernity-centered devastation visited upon the colonized over the last five hundred years by their colonizers, now have a responsibility to structure their conversations so that they have room for that wider spectrum of violence. But how would cultural history look if the camera were to pull back in this way? One intriguing option comes from what Laura Doyle calls "inter-imperiality."[6] From Doyle's temporally expansive viewpoint, which erases the line between premodern and modern, much history suddenly appears as a collision not between colonizer and colonized, but between two colonizers. The immediate effect is a certain demoralization of violence. It's as if the Nahua/Aztec view of the Spanish destruction of Tenochtitlan could now be generalized—as if Europe's desire to avoid Eurocentrism *obliged* its observers to adopt that demoralized view at the expense of Las Casas's Western, moralized denunciation of the Spanish atrocities. The two empires were of course technologically inequal, but *as* empires, which is to say both of them based on conquest and tribute, they would have to be placed on the same moral plane. Assuming (as we have been assuming) that premodern and modern empires can be made part of the same interrogation of atrocity, there would be nothing to choose between the moral character of the one and the moral character of the other. Morally speaking, they would cancel each other out.[7] Even those belonging to neither empire would be trying to negotiate a position between them; being caught in the middle by no means encourages a claim to victimhood or indeed permits the invention of an anti-imperial identity. Even with regard to mass violence, the moral dimension disappears. Atrocity becomes universal. It is again like the weather. Which is to say that it too disappears.

If moral progress is a fairy tale, just as the originary pacifism of the Moriori is, the reality, we might logically conclude, is that we are all Maori, conquering and massacring with more or less success and, if challenged, attributing the conquests and massacres to our customs, our culture, our need to preserve our identity. That is the Nietzschean temptation that Mitchell throws his unconvincing Moriori in the face of. And it is one way of judging the concept of inter-imperiality—no doubt a judgment that pushes the concept farther than it wants to go, but useful at least as a warning. Doyle struggles valiantly to retain some moral purchase on history. She shines a light on scattered moments of slave revolt and proto-feminist and anti-imperial protest. But the main players in her game are empires, and the overwhelming momentum of her coinage goes in the opposite direction: toward a vision of history in which, because one empire is pitted against another, no participant in the conflict has a moral advantage over anyone else. If there is no moral division between perpetrator and victim, then in the strict sense there is no atrocity. Hence a great deal of this revisionist history has a whitewashed feel, as if violence, though everywhere, played no major part in it or, when it did, as if the violence was not something of any moral significance. It's a conclusion that would not have been out of place (among Europeans) in the heyday of European imperialism, when any violence could be downplayed or justified in the name of winning the competition with rival powers, a competition that was inevitable. And it's a conclusion that has a certain appeal in the realist/nihilist climate of the twenty-first century, when all claims to moral judgment are vulnerable to the Nietzschean charge of camouflaging a universal impulse to imperial domination that has never abated and should not be expected to abate.

The alternative I have been gently suggesting is to embrace the indignant history of the invention of the atrocity as a moral achievement, however tainted every stage in its development may be. Otherwise, so I have suggested, the victims of violence risk dropping out of the historical record.

I would not argue that humanists are obliged to display the violent sufferings of the past in brightly lit exhibits, the blood and guts as vividly gruesome as the day bodies were hacked to pieces. But whitewashing the violence out of world history has its own dangers. The common sense about historical atrocity that takes the place of crude blaming is interesting in its own right, and perhaps even consequential in terms of what it might teach if it is extended (and why would it not be?) from atrocity in the past to atrocity in the present. One form it takes is erasure of the line between premodern and modern. If you erase that line, as Doyle does, you also erase the invention or discovery of atrocity as a moral scandal. It seems a high price to pay, but many hardly notice how much is being deducted from their accounts. Because the traditional rationale of the humanities has involved the resuscitating of texts that have been forgotten or have lost their primary audiences or have otherwise been lost to the present, because humanists' work has seemed to require undoing time's work of dissolution, the humanities have always been strangely uncritical of the tacit assumption that the passage of time never results in any sort of improvement or accomplishment, even improvement in attitudes toward the massacre of noncombatants.[8] The entirely laudable impulse to avoid Eurocentrism has offered cover for new versions of this old assumption. Modernity, assumed to be the highest state achieved by human society, and modernism, its cultural embodiment, have of course served as a rich source of undeserved cultural capital and moral smugness for the West, a reason for envy on the part of those anywhere else in the world who see themselves, or feel they are seen by others, as not yet having achieved them. It is understandable, then, to want to divest from the concepts, as critic Susan Stanford Friedman does in her book *Planetary Modernisms: Provocations on Modernity across Time*. It is a myth, Friedman argues, that, thanks to a unique evolutionary trajectory, the West was ever the exclusive possessor of modernity. Modernity should be seen, rather, as a recurrent phenomenon. It is defined by nothing more than moments of accelerated change. It has happened again and again, outside as well as inside Europe. If modernity is so spread across time and space, no one need feel hurt that they are being excluded from it.[9]

The obvious problem here is that if modernity is everywhere, we lose sight of its virtues, which cannot *be* virtues, that is, worth articulating, propagating, and treasuring, unless they are *not* everywhere. And if those virtues are not equally distributed in every time and place, then Friedman is back where she started—valuing some times and places at the expense of others. Friedman tells us that there are multiple modernities, each of them a moment of accelerated technological and social change. But if so, each of her modernities would transmit exactly the same message to its own "tradition" or "before" (the message that I'm better than you are) that Friedman finds unacceptable when transmitted to non-Western "tradition" by Western modernity's "after." Each "tradition" would have the same grounds for complaint. Each would have the same right to demand a better grade, the right that Friedman acknowledges in relation to countries, cultures and periods. One way or the other, modernity, singular or plural, is going to hurt someone's feelings. Everyone cannot be morally above average. Change is not always for the better, but once you decide what *is* better, for example when the change involves disapproval of atrocity, you are entitled to decide, after proper scrutiny, where more of that sort of change has happened and where it hasn't. Making that decision does not commit you to inhabiting the domain of triumphalist myth. Surely it is better to ignore everyone's feelings, whether hurt (tradition) or puffed up with false pride (modern) and instead try as hard as possible to ascertain *what has actually happened* in history, for better or for worse. Friedman's assumptions ensure that her version will not be reliable on what has actually happened in history. Among other reasons, because in seeking to avoid Eurocentrism, she does her diplomatic best to ignore the violence that accompanied non-Western as well as Western cultures and empires. Military violence is not totally absent from her account, but it is very close to invisible. In the case of the Mongol Empire, say, this is quite a feat, though the tide of educated opinion has swung forcefully toward a recognition of Mongol accomplishments.[10] Matthew White ranks Genghis Khan second in the all-time list of atrocity-makers with approximately 40,000,000 dead. He does this although he, like Friedman, is something of a fan of Chinese imperial unification.[11] (Order is better than chaos.) The closest Friedman comes to a statement on imperial coercion is as follows: "Empires typically intensify the rate of rupture and accelerate change in ways that are both dystopic and utopic" (337). What Friedman calls "brutalities" (337) can of course be recognized, but only as a general phenomenon that (1) is balanced in advance by the "utopic" aspects of empire, and in part for that reason, (2) is in no way interesting or worthy of being investigated further.[12]

On the Quai at Smyrna

We know that representations of atrocity were newly in vogue after World War II, and especially during and after the 1960s, with the combined impact of the Holocaust, the dropping of the atomic bomb, and the strong voices raised in and by movements of national liberation. But what about the first half of the twentieth century, the period roughly described as modernism? None of these shocks had yet been felt. In this chapter I glance at two modernist authors whose works describe non-European atrocity, Ernest Hemingway and Ishikawa Tatsuzo, asking what might count for them as a meaningful contextualization of the violence. But first, for purposes of comparison, some words about a more recent account of the atrocity on which Hemingway reported in "On the Quai at Smyrna." The Turkish massacre of Christians in 1922 was arguably an instance of inter-imperiality. What do we gain or lose by contextualizing it, reallocating responsibility for the violence to the empires that were colliding at Smyrna?[13]

Homero Aridjis's *Smyrna in Flames* (originally published in Spanish in 2013) is written in the third person. The novel's last words are its first and only words in the first person: "I still cannot find words to explain, to myself or to others, the Turkish genocide of Asia Minor" (122).[14] The rest of the novel follows its protagonist, Nicias, as he witnesses scene after scene of almost unimaginable cruelty, varied and repeated, all of them involving some combination of the rape, torture, and murder of civilians carried out by Turkish irregulars, or *chettes*, in September 1922. As here:

> The sick, the dying, and the dead had been left to rot on the floor. Others watched the movements of a *chette* recklessly engaged in plunder and rape. Nicias got a glimpse of his hands on the breasts of a little girl. Like a louse he explored her nakedness, slid over her body, bit her, pinched her, pecked her. Dishes and flower vases went crashing. Her father who came between them was stabbed with a knife. The little girl rushed out of a back door. Beside herself with fear, she clung to Nicias's knees. In a mixture of Armenian and Greek she begged him to save her. But the *chette* dragged her back indoors, threw her face down on the rug and penetrated her like a dog. (41)

The scene does not invite contextualization. Even to imagine finding "words to explain," one would have to have absorbed the indigestible enormity of it. That seems too much of an ask. The cruelty and the suffering depicted in vignettes like this overwhelm the usual explanatory categories. In this sense they could be called sublime; they make explanation as such seem inadequate and even inappropriate. Well after it stops appearing as the will of God and should in theory be seen as the potentially understandable result of human action and social organization, atrocity still repels historical contextualization.

The Allied bombing of the German cities during World War II, with which this book began, is not the most cut-and-dried of cases. From the outset, I have confessed myself ambivalent about the enterprise of contextualizing atrocity. Any context—

for example, the urgent need to put an end to Nazism—could reasonably be suspected of wanting not just to explain, but to explain away, actions that should be labeled war crimes. Having a father who was a bomber pilot means having skin in the game. Contextualizing means going easier on the perpetrators; the case against contextualizing will seem more natural for those who have kin among the victims. Aridjis tells us that his novel's third-person protagonist, Nicias, is his father. That avowal may not complicate the author-character relationship, but it encourages the reader to supply some of the explanatory context that Aridjis may have neglected. It may be a small thing, but Nicias seems more than a simple spectator. For someone who is unable to save the victims (the little girl is torn away from his knees), and who is not made to suffer the likely consequences of proximity as the killers and rapists are doing their thing (killers and rapists don't appreciate witnesses), he seems to be in the vicinity of the crime suspiciously often. How does he manage to come away unscathed? It's almost like having a superpower. Where does that power come from?

Looking through Nicias's eyes, Aridjis describes the *chettes*, or irregulars, as "sadistic fiends straight out of a circle of Dante's *Inferno*, primitive brigands Mustafa Kemal had called up from the depths of backward Anatolia" (114). This description tells us something extra. Aridjis perceives the *chettes* as barbarians. This perception is characteristic of a someone who assumes he himself is a privileged metropolitan. To say that the killers have been "called up from the depths of backward Anatolia" is to say that, by contrast with the Greeks of coastal, cosmopolitan Smyrna, they are provincial, backward, left behind by modernity. It is to hint that the Greeks, not the Turks, are the true natives in Smyrna, having lived there for centuries rather than being "called up" at this moment. It is the *chettes* who are the intruders. Meanwhile, Nicias doesn't let us forget that he himself is an educated European. What could be more flagrantly civilized than referring to Dante's *Inferno*? Such references are a motif in the novel, which on occasion will abruptly turn away from the horror (these are among the novel's most arresting passages) both to show Nicias appreciating the beauties of his dying city as they vanish and to reveal him as a man of refinement, capable of pausing implausibly on the run to quote Homer and Euripides to the uncomprehending Turks who are threatening to detain or kill him. (Young Greek men who were not killed on sight were sent on death marches into the interior, supposedly to repair the damage done by the Greek army.) It is not to be expected that someone who went through such an experience would fail to recount it one-sidedly. And yet, as civilized as Nicias may be, his characterization of the Turkish perpetrators as barbarians from the interior of Asia would hardly discourage today's Greeks from responding to these atrocities in kind, which is to say in an uncivilized way. As some would undoubtedly still be eager to do. It also disguises the complicity of Europe in this atrocity.

Would any explanation make a difference to the reader's feelings, the facts being as grisly as they are? Assuming, as I think we must, that scenes like the ones Aridjis describes did indeed happen in Smyrna/Izmir in 1922, could any context be supplied that would matter? Well, maybe. When Greek troops landed at Smyrna in 1919, atrocities were committed against Turkish civilians, though not on anything like the scale of 1922, both by the troops themselves and by Greek locals. "Bands of civilians, not all of them Greek, took advantage of the disorder to plunder and loot the Turkish houses. A mob of Greeks carried off thousands of pounds worth of hides from a Turkish tannery. . . . During the first day, the Turks suffered 300 to 400 casualties, killed and wounded, and the Greeks about 100 . . . Before long the killing and looting had spread through the town and into the surrounding villages" (98). Other atrocities were reported three years later as the Greek army, defeated by Ataturk's forces, pulled back toward Smyrna to be evacuated, executing a scorched-earth strategy as it did so.[15] Aridjis neglects to mention these Greek atrocities, which might indeed help "explain . . . the Turkish genocide." One Turkish motive was presumably vengeance, as historian Michael Llewellyn-Smith suggests: "In the back streets, Turkish civilians and later Turkish troops were taking their revenge for three years of humiliation by the Greeks" (330). Revenge is the most familiar and the most potent form of contextualization. Adding it immediately changes the narrative. The revenge theory assumes that the primary agents of atrocity were after all not the *chettes*, who have just been brought in from elsewhere and have therefore not suffered humiliation, but the Turks of Smyrna, who were there all along and are the ones who presumably did feel humiliated.[16] The perpetrators are no longer barbarians from the interior. They have feelings; they are humanized. It seems like a step in the right direction, if only a tiny one.

No one needs to be reminded how tiny. To see atrocity as retaliation for previous atrocity is to set off a they-started-it race for the origin that has no finish line. Versions of this narrative (minus the concept of atrocity, which had not yet been formulated) have been used to justify history's most massive killing sprees—for example, those of Tamerlane and Alexander the Great, both of them thinking their conquests would make up for a civilizational humiliation of their forefathers. Even if contextualization merely posits that atrocities exist on both sides, the moral seems to be that they balance out; each side has its justification. In that case, it will be harder to hold perpetrators accountable. It makes sense that the human rights position, which aims at accountability above all else, wants to keep context out of its proceedings and is willing to give up on seeking to wring from the cruelty any practical or political wisdom.

Is atrocity the source of any practical or political wisdom? That is one way of phrasing the question by which this book has been animated. Another is whether accountability can coexist with contextualizing. In the case of Smyrna/Izmir, those who care about both contextualizing and accountability might look more closely into the subject of Nicias's perplexing invulnerability. He may seem invulnerable despite the terrible violence all around him only because the text needs a narrator who survives. But his invulnerability also seems connected to his identification with Europe. In this case, that means Europe both as a presumed seat of civilization and as the epicenter of imperialism. European power is a larger and trickier part of this story's context than Aridjis's account allows for. Like Nicias, it was very close to the violence but survived the Smyrna mess with hardly a scratch. Three years earlier, in 1919, the Greek army had debarked at Smyrna, launching an invasion of what was then the Ottoman Empire. It could do so because Greece's Prime Minister had requested and received the go-ahead from the victorious leaders at Versailles, especially Britain. Officially, the Greek army was seeking to protect the Greek minority of Anatolia from Turkish persecution. In actuality the Greek hope was both to bring that large Greek-speaking diaspora into the Greek state and to conquer more territory for that state, which had entered the world a century earlier able to count only a fraction of the region's Greek speakers as its citizens. Had the invasion succeeded, however, the Greek state would have exercised sovereignty over an even larger population of Turkish-speaking Muslims. So how to think of the invasion, which spawned the worst of the anti-Christian atrocities? From one perspective, it was Greece's national initiative, an extension of its still incomplete project of nation-formation, though it looked like (and indeed also was) a late attempt on the part of a minor power to get in on the action of the previous century's major-power colonialism. From another perspective, however, the initiative belonged to the major powers, which were simultaneously trying to control the territory of a rival empire, a loser in World War I that was perhaps permanently weakened by its loss. From this perspective, the moral confusion of Smyrna/Izmir from 1919 to 1922 would result from inter-imperiality, a pattern of conflict in which colonizers do not confront colonized, but it is colonizers on both sides, and any moral high ground is hard to find.[17] To many Greeks, and with some reason, it looks as if Europe was merely making use of Greece as an instrument of its ongoing imperial projects. Meanwhile Turks are taught in school that the events in Smyrna/Izmir in 1922 were not an atrocity at all, but the expulsion of the European invaders that made possible the founding of the modern Turkish republic. Thus it is possible for both Greeks and Turks to blame the deaths in Smyrna on imperial Europe. At a joint conference of Greek and Turkish scholars commemorating the hundredth anniversary of the events in 2022, that was the de facto solution that laid out the terms for a friendly scholarly truce. All of those involved were critical of the conduct of their home nations. Neither group of scholars wanted to push all the blame away from their side, while generosity did not permit either side to allow the other priority in blaming itself. The most comfortable position for all, therefore, was to join in blaming the catastrophe on Great Power interference.[18]

Should European imperialism remain at the center of world history, and thus also of the history of representations of atrocity? That is what seems to follow from Robert Young's preface to the 2016 edition of *Postcolonialism: An Historical Introduction*.[19] Young retains the uniqueness of Western imperialism not, as one might have imagined, by following Marx and distinguishing European from non-European conquest by the presence or absence of modern capitalism, with its uniquely corrosive effect on existing social structures. Rather, he recenters his history in the modern nation-state. Western modernity is still caught in the spotlight and is still the villain, but now its chief representative is the nation-state. If there must be a villain, why should it be the nation-state, and not capitalism? In the US at least, a preference for the state rather than capitalism as the main source of social harm is what distinguishes the right from the left. For Young, who certainly does not align himself with the right, it's the nature of the nation-state to be territorially expansive—expansive in just the way that empires were once thought to be expansive. In Young's revisionary view, it was only a kind of historical luck that stopped most of the newly independent nations of the Third World from following in the tracks of the European nations that had colonized them. The nation-state form inherited from their colonizers was no improvement; the only difference was in timing. Targeting the nation-state as the representative of colonizing modernity allows Young to keep postcolonialism just as relevant to the present, despite the obvious fact that the high point of anti-colonial politics has receded into the past. It also allows him to avoid the double implication that, as far as Indigenous peoples are concerned, (1) they are sometimes the victims of victims, colonized by the colonized, and (2) what they aspire to, as a form of remediation, is often a form of self-determination or national sovereignty. It is also to remain Eurocentric, if only by way of keeping Europe as the focus of critique.

Pointing the finger at powerful foreigners is not always a mistake—in Smyrna/Izmir, there are good grounds for it—but it does tend to help local actors shrug off some of their own responsibility, diverting attention from what they have chosen to do, why they have chosen to do it, and the significance of their own internal divisions. Attention to internal divisions is the obvious programmatic alternative to inter-imperiality, and it should arguably be at the top of every methodological agenda. Between 1919 and 1922 there were both Turks and Greeks who refused to commit themselves to their country's agenda. (I will point out below how children, paradigms of innocent victimhood, can also serve writers as a technical device, calling attention to the internal divisions that make as much sense as can be made of atrocity.) Another item in contextualization's tool kit is national comparison. Comparison is a tool with a sharp edge—the danger of abetting partisan bloodshed is obvious—but it can be useful if handled with proper care, and there are probably some interpretive tasks that can't be accomplished without it[20]—for example, avoiding the paralyzing equivalence between two dirty-handed sides.

If the mere existence of atrocities on both sides is enough to create a moral balance between them, it follows that the actual numbers of the dead on each side will be judged irrelevant. (In "The Embassy of Cambodia," Zadie Smith offers, among other things, a Monty Pythonish satire on the quest to claim for oneself the highest number of genocide fatalities.) But the opposite premise is also possible: that moral equivalence should not be taken for granted and that the numbers therefore *do* remain relevant. (As they do, for example, if you compare the number of those killed by Hamas on October 7, 2023, with the much higher number of Gazans killed by Israel in retaliation in the months that followed.) In the case of Smyrna, "three years of humiliation" are hard to quantify, though the humiliation was no doubt quite real, even in relation to the "four hundred years" of Turkish occupation of Greece. On the other hand, the estimates of the numbers of the dead are extremely unbalanced: hundreds of Turks killed on the "first day" in 1919, but thousands of Christians killed on the first day in 1922. Estimates of Greeks and Armenians killed in Smyrna in September 1922 run from 10,000 to 125,000. The total figures on the two sides could well be roughly proportional to those: hundreds versus thousands. (As was the "exchange of populations" that followed: 1,500,000 Greeks exiled from their homes in Turkey, 400,000 Turks exiled from their homes in Greece). Order of magnitude is one of the criteria that permit Sven Lindqvist, in his *History of Bombing*, to distinguish the German extermination camps from the Allied bombing of the German cities, both of them atrocities, both cases of "the well-organized mass murder of innocent people, sanctioned at the highest level but contrary to international law" (97). In addition to the difference in scale, Lindqvist, citing the work of Peter Englund, offers the fact that "the victims of the Germans were completely defenseless," while the inhabitants of the German cities were not, as evidenced by the cemeteries full of Allied air crews, and the fact that "the British had no plans for a conquest that would require the killing of Germans in order to make room for British settlement" (97). The victim's defenselessness and the perpetrator's project of conquest, both attributes of atrocity that have seemed decisive in prior discussions, return here, allowing Lindqvist to differentiate the two cases without denying that bombing from the air was, also, an atrocity. In Smyrna too, as in the American West, the project of conquest involved the elimination of the conquered population to allow for resettlement. Even within the common and undisputed category of atrocity, it ought to make some difference whether the result and/or the aim was the destruction of an entire civilization.

Writing about the Sand Creek massacre of 1864 in *Oh What a Slaughter: Massacres in the American West, 1846–1890,* McMurtry lays out similar arguments from context. "Few, I imagine, see it as a simple case of white wrong. Though it *was* wrong, it had a context that few not of that region can appreciate now" (93, emphasis in original).[21] It was 1864, he says, and the American Civil War was still going on. The Plains Indians were still "unbroken and undefeated peoples . . . able, and very determined, to wage a vigorous defense of their hunting grounds and their way of life" (94). Culturally, the US government expected an agreement with leaders to protect the "immigrants pouring west," but "no Indian leader had authority over even his own band such as a white executive might possess," meaning that young warriors "*would* run off and raid" (94). "Leadership among the plains [*sic*] tribes was collective but not coercive" (99). Objections can be raised against these bits of historical context, but each of them also has a positive value for anyone who, in today's political context, is motivated to remember the cultural distinctness and autonomy of Native American nationhood in the not so distant past. The same can be said when McMurtry tries out some quantitative comparison: "Judged by world-historical perspectives these massacres were tiny . . . the body count in the six massacres I'm especially interested in still adds up to fewer than one thousand people, barely one-third of the number who died in New York and Washington on September 11, 2001" (2). One may disagree with the implications of a particular act of comparison, like this one, which confines itself to absolute numbers. One should ask what the different killings mean relative to the total population or its ability to sustain its way of life. From this viewpoint, the genocidal killing of the Native Americans is arguably more different from 9/11, and much more significant, than the comparison of absolute casualty figures would suggest.

The comparison of casualty figures comes out in favor of the Greeks. On the other hand, if responsibility for atrocity can be legitimately assessed at the scale of the nation—if, that is, it seems morally responsible or politically wise to think in terms of collective responsibility—then Greeks contemplating Turkish revenge for the humiliation that accompanied the Greek occupation of Smyrna might have to think back to a moment almost exactly a century earlier. The end of the siege of Tripolitsa in late 1821 and Corinth in early 1822, during the Greek struggle for national independence, resulted in the plundering and killing of numerous Turkish noncombatants. In the Peloponnese, as in Anatolia, a substantial portion of the civilian population belonged to the other nationality. Like the Greeks of Anatolia, the Turks of the Peloponnese had lived there for generations. Like the Greeks of Smyrna, they probably did not think of themselves as living on foreign soil. What transpired has to be accounted an atrocity. While engaged in a well-documented frenzy of looting, Greek peasants of the Peloponnese butchered whole Turkish families, taking care not to spare the women and children unless the women could be sold on the market, as many were. According to Mark Mazower's history of the Greek independence struggle, the going post-siege rate for women was 30 to 40 piastres (239). The Greeks did all this openly, in front of many heretofore sympathetic European observers, who had assumed that in this struggle the Greeks were noble victims and the Turks cruel oppressors. Moral standards clearly existed that ruled out violence against women and children. The violence these observers wrote home about shook their solidarity with the Greek cause, though some rationalized it racially as the result of four hundred years of Turkish rule. Others "returned to Marseilles with their tales of disillusionment and massacre" (241), which gave European authorities trying to safeguard the status quo ammunition with which to deter other pro-Greek volunteers. Here too, as in Smyrna a hundred years later, the perpetrators could say they were responding to foreign occupation.[22] And unless we are prepared to estimate the moral difference that the passage of a hundred years should make, we would have to conclude that the noncombatants who suffered in the Peloponnese have the same right to be counted as victims as the noncombatants who suffered in Smyrna/Izmir. In tracing processes like these, a century is not a very long time.

The moral here might seem to be that atrocity does not after all provide any practical or political wisdom. There are victims who are deserving of sympathy on both sides. Both sides are guilty. Side-taking seems like a mistake. Disengagement seems wiser. Smyrna/Izmir had witnessed a clash of rival empires in 1919, but by 1922 the inter-imperial context had been obscured and superseded. Mustafa Kemal's forces were bringing down the Ottoman Empire, not defending or extending it. Yet the location of the atrocity at the fault line between preexisting empires does suggest a moral that could also be expected from the inter-imperiality model. If the reader finds no one in the account of atrocity with whom to identify, that's because there was no one who was deserving of political identification—except, as always, the victims, considered solely *as* victims and not as political actors. Inter-imperiality, which is more interested in actors than in victims, does not encourage attention to atrocity, or indeed to violence. Morally speaking, nothing is at stake. The attitude that a modern observer is therefore invited to take seems to be distanced, spectatorial, apolitical. Enlightened callousness is the kind of response that is to be expected as an alternative to indignation, or a backlash against the side-taking that indignation seems to demand.

Enlightened callousness is one way of describing the subject of Ernest Hemingway's "On the Quai at Smyrna," a 738-word sketch responding soon after the fact to the massacre of 1922.[23] In that sketch, a British naval officer tells an unnamed interlocutor what it was like to observe the waterfront of Smyrna, crowded with refugees, from his ship in the harbor. Here, as in Aridjis, no mention is made of the political context beyond a passing allusion to the possibility that the British navy might have chosen to bombard Smyrna's Turkish quarter. The bombardment would presumably have aimed to stop the killings, though this is not said, and the killings themselves are never mentioned: "We were going to come in, run close along the pier, let go the front and rear anchors and then shell the Turkish quarter of the town. They would have blown us out of the water but we would have blown the town simply to hell" (11). Though presented here as suicidal, the option of blowing the town to hell approximates the policy Gladstone had advised in response to Turkish atrocities in Bulgaria in 1876. Like Gladstone's idea, it too would have answered atrocity with atrocity. The officer erases possible objections to the project of blowing the town simply to hell by personifying its target: the inhabitants of the town are collected into "the Turk." The Greeks on the pier, he says, "never knew about the Turk. They never knew what the old Turk would do" (10). "The Turk" and "the old Turk" seem to refer to military leadership, but neither expression allows for a saving distinction to be made between Turkish soldiers and Turkish civilians. The Turkish civilians who would certainly have died if the Turkish quarter were shelled dissolve into their nation, which is presumed to have deserved its fate. But the bombardment has not happened. The officer speaks as a spectator, not an actor, and by this point spectatorship was government policy. The British had decided to pull back from their earlier involvement. Llewellyn-Smith writes: "What made these scenes the more frightful was the impotence—in the case of officials, impotence as a matter of policy—of the foreigners. British marines stood by, deliberately idle, while Turkish troops goaded and chased their Armenian victims into the sea, then coolly shot them as they swam for safety" (331).[24] Hemingway's text does not report any violence directly, though the vague qualms of conscience it registers might be explained by the violence that goes unreported: "That was the only time in my life I got so I dreamed about things" (11).[25] Not reporting the violence allows readers to keep their distance.

What Hemingway's text does report is what spectatorial impotence sounds like. It does not sound good.[26] The text takes ironic distance from this British officer, an ironic distance that is audible in the officer's casual contempt for "the Turk," but also in his lack of sympathy for the refugees on the quay, some of them dying (one dies while he is examining her). The lack of fellow feeling is underlined by his failure to mention what the refugees are doing on the pier in the first place. The text begins: "The strange thing was, he said, how they screamed every night at midnight" (9). Nothing is said about *why* they screamed (screaming on the pier was attested to by many witnesses), but only *when* they screamed.[27] There are dead babies on the pier, and that is clearly one possible reason for the screaming, but what grabs the officer's attention is not why the babies are dead but only the fact that the screaming comes at midnight. From the officer's point of view, the problem is not what brought them to the waterfront, but only how to stop the screaming: "We used to turn the searchlight on them to quiet them. That always did the trick" (9). As with Ishikawa, the victim's screaming, which is presumably an effect of atrocity, is unbearable to those who hear it, even if (or because) those who hear it might share some responsibility for the suffering. Not being able to bear the effects of atrocity thus becomes a potential cause of further atrocity. For what it's worth, this is also evidence for the historical existence of qualms of conscience, however counterproductive they may be.

In pursuit of what he presumes would make a juicy anecdote, or in flight from the natural feelings that so much suffering might seem obliged to evoke, the British officer wanders from topic to topic without making any connections between them. There is no paragraph break marking a transition between the screaming at midnight and a farcical encounter with a Turkish officer who feels he's been insulted by a British common soldier. No mention is made of the fire, though that is how the Turks name the event, thus opening the deaths to interpretation as a natural disaster. The officer does not want the event classified as a natural disaster ("it wasn't at all like an earthquake or that sort of thing"). He makes it clear that the people on the waterfront correctly see human agents at work behind their situation and that those agents are Turkish. The sentence goes on: "because they never knew about the Turk. They never knew what the old Turk would do. You remember when they ordered us not to come in to take off any more?" (11). This refusal to allow any more refugees to be evacuated by ship makes it seem that, in the officer's eyes, the Turkish authorities are the villains of the piece. And yet that is not the note on which the text ends. It ends with an ironic anecdote about the evacuations that have already happened: "The Greeks were nice chaps too. When they evacuated they had all their baggage animals they couldn't take off with them so they just broke their forelegs and dumped them into the shallow water. All those mules with their forelegs broken pushed over into the shallow water. It was all a pleasant business. My word yes a most pleasant business" (12).

The irony here seems natural enough: it's not a pleasant business to break the legs of mules and dump them in the harbor. We are not told why the Greek refugees, the victims in this scenario, compromise their victimhood by committing this act of seemingly gratuitous cruelty. So that the Turks who have driven them away won't have the use of the mules? So that the mules won't slowly starve? For some other reason? What we know is that in the officer's ironic view, and quite likely also our own, this is not nice. No one in this scene seems very nice. The note on which the text chooses to leave us is, once again, something like a "plague o' both their houses." If moral equivalence between perpetrators and victims is what Hemingway wanted, the final twist, which gives the text a pleasing aesthetic roundness, represents a very unexpected last-minute convergence between his own view and that of the British officer, though he seems to have been ironizing that officer throughout. It is perhaps also what Hemingway's readers wanted to hear, or what he thought they wanted to hear. Either way, it offers an interesting antithesis to Aridjis and a useful if troubling landmark along atrocity's twentieth-century trajectory: an impulse to self-critique (we Great Powers bear some responsibility for the victims) coupled with an impulse toward (American?) disengagement from violence seen finally as the responsibility of other people. Troubling especially for the hypothesis that there has been moral progress with regard to atrocity. Is disengagement what progress looks like?

A somewhat inflected reading of "On the Quai at Smyrna" might assume that the text is indeed ironic about the British officer's ironic distance, adding only that Hemingway is pointing out the unpleasantness of that ironic distance and the impotent spectatorship it entails. From this perspective, the text would be pointing the reader toward its own contextual omissions, thereby seeding in its reader a curiosity about the politics of this presumably exotic place on the margins of Europe rather than either seeking to satisfy the curiosity on the cheap or seeking to make curiosity seem futile. Here the mules in the ending suggest another bit of contextualization, though perhaps a bit of a stretch, that might help restore the scene's place in a significant moral history. If there is a moral weighing and measuring going on, how much should the cruelty to the mules count? Does cruelty to animals balance or even overbalance cruelty to humans? No judgment could be more historically variable. Indeed, cruelty to animals might be thought of as the most obvious test case of moral historicity. In the passage from Hemingway's *A Farewell to Arms* where Fredric Henry is embarrassed by the emptiness of words like "sacred, glorious, and sacrifice and the expression in vain," he goes on to say that "the sacrifices were like the stockyards of Chicago if nothing was done with the meat except to bury it" (9–10), and Nicolaus Mills comments, "the soldiers are being treated like cattle" (10).[28] In the twenty-first century, it has become more plausible to worry that *cattle* are being treated like cattle. We now worry that from the perspective of cattle, history is an undifferentiated, taken-for-granted nightmare of everyday butchery on slaughter-benches both metaphorical and literal. Which is to say, it is not a history in the strong sense at all. Coetzee suggests as much in his novel *Elizabeth Costello*, which insists on the provocative analogy between the Holocaust and the killing of animals for their meat. Others might draw a different conclusion, however. Vegetarianism, like anti-militarism, is now a mass phenomenon. The issue of eating meat posed by *Elizabeth Costello*, like the rise of abolitionism in the eighteenth century or anti-militarism since then, might therefore count on the contrary as evidence that the human race does in fact have a moral history, a history that does not preclude moral improvement even if it makes political commitments more complicated.[29] Where do those who disbelieve in modernity think their own enriched sensibility comes from if not from moral transformations that are distinctively modern?

As he escapes again and again from the marauding Turks, Nicias runs again and again into a former teacher, and the teacher tells him, "The barbarians have arrived" (37).[30] The reference is to Constantine Cavafy's poem "Waiting for the Barbarians" (1904). The barbarians' nonarrival is the nonevent at the center of Cavafy's poem. The barbarians, though fearfully expected by the inhabitants of the unnamed city, never do arrive, and the poem concludes by wondering whether there have ever actually been any barbarians and if not, whether positing their ever-threatening existence was the solution to a problem that besets those who consider themselves civilized, a problem they themselves will now have to deal with in some less dishonest way. Turning its back on Cavafy, *Smyrna in Flames* tells its readers that barbarians do indeed exist, and those barbarians are Turks. Based on the historical record, the novel might as easily have said that the barbarians are the Greeks. But there is political guidance to be taken from accounts of atrocity that do not rely on the concept of the barbarian. If there is a version of distinctively modern or cosmopolitan civility to which the reader of this account can aspire, something to identify with, it would be the higher civility or civilization represented by Cavafy and available to Turks and Greeks alike. It would no doubt be premature to claim that Cavafy's no-barbarians position, articulated at the turning point between the nineteenth and twentieth centuries, is characteristic of educated common sense today. But who can doubt that, by comparison with a century or two ago, there has been a move in that direction?

The Subjectivity of the Perpetrator, the Projectivity of Prolepsis

Like the Greeks in the 1920s, the Japanese in the 1930s could claim that their colonialism was a response to, and an imitation of, the European colonialism that preceded it. That is not the approach Ishikawa Tatsuzo takes in *Soldiers Alive* (1938).[31] Unlike both Hemingway and Aridjis, Ishikawa does that most difficult thing: he accuses his fellow Japanese countrymen of an atrocity committed against the inhabitants of another country—in his case, the rape and slaughter of Chinese civilians during the invasion of China in the 1930s. Ishikawa, a journalist on assignment, was in Nanjing, interviewing the Japanese troops, in January of 1938, in the midst of the six-week massacre that came to be called the Rape of Nanjing, in which some 200,000 to 300,000 Chinese died. As if aware that what they had done would come to count as a world-historical atrocity, the Japanese authorities had placed Nanjing off limits, and Ishikawa said nothing about it. His fictionalized account of the fighting immediately beforehand, published in March of 1938, was nevertheless censored. Ishikawa himself was arrested and, after a widely publicized trial, he was convicted. The court's judgment gives all the evidence against the government that an outsider might need. Ishikawa was guilty, in the court's words, of "disturbing peace and order by describing massacres of noncombatants by Imperial Army soldiers, instances of plunder, and conditions of lax military discipline" (39).[32] The court does not claim that the massacres or any of the rest of it did not happen.

With Ishikawa, as with Tolstoy, the characters who commit the atrocities seem to have no moral understanding of what they are doing. In *Hadji Murat*, as I said, we watch the attack on the Chechen village through the eyes of a Russian who is worrying about his gambling debts and dreaming of attractive women. He sees no killing; the boy bayoneted in the back is invisible to him. In *Soldiers Alive*, the killing does register on the killers' consciousness, but it does not register as a moral scandal. The Japanese soldiers go in search of local women, whom they routinely rape and murder, returning "from their expeditions," we are told, "sporting silver rings on the small fingers of their left hands. 'Where did you get this?' their comrades asked; and each man laughingly replied, 'It's a memento of my late wife'" (122). The joke circulates in the ranks that the silver wedding rings taken from Chinese women are "in exchange for a pistol bullet" (111). Anti-Chinese racism is clearly also a forceful factor here: "They could not overcome their contempt for the Chinese, so stubbornly and deeply was it rooted in their hearts" (127).

At the same time, the deep exploration of subjectivity that is at the innovative heart of modernism, especially in its Japanese variants, is by no means lacking among the Japanese invaders, and some scruples about the killing emerge, if only in a backhanded way. Corporal Kasahara, we are told, is unburdened by "either oversensitivity or the intellectual's habit of self-criticism" (103). "To Corporal Kasahara, killing enemy soldiers was no different than killing carp. The carnage he perpetrated did not affect his emotions in the least. The one emotion that did move him mightily was a virtually instinctive love for his comrades" (103). When we are told that Second Lieutenant Kurata "was already starting to cultivate a character that would enable him to participate calmly in the most gruesome slaughter. That is to say, he was catching up with Corporal Kasahara" (110), Ishikawa is informing the reader both that Kasahara was considered an example to emulate and, more to the point, that the others do not in fact already resemble him—that they, unlike Kasahara, do have some sensitivity to slaughter and some habits of self-criticism. The acts these men commit are monstrous, but Ishikawa finds the subjectivity behind those acts interesting enough to warrant examination.

Along with three other soldiers, First Class Private Kondō breaks down a door; a Chinese woman aims a revolver at them and it misfires. "They were suddenly seized with a furious desire and a savage urge to inflict maximum torment upon this woman who had resisted" (88). Kondō suggests stripping her. "She might be a spy. Maybe she's got something on her" (88). In her purse they find "a piece of paper covered with incomprehensible marks resembling shorthand" (89). One soldier says, "She a spy for sure" (89). Kondō feels "a furious passion" boiling up in him, "whether rage or lust he could not tell," and he stabs her. Kasahara arrives, and Kondō explains: "I was sure she's a spy, so I killed her" (90). Kasahara responds, "You sure wasted a good lay" (90). We know that he could not in fact be "sure" she was a spy; the marks on the piece of paper are "incomprehensible" to him. We know that he does not know what his own feelings are, rage or lust. And we know that the desire to torment her comes in part from the fact that "she had resisted" (88). It is possible that in pulling the trigger she was merely resisting her rape and murder. But Chinese resistance enrages the Japanese soldiers because it undercuts the ideological justification for their presence in China: they are supposed to be liberating their fellow Asians, and the Chinese are supposed to be welcoming their liberators. At the same time, the Japanese express a romantic attachment to the Orientalist image of the Chinese as unchanging and impossible to convert: "Any notion of converting the Chinese to Japanese ways is a dream within a dream within a dream" (142). "He began to feel a boundless love for these Chinese people and their millennia-old spirit" (143). As when the soldiers are confronted with Chinese women, love and violence, lust and rage, are hard to disentangle.

Kondō, a medical college graduate, is a perpetrator of sexual violence to whom the novel gives a rich inner life, tormented by philosophical questions. The night of the murder, he is "preoccupied by the ease with which life yielded to death" (91). This becomes an uncertainty about the medical view of life into which he has been educated, which segues into an uncertainty about the worth of life itself, seen across enemy lines: "Supposing the enemy troops consider my life worthless . . . ?" (91). The upshot is a questioning of the value of thinking itself. Like Primo Levi in Auschwitz, he is tempted by the idea that "Nothing made any sense" (118). Finally, he questions the murder he has committed—but he questions it only in Kasahara's terms. The woman was "a true beauty. Hmmm. Maybe I should have let her live" (92). Violence can be chosen over lust; it can emerge together with lust; it can also emerge out of empathy, as when Hirao and other soldiers can't stand hearing a Chinese woman moaning over the body of her mother, who has been shot, and go off to find her and stab her to death. "They felt a burning sympathy that grew steadily stronger until it yielded to irritation" (115). Afterwards, Hirao thinks of "what war meant to the nation and why it left no margin for criticism," and knows "that killing her, far from alleviating his pain, was likely to make it much worse . . . His one source of great joy was that several soldiers had joined him in killing her. Tears of gratitude to his comrades rolled down his cheeks" (117–18). Like Kasahara, whom he is trying to imitate, he comes to rest on his single strongest emotion and his highest value: love for his fellows, solidarity with his unit.

Like the willingness to sacrifice one's own feelings (presumably, feelings of self-disgust at the killing of noncombatants) for the higher good of the nation, which is appealed to repeatedly, this is of course a kind of ethical thought.[33] A case could be made for it. But the novel ends by beating an abrupt retreat from that version of ethics. Kondō finds himself in a geisha house with Hirao and Kasahara. "An irresistible urge to kill a woman suddenly blazed up within his chest" (195). He says so. Kasahara tells him off. "'Speaking of killing women, Hirao,' said Kasahara, his tongue somewhat tangled, 'what you did back there, you know, killing that girl holding on to her dead mother—that was terrible! That was really rotten, still is. She couldn't help crying, the poor thing'" (195–96). Kondō responds by retelling the story to a geisha. The geisha says that killing women is "really wicked" (197). "'What's wicked about it?' retorted Kondō swiftly. 'Well, women are noncombatants, are they not? A true Japanese fighting man would never kill a woman'" (196). Kondō flings a cup at her. She runs. He fires his pistol at her. The next day he is brought before the company commander. He learns the woman was hit in the arm and will recover. He is questioned and confined to his room. Then he is told he will not be punished. He can go back to his unit. "To advance along with the unit, to go with it to the end of the world—he could think of nothing else" (205). When a Japanese woman suddenly becomes the victim, the limits of an ethic based on all-male bonding become clear even to the Japanese—though perhaps not to the military unit itself. Colonial violence has performed its classic boomerang, returning to strike the society of the colonizers. Even the colonial nation is invited to see that there is a higher standard of ethical judgment than sacrifice in its name.[34]

A Japanese corporal, who has just impulsively stabbed a Chinese boy to death on suspicion that the boy had taken a packet of sugar, says to a nearby interpreter, "Try imagining how I feel!" (125). In the presence of atrocity, feelings are not decisive. Yet feelings are what the novel is made of. That is one way of understanding James Wood's much-discussed review-essay "Hysterical Realism" and its critique of Zadie Smith's *White Teeth* (2000). Wood offered a parody in which one character "was born at the exact second that the bomb was dropped on Hiroshima" (178–79).[35] This barb was clearly intended for Smith, who had timed the birth of her twin protagonists to coincide with a world-historical atrocity. She had gone too far, Wood's parody suggested, in trying to link private feelings and relations, which the novel is good at, with events of the largest public significance, like Hiroshima, which it is not good at. Even with the carefully nuanced attention Ishikawa gives them, the feelings of the Japanese soldiers in *Soldiers Alive* cannot carry the weight of representing the atrocities they commit.

If so, however, this does not leave the novel without resources. Consider the treatment of Japanese atrocities in China in Haruki Murakami's *Wind-Up Bird Chronicle* (1994–95).[36] The example may seem cherry-picked; the plot turns on the guilty secret of the Japanese Army in Manchuria executing Chinese prisoners and the bringing of this secret to light in contemporary Japan. But the local description does not depend on the centrality of atrocity to the plot. Like Tolstoy, Murakami makes use of prolepsis. And as in Tolstoy, prolepsis adds a plot trajectory to minor characters who might not otherwise have one: "'Have you ever played baseball?' the lieutenant asked the young soldier (the one who would eventually have his skull split open with a shovel by a Soviet guard in a mine near Irkutsk)" (518). The soldier whose death is here foretold smashes a Chinese prisoner's head with the bat, as ordered, and then we get more prolepses, the future deaths of more young men who have participated in the executions. The anticipated deaths are not quite a definitive judgment on what they've done, but they are certainly suggestive of an act that would not be judged in the present and has to reach into the future for moral resources. Examples are both strangely numerous and, literarily speaking—given how much we may resist having the details of violence forced on us—strangely *readable*. This makes sense: prolepsis permits you to look away from the violence, thereby sparing your feelings. But in inviting you to look *away*, it also invites you to look *toward*—toward something of interest beyond the violence. This means attaching your feelings to a new object, perhaps so as to have those feelings assuaged by a foretaste of justice that is missing from the present. It's the crystallization of a missing contextualization.

To put this another way, prolepsis interrupts the steady flow of time in order to make a space in it for the future. In that future, we may be offered not only knowledge that is not available to the present, but also categories of moral meaning that are similarly unavailable but that transform our understanding of what we are seeing in front of us now. The need for moral categories that are presently unavailable helps explain the special connection with atrocity. Consider a bit more of the Murakami passage quoted above—that is, more in the series of prolepses in which Murakami gives the future fates of the other Japanese soldiers involved in the execution of Chinese prisoners.

> After they were disarmed by the Soviets, the young paymaster lieutenant would be handed over to the Chinese and hanged for his responsibility in these executions. The corporal would die of the plague in a Siberian concentration camp: he would be thrown into a quarantine shed and left there until dead, though in fact he had merely collapsed from malnutrition and had not

> contracted the plague—not, at least, until he was thrown into the shed. The veterinarian with the mark on his face would die in an accident a year later. A civilian, he would be taken by the Soviets for cooperating with the military and sent to another Siberian camp to do hard labor. He would be working in a deep shaft of a Siberian coal mine when a flood would drown him, along with many soldiers. (521–22)

Only one of these deaths is explicitly linked to "responsibility for these executions." But at a more implicit level, all of them are.

Tolstoy and Ishikawa give us the subjectivity of the participants in the action. Prolepsis is projective in the sense that it gives us a *judgment on the action that is unavailable* to the participants. You could easily miss this because what prolepsis gives you is the future, which the characters by definition cannot know. That is the point of allowing the future to intrude: to give us access, if incomplete access, to moral values they do not yet hold and qualifying factors that to which they have no access. The fact that the judgment thus dispensed is so rough and approximate may well make these deaths look like fates in the pagan sense: delinked from the actions that led up to them, morally undeserved or simply random. It seems more accurate to say that they are calibrated to a situation in which, though Murakami must appeal beyond the jury of his peers and though no supranational court has arisen to replace or supplement a Japanese judgment on Japanese actions, norms are actively at work, within as well as beyond the nation-state. The pressure of those norms, while it remains an intrusion from the future, is nevertheless made palpable.

The value of prolepsis as a vehicle for the representation of atrocity, even when delivered in only in short, single-sentence bursts, becomes visible by contrast both with realism and with melodrama. Consider the first sentence of Kamila Shamsie's 2009 novel *Burnt Shadows*: "Later, the one who survives will remember that day as grey, but on the morning of 9 August itself both the man from Berlin, Konrad Weiss, and the schoolteacher, Hiroko Tanaka, step out of their houses and notice the perfect blueness of the sky, into which white smoke blooms from the chimneys of the munitions factories" (5).[37] This sentence foreshadows the dropping of the atomic bomb on Nagasaki, which happens later that morning and is the novel's central event. It's the results of the bomb that will make the survivor—as yet unnamed, and thus a matter of suspense—remember the day as gray.

It takes nothing away from the seriousness of the event, or the seriousness of Shamsie's treatment of it, to notice that her use of analeptic prolepsis in her first sentence is a grateful nod to a great literary predecessor, Gabriel García Márquez. The famous first sentence of García Márquez's *One Hundred Years of Solitude* (1967) goes like this: "Many years later, as he faced the firing squad, Colonel Aureliano Buendía was to remember that distant afternoon when his father took him to discover ice" (1).[38] What do such sentences accomplish? "Later, the one who survives" is of course a guarantee that someone does survive and will therefore be around to serve as witness. This turns out to be true as well of Colonel Aureliano Buendía even after he faces the firing squad. That which seems to be fated to happen may not happen after all. But survival is an outcome that obviously cannot be taken for granted in the presence of atrocities like the bombing of Nagasaki or, for that matter, the massacre of the striking United Fruit workers later in *One Hundred Years of Solitude*, which is again presented via prolepsis: "Many years later that child would still tell, in spite of people thinking that he was a crazy old man, how Jose Arcadio Segundo had lifted him over his head and hauled him, almost in the air, as if floating on the terror of the crowd, toward a nearby street" (000).

The need for a survivor who can tell the story of killing in which most others do not survive is one practical reason why prolepsis, with or without an act of remembrance, tends to cluster around descriptions of large man-made life-threatening events. But there are more important reasons. Shamsie's sentence makes a quiet, almost imperceptible gesture toward balance. The cloud of smoke from the munitions factories that ends the sentence is a premonition of the much larger mushroom cloud that is shortly to cover the city, but it is also a reminder that this peaceful-looking city is manufacturing munitions, hence is part of a war effort, hence in the eyes of some is not entirely distinguishable from the war's more active battlefields. It hints that the responsibility for this atrocity may be more complex than it appears. In other words, one little sentence contains the elements of an unpredictable conversation about whether, remembered by the survivor as gray, the day's event should in fact be *seen* as gray and not, melodramatically, as black-and-white.

Salman Rushdie's representation of the Amritsar Massacre in *Midnight's Children* (1980) is another example. Rushdie too makes use of prolepsis, which ignores present feelings and guarantees that there is a witness who survives to tell the tale. The British machine guns have begun to fire, the hero's grandfather has escaped the bullets only by sneezing and falling flat on his face, and we get another "years later": "The clasp of his bag is digging into his chest, inflicting upon it a bruise so severe and mysterious that it will not fade until after his death, years later, on the hill of Sankara Acharya or Takht-e-Sulaiman" (34).[39] This prolepsis tells us that the grandfather survives the violence of 1919, something we have reason to doubt, by telling us where and when he *does* die, years later, "on the hill of Sankara Acharya or Takht-e-Sulaiman." But why are two place names given for the site of his death, one of them Hindu and the other Muslim? And why are they separated by an "or"? At the moment of the massacre, what is happening between the British and the Indians seems the only meaningful conflict. Even at this moment of world-historical horror, however, Rushdie intrudes to remind the reader that in fact the confrontation of colonizers and colonized was never the *only* meaningful conflict. You cannot understand modern India, he suggests, without also thinking of the division between Hindus and Muslims, which began before the British came and continued after the British left. Even if British colonialism deliberately made it worse, which by all accounts it did, the religious division cannot be attributed solely to colonial rule. Rushdie urges on us this extra thought in the very act of describing an atrocity that is being committed by the British, which is to say at a moment when the temptation to locate absolute evil in the perpetrators is overwhelming. Prolepsis allows him to do this by stretching the temporality of the moment so as to include a future that will relativize even this great, world-historical, seemingly absolute evil. This impulse toward moral qualification and self-indictment may seem almost indecent, given the horror of what is being alluded to. And yet we should not be sorry to get it.

Other examples are worth mentioning here both for their own artfulness, not the first thing one thinks of with regard to the treatment of atrocity, and to show the surprising scale at which prolepsis is asked to do this work. In Jeffrey Eugenides's *Middlesex* (2002), a Turkish army convoy passes through Smyrna in the midst of the 1922 massacre that Greeks call "the great catastrophe" (*megali katastrophe*) when Turkish troops slaughtered large numbers of Greek and Armenian Christians. The massacre itself (the details of which I spare you, though Eugenides does not) is described in flagrant imitation of *Midnight's Children*. Then we catch a sideways glimpse of Kemal Ataturk, sitting in the convoy's last car. As we get this glimpse we again leap forward to the moment of his death: "Kemal, champion of Westernization and the secular Turkish state, would remain true to those principles to the end, dying at fifty-seven of cirrhosis of the liver" (53).[40] It's a glimpse of the logic of judgment which is otherwise missing from the scene: the death of the author of so much death. A secular logic of alcohol and cirrhosis.

In anticipating a future death, prolepsis can also offer, as a sudden reason to care, the sense of an ending for a character who perhaps would not otherwise have mattered. In Orhan Pamuk's *Snow*, also published in 2002, the massacre in the theater which sets off an anti-Islamic coup is announced by a crescendo of prolepses that foretell the impending fate of a young student at the religious high school: "There was a tense silence, during which Necip raised his beautiful eyes (one of which, in two hours and three minutes, would be shattered by a bullet)" (111).[41] Thirty pages later: "His eyes opened wide (one of them to be shattered twenty-six minutes later, along with his brain)" (143). It is sometimes said about prolepsis in Homer's *Iliad* that it eliminates suspense. Here prolepsis clearly does not eliminate suspense. For minor characters like Necip, there was no suspense to eliminate. If anything, being told in advance what will befall minor characters in the future *adds* suspense; it provokes readerly concern with regard to characters about whose fates readers have not yet committed themselves to feeling much of anything.

William Gardner Smith's account of the Paris massacre of October 17, 1961, in his novel *The Stone Face* (1963) turns from a normal, frivolous evening among the expats to the corpses of Algerian protesters killed that day by French police: "Clyde drank at the Monoco to forget about Jinx; Jinx drank at the select to forget about herself; Doug made love to his State department girl, Babe belched after a gigantic meal and joked off a feeling of guilt, Benson lay drunk and bitter in bed with his mistress, and Ahmed lay dead, his head battered to a pulp by police clubs, on the corner of the rue du Bac and the Boulevard Saint-Germain" (000). Benson lay in bed with his mistress; Ahmed lay dead, beaten to death by the police. The irony of violent death looking so much like ordinary, inconsequential life carries over as Smith pulls back to capture the scale of the atrocity: "His body was one of the many, dead and wounded which lay sprawled on the street. Curled up like a child on his side, face twisted in a grimace, arms still raised protectively over his head, he looked even more youthful than in life. The police did not know he was dead, and tossed his body, along with the others, into a van. The corpses of more than two hundred Algerians, Ahmed's among them, were to be fished out of the Seine the next day and for days afterward" (197).[42] The "were to be" in this final sentence, the slightest of literary touches, again stretches the time of the atrocity proleptically, giving a narrative arc to nameless murdered Algerians who would otherwise have none and making room for connections (like that between the Algerians and Black Americans at home) rather than, as in the liberal model of time's passage, dissolving solidarity and connectedness into isolated and irresponsible individuality.[43]

In Jenny Erpenbeck's *Visitation* (2008), death in the Holocaust is buried in the middle of a sentence that, like the novel itself as a genre, is mainly concerned with more banal matters like real estate and family inheritance: "Two months after

Arthur and Hermine get into the gas truck in Kulmhof outside of Lodz, after Arthur's eyes pop out of their sockets as he asphyxiates, and Hermine in her death throes defecates on the feet of a woman she's never seen before, all their assets, together with the assets remaining in Germany that belonged to their son, Ludwig, who has emigrated, are seized." Unbearable suffering and humiliation are framed by and subordinated to the straightforward clause telling us, with a jump forward in time of two months, that "assets . . . are seized"[44] It's as if we had to learn to see unspeakable violence lying under the surface of the ordinary nonviolent injustices we are more accustomed to, like the seizure of property. The same proleptic framing of violence reappears in Arundhati Roy's *The Ministry of Utmost Happiness* (2017). There it refers to the atrocities committed by the Indian Army in Kashmir. Roy inflates the device to the point where it seems ready to burst, spattering the reader with filthy pent-up history and bringing the novel's forward march to a halt:

> Years later, after the government declared that the insurrection had been contained (although half a million soldiers stayed on just to make sure), after the major militant groups had turned (or been turned) on each other, after pilgrims, tourists and honeymooners from the mainland began to return to the Valley to frolic in the snow (to be heaved up and whisked down steep snow banks—shrieking in sledges manned by former militants), after spies and informers had (for reasons of tidiness and abundant caution) been killed by their handlers, after renegades were absorbed into regular day jobs by the thousands of NGOs working in the Peace Sector, after local businessmen who had made fortunes supplying the army with coal and walnut wood began to invest their money in the fast-growing Hospitality Sector (otherwise known as giving people "Stakes in the Peace Process"), after senior bank managers had appropriated the unclaimed money that remained in the dead militants' bank accounts, after the torture centers were converted into plush homes for politicians, after the martyrs' graveyards grew a little derelict and the number of martyrs had reduced to a trickle (and the number of suicides rose dramatically), after elections were held and democracy was declared, after the Jhelum rose and receded, after the insurrection rose again and was crushed again and rose again and was crushed again and rose again—even after all this, Miss Jebeen's grave remained single-deckered. (325)[45]

The grave referred to here is, once again, that of a small child. She has been shot by the army while sitting on her balcony. The passage continues:

> Her massacre was the second in the city in two months.
>
> Of the seventeen who died that day. Seven were by-standers like Miss Jebeen and her mother (in their case, they were technically by-sitters). They were watching from their balcony, Miss Jebeen, running a slight temperature, sitting on her mother's lap, as thousands of mourners carried the body of Usman Abdullah, a popular university lecturer, through the streets of the city. He had been shot by what the authorities declared to be a "UG"—an unidentified gunman. (325–26)

The mass of this passage—it's a lot to ask the reader to wade through—can perhaps stand in not just for the ongoing history of which the massacre is a part, but also for the mass of examples of further massacres, most of them abbreviated here and others simply omitted, which is to say for the challenging if not indescribable quantity of violent history that each of them takes upon itself to remember. We are asked to imagine how hard it would be to add them up.

Five

Confusions of Self-Indictment

There Is No Why: *Slaughterhouse-Five*

"Shortly before he died, he said to me, 'You know, you never wrote a story with a villain in it'" (10).[1] *Slaughterhouse-Five* (1969), in which this sentence appears, is another story without a villain in it. The lack of a villain is striking given that Vonnegut's most famous novel is famous above all for the exposure it gave to an underacknowledged atrocity: the Allied fire-bombing of Dresden in early 1945, which Vonnegut survived as a prisoner of war. There is a kind of contradiction here. On the one hand, *Slaughterhouse-Five* is arguably one of the most significant instances in world literature of a writer accusing his own side of an atrocity committed against foreigners, in particular foreign noncombatants. At the same time, however, it is also distinctive for abstaining from accusation, and even for embracing (explicitly, via the philosophical aliens of the planet Tralfamadore, but in other ways as well) a no-villains policy that makes accusation look like an earthling's naïve, provincial error. It seems too perfect to be a coincidence: at just the moment when an American novelist blames America for an atrocity, he also backs down from blame as such. He takes refuge, if that word is not too strong, in a vision of history as meaningless, resistant to any causal understanding. As if to say, even in the presence of mass death: it is what it is. Nothing to be seen or done here. Move along. So it goes.

Vonnegut is clearly tempted by this postmodern or anti-moral moral. He confesses, as if to explain the difficulty he had writing about the destruction of Dresden, "there is nothing intelligent to say about a massacre" (24). But he does try to answer his father, and in so doing he displays some uncertainty about his no-prior-villains record. He says he acquired his suspicion of the concept of the villain when he briefly studied anthropology at the University of Chicago after the war. Looking back on his instructors, he recalls: "Another thing they taught was that nobody was ridiculous or bad or disgusting" (10). This is less than wholehearted approbation of anthropology's lessons. A careful reader of *Slaughterhouse-Five* might have trouble locating "bad" characters, but not "ridiculous" or "disgusting" ones. Vonnegut's account of postwar University of Chicago anthropology is remarkably consonant, however, with the posthuman philosophy his protagonist encounters during his visit to the planet Tralfamadore (a plausible stand-in for the University of Chicago) and of which he later becomes an embarrassingly noisy proponent. This cosmic cosmopolitanism chides Earthlings gently for their eagerness to find someone to blame, but also because they think in terms of causal explanation at all.[2] In response to Billy Pilgrim's question, "Why me?"—why has he been kidnapped from Earth and installed as an edifying spectacle in a Tralfamadorean zoo—his captor says, "There is no *why*" (97).

It's hard to know how seriously Vonnegut means his readers to take the Tralfamadorean *Weltanschauung*, which posits that there are "no causes" (112). But another science fiction novel whose plot Vonnegut imagines and summarizes in *Slaughterhouse-Five* posits that there *are* causes—causes of mental disease—but they "couldn't be treated because the causes of the diseases were in the fourth dimension, and three-dimensional Earthling doctors couldn't see those causes at all, or even imagine them" (132). Here Vonnegut refuses to let go of causality, referring obliquely, perhaps, to the PTSD diagnosis that Billy Pilgrim plausibly deserves but never gets, since that diagnosis did not come into its own until after the Vietnam War.[3] The Vietnam War and the killing from the air that it brought into the nation's living rooms every night seems to have allowed Vonnegut to revisit the aerial bombardments of World War II, twenty-odd years later, and to see them as the atrocities they were. The years after 1965 when he was finishing the novel were the years of Operation Rolling Thunder, which Roy Scranton describes as "a forty-four month air attack against North Vietnam that dropped almost a million tons of bombs on 'strategic' military and civilian targets, and killed an estimated 52,000 civilians" (51).[4] Certainly the postcolonial fiction that flourished elsewhere in the Vietnam era also left its imprint on representations of atrocity, though most often it is other-directed rather than self-indicting. As we will see, the massacre of the banana workers in *One Hundred Years of Solitude* (1967) also troubles the apparent simplicity of blame. As a matter of literary history, decolonizing and Cold War struggles outside Europe, often indistinguishable from each other, make the late 1960s a breakthrough period for national self-indictment of atrocity. Yet as with Vonnegut, the reference is often also back to World War II, the impact of which felt unavoidable. With "There is no *why*," Vonnegut puts away his sci-fi toys and makes a troubling link between meaninglessness and high moral seriousness.

He is borrowing, almost word for word, a line from Primo Levi's Holocaust memoir *If This Is a Man/Survival in Auschwitz* (1959). The reference, heavy with Holocaust gravitas, is to a scene from ordinary life for that small minority of arrivals at Auschwitz who are not immediately sent to the gas chambers but instead are put to work and slated to be killed off more slowly. Levi is always thirsty, like his fellow inmates, whose only hydration comes in the form of salty soup. One day, in search of relief, he reaches through the barracks window and snaps off an icicle. Before he can lick it, however, the icicle is batted out of his hand by a passing guard. Levi asks why in German: "Warum?" The guard replies, "Hier ist kein warum": "There is no why here" (24).[5] As Vonnegut's borrowing suggests, the formula "there is no why" has broken free of "here." Taken over for instance by Claude Lanzmann, director of the classic Holocaust documentary *Shoah* (1985), it is offered as a universal guide for traversing a world defined (that's the implication) by the fact that it produced or permitted Auschwitz. His film refuses to enter into explanations of the Holocaust, Lanzmann declares, because there is "an absolute obscenity in the project of understanding."[6] Asking why is obscene even with regard to atrocity, which seems to cry out for some account of causes. Yet this is a truth, Lanzmann suggests, that is drawn directly *from* atrocity, one that seems imposed on the rest of history *by* atrocity, and one that is more and more universally acknowledged.[7]

Given the fallibility of all interpretive efforts, which must always be conceded in advance, epistemological humility seems the best policy. And where what is to be understood is an atrocity, an additional factor comes into play. It is natural to fear that any alleged explanation of atrocity, however partial and provisional, would be taken as disrespect for the experience of the dead, further violation of those who suffered so unimaginably, an inexcusable attempt to diminish their suffering by finding something intelligible and therefore potentially redemptive in it. Not everyone fears that intelligibility will inevitably slide toward redemption, but the risk is widely recognized. Even a hesitant move along the path toward interpretation feels like losing your balance on a treacherous slope with nothing to stop you as you tumble toward humanizing, normalizing, accepting, and finally forgiving the atrocity. To understand everything is to forgive everything.[8] I have already referred to one example. The mechanisms of human rights, concerned as they are to see human rights violations punished and deterred, refuse to contextualize those violations. The assumption appears to be that any background information about the particular motives, cultural values, or built-up resentments that brought perpetrators and victims into lethal proximity might disturb the moral clarity of the act itself, blurring the line between those who were harmed and those who inflicted that harm, and perhaps ending in a blaming of the victims. After all, they started it. Better avoid complications. Stick to the facts of the case. Trying to understand is too dangerous. Paradoxical as it may seem, then, unintelligibility might not be the bitter, hard-to-accept existential truth that is forced on us, as its champions assume, but rather what we choose because it seems the less strenuous and the more comfortable option.

And yet, as the intellectual historian Dominick LaCapra has pointed out, in *If This Is a Man* the person who says "there is no why here" is not Primo Levi himself, but an SS guard.[9] Those who draw a sacred circle around the atrocity, demanding a reverential unintelligibility, are agreeing with the Nazi; they are not making common cause with Levi. On occasion Levi does indeed remind himself that his paltry efforts to understand may only degrade his already weakened will to survive. But his own feelings for the drowned and the saved, the dead and the not-yet dead, don't leave him any less respectful of the project of understanding, despite or because of the complications to which that project gives rise—notably, the fact that survival in Auschwitz demands being brutal to one's fellow sufferers. This is the self-indictment for which his memoir is so well known.

Levi rarely personifies Nazism. But he gives his readers at least one Nazi who might count as a villain. And it is in recollecting the physical presence of this Nazi that Levi comes closest to the goal, never entirely renounced, of comprehending what it is that drives the merciless project of Auschwitz. One day he is called in to be examined on his knowledge of chemistry. The examiner is one Doctor Pannwitz. Pannwitz looks at him with eerily empty eyes. Levi writes: "That look was not one between two men; and if I had known how completely to explain the nature of that look, which came as if across the glass window of an aquarium between two beings who live in different worlds, I would also have explained the essence of the great insanity of the third Germany" (123). Levi goes on to ventriloquize the educated anti-Semite: " 'This something in front of me belongs to a species which it is obviously opportune to suppress. In this particular case, one has to first make sure that it does not contain some utilizable element'" (123). As it happens, Pannwitz decides that Levi does contain a utilizable element. Although Levi is a Jew, belonging to a species that it is opportune to suppress, he is judged to possess valuable knowledge. He is therefore sent to serve in the manufacture of synthetic rubber, an enterprise that Buna, also known as Auschwitz III, was avidly pursuing by means of slave labor and under the direction of IG Farben. (The name Buna derives from the German production process for synthetic rubber.) In other words, what Levi glimpses in Pannwitz is an uneasy mixture of racist dehumanization with economic expediency.[10]

The mixture of racist dehumanization with economic expediency is worth pausing over. Is it the "essence of the great insanity"? That's no doubt too much to credit these two terms with describing. The mixture doesn't correspond to the theory that Levi himself proposes elsewhere: that the camp's intention is "to annihilate us as men in order to kill us more slowly afterwards" (52). Racism should no doubt weigh more heavily in the balance. But even if it is only embryonic, the analysis of Nazi villainy embodied in Pannwitz is a more plausible explanation of Auschwitz than the desire to dehumanize—which assumes, against the evidence, that the Nazis saw Jews as human to begin with.[11] It is more plausible because it includes a recognizable material logic, because it invites the inspection of evidence, and because it is familiar from American slavery and indeed closer to the logic of slavery than to the programmatically impenetrable darkness of Lanzmann's Holocaust. The volatile compound of racism and utilitarianism has a meaningful place on a table of atrocity's history's recurring causes.[12]

Those who are not ready to renounce asking why will have perhaps wondered why he and his fellow inmates are treated so very cruelly given that the Nazis, who do not hesitate to engage in industrial-scale murder, have decided to keep them alive, at least for a time. Like the slapping away of the icicle, it doesn't make much sense. But the discovery of some sense behind the apparent senselessness is an Auschwitz trope. Charlotte Delbo, one of a contingent of women of the French Resistance who were also shipped to Auschwitz, is also bewildered by the meaningless cruelty of a task imposed on them—digging out a ditch and carrying loads of earth in their aprons—until she realizes that the Nazis are using the inmates to plant a garden at the camp entrance.[13] Not worth the beatings and the deaths it entails, but a rational goal. Levi too refers to a rational motive: the Nazis' need for an artificial substitute for rubber. In a time of war, supply lines for natural rubber, an exotic raw material which like so many others came from outside Europe, were unreliable. Levi belonged to the workforce enlisted in the quest for a rubber replacement. And there is also a why behind the paradoxical fact that the Nazis were self-consciously starving this useful workforce to death, the average lifespan in the camp for those not killed at once being about three months. Believing down to the end that they had access to unlimited supplies of fresh slave labor, the Nazi leaders clearly felt they could afford to behave like hypercapitalists, feeding and clothing and sheltering their workers minimally—offering them not subsistence but *less* than subsistence—in order to divert a maximum of resources both to the army and to German civilians at home. The German civilians at home also received, of course, the piles of possessions gathered up from the Jews who were gassed on arrival. The same policy included the clearing of land in Eastern Europe that was slated to be enjoyed eventually by German farmers, a policy that was happily if euphemistically compared to the seizure of lands in the American West from Native Americans. The story is told by the German historian Götz Aly in *Hitler's Beneficiaries: Plunder, Racial War, and the Nazi Welfare State* (2005). In summary:

> By exploiting material wealth confiscated and plundered in a racial war, Hitler's National Socialism achieved an unprecedented level of economic equality and created vast new opportunities for upward mobility for the German people. That made the regime both popular and criminal. The cascade of riches and personal advantages—all derived from crimes against humanity, for which ordinary Germans were not directly responsible but from which they gladly profited—led the majority of the populace to feel that the regime had their best interests at heart. Conversely, the Nazis' genocidal policy gained momentum from the fact that it also improved the material welfare of the German people. (7–8)[14]

Unsurprisingly, historians like Inga Clendinnen have refused to surrender the right to ask why questions. Her project, Clendinnen says in *Reading the Holocaust*, is "to arrive at a clearer understanding of at least some of those persons and processes [implicated in the Holocaust] to be confident that the whole is potentially understandable. This is not a matter of arriving at some 'Aha! Now I comprehend everything!' theory or moment" (4). It is "never complete" (4).[15] "What most disquiets about a too-shrill insistence on the uniqueness of the Holocaust is the danger that, if the Holocaust were indeed to be accepted as unique, it would risk falling out of history—the consultable record of the actions of our species, and the active interrogation of that record—altogether" (16). Unwilling to embrace the hypothesis that the horrors of the mid-twentieth century have discredited once and for all the goal of comprehending, historians, like Levi looking at Doctor Pannwitz, have tended to avoid a mysticism of absolute evil that leaves no room for utilitarian interests like plunder. (To repeat: Pannwitz is an anti-Semite, but he also wants to speed up the production of synthetic rubber. He is a racist, but he is not *just* a racist. His villainy, if that is the right word, is an analyzable compound, not an irreducible element or an inscrutable mystery.) One thing the discipline of history has been especially good at is challenging the identification of atrocities with absolute, homogeneous, irreducible evil.

It does not seem audacious to propose that there are meanings in historical events, if not meanings that escape all controversy, and that this statement applies even to events as significance-threatening as the Holocaust. Does this argument really need to be made? Isn't it pushing on an open door? If the pursuit of meaning in atrocities is not a waste of everyone's time, I would argue that it's because educated common sense, which might seem to take the meaningfulness of historical events for granted, is in fact often quietly swayed by the contrary position. One widespread example is the everyday view that atrocities are an inevitable or at least a predictable result of human nature, which has, always has had, and always will have an irrepressible element of aggressive brutality. Sterling Michael Pavelec, who teaches at the US Air Command and Staff College, writes in *War and Warfare since 1945:* "Mankind is inherently violent, greedy, and selfish, and resorts to violence as a mechanism to prosper" (1).[16] This understanding of human nature makes war "the rule rather than the exception" (1). If so, atrocity is (again) like original sin, and there can be no meaningful history of it, just an ever-unrolling spool of instances.[17]

The determination to be historical is no guarantee that fatalism will be avoided. According to historian Mark Levene, his fellow historians "sometimes fight shy" of massacres because they are "ugly, vicious events, often appearing to lack clear delineation or logic," and thus "throw off course where they do not completely skewer" the project of understanding "the long-term transformation of societies, economies, and polities" (4).[18] The subject of massacre forces some historians to question whether history indeed *exists* in their favored sense—whether what the record shows is indeed a long-term "transformation of societies, economies, and polities" (history in a strong sense) or on the contrary a mere register of "ugly, vicious events," instances of violence that are not susceptible of interpretation except as the products of an ugly, vicious, unchanging human nature. This is the view that Hegel was laying out, in a heroic attempt to overcome it, when he suggested that to others history simply looked like a slaughter-bench. The slaughter-bench perspective, resigned to a future it assumes will mirror the past's unending stream of atrocities, has perhaps escaped critical scrutiny because it fits so neatly into an influential conception of history as composed solely of differences—a conception, more precisely, that is instinctively skeptical about any proposed sameness or connectedness that, like lines of causality, would bridge those differences. Working together with, but at a deeper level than, the explicit commitments to identity with which it is often confused, the vision of history-as-difference expresses itself in the presumption that historical events are as justifiably and irremediably disconnected from each other as are the worldviews of distinct social collectivities. Here Michel Foucault can stand in for a broad region of tacit agreement. Within this region, history resists explanation—not just final explanation, but *any* explanation that is tainted by causality. One unexpected place where this assumption pops up is *Slaughterhouse-Five*. It is arguably because Vonnegut forsakes everyday causal and comparative analysis that, though his intentions with regard to the bombing of Dresden are above reproach, the little he says about it has not held up well. He says the bombing of Dresden was worse than Hiroshima (12). He calls it "the greatest massacre in European history" (128). Neither statement is accurate. The figure he gives for the casualties—130,000 dead—is now seen as wildly inflated (current estimates run from 25,000 to 40,000), and this inflation is no surprise, for on this issue Vonnegut cites David Irving, who later became notorious as a Holocaust denier and advocate for the Nazi cause (238).[19] (For the record, so does Howard Zinn.) Vonnegut also cites (three times) the story that candles and soap were manufactured from the fat of the Nazis' victims—a story that now seems to be apocryphal.[20] The more dramatically exceptional Vonnegut makes the bombing of Dresden, the more he insists that "there is no why," the less relevant the ordinary tools of historical explanation come to seem and the more prone Vonnegut is to fall into demonstrable error.[21]

Willingness to assume that atrocity is off-limits to why questions suggests that Pinker's description of modernity is somewhat optimistic—that the day of violence as "a human problem for humans to solve," welcome as it would be, has not yet arrived. Much progressive opinion today tends to believe that, for the purposes of a discussion of atrocity, modernity means the extermination camp (Giorgio Agamben runs together today's refugee camps with Auschwitz), or the genocidal impulse behind European colonialism (Hitler learned from the genocide of the Native Americans), or both—in short, that modernity is at least as responsible for atrocity as the era that preceded it. If fate and the will of the gods have lost much of their explanatory power, what has arguably replaced them is in part a secular modern fatalism that sees people as, in Vonnegut's words, "the listless playthings of enormous forces" (208). The names of those enormous forces are among our most familiar isms: racism, sexism, imperialism, capitalism, militarism. According to William E. Connolly, even for the ancient Greeks themselves the gods were not "beings" so much as "figures," figures for Greek conceptions of the "diverse forces" that ruled so much of human existence.[22]

After his encounter with these enormous forces in Dresden, Vonnegut's protagonist "found life meaningless" (128). Vonnegut memorably crystallizes that conclusion in the slogan "So it goes." "So it goes" is a catchy translation of "there is no why." The novel repeats it over one hundred times, mainly when deaths are mentioned, hinting each time that we should not be surprised or outraged by these deaths, natural or unnatural.[23] This secular ritual might seem to suggest that the novel too is asserting the meaninglessness of life. Of course, "so it goes" might also be taken as a rhetorical provocation, a way of waking Americans out of their slumbrous passivity, perhaps with special reference to the war in Vietnam, where civilian lives were again being destroyed from the air as Vonnegut was writing. It is hard to believe that in 1969 the author of *Slaughterhouse-Five* was enlisting his writerly talents in an effort to dampen anti-war outrage or encourage fatalism about the mass murder of Vietnamese civilians. At any rate, the novel's allusions to Vietnam help explain a minimalist or pragmatic conception of the meaningful. Those of us who might happily concede that life as such is ultimately meaningless, in the sense that nothing humans do can rest its meaning on the foundation of imperatives or principles issued from outside or above humanity, may still feel that, where atrocity is concerned, standing up against ongoing atrocities and diminishing the likelihood of future atrocities would indeed be meaningful actions—that atrocity-deterrence is a project that could not be rejected out of hand as random, absurd, meaningless.[24] Note that the deterrence of atrocity, which is oriented to the future rather than the past, is not identical with indictment. As human rights specialists have observed, it also sometimes threatens to undermine the enterprise of bringing past malefactors to justice and indeed threatens to create further suffering and further atrocity, as in the case of military humanitarianism. And yet these risks do not invalidate the future-oriented project. And explaining how past atrocities have occurred is an indispensable part of this project.

In one of its allusions to ongoing American atrocities in Vietnam, *Slaughterhouse-Five* tells a story (supposedly the plot of a work of science fiction by another author) about a robot with bad breath who was involved in the dropping of napalm. (Another intersection with the career of Howard Zinn.) The robot "looked like a human being, and could talk and dance and so on, and go out with girls. And nobody held it against him that he dropped jellied gasoline on people, but they found his halitosis unforgivable. But then he cleared that up, and he was welcomed to the human race" (214). It's a tricky little parable. In general, the human race tends to applaud the inclusion of those whom it has heretofore excluded. No such applause is invited here. But what then is the point of the story? A dark reading would fit the parable into a "so it goes" fatalism: human nature is such that the all-too-human race will be quick to blame the one who suffers from bad oral hygiene and but will be much less likely to blame the one who, following their society's own orders, drops jellied gasoline on the inhabitants of some other society. Societies do not tend to blame themselves for violence against other societies. But one cannot ignore the possibility of blaming one's own society. Isn't that what Vonnegut is famous for doing? And his moral can be rephrased in less fatalistic terms: his society needs to learn how to shun those who drop napalm in the way it shuns those who suffer from halitosis. Like the novel, society is better at dealing with halitosis, or aspects of personal conduct for which an individual can be properly held responsible and that can potentially be "cleared up," than it is at dealing with the dropping of napalm, a rather more serious infraction (bad rather than merely disgusting or ridiculous) for which society as a whole might be considered responsible. If the goal is for society to clear up its dropping of napalm the way the robot clears up his halitosis, shunning should perhaps remain an option. Not burning people alive is a very, very desirable good, higher on the scale than universal inclusion, no matter who the excluded are or what they are doing. The moral imperative would be not to give up on villains but to get better at identifying the real ones, especially the collective ones. On the other hand, perhaps the point of behabitive blaming is that it would do without exclusion; it would assume the necessity of somehow continuing to cohabit with perpetrators. One way or the other, at that scale it is hard to conceive what shunning or blaming or indicting would look like if done well, especially in the novel, which is so much better at the world of bad breath than at the world of napalm. That is one point the parable makes, and one reason why as a novelist Vonnegut struggles on the subject of villains.

Class, a modern form of tribute, helps explain modern fatalism. In a class society those who are looted, believing they are free, deliver up their possessions, and sometimes their lives, of their own free will. It is no surprise, then, that the "do and die" fatalism Tennyson projects onto English soldiers in the Crimea, whether as their heroic duty or as their unfortunate destiny, can also be expressed voluntarily by the victims of violence themselves. "I prefer not to reason why" is not the most irrational response of those who feel they are "listless playthings of enormous forces," forces that (at least for the moment) seem beyond their comprehension, beyond their power to avoid or withstand, beyond their power to blame. John Hersey, interviewing survivors of Hiroshima, asks them at the end of his book *Hiroshima* what sense they made of the bombing. Some say they would have had no objection to sacrificing their lives for the sake of the emperor. Others conclude, "It was war and we had to expect it." Hersey adds: "A surprising number of the people of Hiroshima remained more or less indifferent about the ethics of using the bomb. Possibly they were too terrified by it to want to think about it at all. Not many of them even bothered to find out much about what it was like" (117). They had ruled out reasoning why. Hersey gives another source in the original Japanese: '"*Shikata ga nai*,' a Japanese expression as common as, and corresponding to, the Russian word '*nichevo*,' 'it can't be helped, Oh, well. Too bad.'" (117).[25]

Westerners often associate fatalism in the face of atrocity with the religions and races of the non-West. As Primo Levi notes, the inmates of Auschwitz had a term for those of their number who had given up the struggle to survive: *Muselmänner*, or Muslims.[26] Steven Pinker locates fatalism in Europe's own premodern past, but he characteristically does so in a way that encourages a Eurocentric identification between that past or pastness and non-European backwardness, while it also encourages the further implication that modernity, with its secular humanist repudiation of fate, is distinctive to Europe. What we glimpse in Tennyson and Hersey might be described as a deracialization of this stereotype. Here fatalism in the face of atrocity becomes an international language of victims, the language of the domestic underclass, of the powerless of whatever race or place. And if so, one would expect it to persist, as indeed it has, wherever the victimhood and the powerlessness also persist. As Levi puts it, "whoever is too weak, or naked or barefoot, thinks and feels in a different way, and what dominated our thoughts was the paralyzing sensation of being totally helpless in the hands of fate" (184).[27] It's another perspective on "so it goes."

If This Is a Man does not quite repudiate fatalism, but it does turn into a narrative with a meaningful resolution, indeed a sort of a surprise ending. The ending showcases a rediscovered human solidarity. Thus it contradicts Levi's own explicit conclusion: "The work of bestial degradation, begun by the victorious Germans, had been carried to its conclusion by the Germans in defeat" (204). On the same page, Levi writes that "Charles, Arthur, and I felt ourselves become men again" (204). So the bestial degradation had *not* been "carried to its conclusion." This rehumanization happens because, with the Germans gone, the patients on the infection ward have joined together in solidarity to help each other survive. Those who have been working for the good of all are offered an extra slice of bread by those who have not. "Only a day before a similar event would have been inconceivable. The law of the Lager said: 'eat your own bread, and if you can that of your neighbor,' and left no room for gratitude . . . It was the first human gesture that occurred among us. I believe that that moment can be dated as the beginning of the change by which we who had not died slowly changed from Häftlinge to men again" (190). The gift of extra bread is the precise opposite of the ethic of looting.

Aerial bombardment seems to push atrocity beyond the logic of looting. Yet on the modern side of the modern/premodern divide, booty remains a relevant motive. This point can be made, in the vocabulary of Marxism, by saying that exploitation has never entirely superseded expropriation. The classic Marxist theory held, in a left-wing variant of Adam Smith's "gentle commerce," that the passage from feudalism to capitalism meant leaving behind the forcible extraction of surplus at the point of a sword (expropriation) and instead embracing the "free" exchange of labor for wages (exploitation), in which the surplus is again transferred from worker to employer, but this time without any apparent need for coercion. Even among Marxists that theory is now considered problematic. The evidence suggests that the system still cannot do without coercion. Yet something has of course changed. As Nancy Fraser argues, a certain percentage of the population, especially colonized and racialized people, have now won at least minimal political rights. As possessors of political rights, they have largely moved from targets of expropriation to targets of exploitation, and while this leaves much to be desired, it is a nonnegligible achievement. Their status as bearers of rights affords them certain possibilities of self-defensive action. It does not protect them from the nonviolent looting that we call exploitation, but it lowers their risk of falling victim to violent expropriation, hence to atrocity.[28]

The climax of *Slaughterhouse-Five* is not the bombing of Dresden. Though that bombing, announced at the beginning of the novel, has been long delayed, Vonnegut spends very few words on it. There is almost nothing about the bombing itself except as noises off. There is little description of the uninhabited, uninhabitable ruins except for the protagonist's assignment to dig bodies out of what Vonnegut calls corpse mines. The novel's real climax, one page from the end, is an execution which has also been anticipated but is also left undescribed: "Somewhere in there the poor old high school teacher, Edgar Derby, was caught with a teapot he had taken from the catacombs. He was arrested for plundering. He was tried and shot" (274). Derby's death seems more distressing than the novel's other losses, though it too gets its resigned, unsurprised "so it goes." It is distressing because Derby is presented as the novel's only real "character," as if he alone (like *der Letzte* in Levi, hanged for sabotaging a crematorium) has somehow stood up against the "enormous forces" that have turned those around him into "listless playthings"[29] (which he does, undramatically, in a civics-lesson push-back against a Nazi recruiter two days before the bombing). And his death is especially distressing because the motive for the killing is absurd: the taking of a teapot that no one is left to feel the lack of, the taking of a trivial household object in the midst of the world-historical wreckage left by a much, much greater crime.

But there is another, almost imperceptible irony here. The act for which Derby is arrested and executed is plundering. For most of human history, plunder was almost inseparable from atrocity. As I've suggested, it was the promise of plunder that guaranteed that war between armies would spill over into the substantial deaths of noncombatants. The rule against looting is absurd as it is applied to the theft of a teapot, but its application nonetheless shows that a norm has come into existence. The emergence of such norms, which seem so callous in their grotesque universality, is nevertheless an event, and an event on which the literary history of atrocity turns. It is an aspect of modernity, but it also straddles the much-disputed line separating the premodern from the modern. Some scruples concerning the killing of noncombatants and civilizational others clearly exist before modernity. But as the scruples accumulate and increase in intensity, quantity is transformed into quality, and scruples are embodied in the not-quite new, not-quite fully developed genre of literary cosmopolitanism that we see in Vonnegut: national self-indictment of atrocity.[30] It's hard to know whether the absence of villains from *Slaughterhouse-Five* should be seen as an affirmation of higher literary and moral principles or as a representational failure—the failure to clinch the condemnation of one's own. Or if not a failure, then one moment in a process that is far from finished.

The Innocence of Children

Vonnegut describes himself, early in *Slaughterhouse-Five*, as unable to write his Dresden novel or even to remember much about Dresden. What he does remember is "two Russian soldiers who had looted a clock factory. They had a horse-drawn wagon full of clocks. They were happy and drunk" (17). Looting is what sticks in his memory when other memories don't come. "It wasn't much to write a book about" (17). What seems to get him unstuck is the anger of his friend's wife, Mary, who was looking at the war from the viewpoint of children. "So then I understood. It was war that made her so angry. She didn't want her babies or anybody else's babies killed in wars. And she thought wars were partly encouraged by books and movies" (18–19). Vonnegut promises to call his book "The Children's Crusade" (19). Which is indeed the beginning of its long subtitle. And he starts researching the actual Children's Crusade, which began in 1213 and resulted (according to his source) in approximately two million deaths, with half the children involved drowned in shipwrecks and the other half sold into slavery. "I have told my sons," Vonnegut writes, "that they are not under any circumstances to take part in massacres, and that the news of massacres of enemies is not to fill them with satisfaction or glee" (24).

Children are the exemplary noncombatants, hence also the exemplary proof that an atrocity has indeed taken place. That is self-evident. It is less easy to pin down what else they do, for better or worse, in the representation of atrocity. *The Gypsy Goddess* (2014), the first novel by poet, translator, and activist Meena Kandasamy, deals with the Kilvenmani Massacre, which occurred on Christmas Day of 1968. According to critic Ashik Kumar, the village, populated by Adi Dravidars (that is, Dalits), "was burnt down by the hired thugs of the Paddy Producer's Association (made up of the district's landlords)" for the crimes of unionizing and flying Communist Party flags.[31] Forty-four people were killed. Because the atrocity occurred in South India and because its victims were Dalits, Kumar goes on, the event has no place in India's national history. In calling attention to it, Kandasamy is not wasting her time. And yet it has to be said that the description of the massacre is not good writing.

> And in desperation a mother throws her one-year-old son out of the burning hut but the boy is caught by the leering mobsters and chopped into pieces and thrown back in and in that precise yet fleeting moment of loss and rage everyone realizes that they would die if their death meant saving a loved one and that they would die if their death meant staying together and that they would die anyway because it would not be as disastrous as living long enough to share this sight. (164)[32]

Consider the "precise yet fleeting" moment that Kandasamy treats as decisive: the one-year-old who is "chopped in pieces and thrown back in." This is, in Kumar's words, a "physical improbability."[33] It is not absolutely impossible that each individual piece of the chopped-up child was thrown back in. But in that case, having used the word *precise*, the sentence is making a stylistic mistake by taking liberties with its own precision. It presents many separate acts, as many as there are pieces of the child, as if they were all one act. Having stated that the child was chopped in pieces, Kandasamy immediately follows by suggesting, in the same sentence, that the child is still whole. Seeing "precise" and "fleeting" together, one is tempted to conclude that this moment disappears from memory so quickly because it was never actually perceived, hence never actually remembered.

Readers are probably in such a state of outrage by this point that they will not notice any imprecision. Chances are they are skimming. The details are awful, and by now they've got the idea. If this indignant, accusatory prose belongs to a genre, that genre has the temptation to skim hardwired into it. The disadvantage of skimming, however, is that it leaves you unprepared if the accused then try to poke holes in the accusation. Those who are likely to be blamed for the atrocity, for its cover-up, and for long-standing and remunerative affiliations with the social system that encouraged it can hold up instances of narratorial sloppiness as evidence that the testimony itself is unreliable. If something that is represented as having happened *could not* have happened, why should the author be believed? If on the other hand you do *not* skim, you may find the free flow of your feelings snagged on an underwater obstacle. Even in cases where the account is clearly valuable as historical documentation and where the messenger who brings the news deserves credit for testifying against their society's official representatives, who are more likely to take revenge on whistleblowers than to hold perpetrators accountable, the melodramatic absoluteness of dead babies may be counterproductive.

The moral absoluteness that is signaled by the killing of women and children seems so paradigmatic of and even necessary to the genre that women and children may well be added to lists of the victims where in fact they were most likely absent. In *The House of the Pain of Others: Chronicle of a Small Genocide,* a valuably politically confounding account of the massacre of Chinese immigrants in Mexico in the midst of the Mexican revolution, Julian Herbert writes: "It is also a lie that there were Asiatic mothers to be bayoneted in La Laguna. A document cited by Carlos Canstañón mentions only four Chinese women named in the 1910 census in Coahuila . . . the vast majority of the members of the community were male" (54).[34] It needs to be said, however, that more often than not, the extra helpless victims did not need to be added. And perhaps it also needs to be said, although it should be obvious, that contextualizing an atrocity, thereby replacing moral absoluteness with moral relativity, does not mean deciding that the atrocity is immune to judgment. Contextualization may weaken the forensic impulse of the account, but serviceability in a courtroom should not be decisive. Where atrocities are concerned, courtrooms have rarely rendered anything like justice.[35] For better or worse, then, we have to be grateful for those literary representations which do the work of contextualizing, addressing public opinion rather than the courts, and which in any case are almost always too late to play anything other than the long game. The long game entails an effort to understand where the responsibility lies when (as is so often the case) it cannot be said to lie only with those who pull the trigger.

In Hwang Sok-Yong's *The Guest* (2005), a novel about atrocities committed by both sides during the Korean War, there is no avoiding scenes of violence against children.[36] "One of Yohan's men threw my baby, the same way he might kick a soccer ball—my child flew up into the air a little bit before falling back down to the ground a few steps away" (194). "Calling the children 'red brats,' they picked them at random and threw them in the fire. Mothers who tried to jump in the fire to save their children were shot" (100). "Eighty-two women and children were dragged through landlord's front yard to execution site. Were stood on hillside and shot. Sunwon's six-year-old baby brother was shot first. Bullets went through his abdomen. He survived. Muttering that he was a tough one, they used bayonets" (101). Christians clearly do not consider the children of Communists as innocent. "These are Reds, too. With Reds, you gotta dry up their seed" (182). Things are not better on the Communist side. The Communists "descend upon any and all Christian households. Just like before, entire families are executed in their homes" (184).[37]

The idea of children as extensions of the political ideas and identities of their parents, future participants in an ongoing struggle, does nothing to absolve the guilt of the killers, but it does say something important about the kind of society in which the atrocity takes place. It is that society that Hwang keeps in focus. In spite of the novel's title, which suggests nefarious foreign influence, he is careful to show that it is not the foreigners, American or Chinese, who are responsible for the violence. "As it turns out, the atrocities we suffered were committed by none other than ourselves" (9).[38] Again, this is an instance of national self-indictment. Hwang is equally careful to show that the causes were not just ideological divisions. They were also material divisions: the resentments of the dispossessed against the rich, the defense of property and privilege on the part of the wealthier Christians. "You son of a bitch, you took our land—thought you'd be the Party chairman for a thousand, ten thousand years, didn't you?" (195). "You were a fucking homeless piece of dirt and we took you in—we taught you, trained you to handle engines so you could make a living—and you have the *nerve* to tell us to give up our factory!" (202).

Hwang's interest in Ichiro, "a kind of village servant" (124) who becomes empowered during the civil war as "Comrade Pak Ilang" (124), taking advantage so as to beat up the mother and father and steal from their home, is echoed in another classic atrocity novel. Bapsi Sidhwa's *Cracking India* (also published as *Ice-Candy-Man*) deals with the atrocities committed in the course of the Partition of India and Pakistan in 1947. The atrocities often involve children, and they are also narrated from the perspective of children. The most atrocious of them, the virtually person-by-person description of the wiping out of a Muslim village by a heavily armed Sikh mob, are loaded into the inset narrative of a child survivor, "Ranna's Story." Ranna "looked on with a child's boundless acceptance and curiosity as jeering men set her long hair on fire. He saw babies snatched from their mothers, smashed against walls and their howling mother brutally raped and killed" (218–19).[39] Others are narrated from the perspective of our protagonist, a little girl from a prosperous Parsee family: "A naked child, twitching on a spear struck between her shoulders, is waved like a flag: her screamless mouth agape, she is staring straight up at me" (144). But this child "me" is something more than an innocent observer. When a Muslim mob, led by Ice-candyman, a poor but ambitious local figure, comes for the child's Hindu ayah, the family hides her. It is our child narrator who betrays her, telling Ice-candy-man where she is. "Ice-candy-man is crouched before me. 'Don't be scared, Lenny baby,' he says. 'I'm here.' And putting his arms around me he whispers, so that only I can hear: 'I'll protect Ayah with my life! You know I will . . . I know she's here. Where is she?' " Lenny trusts him and tells him. The mob takes the Hindu woman away. "I know I have betrayed Ayah" (194). We are not told exactly what is done to Ayah, but we know that she is never the same afterwards. The scene is paradigmatic of how the child-narrator, as characteristic a device of atrocity representation as prolepsis is, can complicate the responsibility for the violence. Her child protagonist allows Sidhwa to suggest that, although we see violence perpetrated by absolute monsters (the violence we see most clearly is perpetrated by figures of absolute inhumanity), responsibility for the atrocities of Partition cannot so simply be disposed of. An enormous class divide separates Lenny's family from Ice-candy-man. It is that divide that speaks through the narrator. As a child, Lenny obviously cannot be blamed for leaking the knowledge that presumably leads to her ayah's rape and torture. And yet the scene expresses a deeper truth about the inequalities that, as the novel knows, feed the violence—expresses, that is to say, the family's unwilling, structural complicity with and responsibility for violence that the family does not itself participate in and indeed deplores and tries its best to rectify.

Sidhwa's child-narrator device for distributing responsibility for atrocity is repeated with a slight variation in Arundhati Roy's *The God of Small Things*. In the Roy novel, it is two children of a wealthy, factory-owning family, twins, who carry the narrative, and the narrative leads up to the symbolic murder of a Dalit man, Velutha, who is their mother's lover and who is also a Communist. Like the narrator of *Cracking India*, the young boy, Estha, who tells the killers—here, the police—that he and his sister have been abducted by the Dalit, which is not true but is what the police want to hear, does not wish any harm to the victim of violence. On the contrary, he loves Velutha. He knows he is lying even as he is manipulated into doing so, and afterwards he is arguably destroyed by his knowledge of what he has done. As a child, he cannot be blamed either for Velutha's death—the murder of a single individual, so not an atrocity, but symbolic of the treatment of a collectivity—or for society's judgment that Velutha was guilty. And yet in lying to accuse Velutha, Estha is acting out the truth of his family, former feudal landowners fully given over to the caste system that has defined Velutha's status and made him vulnerable to police violence. Giving the (non)responsibility for the atrocity to the child is a way for Roy to say both things at the same time: that he is not responsible and that his family is.[40]

The failure of indictment can of course result from a failure of nerve or lack of clarity about who is to blame, but it can also result from a sense of obscure complicity. The first sentence of Jhumpa Lahiri's story "When Mr. Pirzada Came to Dine" goes like this: "In the autumn of 1971 a man used to come to our house, bearing confections in his pocket and hopes of ascertaining the life or death of his family" (000).[41] The figure of speech Lahiri employs here is zeugma, also known as syllepsis. Zeugma refers to the use of the same verb, here "bearing," to yoke together two very different kinds of objects: here, "confections in his pocket" and "hopes of ascertaining the life or death of his family." The grammatical symmetry calls attention to a drastic asymmetry: here, between a trivial object of great interest to children, candy, and the very nontrivial fate of Mr. Pirzada's family, who are caught up in the atrocity-filled sequence of events by which East Pakistan, invaded by the troops of West Pakistan (to stop its attempt to secede) and then by the Indian army (to stop the flow of refugees across the border), became the independent nation of Bangladesh. The story is narrated from the point of view of a ten-year-old child of Indian parents, living in New England. Candy is meaningful to her; the events in East Pakistan, less so. Another way of tracing the trajectory of modern atrocity representation might be as a movement from description (what the atrocity means for its participants) to reception, the impact of the news of atrocity on someone both far away and not immediately involved—not Mr. Pirzada, whose wife and daughters are at risk, but the child of his hosts. The extra element that the first sentence underlines, apart from spectatorial distance, is the contrast between atrocity far away and the routine of pleasurable consumption at the site where the news is received. Here and now, we are not merely spectators; we tend to the pleasures (and necessities) of daily consumption. In Lahiri's story, what is consumed is candy. In Lydia Davis's "Addie and the Chili," it is a bowl of chili. Faced with distant atrocity, we seem to have limited options—to eat or not to eat. At the end of the Lahiri story, the narrator throws away the hoard of candy she has accumulated from Mr. Pirzada's visits. At the end of the Davis story, the narrator, who has lost her appetite after seeing a documentary about unspecified terrible things done by the United States, gets her appetite back and wishes she had ordered more chili.[42] Both options are merely symbolic; neither is presented as consequential. But from the characters' point of view, eating is real in a way that distant atrocity is not. Philosopher Peter Singer, whose child-drowning-in-a-shallow-pond scenario was inspired by the same 1971 events, tries to overcome the distance by making a case for large and immediate cash payment to alleviate distant hunger.[43] (Not eating is a less optional option there.) But for Singer, the cause of the suffering was a famine, and a famine was an act of God. It was not a man-made atrocity, a political situation that required sides to be taken. (The US government, following the advice of Henry Kissinger, was supporting Pakistan, which perpetrated the atrocities.) A famine called for humanitarianism, not for political intervention. Unlike Singer, Lahiri leaves no doubt that this is indeed an atrocity. "In March, Dacca had been invaded, torched, and shelled by the Pakistani army. Teachers were dragged onto streets and shot, women dragged into barracks and raped. By the end of the summer, three hundred thousand people were said to have died" (23). But Lahiri's sentences are in the passive voice; the agents of this violence, like Secretary of State Henry Kissinger and Pakistan's other US backers, are missing. Aside from a focus on unnecessary consumption, Lahiri and Singer have something else in common: the absence of any indictment of the United States. In this sense, both are representative of a remarkable backing down from accusation in recent writing.

As we've seen, even those modern writers who have thought and felt most deeply about the atrocities committed by their own nations, like Tolstoy and Vonnegut, have had second thoughts about blaming the perpetrators and have been at least somewhat drawn to the antithetical idea—according to Steven Pinker, an idea that has been superseded in the modern period—that atrocity is a kind of fate. Atrocity-as-fate removes the possibility of accusing, indeed removes the possibility of seeing an atrocity *as* an atrocity, seeing it as a moral scandal that deserves to be condemned. Condemnation assumes the freedom to act otherwise. That which is necessary is beyond condemnation. If war is inevitable and atrocity is an inevitable result of war, as has been proposed more than once, then atrocity too is a necessity, if a heartbreaking one.[44] It was consistent of Nietzsche that he both demolished the categories of good and evil and preached *amor fati,* a loving embrace of your fate. When Vonnegut returns to Dresden, trying to unblock the writing of his Dresden novel, one of the two books he brings with him on the plane is Theodore Roethke's *Words for the Wind,* from which he quotes these lines—lines that suddenly look like they are reflections on fate:

> I wake to sleep, and take my waking slow.
> I feel my fate in what I cannot fear.
> I learn by going where I have to go.[45]

I go where I *have* to go, which may not be where I want to go. The place I am fated to go may not be a place I fear to go, though going there means learning something—something I don't already know. If Vonnegut is considering that for him these lines may be about Dresden and returning there, it sounds like he may be fearful enough so as not to rush into the waking consciousness of war crimes. It sounds like for him the nation is still a community of fate, as Max Weber proposed. In which case it is only to be expected that opportunities for national self-indictment will be diluted by fatalism.

Indictment? Gabriel García Márquez and John Berger

The massacre of the striking banana plantation workers in Gabriel García Márquez's *One Hundred Years of Solitude,* probably the single most influential representation of atrocity in modern literary history, seems as distant as possible from national self-accusation. The dead are Colombian, not foreign, and the fact that the killers are serving the interests of a US multinational only emphasizes how other-directed the accusation is. That said, the atrocity description itself displays some features that challenge any simple classification. Up to the moment when the order to fire is given, people in García Márquez's crowd show no evidence of believing that they might be shot. "At that time it all seemed more like a jubilant fair than a waiting crowd"

(326).[46] Ordered to disperse, they jeer their defiance and do not move. Then the machine guns open fire. It all seems unreal; there are the first casualties. In another prolepsis, we get the viewpoint of a child rescued by José Arcadio Segundo: "Many years later that child would still tell, in spite of people thinking he was a crazy old man, how José Arcadio Segundo had lifted him over his head and hauled him, almost in the air, as if floating on the terror of the crowd, toward a nearby street" (328). This is the finale:

> Several voices shouted at the same time:
>
> "Get down! Get down!"
>
> The people in front had already done so, swept down by the wave of bullets. The survivors, instead of getting down, tried to go back to the small square, and the panic became a dragon's tail as one compact wave ran against another which was moving in the opposite direction, toward the other dragon's tail in the street across the way, where the machine guns were also firing without cease. They were penned in, swirling about in a gigantic whirlwind that little by little was being reduced to its epicenter as the edges were systematically being cut off all around like an onion, being peeled by the insatiable and methodical shears of the machine guns. . . . José Arcadio Segundo put [the child] up there at the moment he fell with his face bathed in blood, before the colossal troop wiped out the empty space, the kneeling woman, the light of the high, drought-ridden city, and the whorish world where Úrsula Iguarán had sold so many little candy animals. (329)

This passage has been celebrated for its political power, and justly so. Yet certain details do something other than awaken political indignation. For example, the dark pun on "Get down/had already done so." The prolepsis ("Many years later") that detaches us from the present; "Many years later" reassuringly identifies our point of view with that of a survivor, the child who must survive in order to testify and be thought, years later, a crazy old man. And a similar detachment in the conspicuous metaphors: the dragon's tail, the whirlwind, and the onion. All of these are visible only from a perspective above and outside the massacre. The passage does not look at the massacre through the eyes of the crowd itself. To see what is happening as a whole, the narrator's perspective withdraws to a high place where metaphors like onion and dragon's tail make visual sense. These metaphors seem to require a perspective that is suspiciously close to the perspective of those who are doing the shooting.

From the moment when the shooting begins, the crowd becomes a collection of victims and victims-to-be; no one manifests any intention except to escape. The implication, which is natural enough, is that they have an ordinary life to which they *can* escape, a destination arrival at which would *constitute* escape.[47] But what does García Márquez think, then, about the ordinary life into which the atrocity intrudes? What does he think of the "whorish world" that is "wiped out"—the Spanish verb is *arasar*, "to erase"—by the machine guns? The word *whorish* is not affectionate, and this is striking because for this novel those female characters to whom it might normally be applied have been entirely positive figures. So what is going on? A first hypothesis would be that atrocity comes from outside this world; in other words, that there is no atrocity at the core of this world. As the crowd sees it, in spite of the strong motives for dissatisfaction that led to their organizing against the banana company, the ordinary life they led before the banana company came was good. No complaint is registered against the small-scale enterprise of selling little candy animals, which is quietly allowed to stand for the economic basis of ordinary, pre-banana company life and, in part, for the relative prosperity of the Buendía family. It is only the arrival of the banana company, it seems, that has made a real difference. Unfortunately, the hypothesis that the responsibility of the banana company is all we need to know, politically speaking, is refuted by subsequent events. The banana company will now leave, and yet things in Macondo will get even worse. At no point are the people of Macondo ready to make any changes in their world, or even to recognize that such changes are necessary. They have made their peace with the world as it is. This is why, I think, García Márquez calls the world "whorish." It is why, at the end of the novel, he feels that he himself must abolish this "whorish world," as he abolishes the Buendía family itself. And it is why he does so by "erasing" it in another "whirlwind"—strikingly and bizarrely, using the same words about his authorial gesture that he has used for the machine guns and what they do to the crowd. He locates himself with the perpetrators.

The people of Macondo, in love with the beautiful imperfections of their ordinary lives, do not realize that the state of their world is intolerable. As John Berger puts it in a sentence from an essay on Che Guevara, "the full measure of the truth about [their] conditions was unknown—even by those who suffered it."[48] They are unmotivated to make a revolution, and that is why the revolutionary García Márquez feels he has to realize the world's intolerability for them. Hence the strange rhyme between the massacre scene and the novel's final paragraph. García Márquez has to condemn the whorish world where Ursula sold her little candy animals because the people in the square do not condemn it. It's an exemplary gesture of modernist exasperation, a flinging away of the crooked timber of humanity out of which nothing revolutionary can seemingly be made. In that sense, García Márquez is indeed engaging in national self-accusation when he describes his paradigmatic atrocity, and he is inviting the atrocity descriptions of others to do the same.

In García Márquez, the people are tricked into appearing in the square where they will be massacred. It's a trap. They do not know the truth about their situation. This is not the case for the massacre of striking workers by the army in Milan in May 1898 in John Berger's Booker Prize–winning *G.* There it is the people who create the confrontation with the army. No deception or hypocrisy is involved; what they see is what they get. As in García Márquez, some of the description comes through the viewpoint of a child (here, the eleven-year-old G.), and again it is this child whose escape and survival will offer the massacre scene a kind of minimally positive counterplot. But in this case, no one but the children are trying to escape. And because the crowd has chosen to be there, chooses to stay there and to look straight ahead into the guns, the narrative viewpoint does not have to withdraw from them or rise above them in order to make sense of the event. The narrative looks through their eyes, and what it sees is the intolerability of ordinary life. "The crowd see the city around them with different eyes. They have stopped the factories producing, forced the shops to shut, halted the traffic, occupied the streets. It is they who have built the city and they who maintain it. They are discovering their own creativity . . . They are rejecting all that they habitually and, despite themselves, accept" (80).[49] This is the key sentence: "They are rejecting all that they habitually and, despite themselves, accept." The novel declares that the world as it is, however imbued with their creativity, is intolerable.

Berger makes the reasons for their discontent go deep into ordinary life. Before the bloody confrontation in the streets, the people strike the first blow, attacking tax registers. Why? "The tax on flour is over 50 per cent: on sugar 300 per cent, on meat and milk 20 per cent. Salt is so highly taxed that many peasants never taste it. Meanwhile it is an offense against the excise for those who live by the coast to draw salt water from the sea. Guards have shot at women coming down to the beaches with buckets. It is safest at night. Phosphorescent drops form for a moment along the rim of the bucket, in whose illegal water she will cook tomorrow's pasta" (77).

"It is safest at night" places the narrative inside the point of view of women who are already shot at in their ordinary lives, before they are shot at again on the barricades. "Phosphorescent drops form for a moment along the rim of the bucket" individualizes this point of view, preparing for the "she" of "she will cook," and credits it with a refined aesthetic sensibility. It's the rest of the truth about ordinary life. These are not merely working-class women who cannot afford the salt they want for their cooking, they are also women who observe and appreciate the beauty of phosphorescence on the rim of a bucket. That phosphorescence is rightfully theirs. Ordinary life is intolerable if you are not allowed to take salt water out of the sea. What makes it absolutely intolerable is that the salt water is also beautiful and that the beauty too is fenced off by men with guns. Because the men with guns are there protecting the sea and its salt, there is no ordinary life to escape back to.

Berger sees the demonstration and the killings as coming out of the very nature of the life the strikers live, not from an interruption of their life, like the interruption caused by the banana company. In *G.*, ordinary life is not full, as it is in *One Hundred Years of Solitude*; life is constitutively lacking and unsatisfactory. This gives a different valence to the risk of losing one's life. Atrocity is most often seen as terrible but exceptional. To well-intentioned common sense, atrocity is an exception to the ordinary functioning of civil order, an exception that proves the rule of that order. The rule is that the social order does not normally generate extreme, collective, indiscriminate cruelty. The atrocity confirms the virtues of the normal social order by representing everything that order is not. This understanding is so strong that even García Márquez, who is no liberal, falls into it, rescuing his revolutionary hopes only at the end of the novel and only by a gesture of social erasure that, as I said, is unsettlingly congruent with the atrocity itself. It is this vision of atrocity that I would like to credit Berger with transcending. His alternative is to see atrocity as unexceptional, merely crystallizing or making visible that which is already or generally the case. In *G.*, the dead are less victims than vanquished. The people themselves have decided that ordinary life is not worth living; they do not require a gesture of radical modernist estrangement on the part of their author because they are themselves modernists, dedicated to estrangement from a world that deserves nothing else. To give a twist to Raymond Williams's famous formula that "culture is ordinary," for Berger, atrocity is ordinary.[50]

Six

Strategy from Below

Hiroshima and After

Hersey gives the last words of *Hiroshima* to a child. Earlier he has told us that Toshio Nakamura, who was ten years old when the bomb struck, was "delighted when one of the city's gas-storage tanks went up in a tremendous burst of flame" (69).[1] In the final paragraph, the book remembers his failure to moralize what he has been witnessing and gives that failure some extra emphasis. "It would be impossible to say," Hersey acknowledges, "what horrors were embedded in the minds of the children who lived through the day of the bombing in Hiroshima" (119). Whatever the deep horrors were, they don't get articulated. "On the surface their recollections, months after the disaster, were of an exhilarating adventure" (118). Toshio "was soon able to talk freely, even gaily, about the experience" (118–19). Hersey quotes at length from a "matter-of-fact essay" Toshio wrote for his primary school a few weeks before the bombing's one-year anniversary. The essay begins: "The day before the bomb, I went for a swim. In the morning, I was eating peanuts. I saw a light. I was knocked to little sister's sleeping place. When we were saved I could see only as far as the tram" (119). The essay ends, as Hersey's book does, with the following words: "Next day I went to Taiko Bridge and met my girl friends Kikuki and Murakami. They were looking for their mothers. But Kikuki's mother was wounded and Murakami's mother, alas, was dead" (119). This reference to the two mothers, which strikes the predictable, perhaps inevitable adult note, cannot quite erase the phrase "exhilarating adventure," or for that matter the adverb "gaily." It's as if Hersey did not want to credit the ten-year-old with the melancholy with which the boy's essay in fact concludes—as if the cost in death and suffering were somehow outweighed, in Hersey's own mind, by the child's susceptibility to view the experience as an exhilarating adventure.

Hersey's intention here might be ironic. He might choose to end with an elementary school essay in order to hint at just those terrible aspects of the bombing from which an elementary school child would look away. He might also be suggesting that his own book, which renders its extraordinarily compelling subject matter in deliberately flat, matter-of-fact prose, is itself closer than expected to a child's "matter-of-fact" tale of adventure. *Hiroshima*, an enormously successful publication which has never been out of print since 1946, is also exhilarating. After all, of the six exemplary figures Hersey tracked through the days after the bombing, all of them survivors, four were actively involved in rescuing the less fortunate: two were doctors, and two were priests. What could be more readable than a rescue, or a series of rescues? In that sense Hersey's version of events has something in common with the children's. And like the child's version, Hersey's leaves unresolved the contradiction between suffering (the suffering of the victims) and pleasure (in his case, the pleasure he gives his readers). Ending with the child's unreliable viewpoint also suggests something more important: that the adult victims too are failing in the task of resolution, failing to draw the sorts of conclusions that Hersey himself, his own views kept carefully out of sight, might have preferred that they draw. As far as the ultimate meaning of the bombing is concerned, Hiroshima's adults do not fare much better than its children. "What they thought of their experiences and the use of the atomic bomb was, of course, not unanimous. One feeling they did seem to share, however, was a curious kind of elated community spirit, something like that of the Londoners after their blitz—a pride in the way they and their fellow-survivors had stood up to a dreadful ordeal" (115). An ordeal could of course be an act of God rather than an atrocity, like the collapse of an Inca rope bridge in Thornton Wilder's *The Bridge of San Luis Rey* (1927), the literary model (random victims joined together by a shared disaster) from which Hersey says he took formal inspiration. The word *ordeal* does not distinguish between a misfortune and an injustice. A shift from misfortune to injustice can certainly be extrapolated from the many citizens of Hiroshima who, Hersey says, "continued to feel a hatred for Americans" (117) and from the doctor who told Hersey that those who decided to use the bomb should be hanged as war criminals. But that inference is mentioned only in passing. The longest passage Hersey devotes to the subject, from a

Japanese man who is also a Methodist minister, offers testimony after testimony that, in the eyes of these survivors, Hiroshima's sacrifice was justified. It was "all for the country" (116). It was "manly" (117). It was "for [the] Emperor's sake" (117). These witnesses remain enthusiastic about pursuing the military adventure, whatever the costs to themselves, right down to the moment when they are told the war is over. They do not ask what the war's purpose was. They do not ask how much suffering the war may have caused for others. If Japan had had the atomic bomb, it does not sound as if they would have hesitated to use it, even having seen up close what it can do.

From this angle, the child's unreliability is a perfectly fitting vehicle for Hersey's final words: it underlines the deficiencies of the adult viewpoint—the deficiencies, one might say, of the victim's viewpoint as such. This would be an unexpected conclusion to draw about Hersey, and it would be a troubling consideration to raise about the present book as it moves toward its own conclusion. *Hiroshima*'s biggest selling point was its direct access to those who lived through the bombing. In the year that followed, the Western media had been full of moral and geostrategic reflections of all sorts about the new weapon—the first weapon in history, be it noted, that cannot be used for purely military purposes, cannot be used without killing a considerable number of civilians, and is thus as neatly fitted to the concept of the atrocity as the child-victim. What Hersey provided in 1946 was not self-evidently a self-indictment; it was the experience of being there. But what if the experience of being there, and Hersey's accomplishment in bringing the reader as near as possible to that experience, thus giving readers what they think they want, did not mean learning the best or most responsible lessons from the bombing? And if not, then at what terminus does it arrive? And at what terminus is this book arriving? I have argued that though coming to understand mass violence against noncombatants as an injustice, that is, as an action with unjustified and unjustifiable victims, has been a frustratingly gradual and indirect process, in the end that process has resulted in a palpable moral achievement. But what if victimhood, once invented, turns out to be both morally and epistemologically disappointing, even in the wake of a world-historical atrocity? What if it is lacking indignation, or unwilling to aim its indignation at the most useful targets? If you trust the survivors, it seems like a much lesser achievement, or perhaps not an achievement at all.

The temptation to trust the survivors is overwhelming. In the case of the atomic bomb, Kenzaburo Oe's record of consulting the survivors suggests that the trust was not initially well placed, but with time proved open to correction. Oe's consultation happens in two widely separated stages. In 1963, eighteen years after the bomb was dropped, he journeyed to Hiroshima to report on a rally to abolish nuclear weapons. In *Hiroshima Notes*, first published in Japanese in 1965 and then, after he received the Nobel Prize for Literature in 1994, published in English translation the next year, he writes that as a result of his 1963 visit he "discovered human dignity in Hiroshima" (98).[2] He praises as "moralists" people like the "independent-minded" woman who claimed that drinking alcohol protected survivors from radiation sickness (82). The movement to abolish nuclear weapons is necessary, he resolves, after a great deal of good-faith listening, because the atomic bomb embodies "the absolute evil of war, transcending lesser distinctions such as Japanese or Allies, attacker or attacked" (114). In 1995, however, thirty-two years later and a full fifty years after the bomb was dropped, he reconsiders. In the introduction to the new edition, with help from input from earlier readers, he steps back from what he heard in 1963, and he relativizes or at least contextualizes that apparent absolute. "At the time of writing the essays in this book I was sadly lacking in the attitude and ability needed to recast Hiroshima in an Asian perspective. In that respect I reflected the prevailing Japanese outlook on Hiroshima. In response to criticisms from Korea and the Philippines, however, I have since revised my views of Hiroshima. I have focused more on Japan's wars of aggression against Asian peoples, on understanding the atomic bombings of Hiroshima and Nagasaki as one result of those wars" (9). This means that while criticizing "the United States for dropping their bombs," the A-bomb victims also "hold the Japanese state responsible for their sufferings" (9). It is not wrong to blame the United States, but it would be wrong not also to blame Japanese militarism, especially militarism at the expense of those he now sees as his fellow Asians, or militarism as a historical formation shared by Japan *and* the United States. Note that it is not exclusively his individual exercise of reason or for that matter an individualistic detachment from his homeland that permits this new line of thought. It is also an enlarged sense of belonging. He has added to the circle of his informants; he has listened to people from much further away. Having stretched his sense of belonging to include his fellow Asians, he can now also stretch his blaming so as to aim at multiple targets, one of them his fellow Japanese, and thus to clarify, if also to complicate, what must be done in order to discourage further atrocities. From this perspective, neither Japan nor the US can be a villain in the simple sense. His reasoning, which now includes feedback from a wider circle than the residents of Hiroshima he initially consulted, even the most politicized of them, has taken him to national self-indictment, and also beyond it, in the direction of an attitude towards atrocity that is not yet representative of moral common sense in Japan or anywhere else.

The expansion of the circle of belonging, as it appears in Oe, is no more natural or inevitable than the opposite development, though it is the reverse that is taken for granted by liberal ideology. As we have seen, liberal ideology assumes that time will bring a breaking up of circles, as existing collectivities disperse into isolated individuals, none of whom can properly be held responsible for past atrocities or held to be deserving of reparation for past sufferings. That countermovement is real, and when circles of belonging do enlarge, it is most often over stiff resistance. "In general," Hersey writes, "survivors that day assisted only their relatives or immediate neighbors, for they could not comprehend of tolerate a wider circle of misery" (47). In one of the book's memorable vignettes, Mr. Tamimoto, the Lutheran minister, encounters a group of "wounded people lying at the edge of the river, already partly covered by the flooding tide. Mr. Tamimoto wanted to help them, but the priests [German Jesuits] were afraid that Father Schiffer would die if they didn't hurry, and they urged their ferryman along" (65). Mr. Tamimoto goes back quickly to try to rescue them (they end up drowning), but the point is made. This logic makes itself felt even in Auschwitz. In Delbo's *Auschwitz and After*, the Nazis make the women run, carrying earth for the garden by the entrance, with guards beating them from the sides of the column. The women of the French resistance will do almost anything to stay together: "The Jewish women, believing they are taking more of a beating, slip in between our striped dresses. We are sorry for them. Sorry on account of their attire. They have no aprons. They have been made to turn their coats backwards, buttoned in the back, so they could hold the earth . . . They fill us with pity but we do not want to be separated from each other. We protect one another. Each wishes to remain near a companion" (92).[3] "There are more and more Jewish women in our midst. With each loop, our group breaks apart. We succeed in staying together two by two. These pairs do not leave one another" (93). When the Nazis abandon the camp, in Primo Levi's *If This Is a Man*, the efforts of Levi and two fellow sick bay inmates to keep those around them alive quickly run into their limits: "Dozens of patients arrived, naked and wretched, from a hut threatened by fire: they asked for shelter. It was impossible to take them in. They insisted, begging and threatening in many languages. We had to barricade the door. They dragged themselves elsewhere" (187).[4] After all, so the reasoning goes, if we tried to let everyone in, there would be nothing left of the force that holds those inside together and protects them, or us, to the extent that protection is possible, from the atrocity that defines us. "Many invalids from other wards crowded around the door, but Charles's imposing stature held them back. Nobody, neither us nor them, thought that the inevitable promiscuity with our patients made it extremely dangerous to stay in our room, and that to fall ill of diphtheria in those conditions was more surely fatal than jumping off a fourth floor" (190–91). Levi does not quite say that the reason for not letting them in is the danger of infection.[5]

Zadie Smith: "But How Large Should This Circle Be?"

As a literary history, the present volume may have seemed to be pointing toward a triumphant apotheosis in which humanity unites against atrocity, which comes to be nameable and its perpetrators freely indictable, wherever and whoever they may be. If that is the expectation I have created, my conclusion, however provisional, will be unsatisfying. Like Hersey and Oe, I am struck by how uncertain our common sense about atrocity remains. Contemporary fiction, for example, does not offer much clarity even on the part of the victims of atrocity, let alone its perpetrators. In "Hysterical Realism," his much-discussed critique of Zadie Smith's debut novel *White Teeth* (2000), the critic James Wood offered an amusing parody in which one character "was born at the exact second that the bomb was dropped on Hiroshima." His point, roughly paraphrased, was that fiction should stop using atrocity to invest private lives with public significance. Private lives, private feelings, private relationships are rich and complicated enough, Wood argues, to justify treatment in their own right. They are what fiction is good at. Fiction is not good at doing Hiroshima (whatever that would mean) or making world-historical events seem connected to private lives. The novel does not possess the technical means of assimilating atrocity. It should give up trying.

In her short story "The Embassy of Cambodia" (2013), Smith seems to be offering a delayed response to Wood's keep-atrocity-out-of-fiction advice. What the appearance of the Embassy of Cambodia in the North London neighborhood of Willesden means, instantly, to its neighbors, is atrocity. "I doubt there is a man or woman among us . . . who—upon passing the Embassy of Cambodia for the first time—did not immediately think: 'genocide'" (89).[6] The protagonist of Smith's story is a young woman named Fatou who is from Ivory Coast; take the atrocity away, and hers is that familiar story of an immigrant seeking a more secure life in the metropolis. She is employed as a maid by a South Asian couple. She also passes the Embassy of Cambodia for the first time, and when she does, the story thinks of genocide. We are told the date of this first passage: the 6th of August. The date is then repeated. Readers will recall that August 6th is the anniversary of the dropping of the atomic bomb on Hiroshima. It is hard not to think that in "The Embassy of Cambodia," Smith is looking back over her shoulder at Wood's now somewhat distant polemic, engaging him in a sly debate about whether fiction must indeed be making a mistake if it tries to "do" Hiroshima-level atrocity, whatever that might mean. I asked her, by email, and she responded that she was not aware of any such intention at that time.

Looking backwards from the ending, "The Embassy of Cambodia" reads like the story of a bag lady. The last page shows us a young African woman sitting on a damp London pavement surrounded by plastic bags containing all her worldly belongings. She sits and waits while buses slow and then speed up again when they realize she's not flagging them down and while the people of Willesden, who don't know that her name is Fatou, wonder what she's doing there. The rest of the story tells us what Fatou *is* doing there. Her middle-class South Asian employers speak to and about her in an unabashedly racist way ("'Sometimes she heard her name used as a term of abuse between them. 'You're as black as Fatou.' Or 'You're as stupid as Fatou'" [90]). Her employers hide her passport and retain her wages to cover the supposed cost of "the food and water . . . she would require during her stay" (90). (The words "and water" should alert the reader if the reader were not already alerted). She saves the life of one of the children, who is choking on a marble, and the next day is fired because the parents can't look her in the eye. That's why she's sitting on the pavement with her plastic bags, waiting for the friend who has offered her temporary shelter and being wondered at by the people of Willesden. Smith repeats the phrase "we the people of Willesden," thereby invoking questions of what forming a more perfect union would entail, a union that will now have to exist on a more than national scale. And she links these political questions to the task of fiction as it has often been conceived: negotiating who and what there is room for in "we the people."

As chronicler of the neighborhood, Smith seems to be wondering what if anything her fiction can accomplish by reflecting on atrocity, which is not a neighborhood event. The story's first sentences acknowledge the difficulty. "Who would expect the Embassy of Cambodia? Nobody. Nobody could have expected it, or be expecting it. It's a surprise to us all. The Embassy of Cambodia!" These lines are a wink and a nod to Monty Python's Flying Circus: "Nobody expects the Spanish Inquisition!" The famous and often parodied Monty Python skit (more evidence that parody is on Smith's mind) is of course a serious joke on how unexpected it feels, as you are delivering a message or sewing on a sofa, to be intruded upon by uniformed emissaries of violence from a past historical period and another country. That is one thing Smith's story is about: the incongruousness of atrocity, what it feels like to try to assimilate the knowledge of atrocity, especially atrocity that has happened elsewhere, while going about one's daily business here and now. But Smith also seems to want to say that this incongruousness is unequally divided between the Global North and the Global South. Fatou is not passionately in love with her Nigerian friend Andrew, with whom she will have to cohabit because of her sudden firing and to whom (in a commentary on the marriage plot) the story hints she may well end up married. But the thing she likes best about him is his comment about the difference between African and European reactions to violent death. To Africans, violent death *is* ordinary. To Europeans, it's shocking, and they respond more emotionally. As Andrew puts it, "A tap runs fast the first time you switch it on" (95). It's also a point about fictionalized versions of atrocity: they seem more likely to be taken as excessive by readers who are more secure, less accustomed to mass suffering.

Before being fired and left homeless and penniless, Fatou had also been raped by a Russian guest at the hotel in Ghana where she was working. But she de-dramatizes her own experience of victimhood—perhaps too much so, or more than she probably would if she possessed more cultural capital. Neither the firing nor the rape seems to make her see herself as a victim. Here is that moral once again: victimhood requires empowerment. For her, as for most of us, atrocities are things that happen to other people. Still, she is unusually curious about the victimhood of others. She wants to see her life in comparative context; more precisely, she wants to see the suffering of her fellow Africans in relation to the historical record of atrocities elsewhere. She starts a lengthy conversation with Andrew on the subject of the Holocaust. "But more people died in Rwanda," she says, "And nobody speaks about that!" Andrew agrees, "millions and millions. They hide the true numbers." Fatou suggests that "we" (meaning the Africans) "were born to suffer more than all the rest." She insists: "Chinese people have never been slaves. They are always protected from the worst." Andrew has an answer to this: "What about Hiroshima?" (92). Unlike her author, Fatou doesn't know what happened on August 6th, the day she first noticed the embassy of Cambodia on the high street. She says, "a big wave," confusing Hiroshima with the much more recent and much less deadly Fukushima tsunami and reactor meltdown. Andrew corrects her: "'No, man! Big Bomb. Biggest bomb in the world, made by the USA, of course. They killed five million people in *one second*. You think because your eyes are like this'—he tugged the skin at both temples—'you're always protected? Think again'"(92). There is a lot to correct in Andrew's corrections. But if the conversation is funny, it is uneasily so.[7] It's hard to imagine that Smith wants no more than to entertain the largely secure, largely prosperous readers of the *New*

Yorker, where this story first appeared, encouraging them to feel comfortably superior to these uneducated Africans who don't know the difference between the Chinese and the Japanese.[8]

The humor here takes us back to "Nobody Expects the Spanish Inquisition."[9] For its victims, the Spanish Inquisition was not a joke, but the Pythons shift our attention from its threat to its agents, who are not actually very threatening. They tell us that they obtain obedience by using the weapons of surprise, fear, ruthless efficiency, and so on but don't seem to be able to remember their lines. It's hard to inspire fear when you are obliged to do the grand entrance over again in order to get your lines right. Andrew and Fatou are not potential inquisitors, of course, but there is an analogy nonetheless: if it were said in a different tone of voice or perhaps by white people, much of what is said in their conversation about the Jews and the Chinese might be described, like the Spanish Inquisition, as racist. In the context of this story, it's not a trivial point. If this talk can indeed be described as racism, however, the racism, like the inquisitors, is bumbling—not empowered. And it's in that humorously backhanded way that the story can show that racism is not the prerogative of white people. To judge from its plot, centered on the truly vicious racism of Fatou's employers, who are South Asian and middle class, the idea that anyone of any race can be racist is arguably at or near the center of the story. It's also a version of the argument that can be extracted from the story's title. The Cambodian genocide was of course an instance of Asians massacring their fellow Asians, especially (as Smith reminds us) those fellow Asians who wore glasses.

With some moderately strenuous acrobatics, postcolonial scholars could no doubt find Europeans (and the American bombing during the Vietnam War) at least indirectly responsible for the Cambodian genocide. Smith seems more drawn, however, to the quiet indifference Andrew and Fatou display to the legacy of European colonialism, and this even though European colonialism would seem quite relevant to their own subordinate positions in London and might also have been of help in explaining underlying reasons for the African-on-African violence of the Rwandan genocide. For them and for the story, colonialism seems relegated to ancient history. Something similar is happening, I have tried to suggest, in the realm of educated common sense. Geographical cosmopolitanism has brought in its wake a temporal cosmopolitanism, and with it a need to consider, morally and politically, even *more* ancient history—atrocities going back as far as historians can go. As, with the passing of time, the model of core and periphery, European colonizer and non-European colonized, has become a less reliable guide, or a guide to less of the totality of culture and suffering, we are forced to engage in the premodern period with multiple models of plunder and tribute, and in the modern period with class (which distinguishes Fatou from her employers) as well as race as characteristic modern agents of plunder and tribute, drawing lines between the homeless and the housed and reliably producing a population of bag ladies. Fatou's life, Zadie Smith's childhood (the moment of the Cambodian genocide) and the Spanish Inquisition all take meaning from each other if viewed in a single frame.

As a glimpse into what Smith sees replacing the core-periphery model, Fatou's conversation with Andrew at the café repays closer attention. The conversation is about the comparing of atrocities, but it is also about cosmopolitanism as a way of registering the existence of atrocities. Fatou insists that the Africans have "more pain" than others, like the Chinese. Andrew mentions Hiroshima, confusing the Chinese with the Japanese. He then corrects Fatou, who has confused Hiroshima with Fukushima, by informing her that Hiroshima was the "biggest bomb in the world" and that it killed "five million people in *one second*." In other words, Asians have suffered a lot too. He then tries to clinch his argument: "Tell me, why would God choose us especially for suffering when we, above all others, praise his name. Africa is the fastest-growing Christian continent!" (92). To this Fatou responds, "It's not him . . . It's the Devil" (93).[10] For her the Devil is both the cause of atrocity and, logically enough, the cause of the racism that gets her fired: "Anyone could see the Devil had climbed inside Mrs. Derawal. He was lighting her up with perfect fury" (98). Whether Fatou's devil-based theory of atrocity is heretical or orthodox, in the story it stands as a rejection of Andrew's anti-cosmopolitan version of Christianity, which he has just laid out for her. "The Jews cry for the Jews," Andrew says. "The Russians cry for the Russians. We cry for Africa, because we are Africans . . . Only God cries for us all, because we are *all* his children" (92). I have omitted Andrew's good-humored qualification, which follows "because we are Africans": yes, he and Fatou are both Africans, but "if Nigeria plays Ivory Coast and we beat you into the ground, I'm laughing, man! I can't lie. I'm celebrating! Stomp! Stomp!" (92). Andrew is a kind and tolerant man; his patriotic commitment to Nigeria takes the unimpeachable form of wanting to expose the financial corruption of its government. And yet "Stomp! Stomp!" is more than a humorous throwaway. Taken out of the realm of sports, it stands as evidence against his anti-cosmopolitanism. He believes that because "only God cries for us all" it's only right that we ourselves should cry exclusively for our own nation or (the case of the Asians and Africans, and perhaps the Jews) our own race. But this thought ends in a triumphant "Stomp! Stomp!"—an ominous, violence-threatening tightening of the circle of "we the people." What comes from each race or nation crying and caring for its own is the threat of ultimate violence. The exclusivity of crying and caring is made possible by the belief that there is a God who cares for us all. If there is a God who cares for us all, we don't have to care so much for each other, or for atrocities that have happened far away. It's a logic worthy of a clever Devil. In any case, so tight a circle of crying and caring would likely not have room for Fatou, sitting on the wet pavement. But in the ending, Smith's Willesden does make room in the circle for her. "Many of us walked past her that afternoon, or spotted her as we rode the bus, or through the windscreens of our cars, or from our balconies. Naturally, we wondered what this girl was doing, sitting on damp pavement in the middle of the day. We worried for her" (98).

Fatou's curiosity, we are told, is limited. Smith's narrator, speaking for "we, the people of Willesden," expresses sympathy with its limitations: "The fact is if we followed the history of every little country in the world—in its dramatic as well as its quiet times—we would have no space left in which to live our own lives or to apply ourselves to our necessary tasks, never mind occasional pleasures, like swimming. Surely there is something to be said for drawing a circle around our attention and remaining within that circle. But how large should this circle be?" (91).[11] It's a concession to the Wood critique, but also a questioning of pragmatic exclusiveness as a literary or a moral principle. How large *should* the circle be? How large has it become? Is the reader ready to exclude the victims of atrocity, perhaps including Fatou? And if Fatou cannot be excluded, relatable as she is, will she be included only as an object of worry? What about her role as a paradigmatic vehicle of cosmopolitan curiosity, someone who demands to set her own life in the context of atrocities committed in other times and places? The implication of the ending is that room must be made in "we, the people of Willesden" not just for Fatou as a victim—a status that she rejects—but also for the project of knowledge for which she stands, which sets no limits on atrocity, spatial or temporal.

9/11 Novels

How representative is Zadie Smith? On the evidence of the novels that followed the attacks of September 11, 2001, one might say that, unlike Smith, most novelists *have* given up on trying to assimilate atrocity. (9/11 was an atrocity despite the fact that, taken in context, it was provoked in large part by US policy in the Middle East.) If there is a pattern in the first generation of 9/11 novels, that pattern goes something like this: novelists decide that, seen from the perspective of the attack on the World Trade Center and the innocent lives lost there and elsewhere on September 11, 2001, history at the global scale is chaotic and meaningless. But if the world outside is meaningless, meaning is still to be found inside, in intimacy, behind the door of the family home. In Claire Messud's *The Emperor's Children* (2006), for example, 9/11 interrupts like a moralizing deus ex machina, determined that the events should end in a return to order: an extramarital affair is broken up, an ambitious usurper has his projects foiled, a woman is reunited with her mother.[12] Only one strand of the plot goes the other way: an uncomfortable young man, presumed killed in the towers, is enabled to disappear from his family without leaving a trace. In William Gibson's *Pattern Recognition* (2003), 9/11 provides the needed ethico-emotional excuse for the disappearance of a family member who was missing anyway. Because of the falling towers, both the absent father and the putatively villainous father-surrogate can finally be forgiven.[13] In Joseph O'Neill's *Netherland* (2008), husband and wife split up over their different reactions to 9/11 and to the American government's reactions to it. She says: "Our personal feelings don't come into the picture. There are forces out there" (98). He says he is "a political-ethical idiot" and is clearly pleased to say so; he believes that only personal relations matter. His view wins out, and the couple is reunited.[14] Don DeLillo's *Falling Man* (2007) takes 9/11 as an occasion to send his protagonist home to his estranged wife and child. When the word *world* comes up in *Falling Man*, it's often to indicate that ambitions are being scaled back, life-complicating desires are being abandoned. "Keith used to want more of the world than there was time and means to acquire. He didn't want this anymore, whatever it was he'd wanted" (128).[15] "This was the world now," DeLillo writes. In "a time and space of falling ash and near night," (3) the point seems to be that the novel's field of vision has contracted, not expanded. When the street becomes a world, as the novel's first sentence declares it has, perhaps we can see less rather than more of the world outside our borders and our causal relations to it. Seeing less may even be the goal we strive for. At one point *Falling Man* makes an explicit argument *against* seeing the street as the world. Boldly reconstructing the perspective of one of the hijackers, a perspective that sounds rather like his own, DeLillo bestows on him the ability and impulse to see through the street to the structures of world power behind it. "These people jogging in the park, world domination. These old men who sit in beach chairs, veined white bodies and baseball caps, they control our world" (173). The ability to glimpse "world domination" behind old men in beach chairs is essential if one is to believe that seemingly random violence at any point will in fact injure the enemy as an organic whole. (Of course, the legitimacy of random violence is not the only conclusion one might draw from such global perceptions. And the terrorist shares other perceptions with mainstream common sense.[16]) Better, then, to reject wholeness in favor of the fragmentary. Better for the eye to stop at the veined white bodies and the baseball caps, the things in themselves, cherishing them in their overlooked particularity rather than feeling obliged to pass on to the inhuman structures that may or may not link them together. By this logic, worldliness is not an unambiguous ethical good. Perhaps the novel would be better off doing what the protagonist and his wife do late in *Falling Man*: "falling out of the world" (212).

Readers of American fiction should not be surprised by this anti-worldly moral. In Pynchon's visionary *Gravity's Rainbow* (1973), readers had already become accustomed to the idea that even World War II, the very paradigm of just war, was "a meaningless event" (231).[17] The same was true of less farsighted texts. Rituals of retreat from public meaninglessness to a private or familial zone, whether fully comfortable or (more likely) not, make up an unbroken tradition in the novel before and since 9/11. And often these celebrations of the private are tied to public events that, like 9/11, have some claim to the status of national trauma: the Vietnam War, the Soviet atom bomb test at the beginning of DeLillo's *Underworld* (1997), and the bursting of the dot-com bubble in the late 1990s, to which the title of Jonathan Franzen's *The Corrections* (2001) refers. The sentiment that Franzen puts into the mind of his patriarch, another falling man, as he goes over the side of a cruise ship—"There was no solid thing to reach for but your children" (336)—does something less than justice to the argument of Franzen's novel, but it will certainly stand for many other withdrawals from worldliness.[18]

One way to rationalize such withdrawals is to decide that, whatever one thinks of the righteousness and coherence of American society, the world outside America's borders is still more incomprehensible, if entertainingly so. *Absurdistan,* the title of a novel by Gary Shteyngart (2006), is not a bad term for the generic place where, from the perspective of the American novel, the foreign *is* the absurd, or an inevitable object of satire—which is not to say that for Shteyngart the US lacks its own targets of satire. Another possible term, from DeLillo's *Underworld* (1997), would be "The Museum of the Misshapens." It is there that US visitors can inspect the effects of radioactive testing and waste on two generations of Russian children.[19] To a large extent, the novelistic treatment of historical suffering outside America's borders has resembled visits to such a museum—mercifully short visits. Between comic entertainment at the expense of foreign absurdities and the representation of foreign history as extreme suffering, the latter may sound as if it offers a more earnest educational payoff. But for the most part it too is subject to generic rules that severely limit the instruction it can deliver about the world and America's place in it. One such rule is that history abroad is atrocity, and atrocity abroad can then serve as the motivating event behind a "coming to America" story. In Bharati Mukherjee's *Jasmine* (1989), as in many other narratives of heroic American acculturation, the protagonist's country of origin—here, India—is vividly presented as a place of inscrutable and incurable ethnic violence. Her fiancé is assassinated in a bombing, thus underlining the ineligibility of her homeland as a place to live and reproduce.[20] The more painful the history, the more the protagonist is justified in leaving her home behind and coming to America. America, despite all the nasty obstacles it puts in the way of the would-be immigrant, cannot equal the nastiness of such a history. Thus it can only figure as redemptive.[21] In Junot Diaz's *The Brief Wondrous Life of Oscar Wao* (2007), the prolepsis-rich abominations of the Trujillo dictatorship in effect take over large sections of a novel that initially seems to be about present-day Dominican Americans. The premise is that only this buried history, which explains the family's presence in America, can make sense of the twisted and passionate lives of the younger generation.[22] But it is those American lives, not an ongoing life in the Dominican Republic, that must be made sense of. In Jeffrey Eugenides's *Middlesex* (2002), the Megali Katastrophe of 1922, discussed in the previous chapter, is again represented at some length (and in flagrant imitation of the Amritsar Massacre in Salman Rushdie's *Midnight's Children*). But Eugenides, unlike Rushdie, allows the initial atrocity to dissipate gently into another coming-to-America narrative. It will have grave consequences for the main character's sexual identity, but they too dissolve eventually into the (relative) happiness of perpetual self-fashioning. Unlike the trauma itself, the *scene* of the trauma, that is, the scene of atrocity, disappears.[23]

A similar structure shapes the treatment of the Holocaust in Michael Chabon's *The Amazing Adventures of Kavalier and Clay* (2000). The family left behind in Hitler's Europe motivates attempts at transnational rescue, but also attempts at upward mobility. One might say that upward mobility in the US is legitimated as a form of rescue directed at the victims of atrocity abroad. The protagonists' success depends on inventing a new comic book super hero. The secret of a new super hero is the proper motivation: "We need to figure out what is the why" (84).[24] The "why" for the super hero, as for Kavalier, is what Hitler is doing to the Jews. Structurally speaking, then, the Holocaust figures as the secret of an immigrant's upward mobility. The same point could be made about Dave Eggers's *What Is the What* (2006), the testimony of a boy who survives the ethnic cleansing in Sudan's Darfur region.[25] Here the proportions are very different—much of the novel centers on trying to understand the complexity of African events. Non-American suffering and injustice are better balanced by attention to the domestic varieties of each. But the same underlying schema, however inflected with irony, remains visible. Step one: atrocity in a foreign country. Step two: escape to relative safety in the metropolis. This may represent personal progress, but it does not suggest anything like progress in the realm of collective vision.

In world literature after 1965, there is of course a great deal of atrocity description, and even a fair amount of national self-indictment. We have already seen this in Haruki Murakami's *The Wind-Up Bird Chronicle*. Yambo Ouologuem's *Bound to Violence*, published in French in 1968, begins the violent phantasmagoria of the precolonial Empire of Nakem in the year 1202: "In that age of feudalism, large communities of slaves celebrated the justice of their overlords by forced labor and by looking on inert as multitudes of their brothers, smeared with the blood of butchered children and of disemboweled expectant mothers, were immured alive . . . That is what happened at Tillabéri-Bentia, at Granta, at Grosso, at Gagol-Gosso, and in many places mentioned in the *Tarik Al-Fetach* and the *Tarik al-Sudan* of the Arab historians" (4). "But there is nothing unusual in this story: many others relate how terror enslaved populations and stifled every attempt at rebellion throughout the Empire" (5).[26] Amitav Ghosh's *The Hungry Tide* (2004) turns on the Marichjhapi Massacre of Hindu Dalit refugees in 1979.[27] Boubacar Boris Diop's *Murambi, The Book of Bones* (2006), which deals with the Rwandan genocide of 1994, cannot strictly speaking be described as national self-indictment—Diop is Senegalese, not Rwandan—but the plot turns on the discovery that one of the killers is a family member; the novel insists on behalf of Africa and the rest of the world that Rwandans take their share of responsibility for the mass killing.[28] It is worth speculating that novelists from the Global South, taking a step beyond the anti-imperialism that Fredric Jameson called "national allegory,"[29] have been more ambitious than their more private, self-involved counterparts in the Global North in this respect as well: they have produced a richer crop of national indictments, indictments both of the self and of the other.

Is War More Democratic?

In *Total Mobilization: World War II and American Literature*, Roy Scranton takes a closer look at one of the most recognized American classics of anti-war fiction, Joseph Heller's *Catch-22* (1961).[30] The moral center of that novel is the death of Snowden, a crewman on the plane where Yossarian serves as bombardier. It's Snowden's suffering, his guts spilling out from under his flak jacket as he whimpers in agony, that triggers Yossarian's decision not to fly any more missions. But for all its power, this scenario is morally off kilter. There is no atrocity here. As Scranton observes, there is no room in Yossarian's mind for the victims of the bombs his plane is dropping.[31] Snowden may be a victim, but he is also a killer. He is flying on a plane full of killers. Yet it is as victims—as the *sole* victims—that those killers saw themselves, and were seen by the people at home. Scanning novels and films of the postwar period, Scranton generalizes: "Creating sympathy with men responsible for murdering thousands of unarmed civilians is one of the central effects of much canonical American literature of World War II" (48). It could do so in part because of a peculiarity of bombing from the air: while eliminating the traditional associations linking war to looting and sexual violence, it also eliminated the seemingly unavoidable association with belligerence. It became plausible to think of air crews merely as targets of the aggression of others, putting themselves at risk—as they certainly did—but not themselves committing acts of violence. Here the child returns to the representation of atrocity, this time cast in another role. It is as innocent children that postwar literature tends to treat the bomber crews. "To help underline their innocence, Jarrell portrays the men of the 'Eighth Air Force' as children—playing with a puppy, 'as puppies,' playing games, goofing off, totally lacking any adult sexuality or aggression . . . Characterizing American soldiers as innocent children is a common enough trope. Paul Fussell and Kurt Vonnegut both called World War II a children's crusade" (58). In the case of the bomber crews, sitting helplessly in a thin metal shell exposed to fighters and flak, the infantilization seems almost overdetermined.

Scranton is right that "no agent of violence can be deemed innocent or faultless, even if that agent has been drafted against his or her will to fight in a war ultimately considered just. We must understand the soldier first, foremost, and always as an agent of state power . . . Soldiers are the state's killers" (62). But his theory of how the bomber crews serve as "scapegoats . . . for wartime atrocities" (46) also complicates the very idea of indictment for atrocity. It assumes not merely that the crews were taking risks that the people back home did not want to take themselves, and thus were scapegoats in that sense, but also that they made a moral sacrifice by committing violence of which the people back home *disapproved*. (Note that the idea of the killing of enemy civilians as a moral sacrifice made on behalf of the nation also pervades the subjectivity of the troops in Ishikawa's *Soldiers Alive*.) "A community projects its collective blood guilt onto the soldier it sent to do its killing," Scranton writes, "then reinterprets that projection as both a judgment against the soldier and a judgment against itself for having victimized the soldier . . . Yet by being transformed thus from the agent of collective violence into its blameless victim, the soldier is purified of his own blood guilt and takes the place of the original victim of violence, who has by this substitution effectively been erased" (42).[32] For Scranton, this all seems part of the process by which atrocity itself is erased. The erasure is a by-product of national mythmaking. "The bombers who kill civilians in foreign cities threaten our demand for goodness in our heroes," as Daniel Swift puts it (42).[33] But the scapegoating also seems to be *needed* (so one supposes) because society felt guilty for the murder of civilians. If society in the 1940s was indeed dealing with guilt about the murder of German civilians, which is to say that it acknowledged, however backhandedly, that the killing of civilians was wrong, then that guilt would mark a notable coordinate in moral history and would have to affect history's subsequent judgment of the bombing.

Were there pertinent moral standards in place? Technically, there was no law against the bombing of civilians, and the Roman adage applied: no crime and no punishment in the absence of a law. But as A. C. Grayling notes, Chamberlain "had given an assurance two days before the outbreak of war, that Britain would not bomb civilians" (24).[34] Military historians like Tami Davis Biddle and Richard Overy offer considerable evidence that, if the bomb crews in the air were oblivious to the people on the ground, the same was not entirely true for public opinion, especially in the UK.[35] Biddle mentions the desire of Churchill's government to avoid "stirring public discomfort" (219), including "religious and humanitarian opinion" (221). As the results of the February 1945 raids on Dresden "became known in Britain, questions were raised about the means and ends of the strategic bombing campaign . . . Was the raid, which took such a heavy toll on noncombatants, really warranted, especially at what was clearly a late stage of the war?" (256). The word *terror* was used; Churchill himself questioned the bombing of German cities "simply for the sake of increasing the terror" (256). As a historian, Churchill was sufficiently worried about history's judgment to omit what he could; "the entire episode of Dresden is missing from his history of the Second World War" (215). Given the attention the issue received in Parliament and in the British press, it seems hard to imagine that American crews based in Britain had absolutely no inkling. Whether it is the government or the historians who address the issue, the moment of arrival at decisive awareness is forever being declared and then recalculated. "Not until Jim Goodson, Max Woolley and Jim McCubbin were shot down," Gerald Astor writes in *The Mighty Eighth*, "and saw not only the carnage but personally came under the hammer of bombs dropped in their vicinity or experienced fighters strafing their trains did they come to have feelings about the effect of their efforts" (458).[36] "By the time of Dresden and probably much earlier, the airmen knew their destruction was not limited to strategic targets" (419). One pilot confesses freely: "The aiming point was the center of Berlin and I don't think this was bombing a military target. But I personally felt no remorse. They brought Hitler to power and supported him and sealed their fate" (420). Another pilot, flying through dense clouds, unsure whether the city below was in Germany or Switzerland, records his crew's very tentative scruples: "We didn't drop our bombs for our navigator had very strong reservations" (424). It is good that reservations are recorded. It is less good that, if the city had been in Germany, those reservations would seemingly have been superfluous.

Unlike the Royal Air Force, which flew night missions with little visibility and knew very well from the outset that it was killing civilians, the Eighth Air Force, to which my father's 305th Bomb Group belonged, flew in the daytime and, especially with the help of the new Norden bombsight, was supposed to be able to see what it was bombing.[37] My father told me that he was told he was bombing only military and industrial targets, and to a remarkable extent that turns out to be true, at least as a matter of contrast with the RAF, at least initially. That was to change radically when US bombers (not the Eighth Air Force) attacked Japan. But the line had become blurred before then, and perhaps well before then. In February 1945, when my father was flying his first missions, a new directive placed "Berlin, Leipzig, and Dresden on the target priority list just below oil" (254).[38] To take cities as targets was to take civilians as targets. "On February 17 an Associated Press war correspondent had issued a dispatch (which had inexplicably cleared the censors) stating that the Allied air chiefs "had made the long-awaited decision to adopt a deliberate terror bombing of German population centres as a ruthless expedient to hastening Hitler's doom" (258).

> Members of the American press, who generally took a pro-air power stance and seemed to be enamored of the "precision bombing" image, rarely challenged the official USAAF interpretation of events, even as their stories described American bomb damage in terms of acres or square miles destroyed . . . During the war even liberal and religious journals of opinion were, generally, either supportive of the of or silent on American strategic bombing. *The New Republic*, for instance, largely dodged the issue of bombing from 1943 to 1945 . . . In April 1943 the journal did, however, run a short news brief pointing out that two respected British papers (*The New States-*

> *man* and *The Tribune*) had printed stories indicating that American bombing was killing innocent civilians. Disinclined to give credence to the British view, which conflicted with their own interpretation of events, the editors suggested that the newspapers had been "misled." (258)

Was it possible to take a critical perspective on the bombing of civilians at that time and place? Yes, it was. The months during which my father was flying his missions were also months of "public scrutiny."[39] On the wall of my office, above the framed list of my father's missions and a photo of his B-17 in the air, taken by his wingman and sent to me after his death, there is evidence of the only moment of macho posturing I can remember from my father's war stories: a bayonet in its scabbard. If he were ever shot down, he said, and they came for him, this is what would be waiting for them: six inches of cold steel. The line was delivered with a smile, but it suggests an awareness that there were people on the ground who were seriously displeased that bombs were being dropped on them. Several of Gerald Astor's stories feature airmen who, having bailed out, are attacked by "angry civilians" (432) and are saved from their clutches by German soldiers. Astor does not wonder why the civilians were so angry. According to Jörg Friedrich, "Ten days before the first V1 was fired, Goebbels recommended that the German take reprisal into their own hands . . . Parents of children who had been shot killed the pilots who had performed emergency landings or bailed out. 'Police and Wehrmacht could hardly intervene against the German people when they give child murderers what they deserve.' The party chancellor instructed the gauleiters not to obstruct the 'people's justice against Anglo-American murderers.' The license to lynch encompassed strafers and bomber pilots to the same degree" (433).[40] "More than one hundred pilots were lynched in the last year of the war," Friedrich goes on, "sometimes in complicity with Wehrmacht institutions, and sometimes police and soldiers saved the prisoners from such raging vengeance" (433–34). He documents multiple examples of both lynchings and rescues. "The peak of popular lynching occurred in March 1945, with thirty-seven killings" (310). It was a month when my father flew seven missions. The bayonet story suggests that awareness of the lynchings may have worked its way back to base.

According to Friedrich, prisoners of war like Vonnegut and William Spanos, also in Dresden during that bombing, as well as foreign workers, had mixed reactions to the bombing: "In Düsseldorf and Duisberg prisoners impulsively offered their services. 'This is not war anymore, it is murder.' Others said, 'Our friends are here!'" (430). Meaning, apparently, that the bombers were their friends. The point is not just that German morale was not broken, as all authorities seem to agree. It is that no useful conclusions were drawn by those on the ground at all. Fatalism was one response. The idea of a "community of fate" (*Schicksalsgemeinschaft*), beloved by the Nazis, seems to have implied that "the final struggles would test their racial qualities to extremes," as in the mentality "victory or death" (308).[41] But as in Hiroshima, fatalism also took other forms: "Most of the home intelligence reports over the last year of the war show that ordinary Germans felt themselves to be trapped between a rock and a hard place" (308). They were more afraid of the advancing Russian troops they had not yet seen than of the bombings they had. According to Nossack, Germans saw the enemy as "an instrument of unknowable forces that sought to annihilate us" (quoted by Overy, 311). As in Hiroshima, the view from below does not seem to have produced any corrective to the reflex nationalism on both sides. The victims too get stuck at "us versus them" as the only clarity in an otherwise incomprehensible universe. And if so, then the perpetrators can again conclude (as the Athenians perhaps concluded from the nonanswer they got from the Melians) that the victims would have done the same to them, had they the opportunity. And in that case, progress toward a universalistic judgment of atrocity would be too much to expect.

In the twenty-first century, how far has American common sense come about the bombing? Writing in 2001, Stephen E. Ambrose puts the accusation in the mouths of "critics of the AAF," speaking up after the war was over (247), and he uses the literary device of free indirect discourse so that the reader can't quite tell where he himself stands: "It would have avoided the worst accusation of all, that in World War II the United States used a method of making war that killed hundreds of thousands of civilians and destroyed uncountable historic buildings, factories, and residences, without doing much of anything to win the war while creating the worst legacy of the war, made much more frightful with the development of the atomic bomb and the beginning of the Cold War—making civilians into targets" (247).[42] The next sentence is no longer "would have" avoided the accusation, but a simple declarative, implicitly accepting that accusation: "Perhaps 305,000 German were killed in the bombings, another 780,000 seriously injured" (247).[43] Scranton quotes Howard Zinn, writing in 2004, "World War II is not simply and purely a 'good war.' It was accompanied by too many atrocities on our side—too many bombings of civilian populations. There were too many betrayals of the principles for which the war was supposed to have been fought" (242).[44] A. C. Grayling, writing in 2006, quotes an official Air Force document: "The official US Air Force doctrine suggests that the morale of the civilian population may, in itself, legitimately be targeted since the weakening of the will to fight would offer a miliary advantage" (275).[45] One suspects that the default setting in the US remains American righteousness, but if so, it is a somewhat troubled righteousness. The pilot of the Steven Spielberg/Tom Hanks series "Masters of the Air," which dropped on January 26, 2024, centers on a first mission that lays out what looks like the controlling moral framework for the Eighth Air Force's bombing campaign. The target of the mission is the submarine pens at Bremen—a strictly military target. The submarines, the pilots are told, are sinking merchant ships bringing supplies that are necessary to keep the war going. An airtight argument, and one bearing a certain resonance with 2024: what could be wrong with protecting global commerce? When the planes get over the target, however, they find it obscured by heavy clouds. What to do? The squadron commander announces that they are not going to drop their bombs if they can't see their target. The mission has already lost three planes, but it is scrubbed. Implicit here, but not articulated: OK, this is Germany, but we don't just drop bombs on Germany. We'll drop them in the Channel on the way home. They will be wasted, but better to waste them than to hit innocent civilians. Without any mention of civilians, there has been a quiet attempt to refute moral arguments against the killing of civilians. Which is to say that there has been a muted acknowledgment that those arguments are felt to be there and pressing.[46]

This book began with a sense that a better narrative is possible. Alexander Kluge was a child when Halberstadt was bombed on April 8, 1945, but in *Air Raid* he does not share his childhood experience. He does not give a first-person account; he does not talk about what his family went through. Nor does he seem to trust the testimony of his fellow victims. The closest thing to victimhood he offers is the experience of a young mother named Gerda Baethe, a primary-school teacher who has been "conscripted" (he says) "as a munitions worker." She suddenly hears the waves of bombers coming overhead and hears and feels the bombs dropping around her house and must decide what to do to protect her three children, aged nine, seven, and five. Calling the section "Strategy from Below," Kluge frames it in terms of agency—an agency that seems entirely absent. He says, "There was no time." There is no time for Gerda to do more than pick up a piece of tin guttering and a shovel, hoping to use them to protect her children from the flames. The flames are everywhere. It gets very hot. The children are crying. Under the circumstances, what can "strategy from below" possibly mean? It can only mean an impossible expansion of time, beginning with a movement *back* in time. Kluge writes: "In order to open up a strategic perspective, such as on 8 April, Gerda Baethe, 'well toasted,' especially during the night, when the heat was at its worst, in her shelter wished to have, then since 1918, 70,000 teachers, all like her, would have had to teach hard for 20 years in each of the countries involved in the First World War; but also at the national level—pressure on press, government; then the young people educated in this way would have been able to seize the reins or sceptre" (000).[47]

Kluge insists, as if responding to Thucydides, that the operative question is not what is to be suffered, but what is to be done. Gerda is in a situation where there are no good options. You might say that she has no agency at all—nothing meaningful to choose that will make a difference to her ability to shield her children as the bombs fall around them. But Kluge refuses to conclude, with the Athenians on Melos, that Gerda and her children are the weak, so they will simply suffer what they must suffer. And they will suffer, of course. Strategy from below is real, but it is in the conditional. It exists in the past, which is to say that the past exists as a significant site of agency that *would have* made a difference. Since 1918, 70,000 teachers like Gerda "*would have had* to teach hard." And Gerda then translates this past, suddenly opened up to her, as an imperative for the future: "Gerda swore to herself in those moments of time shortage," especially during the "respite of ten minutes" between the third and fourth wave of the bombers, "that in future she wanted to lay the foundations of" an "organization" that would teach about the past in order to stop such things from happening in the future—a future that is now, with the fires burning around her children, her own present. Kluge writes: "Eight hundred years of strategy from below would then shatter eight hundred past years of strategy from above, not with a length of gutter, not with a shovel and not by mere wishing and waiting" (33).

Eight hundred years. The implication seems to be that in a situation in which "there is no time," a situation of ultimate urgency, one thing that is needed is much more time. Going back in time, in an impossible past conditional, so as to have done something that has not in fact been done. (This is a version of the much-noticed moment in *Slaughterhouse-Five* when Vonnegut runs a film of World War II bombardment in reverse.) Kluge is also going back in time in an entirely practicable fashion so as to see a shape in history that cannot be visible in the moment and to see the bombing within that history. The circle must be expanded in time as well as in space. It's a version of what was suggested above about the ancient rhetorical trope of prolepsis: we cannot understand atrocity if we live only in the present. In order to understand atrocity, we have to live and feel beyond our present, beyond our own little lifetime. "Eight hundred years"—what happened eight hundred years ago? It seems plausible, especially thinking back on my time-traveling conversation with him in the hotel lobby, that Kluge is reaching all the way back to the period of the Crusades—number 30 on Matthew White's list of the world's one hundred worst atrocities, with over three million dead. If so, Kluge would be thinking of atrocities that were committed by the Germans themselves, against Europeans as well as non-Europeans, well before there were airplanes or drones. And he would be choosing to think of them even as he himself and his family and their neighbors are being bombed.

It seems worth adding here that, at a smaller scale, this is the same principle that is at work when Primo Levi chooses to step outside the self-imposed austerity of his writing. Levi omits the gas chambers because he didn't see them with his own eyes; he almost always restricts himself to the here and now. His few proleptic forays into the future, however unstressed, are therefore noticeable. "At that time I had not yet been taught the doctrine I was later to learn so hurriedly in the Lager: that man is bound to pursue his own ends by all possible means, while he who errs but once pays dearly" (3–4).[48] On the train from Italy to Auschwitz, he again jumps forward: "Among the forty-five people in my wagon only four saw their homes again; and it was by far the most fortunate wagon" (9). Today, he says, "we know that of our convoy no more than ninety-six men and twenty-nine women entered the respective camps of Monowitz-Buna and Birkenau, and that of all the others, more than five hundred in number, not one was living two days later" (11–12). These are facts that he could not have known until later, when he had survived, when he was back in Italy. Such statistics are an almost imperceptible form of prolepsis, a stretching of time to make room for a perception or judgment that would otherwise be impossible.[49] As time stretches, so do the limits of the communities to which we belong and the responsibilities that go with belonging to them. It is hard to imagine that Kluge could have achieved his moral generosity without feeling that he belonged, for better or worse, to a national history that went back a long way and entangled him in more violence than his childhood had given him the time for.

It is perhaps in the same spirit that Jörg Friedrich's account of the bombing of Halberstadt pauses, before the bombs fall, to sketch out some of the city's early history, which it presents as "carved into the beams of the buildings—combustible material" (309).[50] The main episode is a "feud over disputed fiefs" between Henry the Lion and Bishop Ulrich in the twelfth century. Henry loses a battle and in 1180 is divested of all his fiefs. Ulrich invades. Henry responds "by destroying Halberstadt . . . A thousand residents were slaughtered. The number is not known, but certainly a large segment of the Halberstadt population had been exterminated" (308–9). The next episode sees Halberstadt drawn "into the cauldron of the Thirty Years' War. Sacking and pillaging by Tilly and Wallenstein were roughly the same as being saved from it by the Swedes" (309). After offering this background violence, which we have followed in an earlier chapter, Friedrich finally gets to the destruction of Halberstadt (three-quarters of it, he estimates, and between 1,800 and 3,000 people) by the B-17s of the Eighth Air Force, which were experimenting with a new bombing pattern called "the fan . . . the most exact way of destroying an area on the ground" (309). The cultural heritage that was destroyed in Halberstadt on April 8, 1945—in figures "carved into the beams of the buildings"—was a heritage of extreme violence. Why add that violent past? It's a kind of supplement, if an ambiguous one. On the one hand, it does the obvious: it bemoans the irreparable cultural losses caused by the bombing. On the other hand, it also remembers how terrible the historical memory was, thus relativizing the terrible violence that is about to descend on Kluge's town. The long view, in Friedrich as in Kluge, is appealing because the short view is distorting—distorting not just about the destruction of Halberstadt, but about the larger history to which the bombing belongs.

In *Governing from the Skies: A Global History of Aerial Bombing*, Thomas Hippler quotes Giulio Douhet (1869–1930), the Italian general who would become the most important theorist of strategic bombing, to the effect that "the distinction between belligerents and non-belligerents no longer exists now, since all are working for the war, and the loss of a worker may well be more serious than the loss of a soldier" (83).[51] It is true, of course, that theorists of aerial bombardment were trying to whittle down their moral responsibility by splitting off from the category of the noncombatant those workers who were making a significant contribution to the war effort. Overy: "It has never proved possible to calculate the number of workers killed, rather than nonworkers (elderly, women with families, children, etc.)" (225).[52] But it does not follow that, contemplating the shape of modern history, we must conclude that war had become "more democratic" (84).[53] It is also true, as others have observed, that Europe practiced aerial bombardment in its colonies, where civilians were considered fair game. But did they have to learn the lesson in the colonies that war was no longer a matter of statecraft, but "the business of the whole people" (xvi)? Was it in the colonies that war became the business of the whole people, "became more 'democratic'?" (84). What is wrong with this history, and even grotesquely wrong, is the assumption that until recently, or at any rate before European violence against the colonialized, war was *not* the business of a whole people. What do the adherents of this theory think happened to the nonbelligerent inhabitants of a city that was sacked in the medieval or early modern period, as Halberstadt was?

In the course of the twentieth century, Eric Hobsbawm writes, "the burden of war shifted increasingly from armed forces to civilians, who were not only its victims, but increasingly the object of military or military-political operations. The contrast between the First World War and the Second is dramatic: only five per cent of those who died in World War I were civilians; in World War II the figure increased to 66 per cent. It is generally supposed that 80 to 90 per cent of those affected by war today are civilians" (16).[54] I have no reason to think this is not accurate. But it does not follow, as Hobsbawm goes on to say, that "The 20th century was the most murderous in recorded history" (16). More important, the general shape that such comments give to history, politically inspiring as they may be, is profoundly misleading. When were civilians ever off limits to violence? When was war ever not "democratic" in the sense that civilians were in harm's way, always and inevitably exposed to violence? To avoid these questions is to avoid recognizing such moral achievements as humanity has to its credit, however frail and unsatisfying, including the invention of the concept of atrocity.

Arguing in favor of history seems like wasted effort. Who doesn't already believe in history? Well, it depends on what the term is taken to mean. What I take it to mean in this book is allowing mass violence to cut through the welter of wildly disparate events, opening those events up to moral judgment—judgment that is itself historically variable, developing, and unfinished, hence is perhaps less peremptory than judgment based on universal principles, but (this is crucial) remains capable of organizing events into a narrative. As a matter of how everyday sentences are manufactured, clearly not everyone believes in history in this sense. The first sentence of the first chapter of a distinguished recent discussion of world literature provides the following reasons why Alexander of Macedonia, who brought the *Iliad* with him on his campaigns, came to be called Alexander the Great: "Alexander of Macedonia is called the great because he managed to unify the proud Greek city-states, conquer every kingdom between Greece and Egypt, defeat the mighty Persian army, and create an empire that stretched all the way to India—in less than thirteen years" (3).[55] This sentence is likely to pass unnoticed, its admiration for past greatness calibrated to the vast amounts of time that have gone by, even though the same reasons for greatness would also work, if applied to other times and places, as evidence for the accomplishments of more recent conquerors, unifiers, and empire-builders who are not referred to as great. Adolf Hitler also had some impressive territorial acquisitions to his name, and he "managed" them in even less than thirteen years. In Alexander's case, the body count, though proportionately higher than Hitler's, has dropped from sight.[56] Indignation about violence in the distant past, even very massive violence, is assumed to be an obvious error of critical tact, if an error of an unnamed kind. This assumption seems pragmatically unassailable. There is nothing jarring to common sense about the placidity of tone here, which inhabits an indignation-free zone marked off by tolerance at one end and reverence at the other. The polemical term for it would be cultural relativism—relativism in time.

As we have seen, the Maori explained their ethnic cleansing of the Moriori as "according to our custom." Respect for custom, or culture, does not require that violence be ignored, but it pushes violence into the background, allowing other things to capture the spotlight. It is particularly efficacious with what Burke called old violence. Judgment of the bloody conquests of Alexander the Great is not disabled merely by the time that has gone by, but also by respect for cultural difference—respect for a culture that respected conquest. We see the same principle in Jill Lepore's account of atrocity in King Philip's War. Both sides, settlers and Natives, committed atrocities. Both sides reconciled themselves to the atrocities they committed, Lepore argues, by telling themselves they were carrying out the will of their gods. The Nipmuck ritual before battle involved listening to the powwaw, or shaman, and calling "upon the power of animal and other spirits, or manitou, to aid them in battle, and sought, from the powwaw, prophecy of victory" (98).[57] "Just as Puritan ministers interpreted signs from God, so Algonquian powwaws looked for messages from the spirit world . . . And when a violent seaside storm blew down houses in August 1675, Nathaniel Saltonstall wrote that 'the Indians afterwards reported that they had caused it by their *Pawwaw*' " (101). When Roger Williams angrily demanded in March 1676 why the Narragansetts were burning down his house, along with much of the rest of Providence, they gave three reasons. Their first answer, enigmatic but evocative, is that they were "in a strange way." The second, which seems more to the point from our present point of view, is that the English "had forced them to it." And the third is "that God was [with] them and Had forsaken us for they had so prospered in Killing and Burning us far beyond What we did against them" (120). When she draws her conclusions from this dialogue, Lepore ignores answer 2, which seems to require a taking of sides, and pivots instead toward answer 3, which suggests that there is a symmetry between the two sides. Both sides believed, or wanted to believe, that violence was the will of their gods. Lepore might have said that the English listened to their god instead of doing what they should have done: listen to the Indians. Instead, she says that both sides believed that "they were fighting to save their lives—and their religions," and both were feeling in a strange way—"disoriented by loss, fear, and gods who had forsaken them" (121). In subjectivity and religion, which is to say cultural identity, the two sides are morally equivalent. One is a culture of property, land-clearing, and settlement; the other is a nomadic culture that sees no need to build permanent dwellings or mark permanent boundaries. Culture, to which each side had an equal right, is a way of maintaining a balance between them. No side takes more than a precise half of the blame.[58] The fact that there are invaders and invaded disappears.

From one perspective, moral equivalence is a way for Lepore to refuse to congratulate the white, Western present on its putative moral superiority or the progress it has supposedly made. From another angle, the recognition of moral or cultural equality between the two sides could be seen as her own definition of moral progress, which remains a feather in the West's cap. What distinguishes moral progress is the refusal to take sides, the refusal to blame. Those who refuse to blame (wouldn't that be us?) are quietly presumed to be the most evolved, the most civilized, the most ironic, the most modern. In putting it this way, I will sound as if I am denouncing the positing of *any* criterion of progress. If I were, my argument would no doubt be more palatable. But what I am trying to denounce, from the perspective of atrocity, is the identification of moral progress with depoliticization.

Nothing could be more respectable in the humanities than respect for culture, especially the culture of others who are distanced from us in time, space, or social situation. That respect includes a selective willingness to forgive and forget. It is a large part of the undeclared protocols by which the humanities negotiate their relation to the texts they teach. Under no foreseeable circumstances could the humanities do without those protocols, or (since they are anything but explicit) something like them. Yet it follows that the humanities live with a permanent if inconstant impulse to depoliticize the past—in effect, to accept culture as fate. Anyone dissatisfied with the moral equivalence that Lepore establishes between the cultures of the settlers and the Indians will be motivated to look under the hood of those protocols. They will be motivated (to switch metaphors) to keep some flicker of outrage alive even when (as with Alexander's invasion of Persia) there is no side to be taken that is fully populated—that is, there is no culture to be wholeheartedly embraced—and the only side to be taken, looking into the future, is the very partially populated, only very slowly populating side that is anti-conquest, gathering solidarities as it moves.

Before he became the high-theory Hayden White of *Metahistory*, Hayden White did not hesitate to blame Alexander the Great, and his manner of doing so deserves to be cited here as a counterpoint to the reverential introduction to the *Iliad*-reading Alexander cited above and as a reminder of historical continuities that the general admiration for Foucault need not mean surrendering. White blamed Alexander for the decline of the Greek polis and the decline of Greek humanism.[59] In pursuit of his plan, "the amalgamation of the Greek and Persian cultures into a new, homogeneous civilization in which the best elements of each would be saved for the general human benefit" (45), Alexander "did not shrink from using terroristic methods" (45). "To provide a religious cement for this new cultural agglomeration, he took over the notion of the god-king, forcing even the Greek states to recognize him as the son of Zeus-Ammon" (45). "In exchange for political stability, Greeks and Persians alike were to surrender political freedom" (46).

> The conquest of Greece by Macedonia and of Persia by Alexander's combined Macedonian-Greek force marked the end of Hellenic civilization properly so called. The main achievements of Greek civilization had been produced by men organized in autonomous city-states. When the city-states lost their autonomy, Greek culture lost much of its original creative tension and power . . . Loss of faith in the city-state meant loss of faith in the ability of men—unaided by some kind of supernatural power—to build a life adequate to human needs. Thus the decline of the Greek city-state was accompanied by a revival of religious feeling, manifested above all by appeals for salvation to supermen, heroes, or agents of the gods to do what ordinary men were incapable of doing . . . Greek acceptance of Alexander's claim to godhead signaled the political bankruptcy of Greek humanism. (47)

For all its imperfections, humanism is of course one way of positing a degree of continuity between resistance to old violence and resistance to new violence.[60]

Set against the nonjudgmental, anti-progressive paradigm, the querying of history to which the later Hayden White made his own epoch-making contribution, I hope the positing of narrative continuity here will merit at least a second look. It does not pretend either that modernity is whole or unambiguous in its blessings or that a blessingless premodernity can be neatly distinguished from it. Rather than treating victimhood, indignation, and abhorrence as natural givens, it treats them as historical products and it values the history that has produced them, the (modern) history in which atrocity emerges as a moral scandal. The emergence of the concept of atrocity has a disorienting effect on established habits of political position-taking, there is no doubt of that. But Orientalism and Occidentalism have by no means disappeared, and the new habits of position-taking that are called for can still draw on the muscle memory that the past half century has learned from them.

It seems possible that only such a history could stand up to the undying and indeed very current power of the moral that has been deduced from Thucydides: the conviction that if the shoe were on the other foot, the survivors would do, and the victims would have done, the same thing that was done to them by the perpetrators. "All I said," Israeli Brigade Commander Gutman tells the Palestinian dignitaries in Lydda in July 1948, speaking of his Palestinian prisoners, "is that we will do to you what you would do to us" (22).[61] If this is indeed the rule, those who complain about atrocity have a much, much weaker case. The way of the world is that power gets its way. A literary history does not have to make the contrary case; it does not require evidence that those with the power to commit atrocity have in fact failed to do so, or that they have failed to do so for moral rather than practical reasons. In fact, such evidence is not absolutely beyond the reach of history. The Melians might have responded to the Athenians that the Athenians had countermanded their own decision to commit genocide, as they did in the case of Mytiline. Historians of World War II could bring up the fact that the Allies did not use poison gas, as they contemplated doing (197–98).[62] Other historians could speak their piece about the abolition of slavery, the rise of equal rights for women and sexual minorities, the rise of vegetarianism, and so on. But welcome as such real-world examples would be, this book has not been trying to argue on that level. The would-be historian of literature must be content with such a grip on the moral record as literature can claim, anemic though it may seem. The record offers evidence that minds have changed, if only discontinuously, if never enough and never for impeccable reasons. The record tells us that there is no firm, unwavering line between victims and perpetrators or between a modern secular view of atrocity and premodern will-of-the-gods fatalism. Fatalism will stay modern as long as inequalities of power stay as fatal as they have been. Yet there is a trajectory here. The representations of atrocity laid out are not just one damn bit of bloodshed after another. This is a history: it begins in a past that is morally quite different from the present, but also continuous enough with the present so that acknowledging it is not an exercise in either perpetual self-flagellation or ultimate self-congratulation. Membership in that history is optional, but the fees are quite low, and the benefits are not negligible. When the Melians are informed by the Athenians that, had they the power, they would do the same thing that is about to be done to them, for that is the rule that has always existed and will always exist, they are silent. The advantages of recognizing oneself within this moral history include having in hand a reply that the Melians were unable to give.

Epilogue

I didn't want to see the raw footage of Hamas's October 7, 2023, attack on Israeli villages and military bases near the Gaza border. I had heard how horrific the footage was, and I had seen some snippets on the television news as well as accounts by tearful survivors and the relatives of hostages. But after doing a teach-in on behalf of the Palestinian victims of the Israeli bombing of Gaza, having attended a couple of pro-Palestinian rallies organized by Jewish Voice for Peace and Within Our Lifetime, one a Jewish organization and the other Palestinian, and having spent a night tossing and turning and even dreaming of Gaza, I decided that I could not continue not to watch that footage. Having the political commitments I have, and having submitted a manuscript on atrocity that was just then being evaluated by the readers of an academic press (the book you are now reading, or consulting), I felt I had no choice but to put myself through it. So I went on YouTube. For better or worse, I found that much of the raw footage had not yet been released. But the edited segments that were available were horrible enough. Having seen them, I doubt anyone can forget them. This was an atrocity.

There is probably no record of any past atrocity that vies with this atrocity in sheer unforgettable horror. That's not because this one was worse—that's a competition it's better not to enter into—but because the accounts of past atrocity with which this book has been concerned are verbal, not visual. It may not be impossible for the verbal account of a killing to be more gut-wrenching than a video of the same event, but the odds are in the video's favor, and that's why video is more regulated, with no objections from me. Also, even visual accounts of atrocity, like the Holocaust photographs that caused Susan Sontag such anguish as a child, were taken after the fact. Today, in the age of the cell phone and the surveillance camera, someone with no advance warning can capture atrocities in real time, including the killing of their own families; on occasion, they can film their own death. *New York Times* opinion writer Bret Stephens, who was shown a forty-six-minute cut of the Gaza footage at Israeli army headquarters in Tel Aviv, a version "assembled from security cameras, smartphone videos recorded by victims and survivors, and the GoPro footage taken by the terrorists themselves," offers his readers a verbal selection of telling moments: "I watched as one terrorist murdered a father with a hand grenade and then raided his fridge while two orphaned boys whimpered in fear. I watched another who tried to behead a wounded Thai field worker with a garden hoe while shouting 'Allahu akbar.' I listened to a third who, in a phone call to his parents, boasted, 'I killed more than 10 Jews with my bare hands!' "[1]

These scenes are horrible and immediate enough. Immediate, in the sense that they back up Stephens's argument that, though Hamas may have had longer-term strategic objectives, like "derailing the Israeli-Saudi peace deal," "not the least of their intentions was to kill Jews" (6). Killing Jews for the sake of killing Jews: out of anti-Semitism or sheer, incomprehensible ferocity. That's what Stephens suggests. What you see is what you get: the killers are monsters. This is true to an important degree of any and all accounts of atrocity. It's what makes them atrocities. Looked at up close, they are unbearable, and there is no real alternative to deciding that the perpetrators are inhuman monsters even when, as in this case, certain accusations turned out to have been falsified and certain human motives can be supplied. The Israeli army, which showed the footage to Stephens, has rarely been pleased when questions of human rights were brought to bear on them, but in this case a human rights perspective might help them make a point they want made. From a human rights perspective, at least in its absolute version, the context that might help explain a violation of human rights is judged to be irrelevant. Attention need not be paid to motives or other contexts. All the observer wants is evidence of what was done and to whom. Just what Stephens provides.

In controversies over the violence in and around Gaza in the fall of 2023 and afterwards, the unassuming word *context* has stepped forward into a harshly politicized limelight; context has been something one suddenly was asked to be for or against. Defenders of the Palestinian cause have insisted that this history did not begin on October 7, 2023—that to understand the violence of that day, you need to remember sixteen years of Israeli blockade of Gaza and the profound, relentless, and many-sided distress it has imposed on the population; the recurrent bombings and invasions, as in 2014, which Israel has called "mowing the lawn," with over two thousand deaths on that occasion alone; the shootings of unarmed demonstrators at the Gaza border during the "Great March of Return" in 2018; the ever-increasing pogroms (no lesser word will do) on the West Bank, in which settlers have killed more Palestinians while grabbing more and more of their land; and for that matter the exclusion of Muslims from praying at the Al-Aqsa Mosque in Jerusalem. On the Israeli side, the word *context* has been ridiculed as an evasion; readers are asked to look at the murders alone, trusting only the evidence of their own eyes. It may seem perverse, therefore, to point out that bits of contextual evidence—certainly not conclusive evidence of anything, and yet not negligible either—are to be noticed even in the passage I quoted from Stephens. The wounded Thai worker whom the Hamas killer is trying to behead with a garden hoe might suggest, to a Gazan, Israel's cutting off of employment for Gazans in agriculture and construction, thereby raising joblessness and hopelessness to stratospheric levels, and their replacement by foreign workers who have no idea of the politics behind their hiring and could be relied on not to make trouble. If the Hamas killers wanted only to kill as many Jews as possible and were moved by no human sentiments whatever, the two orphaned boys whimpering in fear would be dead. The raid on the fridge might be a sign of callous indifference to what the killer has just done, like Ron Haviv's famous photo of a Bosnian Serb, seen from behind, kicking the corpse of the women he's just murdered, his cigarette delicately tilted to the side. As seen with frigid aestheticism, or from Mars, the raid on the fridge might also be a reminder of how hungry the people of Gaza have been kept, including its children, and for how long.

The Israeli side of course has its own version of context, a version in which Hamas is responsible for everything, very much including the many Gazan civilians the Israelis have reluctantly murdered.[2] Contexts are always multiple, and they are always controversial. Those of us who want atrocities to be self-evident and uncontroversial will always be tempted, therefore, to rule context irrelevant. Like the observer of human rights violations, we do not want to become enmired in a self-renewing cycle of "they started it, and our violence is just a response to theirs." At the same time, who does not feel the wicked pull of the urge to retaliate? Revenge is the ur-context. On the subject of context, this book began in ambivalence—indeed, ambivalence about context is one of the strongest motives for writing it. (Everyone is against atrocity. What is there to say? Aren't you wasting your time?) As I have said, my father was a bomber pilot in World War II. He was fighting the Nazis. That was a very good thing to do. He was also bombing cities. That meant he was killing large numbers of noncombatants, including children, as his squadron did at Halberstadt. That is not a good thing to do. How much should the context matter? Can the justice of the cause erase the fact of the atrocity? The killing of 1,200 Israelis, the majority of them noncombatants, including children, on October 7, 2023, was an atrocity. (The Israelis began by claiming 1,400 dead, but such is perhaps the fog of war; anyway, enough civilians died for this to count as an atrocity.) So was the killing of thousands and thousands of Gazans in the months afterwards, a good proportion of them children. (As I write, the numbers in Gaza continue to mount; patients in wheelchairs and the doctors trying to treat them have been shot by Israeli soldiers in a hospital; Gazans have been forced into "safe areas" and those safe areas have then been bombed and strafed.) An atrocity—but so was the killing of German civilians, including some conscripted laborers from other countries, in the bombing of the German cities. Can you judge the justice of the cause by the fact that an atrocity was committed on behalf of that cause? Can comparing the number of atrocities or the number of casualties on each side be determinative? What does the fact of an atrocity tell you, if anything, about the history to which it belongs? These questions have tortured and informed this book. My conclusion, which I state at the risk of seeming to undermine the argument of this book, is that the fact that a given actor or movement is responsible for committing an atrocity is not enough reason for deciding not to support that actor or movement. Atrocity is not determinative.

In that case, should we try to do without the concept altogether? "We rarely pause to consider," Marco D'Eramo writes, "that up until the end of the nineteenth century," categories like " 'atrocity,' 'massacre,' 'genocide,' 'ethnic cleansing,' 'torture,' and 'crimes against humanity' . . . were alien to political discourse."[3] Until quite recently, that is, there was no place in political discourse for the concept of atrocity. Political discourse had no need for it, D'Eramo suggests; utter mercilessness toward anyone considered to be an enemy was already assumed to be the inevitable result of collective violence. "Acts committed during war were never considered more culpable than the war itself. Vanquished enemies were enslaved or deported, but they weren't cast as criminals; defeat—and everything it implied—was punishment enough." Like Foucault's account of punishment in *Discipline and Punish*, which seems to have inspired him, and for that matter like Foucault's heavily weighted juxtaposition of (pro) Greek and (anti) Christian discourses of sexuality, D'Eramo's contrast between premodern and modern discourses of violence uses the premodern past to level an implicit accusation against modernity. By inventing the category of the atrocity, he suggests, modernity has burdened actions already penalized by defeat (since victors are never penalized), with a further and unwarranted punishment. When we use the term, we construct monsters, and we do so in order to make ourselves, and the levels of violence we see around us, seem normal. That is a mistake. We too should assume that relentless and promiscuous bloodshed is not a special case but the inevitable result of warfare. Taking our directions from premodernity's indifference to the concept of atrocity, we too should remove that concept from circulation.

I conclude this book with a skeptical view of atrocity because skepticism about the usefulness of the concept is the most plausible alternative to the argument of the foregoing chapters, and one in which I myself see much merit. The proposition that there is nothing more culpable about committing an atrocity than about warfare itself—that war *is* atrocity—could count as an argument against war, and since war is of course the cause of much and perhaps most atrocity, there would be reason to welcome this fortification of the anti-war case. At the same time, however, D'Eramo's proposition also implies that in the meantime, while wars remain ongoing, no extra culpability should be assigned to the mass killing of noncombatants. Indeed, such killings should be paid no special attention. Any special attention that *is* paid to them should excite not indignation, but skepticism. This line of argument calls for a moment of reflection. Atrocity and war: Is it really a distinction without a difference? Would it be better to stop using the concept altogether? It's a practical question, but also (and more importantly for the purposes of this book) a historical one.

On the practical level, D'Eramo is clearly right that the concept of atrocity is fraught with dangers. (I make the same point in the first pages of this book). He is right to emphasize that a great deal of misguided violence has resulted from accusations of atrocity, many of them groundless. Even when accusations are grounded, violent retaliation has been highly selective. Friends and powerful enemies are rarely singled out; the frail and the alien are always convenient. It was a stroke of good luck that when Timothy McVeigh set off a bomb outside the federal building in Oklahoma City in 1995, killing 168 people, 19 of them children, and so-called terrorist experts like Steven Emerson instantly pointed their fingers at the Middle East, there was no retaliatory violence against Muslims inside or outside the United States.

Yes, accusations of atrocity can also hinder the cause of peace, especially when (as D'Eramo says) the category is loosely and irresponsibly applied: "The Uyghurs are certainly persecuted and oppressed by the Chinese state, but the persistent use of 'atrocities' by the Western security establishment is a semantic escalation that signals a political transition: away from peaceful diplomacy, towards New Cold War confrontation." In practice, it's also true that the humanitarian vocabulary tends to throw a moralistic disguise over the actual workings of power.

On the other hand, how power actually works, and how it *has* worked, is a matter for historical analysis. Whatever the implications for policy—that's a complicated question, and one I have not addressed here—getting as accurate a picture as possible of the relevant history is a distinct if related enterprise, and it is that enterprise with which this book has been concerned. On this point D'Eramo's historical sketch, despite its brevity, allows me to be more precise about my alternative outline of the relations between power and atrocity. For D'Eramo, the truth about why wars are fought, and thus the truth about why what we now call atrocities are committed, is "simply and purely to accrue more power." It's in this sense that D'Eramo can claim, in his brief story of before and after, that political discourse was more honest before the term atrocity emerged. "Why is it that atrocities hardly appear as an issue in the fifty preceding centuries? Because atrocities were taken for granted. It was common knowledge that power kills, tortures, sweeps away." But how smart *was* that common knowledge? What would it mean to take atrocities for granted not just in the present, but in one's vision of world history? D'Eramo leans heavily on Foucault in his understanding of power and in his desire to slap down the confident progressivism of the liberals—and also perhaps the less confident progressivism of the Marxists. About power, it seems worth mentioning that in *Discipline and Punish*, Foucault is very explicit about the existence of what he calls "counter-power," which was visible at moments of public execution and which pushed back against the power of the sovereign.[4] Yet (as I said in the introduction) when Foucault discusses the term *atrocity*, he notices its presence only in the vocabulary the sovereign applies to great crimes. He does not consider it as a concept that some emergent counter-power might potentially apply (as it was in fact applied) to the sovereign himself. He does not consider it as a way of contesting the excesses of sovereign power. This is not the place to engage at any length with debates over Foucault's conception of power, but I note in passing that, whether one approves of it or not, his notorious prohibition on theorizing the transitions and continuities between one regime of power and the next is something of an obstacle to the would-be historian of representations of atrocity. Without an analysis of transitions and continuities, power will always *look like* the same thing, whether it is or (as seems more likely) is not at all the same thing, and indeed has genuinely and significantly changed its composition and conduct under pressure from the forces in which it is enmeshed, including the naming and shaming of atrocity. To think of power as always itself and always absolutely sovereign is to think of power theologically.

Like Foucault, D'Eramo wants to challenge mainstream liberalism, which as he sees it exploits the concept of atrocity in its own interests. His historicization of the concept is the dark negative of Steven Pinker's cheerful story of the modern decline of violence. For both, consciousness of atrocity did not exist, *could* not exist before the advent of modernity. For Pinker, modernity is the hero; for D'Eramo, modernity is the villain. As will I hope be clear by now, this book has tried to take its distance from liberal self-congratulation, but on this point it is certainly closer to Pinker, for all his sins. D'Eramo wants to argue that because war is atrocity, the absence of the concept in premodernity is morally superior to modernity's dependence on it. In order to defend this case, however, D'Eramo would have to show that premodernity saw war itself as immoral. He would have to show that there was a premodern rejection of collective violence. Evidence for that proposition would be hard to come by. The absence of a concept of atrocity is hard to distinguish from an inability to imagine a world without collective violence. "One searches in vain," Kristofer J. Petersen-Overton writes in a survey of two millennia of thought, "for a morally grounded opposition to forms of violence thought to go too far" (5).[5] Recall that in the premodern period conquest was universally seen as a heroic deed that bestowed on the conqueror legitimate rule over the inhabitants whose territory had been conquered. If so, then war was emphatically *not* seen as culpable, and (continuing to argue on an absurd level of generality) the glorification of premodern attitudes to war would be a glorification of violence itself. Or if glorification seems too strong a word, we can think of it as a lack of indignation against "violence, plunder, rapine and disorders in souldiers," such as we witnessed in Simplicius's farmyard.

There is something to be said for the lack of indignation. It's arguably this deep-seated moral passivity with regard to violence, violence understood as uncontrollable, that allowed Christians to admire the extremely bloody sacking and pillaging carried out by the Muslim conqueror Tamerlane (Timur, or Tamburlaine), their admiration miraculously undistracted by the Orientalism that elsewhere ruled their putatively moral responses to non-Christians. Tamerlane's name comes up in Karl Marx's "The British Rule in India," indicating an uncertainty in the indignation that might otherwise seem to be the text's exclusive and unquestionable doctrine. This observation can serve as a reminder—perhaps a necessary one, given the number of references I have made above to Hegel's slaughter-bench metaphor—that rejecting the Nietzschean-Foucaultian crypto-theology of power and its contempt for the slave morality of victimhood does not mean embracing a redemptive Hegelian vision of violence in which the emergence of indignation would appear as a secular embodiment of Christian providence, in other words as another version of theology. What I happily borrow from Hegel, in the chapter on plunder and elsewhere, is not the teleology, but the assumption that morals can only emerge in tandem with society's various stages of material development. As I have tried to show, history progresses, when it does progress, by its bad side. It's not that there's nothing to cheer at when indignation makes its appearance, but cheering cannot be the only reaction called for when indignation arises from attachments to the newly centralized state with its monopoly on the legitimate exercise of violence or to an endangered feudal hierarchy.

Yet something has been achieved when, for example, the Israeli journalist Ari Shavit offers an account of the massacre of Palestinian civilians by young Israeli soldiers in Lydda in 1948. Shavit's *My Promised Land* is a Zionist text, but it deserves to count, along with classics like S. Yizhar's *Khirbet Khizeh*, as one of Israel's national self-indictments of atrocity. Shavit admits that the violence in Lydda was not (simply) caused by a few tragic mistakes and misunderstandings—this was the common Israeli view, when the deaths were admitted at all—but was the result of careful deliberation and malicious forethought. He also admits that he, Shavit, cannot denounce the decision to expel the Palestinians, because he is a beneficiary of it. He doesn't want to be "one of those bleeding-heart Israeli liberals of later years who condemn what they did in Lydda but enjoy the fruits of their deed" (131).[6] What is most fascinating about this display of ambivalence, however, is that Shavit spends so little time on the Palestinian dead and so much time on the plundering of Palestinian possessions. "On one of the doors is a handwritten sign that reads EAT, DRINK, AND LOOT, FOR TOMORROW WE DIE" (115–16). Shavit shows in detail that the looting, like the expulsion of the Palestinian population, was not incidental, but part of a deliberate policy to take over Palestinian lands: "They returned at sunrise, riding looted donkeys, wearing looted kaffiyehs, carrying looted strings of beads" (115). After another battle, a battle in which prisoners and civilians have been executed in large numbers, one of the participants writes home in a letter: "Even in all the excitement, I see the wrong in all these looted possessions, and at the end of the day, it disgusts me, sickens me. I cannot recognize the guys anymore. All of them are drunk with victory and driven by the lust for loot" (116). When he finally gets to the massacre of civilians at Lydda, Shavit records a witness who "sees soldiers forcing those marching to hand over cash and wristwatches" (127). "So now the young soldiers can ride looted bicycles all over town and break into Lydda's luxury stores to take cameras, gramophones, radios, carpets, hookahs, and fine copperware. They confiscate trucks, tractors, combines, and orange grove pumps for their future kibbutz" (126).[7] His shame at the looting should not be more acute than his shame at the expulsions and the killings. It's not how an ideal moral history would go.[8] The paradox of cosmopolitics remains: in order to accuse, you must feel you belong to the entity accused; but if you do belong, full-throated, unambivalent accusation is perhaps not to be expected. Shavit deserves less credit than Vonnegut. Still, even his chapter is an improvement over the Bible's account of the killing of the Midianites.

In a passage from his short story "Thursday," George Saunders sums up "earth's tiresome history" in a way that will be tempting for anyone who feels a similar urge to sum up and who knows at the same time that any truthful summary will have to be heavy on "violence, plunder, rapine and disorders in souldiers":

> Early on, countless generations of men in crude leather sandals had driven swords into other men in sandals, as the downtrodden women of the stabbed men looked on, dreading their coming ravishment, after which some slightly more sophisticated men, in leggings and cravats, had driven sabres into some other men in leggings and cravats, as their downtrodden women coughed into delicate handkerchiefs, dreading their coming ravishment, and even in good times the poor sickened, the rich feasted, men beat horses, lions ate baby gazelles, and for what? To what end? Had it all been just a pointless, random, meaningless disposition of energy? (57)[9]

Hegel too would ask "to what end?" Saunders's final sentence is a paraphrase of the famous slaughter-bench passage: "But even regarding History as the slaughter-bench at which the happiness of peoples, the wisdom of States, and the virtue of individuals have been victimised—the question involuntarily arises—to what principle, to what final aim these enormous sacrifices have been offered" (66).[10] Talk of a "principle" or "final aim" (what history intended all along) has clearly passed its sell-by date. Today it's a toss-up as to whether it would sound more ridiculous or more obscene. But the alternative to such talk is not the conclusion that this has been "a pointless, random, meaningless disposition of energy," as if to sum up Earth's tiresome history all we had to do was take one senseless shooting spree and multiply it by a million.

No shooting spree is truly senseless. You begin with the availability of guns, and you work back from there. Family upbringing, pervasive racism, class and gender divisions, a capitalism that claims to be a force for peace and yet when threatened reaches for its gun. (The force behind capitalism is force.) The point is not to make a comprehensive list of sense-making factors, each one relative but also relevant. It is only to suggest that even violence at the largest scale can't be assumed to defy all efforts of explanation. To say that there is no complete or satisfying explanation is not to say that there is no explanation. I considered and rejected "No Explanation" as a title for this book; it's too polemical for a book that is less interested in polemic than in getting the known but neglected facts of bloodshed back into working assumptions about the shape of history. To concede that so much has not been explained is to say that the labor of trying to explain, if only as a matter of long-term moral retrospect, must go on so that one day there will be less that cries out so bitterly for explanation.

Acknowledgments

The writing of this book was stopped cold by the COVID-19 pandemic, and I owe debts to people from before those years that I will not remember in enough detail, though I'm sure they have left their imprint in the final version. I am thinking of kind invitations and fruitful conversations from Avi Alpert, Amanda Anderson, Jonathan Arac, Nancy Armstrong, Etienne Balibar, Tim Bewes, Paul Bové, Leonard Cassuto, Joseph Cleary, Margaret Cohen, Eleni Coundouriotis, Marco D'Eramo, Gaurav Desai, Richard Dienst, Costas Douzinas, Jason Fitzgerald, Lauren Goodlad, May Hawas, Stefan Helgesson, Ken Hirschkop, Bonnie Honig, Paolo Horta, David Kurnick, Christina Lupton, David Marcus, Giorgio Mariani, David Palumbo-Liu, Klaus Petersen, Anjali Prabhu, Barnaby Raine, Zach Samalin, Nikil Saval, David Shumway, Peter Simonsen, Ann Laura Stoler, Valerie Traub, Lauren Walsh, and Jeffrey Williams.

Erica Wetter was the ideal editor; I couldn't have asked anything more from her or her excellent colleagues. Recognizing the significant points raised by Stanford's anonymous reviewers did not make my life easier, but I think it did make the book better.

Among the various students who tolerated my obsessiveness in "The Literary History of Atrocity" and pushed me to think new thoughts, I would like to single out Sam Hyman and Melissa Kalyoncu.

On one occasion I was lucky to receive extremely insightful and good-hearted pushback from Robert Young. Christian Thorne, my colleague on the editorial board of the journal *boundary 2*, was astonishingly generous and astonishingly on point in his suggestions. On many, many occasions I was blessed with mixed but amicable commentaries from Jonathan Arac, Laura Kipnis, Tom Kruse, James Livingston, Scott Malcomson, and John McClure. Pretty much every day I have been able to count on make-or-break intellectual and emotional support from breakfast seminars and afternoon breaks with Elsa Stamatopoulou. Kaet Heupel's contribution is not limited to her father sweetly handing me a copy of Gerald Astor's *The Mighty Eighth*. Sophia Stamatopoulou-Robbins, on whom too many demands are always being made, has always managed nonetheless to make time to tell me what only her eye could see.

I don't imagine I will ever know how much this project owes to my father, who like so many veterans did not talk much about the war, or to the loss of my son Andreas at the age of twenty-five in December 2014. I had never felt that kind of pain before; maybe feeling it nudged me gently toward the pain of others. Which Andreas himself felt more than was good for him.

This book is dedicated to Lynne Robbins, who has always shown those around her that love and knowledge go well together.

Notes

Preface

1. There are no doubt times and places where the cost of leaving one's family undefended would be too high. The undeservedly privileged cannot always be expected to surrender their privileges when asked nicely and firmly, though one hopes they will. A high price is paid by resistance to occupation (for example, resistance to the Nazi occupation of Europe), but that does not mean it is a mistake.

2. George Orwell, *Diaries,* ed. Peter Davison (New York: Liveright, 2013), 387.

3. Ibid., 387.

4. There is no such thing as a set of facts from which only one political conclusion can be reasonably drawn. Take the example of the war against the Nazis. By June 1942, few if any members of the Left in Britain were still reluctant to join capitalist England in its struggle against fascist Germany. But at the moment when Orwell transcribed the BBC report about Lidice, he was working at the BBC World Service, broadcasting to South Asia. His task was to bring Indians into the war. As he was well aware, he was asking his listeners to side with their colonizers, whom they knew, in a war against Germany, about which they probably knew much less. That may explain some of his otherwise misguided irritation about how the news of atrocity is received. For an equally irritated reaction to Orwell's obtuseness on the subject of atrocity, see Mary McCarthy, "The Writing on the Wall," in *Writing on the Wall and Other Literary Essays* (San Diego, CA: Harvest/HBJ, 1970), 154–55.

5. As Orwell was to put it four years later in "Politics and the English Language":

"In our age there is no such thing as 'keeping out of politics.' All issues are political issues, and politics itself is a mass of lies, evasions, folly, hatred and schizophrenia." George Orwell, "Politics and the English Language," in *The Collected Essays, Journalism and Letters of George Orwell,* vol. 4, *In Front of Your Nose, 1945–1950,* ed. Sonia Orwell and Ian Angus (New York: Harcourt Brace Jovanovich, 1968), 137.

6. Rebecca Meade, "How Nasty Was Nero, Really?" *New Yorker,* June 14, 2021. Nero may owe his special place in such discussions to the fact that he was perceived not merely to be cruel, but to take pleasure in cruelty, thereby raising a different set of questions, and to the fact that his tutor was Seneca.

7. Candida Moss, *The Myth of Persecution: How Early Christians Invented a Story of Martyrdom* (New York: Harper, 2013). More often than not martyrs were individuals, hence not perfect examples of atrocity.

8. Agrippa D'Aubigné, *Les Tragiques* (Paris: Garnier-Flammarion, 1968).

9. Etienne Balibar, *Violence and Civility: On the Limits of Political Philosophy,* trans. G. M. Goshgarian (New York: Columbia University Press, 2015).

10. According to the *Oxford English Dictionary, sensational* means "violently exciting" or "calculated to produce a startling impression." The OED's choice of the word *calculated* here—perhaps a reminder of the popular "sensation" novels of the nineteenth century, when "sensational" became the brand name of a successful literary commodity—suggests a cause for suspicion. Someone is deliberately trying to excite your feelings, and you may well react by questioning their motives.

11. Siep Stuurman, *The Invention of Humanity: Equality and Cultural Difference in World History* (Cambridge, MA: Harvard University Press, 2017). "At the dawn of history," Stuurman writes, "the inferiority of the stranger was self-evident" (2).

12. Then there is the rhetorical tradition that the Romans called *vituperatio,* which put no limits on what you could say to malign an opponent. The example comes from Rebecca Meade on Nero. This rhetoric has by no means disappeared from current usage (cue social media), but no number of examples of vituperation would suffice to make this book worth writing.

13. On Gladstone's pamphlet and the political crisis it caused, see Gary J. Bass, *Freedom's Battle: The Origins of Humanitarian Intervention* (New York: Knopf, 2008), 270–71 and passim. Followers of Gladstone came to be called atrocitarians. "The fact that self-styled *komitacis*—'freedom-fighters'—armed bands of 'Christian' Serb, Greeks and Bulgarians were busily massacring Muslims never seems to enter into the equation. Nor that the persistent and widespread nature of such atrocities, not only in the Balkans but in other eras of the Ottoman empire, was, in large part, due to the destabilizing influence of the Great Powers, Britain included" (26–27). Mark Levene, introduction to *The Massacre in History,* ed. Mark Levene and Penny Roberts (New York: Berghahn Books, 1999).

Introduction

1. Alexander Kluge, *Air Raid,* trans. Martin Chalmers (London: Seagull, 2014).

2. Edmund Burke, letter to Captain Thomas Mercer, February 1790, quoted in David Bromwich, ed., *Edmund Burke on Empire, Liberty, and Reform: Speeches and Letters* (New Haven, CT: Yale University Press, 2000), 30.

3. W. G. Sebald, *On the Natural History of Destruction*, trans. Anthea Bell (New York: Random House, 2003). More recent research suggests that the number of civilians killed in the Allied bombings was closer to 353,000, or "a little over half the figure of 625,000 arrived at in the 1950s." Richard Overy, *The Bombers and the Bombed: Allied Air War over Europe, 1940–1945* (New York, Viking Penguin, 2013), 307. It's unclear that the smaller figure makes any moral difference.

4. Walter Benjamin, "The Storyteller," in *Illuminations* (New York: Schocken, 1969), 83–109.

5. Susan Neiman, *Learning from the Germans: Race and the Memory of Evil* (New York: Farrar Straus and Giroux, 2019).

6. In the revised edition of *Evil in Modern Thought*, Neiman reflects at length on the attacks of September 11, 2001, but does not elaborate on the reasons behind them that implicated U.S. policy in the Middle East. Susan Neiman, *Evil in Modern Thought: An Alternative History of Philosophy* (Princeton, NJ: Princeton University Press, 2015).

7. I took a first run at this subject in "Bad Atrocity Writing," *n+1*, no. 32 (Fall 2018): 12–22.

8. Amnesty International, "Human Rights in Nicaragua" (1986), in *Human Rights Reader*, ed. Walter Laqueur and Barry Rubin, 385–91 (New York: New American Library, 1989), 389–90.

9. Walter Benn Michaels, *The Trouble with Diversity: How We Learned to Love Identity and Ignore Inequality* (New York: Metropolitan Books, 2006, 122.

10. Nikil Saval, "American Carnage," *Bookforum,* Summer 2018: 26.

11. Gopal Balakrishnan, *Antagonistics: Capitalism and Power in an Age of War* (London: Verso, 2009).

12. Lawrence L. Langer, *The Age of Atrocity: Death in Modern Literature* (Boston: Beacon Press, 1978).

13. Steven Pinker's moral character may not be relevant for a consideration of his arguments, but those who are interested might want to consult Michael Massing, "How Jeffrey Epstein Captivated Harvard," *The Nation*, August 7–14, 2023, 14–27.

14. Priyamvada Gopal, *Insurgent Empire: Anticolonialism and the Making of British Dissent* (London: Verso, 2019).

15. Christopher Goscha, *Vietnam: A New History* (New York: Basic Books, 2016), 33.

16. It is worth noting that, faithful to his own secular principles, Said set himself apart from the sort of original-sin style condemnations of the West with which *Orientalism* is still sometimes associated. As he knew very well, the record is more various. Ten

years before *Orientalism*, Bernard Porter had published *Critics of Empire: British Radicals and the Imperial Challenge* (1968). Edward Thompson's *The Other Side of the Medal*, originally published in 1925, when the furor surrounding the Amritsar Massacre of 1919 was still fresh and was not restricted to India, was republished in 1989. On the supposed century-spanning consensus in support of colonialism and the violence it perpetrated, it seems as if the time has come for a correction. Jennifer Pitts's *A Turn to Empire: The Rise of Imperial Liberalism in Britain and France* (2005) is one example among many. It traces the rise of European support for imperialism in the nineteenth century, a readiness to legitimize even its bloodiest atrocities. But, logically enough, Pitts also assumes an Enlightenment starting point against which this "turn to empire" could be defined, which is to say a prior moment in which European criticism of European empire was not anomalous but more or less normal, if never an expression of majority opinion. Mention is occasionally made these days of Jeremy Bentham's 1793 address to the leaders of the French Revolution, "Emancipate Your Colonies!" If one is asking, as I am, when and how and why it became possible to accuse one's own countrymen of atrocities committed against others (something that for the record Bentham does not do—he assumes the English behave better in their colonies), the period before the high imperialism of the nineteenth century thus becomes more interesting even if it also risks playing into residual European complacency about Europe's Enlightenment heritage. Bernard Porter, *Critics of Empire: British Radicals and the Imperial Challenge* (London: I. B. Tauris, 2008); Edward Thompson, *The Other Side of the Medal,* ed. Mulk Raj Anand, afterword by Sumit Sarkar (New Delhi: Sterling Publishers, 1989); Jennifer Pitts, *A Turn to Empire: The Rise of Imperial Liberalism in Britain and* France (Princeton, NJ: Princeton University Press, 2005). Other notable books in this revisionist mode include Richard Seymour, *American Insurgents: A Brief History of American Anti-Imperialism.* (Chicago: Haymarket, 2012) and Gopal, *Insurgent Empire.*

17. Adriana Cavarero, *Horrorism: Naming Contemporary Violence,* trans. William McCuaig (New York: Columbia University Press, 2011).

18. Enzo Traverso, *Left-Wing Melancholia: Marxism, History, and Memory* (New York: Columbia University Press, 2016), xv.

19. Claudia Card, *The Atrocity Paradigm* (New York: Oxford University Press, 2002). "Why take atrocities as paradigms? Many evils lack the scale of an atrocity. Not every murder is an atrocity, although murder is also a paradigm of evil. Atrocities shock, at least when we first learn of them. They seem monstrous. We recoil from visual images and details. Many think no one should have to suffer them, not even evildoers. It is not for their sensationalism, however, that I choose atrocities as my paradigms. I choose them for three reasons: 1) because they are uncontroversially evil, 2) because they deserve priority of attention (more than philosophers have given them so far), and 3) because the core features of evils tend to be writ large in the case of atrocities, making them easier to identify and appreciate" (9).

20. See the discussions of Eichmann's intentionality in Claudia Card and Susan Neiman, each of whom revises earlier views.

21. Card, *The Atrocity Paradigm*

22. Claudia Card, *Confronting Evils: Terrorism, Torture, Genocide* (Cambridge: Cambridge University Press, 2010).

23. Marilyn B. Young, "An Incident at No Gun Ri," in *Crimes of War: Guilt and Denial in the Twentieth Century*, ed. Omer Bartov, Atina Grossmann, and Mary Nolan, 242–58 (New York: The New Press, 2002).

24. Michel Foucault, *Discipline and Punish: The Birth of the Prison*, trans. Alan Sheridan (New York: Vintage Books, 1979, 56–57.

25. Etienne Balibar, *Violence and Civility: On the Limits of Political Philosophy*, trans. G. M. Goshgarian (New York: Columbia University Press, 2015); David Simpson, *Engaging Violence: Civility and the Reach of Literature* (Stanford, CA: Stanford University Press, 2022).

26. Norbert Elias, *Power and Civility*, vol. 2, *The Civilizing Process*, trans. Edmund Jephcott (New York: Pantheon, [1939] 1982).

27. Martin Thomas and Richard Toye, *Arguing about Empire: Imperial Rhetoric in Britain and France, 1882–1956*. (Oxford: Oxford University Press, 2017).

28. I mark a special debt here to Philip Kitcher's "Munich Lectures in Ethics" on moral progress and to his extensive discussion in particular of the abolition of slavery. Kitcher rejects the idea of moral progress "toward" in favor of progress "from"—as measured by movement toward "the discovery of previously unrecognized moral truths" (15) —some fixed point or objective moral truth and replaces it with movement away from conduct that is acknowledged to be problematic. Atrocity—mass violence against noncombatants—would seem to meet his criteria for a problem such that "*anyone* placed in the pertinent circumstances would seek relief" (27). But perhaps this position identifies the right opinion with what is universally believed. My own position is closer to that of Amia Srinivasan, who shifts the issue from the idea that "the key to moral change is ideological (a matter of better beliefs)" to the idea that the key to moral change is "material (a matter of better practices)" (105). This phrase offers a useful gloss on what I will mean by "material." Srinivasan goes on: "The history of moral progress (again, such as it is) has not been fundamentally a history of conversation at all, but a history of power" (109). I will give more significance than Srinivasan to dialectically intriguing cases in which those shifts in both morals and practices are not necessarily progressive and the "moral truths" that appear do so *in reaction against* what we might call "progressive shifts." Like Jaeggi, who pays attention to "power-driven structural and functional obstacles to progress" (120), I try not to let power drop out of my sketch of humanity's moral history; it's especially relevant to the trajectory of modern fatalism. Philip Kitcher, *Moral Progress,* with Amia Srinivasan, Susan Neiman, and Rahel Jaeggi, ed. Jan-Christoph Heilinger (Oxford: Oxford University Press, 2021).

29. Caroline Elkins, *Legacy of Violence: A History of the British Empire* (New York: Knopf, 2022).

30. Arno J. Mayer, *Why Did the Heavens Not Darken: The "Final Solution" in His-*

tory (New York: Pantheon, 1988). "In the face of irreversible military setbacks and material shortages, the line between egregious exploitation and outright exterminism kept wearing thin. Indeed, ultimately the execrable living, sanitary, and working conditions in the concentration camps and ghettos took a greater toll of life than the willful executions and gassings in the extermination centers . . . as of late 1941 the drive for full economic mobilization provided a universally plausible justification for deportation, resettlement, and hyperexploitation" (349). People thought, wrongly, that "self-interest and the rational imperatives of war effort would keep the Nazi fury within bounds. Especially in the antechambers of hell it was difficult, if not impossible, to fathom the intrinsic coexistence of the calculated utilization of labor and outright murder" (349). "The SS leaders were in the first instance auxiliaries in the war of conquest and ideology against the Soviet Union" (349). "Any attempt to explicate Auschwitz requires facing up to this diabolic fusion between, on the one hand, the ideological and institutional press for extermination and, on the other hand, the contingent exigencies of an intractable and failing total war" (354).

31. Ann V. Murphy, *Violence and the Philosophical Imaginary* (Albany: State University of New York Press, 2012).

32. James Dawes, *That the World May Know: Bearing Witness to Atrocity* (Cambridge, MA: Harvard University Press, 2007).

33. Nicolaus Mills and Kira Brenner, eds., *The New Killing Fields: Massacre and the Politics of Intervention* (New York: Basic Books, 2002), a book that argues for humanitarian intervention to prevent atrocity, asks, "How should the international community act when governments massacre their own people?" (5). My concern, by contrast, is not with the reaction of outsiders ("the international community") to violence committed by someone else, but (to repeat) with violence committed by one's own government or collectivity—which might include, it is worth noting, the violence that is called for in the name of humanitarian intervention.

34. Bartolomé de Las Casas, *Short Account of the Destruction of the Indies,* ed. and trans. Nigel Griffin, with an introduction by Anthony Pagden (New York: Penguin, 1992).

35. Quoted from Sumit Sarkar's afterword to Thompson, *The Other Side of the Medal,* 88. The original review was B. Shiva Rao, *Lansbury's London Weekly,* December 19, 1925.

36. On the idea that atrocity stories create further atrocities, Thompson writes: "There can be no doubt that the dramatic and heightened fashion in which the Mutiny has been pictured to us has been responsible for deeds that would have been impossible to Englishmen in their right frame of mind" (48). Cawnpore as an example of retribution for the news of atrocities committed by others against "us." "Atrocity and counter-atrocity acted and reacted. The two cruellest massacres of Europeans, those of Jhansi and Cawnpore, occurred long after a policy of indiscriminate vengeance had been put into operation" (59). Thompson, *The Other Side of the Medal.*

37. For a useful discussion of Zinn's reception, including critiques from the left as well as the right, see Nick Witham, "Howard Zinn and the Politics of Popular History," *Chronicle of Higher Education*, July 17, 2023.

38. Martin Duberman, *Howard Zinn: A Life on the Left* (New York: New Press, 2021).

39. Note how, as if in tribute to the suffering below that is invisible from above, Duberman's own language falls apart. The nouns are jumbled, the prepositions and objects don't fit together; the screams and atrocities (two very different kinds of things) are separated off from the dead children.

40. During this trip to Royan, Duberman says, Zinn poked around in the archives and decided the bombing had been "a deadly work of obvious uselessness" (16). In other words, its uselessness was not obvious to him in the midst of the bombing itself. Zinn writes about this episode in "Hiroshima and Royan" (269) in Howard Zinn, *The Politics of History*, 2nd ed. (Urbana: University of Illinois Press, [1970] 1990), 250–74.

41. Howard Zinn, *A People's History of the United States* (New York: Harper and Row, 1980).

Chapter One

1. Raymond Williams, *Politics and Letters: Interviews with New Left Review* (London: Verso, 1981), 170. There is a vast literature on famine as atrocity. One example among many is Yang Jisheng, *Tombstone: The Great Chinese Famine 1958–1962*, trans. Stacy Mosher and Guo Jian (New York: Farrar, Straus and Giroux, 2012).

2. Stephen Pinker, *The Better Angels of Our Nature: Why Violence Has Declined* (New York: Viking, 2011) neglects the violence of colonialism (which gets no mention in the book's otherwise ample index). It omits from its portrait of an increasingly secularized modernity the hyper-religiosity of the United States. It expresses unwarranted confidence in global commerce as a factor supposedly blocking militarist adventures. It overestimates the overall peacefulness of the contemporary world. The book has no entry in its index for *militarism*. Pinker follows Adam Smith in positing that colonial conquest is extrinsic to the working of the modern market; capitalism does not favor or require systematic violence. Thus militarism (as opposed to "martial culture," for him an ancient vestige) shows up in the book only in the nineteenth century, and only as a newfangled glorification of war (as cleansing storm) that is quickly eclipsed by a rising pacifism. World War I, Pinker argues, put an end to "romantic militarism."

3. A straw in the wind: the fact that in Emily St. John Mandel's popular novel *Station Eleven* the phrase "everything happens for a reason" is taken as self-evident proof of mental decrepitude. Emily St. John Mandel, *Station Eleven* (New York: Vintage, 2014), 260–61.

4. Matthew White, *The Great Big Book of Horrible Things: The Definitive Chronicle of History's 100 Worst Atrocities* (New York: Norton, 2012).

5. The idea of a history-spanning list of atrocities is humorous in itself, but White

also makes humor a goal. "People don't argue about nice history. They argue about who killed whose grandfather" (xiii). "Thuggish warlords like to be named after iron and steel" (533). "A terrorist act sparked the First World War, but terrorism itself is small potatoes" (535).

6. In that sense, the list is a Nietzschean or Hayden-Whitean argument against history, considered as a narrativizing of events around a subject or subjects and, most important, as a framework in which action might be perceived as meaningful. Of course, this can also work as a poetic mode that has its own more oblique incentive to action.

7. Edmund Burke, letter to Captain Thomas Mercer, February 1790, quoted in David Bromwich, *Edmund Burke on Empire, Liberty, and Reform: Speeches and Letters* (New Haven, CT: Yale University Press, 2000), 30. Burke was trying to exculpate the property-owning families around him who were often described as "great," where "great" meant that they owned a great deal of property and wielded a great deal of power. It was the power of those families that had put him in Parliament. He was enlisting time as his ally in shoring up their position and his own, and time has obliged.

8. Jeremy Waldron, "Redressing Historical Injustice," *University of Toronto Law Journal* 52 (2002): 158–59.

9. I borrow the line, with a certain embarrassment at leaning so heavily on the authority of the same source, from *Monty Python and the Holy Grail.*

10. It seems obvious that the passage of time is not morally empty or irrelevant. Yet the case seems to need making, and repeating. I have tried to make it myself, for example by pointing out the damage done when it is ignored. For example, by Martha Nussbaum, in a commentary on Theodor Fontane's 1895 novel *Effi Briest*, in which a husband shoots and kills the man with whom his much younger wife had had a brief affair seven years earlier. I complain that Nussbaum "says nothing about the fact that Effi's affair happened in the relatively distant past. She does not ask whether the husband's code of honor is any more at fault in its judgment of an affair that ended years before than it would have been in judging an affair that was still going on, or whether it is any different in this respect from Kantian ethics. When she demands 'forgiveness,' she does not indicate that time might make forgiving less difficult. The passage of time is of no visible significance. And its insignificance has ethical consequences. Nussbaum tells us that we are supposed to love with the sort of love represented by the faithful dog Rollo, love that is not affected by time. But if love is forever, we might well conclude that should there be genuine cause for blame, blame too would be forever. Effi's conduct would be no less blameworthy if it had happened six days ago or six years ago or six hundred years ago." Ditto for the argument in favor of shooting her former lover. Bruce Robbins, "Temporizing: Time and Politics in the Humanities and Human Rights," *boundary 2* 32, no. 1 (2005): 191–208.

11. The case would need to be made that the intervening changes include the wealth and power that accrued to the beneficiaries of the original injustice and were passed along to their descendants. The beneficiaries would have to be persuaded that they

belong to a valid, analytically visible collectivity even if they don't actively acknowledge their membership in it. Faced with such an assertion, there will of course be skeptics. Efforts can be made to address that skepticism. In the case of relatively recent history, the continuities can be empirically verified both for the perpetrators and, negatively, for the victims, as can be demonstrated with regard to Germany's role in Greek belt-tightening in the 1940s and again in the 2000s. Still, there are obviously limits to how far the line of continuity can be reasonably stretched. See Bruce Robbins, *The Beneficiary* (Durham, NC: Duke University Press, 2017).

12. David Rieff, *In Praise of Forgetting: Historical Memory and Its Ironies* (New Haven, CT: Yale University Press, 2016).

13. Peter A. French, "Morally Blaming Whole Populations," in *Philosophy, Morality, and International Affairs*, ed. Virginia Held, Sidney Morgenbesser, and Thomas Nagel, 266–85 (New York: Oxford University Press, 1974).

14. J. L. Austin, *How to Do Things with Words*, ed. J. O. Urmson (New York: Oxford University Press, 1962).

15. French: "Anyone sincerely saying [that the American people are to blame for the Vietnam atrocities] must be able to show that (1) there exists a recognizable or referable collectivity designated by the term 'the American people'; (2) that events describable as 'atrocities' took place in Vietnam; (3) that a causal relationship can be drawn from acts of the collectivity to the 'atrocities' in question; (4) that the American people should have acted (collectively) in a manner different from the manner in which they did act; (5) that the American people were not completely unaware of the nature of their behavior (that is, the American people did not believe they were authorizing a cultural exchange of ballet troupes with the Vietnamese); and (6) that the collectivity could have acted (had the ability and opportunity of acting) in those alternative ways cited in (4), that is, there were conceivable alternative courses of collective action which had they been tried would have made less likely the perpetration of atrocities in Vietnam" (282). It is not impossible to imagine fulfilling all these conditions.

16. See Alastair Hunt, Stephanie DeGooyer, Werner Hamacher, and Samuel Moyn, *The Right to Have Rights,* with an afterword by Astra Taylor (London: Verso, 2018.)

17. The other factors he adduces are the pacifying power of mutually profitable economic exchange between nations, or "gentle commerce" (Pinker, *Better Angels,* 682), increases in secularism, the empowerment of women, and cosmopolitan empathy. One need not agree with Pinker that violence has indeed declined or that capitalism no longer relies on it in order to recognize that these are factors that have made some degree of difference.

18. As will perhaps be obvious, "women and children" is not a fixed description. There is some variation in the category of those who need not or should not or merely will not be killed. The Bible here distinguishes between women who have and have not had sex. Sometimes old people are included, sometimes they are not. In *Njal's Saga,* written in Iceland around 1280, the leader of the band that is besieging Njal's house

and about to burn its inhabitants to death makes a different exception: "I shall give the women, the children, and the menservants permission to leave" (237). The addition of the menservants to this list suggests the possibility that some supposed scruples might indicate only that those spared would bestow no credit on their killers. *Njal's Saga*, trans. Carl F. Bayerschmidt and Lee M. Hollander (Ware: Wordsworth Editions, 1998). Grotius adds priests and scholars to the list of those who should be off-limits on the grounds that their mode of life makes them arms-averse.

19. For a fascinating feminist take on the Midianite story, see Helen M. Kinsella, *The Image before the Weapon: A Critical History of the Distinction between Combatant and Civilian* (Ithaca, NY, and London: Cornell University Press, 2011).

20. Regina M. Schwartz, in *The Curse of Cain: The Violent Legacy of Monotheism* (Chicago: University of Chicago Press, 1997), asks "Why the violence?" and answers: "When everything is in short supply, it must all be competed for—land, prosperity, favor, even identity itself. In many biblical narratives, the one God is not imagined as infinitely giving, but as strangely withholding. Everyone does not receive divine blessings. Some are cursed—with dearth and with death—as though there were a cosmic shortage of prosperity . . . Scarcity is encoded in the Bible as a principle of Oneness (one land, one people, one nation) and in monotheistic thinking (one Deity), it becomes a demand of exclusive allegiance that threatens with the violence of exclusion" (xi).

21. Julius Caesar, *Seven Commentaries on the Gallic War*, trans. with an introduction and notes by Carolyn Hammond (Oxford: Oxford University Press, 1996).

22. Seneca: "A child can be excused [from violence] by his age, a woman by her sex." "On Anger," in *Moral and Political Essays*, ed. John M. Cooper and F. F. Procopé, trans. John M. Cooper (New York: Cambridge University Press, 2010), 101. I'm grateful to Kristofer J. Petersen-Overton for the reference.

23. White, *The Great Big Book of Horrible Things.*

24. Josephus, *The Jewish War*, trans. Martin Hammond (Oxford: Oxford University Press, 2017).

25. Kristofer J. Petersen-Overton, "The Bull of Phalaris: Atrocity in the Canon," APSA Preprints, January 8, 2020, https://preprints.apsanet.org/engage/api-gateway/apsa/assets/orp/resource/item/5e15f685afc3ff001967352f/original/the-bull-of-phalaris-atrocity-in-the-canon.pdf.

26. Ibid.

27. This conclusion sends us back to the Melian dialogue's most famous and most brutal line: the Athenians inform the Melians that the strong do what they can, while the weak suffer what they must. The line has been taken as the slogan of realism in international relations: the assumption that, whatever its high-toned sentiments, each nation will necessarily pursue its self-interest. But as a statement about necessity, it is not quite as self-evident as it might seem. On second glance, one notes that though "must" applies to the Melians, there is no "must" for the Athenians. The line does not attribute any necessity to the strong. Elsewhere in the dialogue Thucydides has the

Athenians mention what might well count from their perspective as necessity: as an empire, they can't afford to look weak in the eyes of the colonies from which they extract tribute. Otherwise, other cities would do what the Melians are doing, and the system of tribute-extraction would break down. In the famous generalization itself, however, necessity applies only to the weak. Necessity is not universal.

28. Translation modified. Thucydides, *History of the Peloponnesian War.*

29. Miguel León-Portilla, ed., *The Broken Spears: The Aztec Account of the Conquest of Mexico*, expanded edition (Boston: Beacon Press, 2006).

30. J. Jorge Klor de Alva, foreword to *Broken Spears.*

31. I spell out what I take to be disciplinary common sense. A given text or event will not be evaluated simply or fully by the ethical standards of the present. The assumption is that other times had other ethical standards. Knowledge of those other standards should have at least some impact on how the object under scrutiny will be appraised—how much and what sort of an impact remaining legitimate and in fact urgent questions.

32. The language of norms, irritating to some and not without justification, could perhaps be translated into the language of solidarity. From this perspective, the normative history of cosmopolitanism, including resistance to atrocity, could be rephrased in terms of expanding solidarities.

33. "The history of the Mexica was a history of conquest." J. H. Elliott, "Mastering the Glyphs," *New York Review of Books,* December 2, 2021, 32. For a more elaborate scholarly account, see Inga Clendinnen, *Aztecs: An Interpretation* (Cambridge: Cambridge University Press, 1991).

34. Bartolomé de Las Casas, *Short Account of the Destruction of the Indies,* ed. and trans. Nigel Griffin, with an introduction by Anthony Pagden (New York: Penguin, 1992).

35. The transition from misfortune to injustice can also be traced through the genealogy of the word *qualms*, another category for the material dealt with in this chapter. The word is of obscure origin, but in medieval usage it suggested widespread death by slaughter or pestilence. Later it came to suggest swoons or fits of faintness before coming to signify scruples of conscience. This is not merely a transition from the literal to the abstract, but from vulnerability to accident or illness, coming from without, to vulnerability to self-imposed moral norms.

36. Bartolomé de las Casas, *Short Account of the Destruction of the Indies.* The invocation of God's justice against the Spaniards comes up more than once: "May God have mercy on him and may He be satisfied with the terrible death which He visited on him" (on Alvarado, killed in a skirmish with the Indigenous people, 64).

37. Seeing not just God's will but God's *justice* in large-scale violent death, however inconsistent and baffling to modern eyes, is not the same thing as seeing the violence as incomprehensible or amoral, and the question of the unexpected revisions to Pinker's narrative it might entail is worth further thought.

38. Stuart B. Schwartz, ed. *Victors and Vanquished: Spanish and Nahua Views of the Conquest of Mexico* (Boston: Bedford/St. Martin's, 2000), 213.

39. Jill Lepore, *The Name of War: King Philip's War and the Origins of American Identity* (New York: Vintage, 1998). 120, 105.

40. Yves Winter, "Conquest," *Political Concepts* (Winter 2012), https://www.politicalconcepts.org/conquest-winter/.

41. S. Yizhar, *Khirbet Khizeh*, trans. Nicholas de Lange and Yaacob Dweck, afterword by David Shulman (Jerusalem: Ibis Editions, 2008).

42. Susan Neiman, *Evil in Modern Thought: An Alternative History of Philosophy* (Princeton, NJ: Princeton University Press, 2015).

43. *Arab Historians of the Crusades*, selected and trans from the Arabic by Francesco Gabrieli, trans. from the Italian by E .J. Costello (New York: Dorset Press, 1969). See also William R. Polk, Jr., *Crusade and Jihad: The Thousand Year War between the Muslim World and the Global North* (New Haven, CT: Yale University Press, 2018).

44. Geraldine Heng, "Reinventing Race, Colonization, and Globalisms across Deep Time: Lessons from the *Longue Durée*," *PMLA* 130, no. 2 (2015): 358–366. Heng is quoting Raymond d'Aguiliers, *Historia Francorum qui ceperunt Iherusalem*, trans. John H. Hill and Laurita L. Hill, Memoirs of the American Philosophical Society, no. 71 (Philadelphia: American Philosophical Society, 1968). *Le "Liber" de Raymond d'Aguilers,* ed. John Hugh Hill and Laurita L. Hill (Paris: Geuthner, 1969). See also John France, ed., *The Crusades and Their Sources: Essays Presented to Bernard Hamilton* (New York: Routledge, 2016).

45. Robert Irwin, "Whose Crusades?" *New York Review of Books,* February 13, 2020, 28–29. Irwin also gives examples where Christian chroniclers of the Crusades repeated passages from the book of Maccabees. And he cites Raymond of Aguilers picking his way through "corpses and blood that reached up to his knees" (28).

46. On Saladin see for example M. Jubb, *The Legend of Saladin in Western Literature and Historiography* (Lewiston, Queenston & Lampeter 2000).

47. Winter, "Conquest."

48. Pinker, *Better Angels*.

49. Klor de Alva, foreword to *The Broken Spears: Visión de los vencidos*, or "Vision of the Vanquished," published by the Mexican historian Miguel Léon-Portilla in 1959, was given the title *The Broken Spears* when it was translated into English in 1962. Since then there has been an enormous amount of scholarship on Nahuatl accounts of their defeat (and survival), much of it influenced by Léon-Portilla. See for example James Lockhart's *We People Here: Nahuatl Accounts of the Conquest of Mexico* (Berkeley: University of California Press, 1993) and Camilla Townsend, *Fifth Sun: A New History of the Aztecs* (New York: Oxford University Press, 2021). The new scholarship is usefully summarized in Elliott, "Mastering the Glyphs," 31–33.

50. *Arab Historians of the Crusades.*

51. David Quint, *Epic and Empire: Politics and Generic Form from Virgil to Milton*

(Princeton, NJ: Princeton University Press, 1993). Quint's Tasso is even worse: he is not merely "an apologist for papal supremacy," but also an upholder of "this supremacy at the expense of Italian political aspirations" (214). Torquato Tasso, *Jerusalem Delivered: An English Prose Translation,* trans. Ralph Nash (Detroit, MI: Wayne State University Press, 1987). *Jerusalem Delivered,* trans. Anthony E. Esolen (Baltimore: Johns Hopkins University Press, 2000).

52. I take this opportunity to express my extreme gratitude to Christian Thorne, who picked out this episode for my delectation and analyzed it for me in superb detail.

53. Christian Thorne, in a personal communication, notes that Anthony Esolen's modern verse translation has "glorious" in the place of "sorrowful," which throws the whole thing even more out of whack. It's possible that there exists a textual variant; Tasso rewrote the poem more than once.

54. Thorne's further comments are too apt not to include here. "And then you can see Tasso trying to get the poem to snap back into place. Rinaldo—Renaud, the character Tasso has borrowed from the medieval Charlemagne epics—goes on an Achilles-like berserker tear, but he does *not* contribute to the "massacre": "His noble sword swings only against the sword / and scorns brutality against the unarmed" (19.32). This brings him very close to the period's preferred vision of Aeneas—as the warrior who can temper the wrath of Achilles with piety. A berserker-Viking, yes, but an oddly disciplined berserker-Viking. We seem to have our exemplary Counter-Reformation soldier, though a big problem remains, which is that the poem has just made it clear that Rinaldo's conduct is exceptional."

55. Nicolaus Mills and Kira Brenner, eds., *The New Killing Fields: Massacre and the Politics of Intervention* (New York: Basic Books, 2002).

56. In the Hemingway passage, Mills comments, "the soldiers are being treated like cattle" (10). In the twenty-first century, it has become more plausible to worry, as well, that *cattle* are being treated like cattle, and that from the perspective of cattle, all of human history is an undifferentiated, taken-for-granted nightmare of everyday butchery on slaughter-benches both literal and metaphorical. Which is to say, not a history at all. Coetzee suggests as much in *Elizabeth Costello.* Although others might say that *Elizabeth Costello,* like abolitionism in the eighteenth century and *Orientalism* in 1978, offers a contrary vision and thus ought to count as evidence that the human race does in fact have a moral history.

57. Before the fiesta, the chief of the armory says to Motecuhzoma in the *Codex Aubin* that they should not trust the Spaniards and should keep their weapons close at hand. Motecuhzoma replies, "Are we at war with them? I tell you, we can trust them" (81). The narrative ends with a priest asking bitterly, "Who said we are not at war? Who said we could trust them?" Here the issue is not justice, but whether there is a war going on and, above all, whether the Spaniards could be trusted. The assumption seems to be that if one is at war, there can be no treachery; enemies can never be trusted.

Chapter Two

1. Matthew White: "About 350,000 soldiers died in the Thirty Years' War, but civilian deaths outnumbered these by 20 to 1. Compare that to World War II, where civilian deaths outnumbered military deaths by a mere 2 to 1 even though the extermination of peoples and the destruction of cities was open policy. How was it possible for so many civilians to have died in the Thirty Years' War when the number who died in the Sack of Magdeburg, 25,000, stands out as uniquely horrible? Simple. Armies lived off the land . . . Every army, both friend and foe, left starving peasants in their wake" (219). *The Great Big Book of Horrible Things: The Definitive Chronicle of History's 100 Worst Atrocities* (New York: Norton, 2012).

2. Johann Jakob Christoffel von Grimmelshausen, *Simplicissimus,* trans. with an introduction by Mike Mitchell (Sawtry: Dedalus, [1668] 1999).

3. Until the 1540s, "massacre" meant "the butcher's chopping block . . . It became the peculiarly (though not uniquely Protestant term for the popular sectarian hatreds which would be the bloody litany of the French civil wars of the second half of the century, culminating, of course, in the most spectacular moment, the ecktype massacre, that of St. Bartholomew, in August 1572" (69). Mark Greenglass, "Hidden Transcripts: Secret Histories and Personal Testimonies of Religious Violence in the French Wars of Religion," *The Massacre in History*, ed. Mark Levene and Penny Roberts, 69–88 (New York: Berghahn Books, 1999).

4. These signs are not entirely unambiguous. The "Swedish ale" might be some other army's belittling of the quality of Swedish brewing. "Pastor" (*Pfarrer* in German) might refer to a clergyman of either Catholic or Protestant denomination.

5. According to Kevin Cramer, nineteenth-century Protestant writers quoted Grimmelshausen's atrocity description but attributed the violence to the Catholics. Kevin Cramer, *The Thirty Years' War and Modern Memory* (Lincoln: University of Nebraska Press, 2007).

6. James C. Scott, *The Moral Economy of the Peasant: Rebellion and Subsistence in Southeast Asia* New Haven, CT: Yale University Press, 1976).

7. Eric Hobsbawm, introduction to Karl Marx and Fredrick Engels, *The Communist Manifesto: A Modern Edition* (London: Verso, 1998).

8. It's the same point Marx made, again notoriously, about the nineteenth-century French peasantry in *The Eighteenth Brumaire*: "They cannot represent themselves; they must be represented." Karl Marx, *The Eighteenth Brumaire,* in *The Marx-Engels Reader,* ed. Robert C. Tucker (New York: Norton, 1978). As Aijaz Ahmad has observed, this point should be taken not as a put-down, but as impartial political analysis. There were peasant uprisings, of course. But even the most justified indignation, if it cannot be translated into sustained political leverage, may have trouble expressing itself or indeed giving proof of its existence.

9. Grimmelshausen, *Simplicissimus*, 12.

10. Catherine Nichols and Marina Benjamin, "The Good Guy/Bad Guy Myth,"

January 25, 2018, *Aeon*, https://aeon.co/essays/why-is-pop-culture-obsessed-with-battles-between-good-and-evil.

11. Siep Stuurman, *The Invention of Humanity: Equality and Cultural Difference in World History* (Cambridge, MA: Harvard University Press, 2017). "At the dawn of history," Stuurman writes, "the inferiority of the stranger was self-evident" (2).

12. Michael Freeman, "Genocide," in *Dictionary of Ethics, Theology and Society*, ed. Paul A. B. Clarke and Andrew Linzey (New York: Routledge, 1996), 403.

13. David Johnston, *A Brief History of Justice* (New York: Wiley/Blackwell, 2011), 15

14. Julius Caesar, *Seven Commentaries on the Gallic War*, trans. with an introduction and notes by Carolyn Hammond (Oxford: Oxford University Press, 1996). It's perhaps worth noting that, in formal terms, the genre of military adventure works against racist portrayal. The value of one's victories depends on having worthy adversaries.

15. Josephine Quinn, "Caesar Bloody Caesar," *New York Review of Books*, March 22, 2018.

16. Josephus, *The Jewish War*, trans. Martin Hammond (Oxford: Oxford University Press, 2017).

17. Friedrich Schiller, *History of the Thirty Years' War*, trans. Rev. AJW Morrison (New York: Harper's, 1861).

18. Teodor Shanin, "Peasantry as a Political Factor," in *Peasants and Peasant Societies: Selected Readings*, ed. Teodor Shanin (Harmondsworth: Penguin, 1971), 238. Here Shanin is of course thinking of a later date when armies did wear uniforms, but the point is the same.

19. Jean Franco, *Cruel Modernity* (Durham, NC: Duke University Press, 2013).

20. The classic Marxist theory held, in a left-wing variant of Adam Smith's "gentle commerce," that the passage from feudalism to capitalism meant leaving behind the forcible extraction of surplus at the point of a sword (expropriation) and instead embracing the "free" exchange of labor for wages (exploitation), in which the surplus is again transferred from worker to employer, but this time without any apparent need for coercion. That theory is no longer considered viable.

21. Nancy Fraser, "Is Capitalism Necessarily Racist?" *politicsslashletters*, May 20, 2019, http://quarterly.politicsslashletters.org/is-capitalism-necessarily-racist/.

22. Jane Burbank and Frederick Cooper, *Empires in World History: Power and the Politics of Difference* (Princeton, NJ: Princeton University Press, 2010). The new global history is an interesting place to look on the question of how, where, and how much violence is the cause of significant change. Yuval Noah Harari's *Sapiens: A Brief History of Humankind* (New York: Harper, 2015) follows a series of revolutionary ruptures and is confident, as Christian is, that they happened because they corresponded to a history of violence. For Harari, the determining gift that language bestows on humankind is a vastly multiplied capacity to commit violence, initially in arranging the extinction of other species and then, of course, against other humans. Sven Beckert's

Empire of Cotton: A Global History (New York: Knopf, 2014) is animated by a desire to show how modern capitalism continued to depend on violence and coercion, but also by some doubt as to whether that dependence could ever be overcome.

23. It has been argued that empires are more tolerant of diversity than nation-states. If so, the empire's drive to expand and conquer, which puts atrocity at its heart, would perhaps be evenly matched by the nation-state's insistence on homogeneity, another atrocity-producing factor. See for example Burbank and Cooper, *Empires in World History*.

24. I take this quote from Annabel Brett, "The Space of Politics and the Space of War in Hugo Grotius's *De iure belli ac pacis*," *Global Intellectual History* 1, no. 1 (2016): 51.

25. As a related factor, Steven Pinker would no doubt want to mention Adam Smith's "gentle commerce," which promised (reliably or not) that material abundance could be had without violent expropriation, thereby helping to establish norms (whether the norms were respected or not is another question) of everyday nonviolence.

26. Norbert Elias, *Power and Civility*, vol. 2, *The Civilizing Process*, trans. Edmund Jephcott (New York: Pantheon, [1939] 1982).

27. David Graeber and David Wengrow, *The Dawn of Everything: A New History of Humanity* (New York: Farrar, Straus and Giroux, 2021).

28. White, *The Great Big Book of Horrible Things*.

29. Vicky Osterweil distinguishes looting from plunder, praising it as "a method of direct redistribution of wealth, from the store owners and capitalists to the poor" (10). This is a helpful reminder that it depends who is looting from whom. But in defending the agency of the poor, Osterweil ignores the history of the poor, who have most often been on the receiving end of violence, and radically simplifies the political lines even in the present: "Looting attacks some of the core beliefs and structures of cisheteropatriarchal racial capitalist society, and so frightens and disturbs nearly everyone, even some of its participants" (10). Vicky Osterweil, *In Defense of Looting: A Riotous History of Uncivil Action* (New York: Bold Type Books, 2020).

30. Gareth Williams, "Raiding and Warfare," in *The Viking World*, ed. Stefan Brink in collaboration with Neil Price, 193–203 (London: Routledge, 2008). Of course, only a small proportion of the *American* population is made up of warriors, but that has not held the US back from various military adventures, adventures on which, some would say, our system also depends.

31. Williams, "Raiding and Warfare.".

32. Stephen Howe, *Empire: A Very Short Introduction* (New York: Oxford University Press, 2002). Anthony Pagden makes much the same point: "This is a very short book on a very big subject—so big indeed that it could simply be described as the history of the world. It is the story of the transformation of groups of peoples into the massive states we call empires" (ix). Anthony Pagden, *Peoples and Empires: A Short History of European Migration, Exploration, and Conquest, from Greece to the Present* (New York: Modern Library, 2001).

33. Pagden, *Peoples and Empires.*

34. The passage continues: "Some months later, after an orgiastic banquet, and urged on by the courtesan Thais (later to become the wife of Ptolemy), Alexander and his entourage burned down the great palace of the Persian King of Kings. It was, or so the Greek historians claimed, the final act of revenge for Xerxes' spoliation of the Acropolis in Athens" (9). Note the string of extenuating circumstances, all of them working against any systematic understanding. Either atrocity is forced on Alexander by his greedy men, or it is personal revenge, or it is urged on him by a woman, or he was inebriated and didn't know what he was doing.

35. Josephine Quinn, "Caesar Bloody Caesar," *New York Review of Books,* March 22, 2018.

36. Julius Caesar, *Seven Commentaries on the Gallic War.*

37. Carolyn Hammond goes on: "The part actually played by expectations of enrichment in the motivation of the Roman soldier is impossible to quantify" (xxiv).

38. Grayling, *Among the Dead Cities*, 221.

39. On the relation between Josephus and Thucydides and how each interpreted violence, see Susan Buck-Morss's eye-opening *Year 1: A Philosophical Recounting* (Cambridge, MA: MIT Press, 2021).

40. Josephus, *The Jewish War.*

41. Alexander Kluge, *Air Raid,* trans. Martin Chalmers (London: Seagull, 2014).

42. Martin van Creveld, *Supplying War: Logistics from Wallenstein to Patton*, 2nd ed. (Cambridge: Cambridge University Press, [1977] 2004). Van Creveld quotes a letter in which the Swedish king Gustavus Adolphus, whose invading army performed the actions on which the scene in Grimmelshausen's farmyard is likely based, writes: "At this very moment . . . we have nothing left to satisfy the men except what they can rob and plunder" (14).

43. The reasons the US Army Air Corps gave, years later, for the bombing of Halberstadt come close to certifiable insanity. The city had no strategic value; the end of the war in Europe was a few days away; the city was about to be occupied by Allied troops. Thousands of civilians died because orders could not be countermanded and, with cloud cover over the preferred targets, it was assumed that the bombs had to be dropped on *some* target, not on uninhabited land. Yet Kluge, like Vonnegut, draws back from accusation. And he finds traces of reason amidst the absurdity. I will say more below about the rationality Kluge discovers in his fellow citizens as they waited under the bombs and tried to decide what to do to protect their families, and what they thought about the long history of atrocity that was just then passing overhead.

44. David A. Bell, *The First Total War: Napoleon's Europe and the Birth of Warfare as We Know It* (Boston: Houghton Mifflin, 2007).

45. Here moral history did not progress by its most attractive side. (Does it ever?) In this domain, however, progress cannot plausibly be denied. In March 2010 a mock trial was held, US Supreme Court justices Samuel Alito and Ruth Bader Ginsburg presid-

ing, to determine Henry's responsibility for the killing of the French prisoners. He was found guilty. The basis of the verdict was "evolving standards of civilization." The phrase will raise hackles, but I would stand by it, raising only a question that will perhaps seem less important, though it is important for the purposes of this book. There is some ambiguity in the mock court's judgment. Was Henry guilty only by the standards of civilization of 2010, that is, as they have evolved *since* 1415, meaning that he would not have been guilty at the time? This would certainly indicate progress. Or was the mock court saying that standards had *already* evolved sufficiently by 1415 for Henry to have been judged guilty? This would also suggest moral progress, but one following a more complex timeline than, say, Pinker's. It seems more likely that it was the first interpretation that was intended, not the second. https://dctheatrescene.com/2010/03/18/high-court-rules-for-french-at-agincourt/. Merrick Garland and Brett Kavanaugh were both involved in the mock trial. It is worth adding that there is no consciousness in Shakespeare's *Henry V* (ca. 1599), which preserves the memory of Agincourt in the "We few, we happy few, we band of brothers" speech that King Henry gives on the eve of the battle, that the battle's occasion was an English invasion of France and might be morally questionable on those grounds. The mock trial, however, did indeed raise that question. On invasions and conquests, standards of civilization have changed.

46. Jill Lepore, *The Name of War: King Philip's War and the Origins of American Identity* (New York: Vintage, 1998).

47. Peter Linebaugh and Marcus Rediker, *The Many-Headed Hydra: Sailors, Slaves, Commoners, and the Hidden History of the Revolutionary Atlantic* (Boston: Beacon Press, 2000).

48. I got this story thanks to Steven Newcomb, "Our Lenape Ancestors Were Slaughtered at Bowling Green Massacre," *Indian Country Media Network,* February 6, 2017. The full account is in David Peterson de Vries, *Voyages from Holland to America, AD 1632 to 1664*, trans. Henry C. Murphy (New York: Klaus Reprint, [1853] 1971), 169–70. For useful context and commentary see Charles McKew Parr, *The Voyages of David de Vries, Navigator and Adventurer* (New York: Thomas Y. Crowell, 1969).

49. Bartolomé de Las Casas, *Short Account of the Destruction of the Indies,* ed. and trans. Nigel Griffin, with an introduction by Anthony Pagden (New York: Penguin, 1992).

50. Nicholas B. Dirks, *The Scandal of Empire: India and the Creation of Imperial Britain* (Cambridge, MA: Harvard University Press, 2006), 111. Dirks is quoting from Edmund Burke, *Writings and Speeches of Edmund Burke*, vol. 6 (Boston: Little Brown, 1901).

51. Las Casas, *A Short Account of the Destruction of the Indies.*

52. Some will hesitate to embrace this argument on the grounds that it takes too uncritical a view of the modern state. I certainly do not intend to idealize the modern state, which as everyone knows is directly responsible for far too many atrocities. Still, taking the long view, as I have been trying to do, and thereby bringing into the same

frame atrocities with which we are less familiar, atrocities which are almost too distant in time to count as atrocities at all, allows us to see processes that are no less real for being excluded from the usual vivid and compelling close-ups. What is being proposed here is only that ideals do make a verifiable entrance into history and that they exert a certain force on the events around them. They do so under circumstances that they do not control or define. Hence the results are often ambiguous, unintended, and self-contradictory. As I have suggested, the state only stands against plunder initially (later, things will change) because it represents and defends an existing social hierarchy, a hierarchy that the upstarts who kill and plunder in pursuit of self-enrichment are subverting. In other words, the literary history of atrocity does not follow the virtuous and praiseworthy enlargement of empathy and a steadily more inclusive embrace of humanity, as suggested for example by Stuurman's *The Invention of Humanity.* In this case, qualms about atrocity abroad come in large part from qualms about social leveling at home. Here as so often, history progresses, if and when it does progress, by its bad side. This is not a history that will or should make anyone happy. If the authorities sense that they would be shamed by looting represents moral progress in even the smallest degree, it is progress purchased at a very high price. But it's unclear that progress ever comes much cheaper.

53. When Uday Mehta says that Burke was alone, and then repeats the "Burke was alone" formula—"He was alone in recognizing" that "'the history of England [was] not in England but in America and Asia'" (154–55)—he is building Burke up at the expense of downplaying the possibility that the (Enlightenment) thinkers around Burke were also capable of transcending narrow ethnocentrism. To see Burke as a miracle is to deny those who, for whatever reason, listened to him and were clearly prepared to do so. Uday Singh Mehta, *Liberalism and Empire: A Study in Nineteenth-Century British Liberal Thought* (Chicago: University of Chicago Press, 1999). "Burke was alone," Mehta writes, "in asking how traditional British liberties could be reconciled with 'that vast, heterogeneous, intricate Mass of Interests, which at this day forms the Body of British Power'" (154–55). On Enlightenment anti-imperial thinking and Burke's relation to it, see for example Jennifer Pitts, *A Turn to Empire: The Rise of Imperial Liberalism in Britain and America* (Princeton, NJ: Princeton University Press, 2005).

54. Sara Suleri, *The Rhetoric of English India* (Chicago and London: University of Chicago Press, 1992).

55. Foxe's bill, the bulk of it written by Burke, tried to create a body that would be a "prudent conduit between the merchant's desire to act as a state and the state's desire to own the power of the merchant" (Suleri, 25).

56. Dirks, *The Scandal of Empire.*

57. Isaac Kramnick, *The Rage of Edmund Burke: Portrait of an Ambivalent Conservative* (New York: Basic Books, 1977). Kramnick: "He was, he told the House, proud of 'my own virtue and self-denial.' He repressed his sexual passion, denied his conquer-

ing masculinity, while all around him men gratified themselves and in so doing inflicted pain and suffering . . . It was his embodiment of free and explosive satisfaction of sexual passion that infuriated Burke as much as anything else about Hastings" (139). Another possible response is given in Parliament itself. "His colleagues in the Commons had obviously had their fill of Burke's preoccupation with naked women for, on one occasion when he was talking of the princesses [of Oudi], according to the parliamentary reporter, 'the House laughed' " (138).

58. When he talks about "the original inhabitants of Hindustan" (301) he immediately starts to lay out the hereditary rules of caste, seen from the perspective of "the highest orders," explaining that since the highest orders are forbidden even from mixing at meals with the lower orders, and can lose caste if they do (which would mean being "thrown at once out of all society" (302), it is incumbent upon the British to save them from "involuntary sufferings, disgraces, and pollutions" (302). Burke accuses Hastings of violating the rules of caste by allowing the lower orders to sit in judgment on the higher: "He has put his own menial domestic servant . . .—a wretch grossly ignorant—the common instrument of his bribery and peculation—" (302) to decide on the affairs of their betters. (Edmund Burke, "Opening of the Impeachment, Third Day," in *Writings and Speeches of Edmund Burke*, vol. 3 (Boston: Little Brown, 1901), 300–302. To a large extent, then, the Indians were placeholders, valued less for their own humanity than for what they permitted Burke to say about England's representatives in India.

59. The first sentence of his *Short Account of the Destruction of the Indies*, by far his best-known work, begins as follows: "As Divine Providence has ordained that the world shall, for the benefit and proper government of the human race, be divided into kingdoms and peoples and that these shall be ruled by kings . . ." There is no evidence that this is merely flattery, intended to further his appeal to King Philip of Spain (the Holy Roman Emperor Charles V) to intercede against those who are mistreating the Indigenous peoples of the Americas. Las Casas is no democrat, intent on questioning the divine right of kings. The Indigenous are worthy of better treatment, he argues, because they are innocent and submissive, "utterly faithful both to their own native lords and to the Spaniards in whose service they now find themselves" (9–10).

60. Las Casas, *A Short Account of the Destruction of the Indies.*

61. David Quint, *Epic and Empire: Politics and Generic Form from Virgil to Milton* (Princeton, NJ: Princeton University Press, 1993).

62. Alonso de Ercilla, *La Araucana*, trans. Cyrus Moore (Eikonica Press, 2022).

63. This definition is no doubt too strict. Those trying to repel invaders can and should be allowed into the category of victims. One interesting example of a confrontation that does not become an atrocity or an atrocity description because of the forceful and effective response of the striking community, the world-be victims, comes in Sembene Ousmane, *God's Bits of Wood*, trans. Francis Price (London: Heinemann, 1962).

64. Quint, *Epic and Empire*. "The language of chance and luck—another legacy from the Pharsalia that runs through the Araucana—denies any ideological explanation for political and military success" (Quint, 178). In other words, this is the anti-Pinker, anti-fate tradition, and it needs to be played up, if only for its place in the counter-tradition of Lucan and Ercilla.

65. Josiah Ober, "The Rules of War in Classical Ancient Greece," in *The Athenian Revolution* (Princeton, NJ: Princeton University Press, 1998).

Chapter Three

1. Charles Dickens and Wilkie Collins, "On the Perils of Certain English Prisoners," *The Works of Charles Dickens* (New York: Collier, 1880).

2. Rudyard Kipling, "Loot," *Barrack-Room Ballads* (New York: Doubleday, 1915). The poem also offers helpful advice to soldiers on how to outwit civilians trying to hide their possessions as well as officers trying to seize the loot for themselves.

3. For an extended and aspirationally sympathetic commentary, see Gary J. Bass, *Freedom's Battle: The Origins of Humanitarian Intervention* (New York: Knopf, 2008), ch. 21. See also the review of Bass's book by Samuel Moyn, "Spectacular Wrongs," *The Nation*, October 13, 2008, 30–36.

4. Atrocity could no longer be seen, therefore, as fate. And in the abstract, this was a good thing for humanity. In other senses, of course, humanity had less reason to congratulate itself. The British sense of entitlement to intervene anywhere in the world, which Gladstone's pamphlet invigorated, would subsequently be used to pick and choose targets on grounds which were rarely impartial or disinterested. Unsurprisingly, the consequences of those interventions tended to favor Britain's own political interests, often expansionist ones involving some quotient of violent coercion. The United States has kept to the same script in matters of what has come to be called humanitarian intervention.

5. On the shelling of Alexandria, see Michael D. Berdine, The *Accidental Tourist, Wilfrid Scawen Blunt, and the British Invasion of Egypt in 1882* (New York, Routledge, 2005) and Wilfrid Scawen Blunt, *Secret History of the English Occupation of Egypt* (London: Unwin, 1907). The figure of 30 percent comes from William Wright, *A Tidy Little War: The British Invasion of Egypt, 1882* (Stroud, Gloucestershire: Spellmount), 107.

6. On *determine* see Raymond Williams, *Keywords: A Vocabulary of Culture and Society* (London: Croom Helm, 1976).

7. Gladstone, "Bulgarian Horrors" (London: J. Murray, 1876).Given such unspeakable evil, given that "the bodies of slain women and children lie in multitudes, unburied and exposed," how could "the well-oiled machinery of our luxurious, indifferent life" continue to work "smoothly on"? There has been no serious attempt to dispute the reality of the atrocities committed. Gladstone mocks Disraeli's attempt to complicate matters by claiming that the Bulgarians too have committed atrocities. "I have care-

fully investigated this point," Gladstone says; "and I am unable to find that the Bulgarians committed any outrages or atrocities, or any acts which deserve that name."

8. Cecil Woodham-Smith, *The Reason Why: The Story of the Fatal Charge of the Light Brigade* (London: Penguin, 1953/1958).

9. On Tennyson and class, see Stefanie Markovitz, *The Crimean War in the British Imagination* (New York: Cambridge University Press, 2009). See also Jerome McGann, "Tennyson and the History of Criticism," in *The Beauty of Inflections* (New York: Oxford University Press, 1985). Tennyson could be credited with undercutting his own patriotism if "theirs not to reason why" is taken not as dictating to the soldiers their moral duty but only indicating the soldiers' sad fate.

10. "Sir Charles Trevelyan, 1st Baronet," Wikipedia, last modified May 27, 2024, https://en.wikipedia.org/wiki/Sir_Charles_Trevelyan,_1st_Baronet.

11. Patrick Brantlinger, "The Famine," *Victorian Literature and Culture* (2004), 193–207. "Obviously the Famine was caused partly by an infestation of the potato crop that nobody could have predicted and that no one knew how to prevent, so to that extent blame made no sense. Nature or, for many nineteenth-century observers, providence was the ultimate cause of the potato blight—and providence, of course, could only be praised" (194). On the Irish famine, see also Cormac Ó Gráda, "Famine and the Changing Role of NGOs: An Irish Perspective," *European Review of History* 22, no. 6 (2015): 963–70, DOI:10.1080/13507486.2015.1048192, and Peter Gray, "Famine and Land in Ireland and India, 1845–1880, James Caird and the Political Economy of the Hunger," *Historical Journal* 49, no. 1 (2006): 193–215.

12. Christopher Herbert, *War of No Pity: The Indian Mutiny and Victorian Trauma* (Princeton, NJ, and London: Princeton University Press, 2008). Priyamvada Gopal makes it clear that Herbert's broader critique of Said is based on a caricature of Said's position and, perhaps more important, that Herbert is wrong to imply that "imperialism was a self-correcting system, constitutively plagued by its own wrongness. If it was indeed the case that a constantly uneasy conscience redeems Victorian culture, then we must ask why it took events entailing violent anticolonial insurgency for a 'faculty of searching self-scrutiny' to be awakened" (51). What Gopal calls "rebel agency" is of course a crucial explanatory factor. But there were also domestic factors, some of them less pious or praiseworthy than an alert conscience. One is capitalist ideology, which pleads the case that violent conquest has now been replaced by nonviolent commerce. Priyamvada Gopal, *Insurgent Empire: Anticolonialism and the Making of British Dissent* (London: Verso, 2019).

13. Bernard Porter, *Critics of Empire: British Radicals and the Imperial Challenge* (London: I. B. Tauris, 1968). As Porter shows, however, Fabian ideas do not deserve to be described as anti-imperialistic. In the preface to the second edition (2007), Porter adds a point he had not made in 1968: that "most contemporary Britons were probably not very *enthusiastic* imperialists, and maybe not imperialists at all, in any sense, but unconcerned and apathetic, even in the years covered by this book, which were surely the most 'imperialistic' in British history" (xxix).

14. Porter, *Critics of Empire.*

15. George Eliot, *Middlemarch* (Harmondsworth: Penguin, 2003).

16. Here a comparison offers itself with the reference to Tamburlaine at the very end of Karl Marx's English-language essay "The British Rule in India" (1854), in *The Marx-Engels Reader*, ed. Robert C. Tucker, 653–58 (New York: Norton, 1978). After denouncing British rule thoroughly and passionately, Marx ends by suggesting that the violent disruption of Indian society that has resulted from the British conquest, however painful and deplorable, might in the long run be necessary to the cause of world revolution. This sounds, of course, like an appeal to a secular providence, though one might also say he is only arguing that X will have to happen in order for Y to happen. The fatefulness is also lightened by the reference to Tamburlaine (another conqueror of India), which reminds the reader that Tamburlaine, or Timur, was responsible for "myriad" or countless deaths. The Goethe lyric from which these lines are taken is about the flowers that had to be cut in order to manufacture perfume that the beloved likes so much. In other words, it too is banter. In English: "Should this torture then torment us/Since it brings us greater pleasure?/Were not through the rule of Timur/Souls devoured without measure?" In German: "Sollte diese Dual uns quälen/Da sie unsre Lust vermehrt,/Hat nicht Myriaden Seelen/Timurs Herrschaft aufgezehrt?"

17. Larry McMurtry, *Oh What a Slaughter: Massacres in the American West, 1846–1890* (New York: Simon & Schuster, 2005).

18. Herbert, *War of No Pity.*

19. Patrick Brantlinger, "The Well at Cawnpore: Literary Representations of the Indian Mutiny of 1857," in *Rule of Darkness: British Literature and Imperialism, 1830–1914*, 199–224 (Syracuse, NY: Cornell University Press, 1988).

20. William Howard Russell, *My Diary in India in the Year 1859–9,* vol. 1 (London: Routledge, Warne, and Routledge, 1860). In Russell, as in Las Casas and Burke, there is a sharp focus on profiteering. "The action of the Government in matters of improvement is only excited by considerations of revenue . . . the grave, unhappy doubt which settles on my mind is, whether India is the better for our rule, so far as regards the social condition of the great mass of the people. We have put down widow-burning, we have sought to check infanticide; but I have traveled hundreds of miles through a country peopled with beggars and covered with wigwam villages" (195).

21. Wilfrid Blunt, *Secret History of the English Occupation of Egypt* (London: Unwin, 1907).

22. Berdine, *The Accidental Tourist*, 193.

23. "What began as an argument between a donkey boy and a Maltese in Alexandria at one o'clock in the afternoon, turned into a riot. After troops were finally brought in and the disturbance quelled four hours later, over two hundred people were dead and many more injured. Included in the dead were a petty officer from the British ship H.M.S. Superb and two hundred more Europeans. Also, the British Consul in Alexandria, Sir Charles Cookson 'was seriously injured and the Italian and Greek consuls received minor injuries.' As Blunt pointed out, 'it was the first act of popular violence

which, during the whole history of the year's revolution in Egypt, had been committed, and the news of it, spread throughout Europe by telegraph, produced, especially in England, a great sensation.'" Berdine, *The Accidental Tourist*, 205.

24. Jennifer Pitts, *A Turn to Empire: The Rise of Imperial Liberalism in Britain and France* (Princeton, NJ: Princeton University Press, 2005).

25. Samuel Bamford, *Passages in the Life of a Radical*, vols. 1 and 2. Originally published in 1842 by Henry Dunckley ("Verax").

26. Bamford's description of the silence that falls over the field ten minutes later is impressive: "The yeomanry had dismounted—some were easing their horses' girths, others adjusting their accoutrements, and some were wiping their sabres. Several mounds of human beings still remained where they had fallen, crushed down and smothered. Some of these were still groaning, others with staring eyes, were gasping for breath, and others would never breathe more. All was silent save those low sounds" (120).

27. Rhetorically, this resembles Wilfrid Blunt's mode of address to Prime Minister Gladstone, whom he despised, in his effort to win support for the Egyptian national movement: "You, sir, I think, once expressed to me your belief that the nations of the East could only regenerate themselves by a spontaneous resumption of their lost national will, and behold in Egypt that *Will* has arisen and is now struggling to find words which may persuade Europe of its existence" (quoted in Gopal, *Insurgent Empire,* 146). Both parties to the exchange were empowered, and the nation was a concept that empowered them.

28. Christine Gledhill and Linda Williams, eds., *Melodrama Unbound: Across History, Media, and National Cultures* (New York: Columbia University Press, 2018).

29. Jeremy Bentham, "Emancipate Your Colonies! Addressed to the National Convention of France, 1793" (London: Robert Heward, 1830).

30. Quoted in Herbert, *War of No Pity,* 11.

31. Leo Tolstoy, *Hadji Murat*, trans. Richard Pevear and Larissa Volokhonsky (New York: Vintage, 2009).

32. Leo Tolstoy, "The Raid," in *The Death of Ivan Ilyich and Other Stories* (Harmondsworth: Penguin, 2009).

33. McMurtry, *Oh What a Slaughter.* McMurtry notes that after an 1824 massacre in what is now Indiana in which nine Indians were killed, the government passed a law making Indian-killing a crime, and three white men were hanged. Otherwise, the law did not prevent the killing of Indians. "Many more Indians were killed, by many more whites; it was to be a good long time in America before white men were judicially punished for killing Indians" (17). "None of the massacres was effectively covered up, though the Sacramento River Massacre was overlooked for a very long time. But the lesson, if it is a lesson, is that blood—in time, and often, not that much time—will out. In case after case the dead had managed to assert a surprising potency" (4).

34. Gopal, *Insurgent Empire.*

35. Karl Jacoby, *Shadows at Dawn: An Apache Massacre and the Violence of History* (New York: Penguin, 2008).

36. McMurtry, *Oh What a Slaughter.*

37. Ned Blackhawk, *Violence over the Land: Indians and Empires in the Early American West* (Cambridge, MA: Harvard University Press, 2006).

38. Pekka Hämalainen, *The Comanche Empire* (New Haven, CT: Yale University Press, 2008).

39. Sebastian Conrad in *What Is Global History?* (Princeton, NJ: Princeton University Press, 2016) objects to Hämäläinen's use of the word *empire* to describe the Comanches raiding, control of territory, and subduing of neighboring tribes, all of this as a way of evading the "standard narrative of Native Americans as victims of European expansion" (194). "Is it helpful to speak of a Comanche empire? Or does it force the Comanche economy, based on bison hunting and on occasional raids, into a conceptual Procrustean bed, and thus distort historical reality?" (194). But what's the problem for Conrad? Is it the fact that saying "empire" subsumes "the Comanche experience under a terminology alien to it" (194)? If so, the problem could be solved by adopting "indigenous categories" (195). But that's clearly not the problem, and using "indigenous categories" is clearly not the solution! The problem (though Conrad doesn't quite say so) is an exaggerated desire to play up "native agency" (195), thus leveling the Comanche with rival Spanish and American imperialisms.

40. David Christian, *Maps of Time: An Introduction to Big History* (Berkeley: University of California Press, 2004).

41. David Mitchell, *Cloud Atlas* (New York: Random House, 2004). While time in the novel is much deeper than usual in various ways, including its linguistic dimension—you have to learn to decipher "Kona got Kona law but they ain't got one flea o' Civ'lize" (286) and "Such bar'bric buggahs are them painted Konas, bros" (299)—Mitchell's time is morally shallow. More precisely, time is morally irrelevant.

42. Even Christian, in his neo-evolutionist book *Maps of Time*, puts the word *barbarians* in scare quotes and explains the wall-building and gate-defending that the term evokes in terms of struggles between agrarians and pastoralists.

43. Jared Diamond, *Guns, Germs, and Steel: The Fates of Human Societies* (New York: Norton, 1997). Diamond's interest lies in why the Maori were able to conquer so completely, though the two groups had a common origin. The crops which the Moriori were used to growing wouldn't grow in the cold climate of Chatham Island, so the Moriori colonists "had no alternative except to revert to being hunter-gatherers" (55). This meant, for Diamond, that they had little social organization and primitive weapons, while the Maori were from a densely populated farming society and thus were used to "ferocious wars." "These opposite evolutionary courses sealed the outcome of their eventual collision" (54).

44. Michael King and Robin Morrison, *A Land Apart: The Chatham Islands of New Zealand* (Auckland: Random Century, 1990). "Contrary to more than a century

of European speculation, there is no mystery about who the Moriori were nor where they came from. They were Polynesian, like the New Zealand Maori. They sailed to the Chathams from New Zealand (their ancient living sites contain flake tools made from New Zealand obsidian and argillite). Their ancestors were also the Polynesian ancestors of the Maori. But they became Moriori on the Chathams, while on the New Zealand mainland they became Maori" (11). "The cultures developed differently and by the eighteenth century the Moriori had outlawed group warfare to settle disputes in favor of individual hand-to-hand combat" (11). "The major disruption to Moriori life and culture . . . was the decision of two hapu of Te Ati Awa to colonize the Chathams in 1835. Ngati Mutunga and Bgati Tama commandeered a vessel in Port Nicholson and moved 900 of their people to Chatham Island. There they killed about 300 Moriori, to establish their right of ownership by conquest, and enslaved the survivors. It was after this trauma that Moriori numbers plummeted: from 1600 in 1835, to 268 in 1848, to 32 in 1883, to 12 in 1900" (4).

45. Arguably this gesture could also count as an instance of the familiar imperialist habit of idealizing one Indigenous people, preferably a minority, as victims of the colonized majority, who can thus be demonized. This is what the French have been accused of doing, rightly or wrongly, with the Berbers/Amazigh in relation to the Arabs of North Africa. See Patricia M. E. Lorcin, *Imperial Identities: Stereotyping, Prejudice, and Race in Colonial Algeria*, new ed. (Lincoln: University of Nebraska Press, 2014). When Assia Djebar describes the asphyxiation of an entire tribe, which has taken refuge in a network of caves, by the French army in 1840, she chooses to keep the line between Arab and Berber, though important elsewhere in her novel, out of the atrocity account. Assia Djebar, *Fantasia: An Algerian Cavalcade*, trans. Dorothy S. Blair (London: Quartet, 1985).

46. As Mitchell in *Cloud Atlas* sees them, the Moriori resemble the heroic protofeminists and anti-colonial rebels whose existence Doyle loyally asserts, although her inter-imperial framework leaves no actual historical place for them to have even stated their values and goals (which may have been merely to *have* slaves rather than *be* slaves, for example), let alone to have achieved anything. In both cases, what we see is a moralized history in which the purity of victimhood excludes the vicissitudes of actual historical existence, including the possibility that struggle will result in some change to the situation on the ground, some political achievement.

47. Mitchell's interest in eternal recurrence was noticed by James Wood in a 2010 review of *The Thousand Autumns* and has probably been noticed a good deal since then. James Wood, "The Floating Library," *New Yorker*, June 28, 2010, https://www.newyorker.com/magazine/2010/07/05/the-floating-library.

48. Thus it ever was, so ever shall it be: here the point is not the merging of will to power into eternal recurrence but eternal recurrence as a denial of Mitchell's own ostensible moral, an emancipationist moral. The idealization of art in Frobisher's suicide note is more consistent with the Nietzschean anti-humanist framework: it proposes first that

the art he has created is great; second, that "people are obscenities"; and third, that history repeats itself: "Nietzsche's gramophone record. When it ends, the Old One plays it again and again, for an eternity of eternities" (471). The only reason—given on the last page—for not simply enjoying the privileges of the strong is an ecological one: "Why fight the 'natural' . . . order of things? Why? Because of this:—one fine day, a purely predatory world shall consume itself" (509). Here linear, non-Nietzschean time reasserts itself, but not so as to introduce either plot reversal or development between the strong and the weak or moral development in terms of civilized or anti-barbaric norms of behavior. Linear history is permitted to return only, it seems, in the domain of the environment: in other words, as the prospect of an ecological apocalypse in which no one will win and all will lose. Sonmi, the rebellious fabricant who is worshiped by succeeding generations as a god, refers to a "game beyond the endgame." The only game beyond the endgame that the novel can imagine is collective ecological suicide.

49. This unwillingness could be classified as a tribute to what used to be called the Third World. The anthropologist Marshall Sahlins, writing about Maori cosmology, describes it in explicitly Nietzschean terms: "The Maori world unfurls as an eternal return, the recurrent manifestation of the same experiences." Marshall Sahlins, *Islands of History* (Chicago: University of Chicago Press, 1985, 57–59). One reading of *Cloud Atlas*, which might also be described as Third Worldist, credits Mitchell with taking his distance from what it calls "the dominance of linear time in Western culture." I quote from its conclusion: "The telescoping of time in *Cloud Atlas*, emphasising the interrelationship between past and future, seems to echo Trask's assertion that, 'As for nationalist Hawaiians, we know our future lies in the ways of our ancestors, not in the colonial world of *haole* experts . . . We do not want to be "liberated" from our past because it is the source of our understanding of the cosmos and of our *mana*' " (164). The obvious problem with this reading is that Mitchell's foray into deep time seems at least equally intended, morally speaking, to let European civilization off the hook. In the novel's penultimate future society, the villains who literally cannibalize their "fabricant" working class are Koreans.

50. For a more characteristic expression of contemporary views on the barbarian, see for example Peter S. Wells, *The Barbarians Speak: How the Conquered Peoples Shaped Roman Europe* (Princeton, NJ: Princeton University Press, 1999).

51. It is worth noting that other versions of non-Eurocentric cosmopolitanism, as in Sheldon Pollock (on the Sanskrit cosmopolis) and Amitav Ghosh (on pre-modern trade interaction in the Indian Ocean) also seem inclined to generate primal pacifisms, as if violence in those areas only began with the arrival of the Europeans.

52. Barbara Ehrenreich, *Blood Rites: Origins and History of the Passions of War* (New York, Metropolitan Books, 1997).

53. Winder, Virginia. "Conflict and Protest—Pacifist of Parihaka—Te Whiti o Rongomai," *Puke Ariki*, http://www.pukeariki.com/en/stories/conflict/pacifistofparihaka.htm.

Chapter Four

1. Dierk Walter, *Colonial Violence: European Empires and the Use of Force*, trans. Peter Lewis (Oxford: Oxford University Press, 2017). It must be said that Walter has a somewhat loose idea of what it means to regulate violence: "Indian war practices, in common with those of every civilization, were . . . quite clearly regulated" (158).

2. Roxanne Dunbar-Ortiz, *An Indigenous Peoples' History of the United States* (Boston: Beacon Press, 2014). It should perhaps be added that norms were easier to maintain if the enemies with which Indigenous tribes sometimes found themselves at war were relatively close neighbors with whom they shared certain cultural assumptions.

3. Jill Lepore, *The Name of War: King Philip's War and the Origins of American Identity* (New York: Vintage, 1998). One would of course like to know whether, when one Native American tribe went to war with another, they saw the differences between them as comparable to the lines separating Native Americans from the English.

4. Upinder Singh, *Political Violence in Ancient India* (Cambridge, MA: Harvard University Press, 2017). Yet Singh does not pretend that this position was representative of ancient India or of the ancient world in general. Ashoka's "rejection of war" makes him "a misfit in the ancient world" (55). At the borders, or beyond them, scruples did tend to disappear. According to Wikipedia, "In about 260 BCE, Ashoka waged a destructive war against the state of Kalinga (modern Odisha). He conquered Kalinga, which none of his ancestors had done. . . . Legends state he converted after witnessing the mass deaths of the Kalinga War, which he himself had waged out of a desire for conquest. Ashoka reflected on the war in Kalinga, which reportedly had resulted in more than 100,000 deaths and 150,000 deportations, ending at around 200,000 deaths."

5. Ashoka's rejection of violence "did not rule out the use of force against recalcitrant people who lived on the borders or in the forests" (50). Here, as so often atrocity can't be jarred loose from issues of "incomplete pacification and consolidation" (51). Even Ashoka cannot renounce atrocity against the so-called forest people "who, in fact, posed a serious impediment and challenge to the expansion of all premodern Indian states" (269). Singh, *Political Violence in Ancient India*.

6. Laura Doyle, *Inter-Imperiality: Vying Empires, Gendered Labor, and the Literary Arts of Alliance* (Durham, NC: Duke University Press, 2020).

7. At any rate, this is a conclusion that is being drawn in and around the domain of world literature. World literature's critique of the colonizer/colonized encounter as a paradigm of world history is familiar: that paradigm holds true at best, the critique runs, for some regions and some history since 1500, but it does not hold at all for many areas of the world or for history before 1500.

8. On the flagrant self-contradictions to which this leads—isn't the teaching of the cultures of racial, ethnic, and sexual minorities a kind of progress?—see my *Criticism and Politics: A Polemical Introduction* (Stanford, CA: Stanford University Press, 2022).

9. Susan Stanford Friedman, *Planetary Modernisms: Provocations on Modernity across Time* (New York: Columbia University Press, 2015).

10. Among the revisionist works celebrating the accomplishments of the conquering Mongols by downplaying the cost of conquest are Jack Weatherford, *Genghis Khan and the Making of the Modern World* (New York: Broadway Books, 2004); Kenneth W. Harl, *Empires of the Steppes: A History of the Nomadic Tribes Who Shaped Civilization* (London: Bloomsbury, 2023); Anthony Sattin, *Nomads: The Wanderers Who Shaped Our World* (New York: Norton, 2022); Nicholas Morton, *The Mongol Storm: Making and Breaking Empires in the Medieval Near East* (New York: Basic Books, 2022); and Marie Favereau, *The Horde: How the Mongols Changed the World* (Cambridge, MA: Belknap Press of Harvard University Press, 2021). The general tenor can be seen from a reviewer's summary: "Yes, they overran cities, but state formation often demanded it. And, yes, they enslaved, but so did lots of societies, and many were much crueler" (58). Manvir Singh, "Genghis the Good," *New Yorker*, January 1 and 8, 2024, 58–61.

11. Matthew White, *The Great Big Book of Horrible Things: The Definitive Chronicle of History's 100 Worst Atrocities* (New York: Norton, 2012).

12. Stanford Friedman, *Planetary Modernism.*

13. For another Anglophone view of the events, see Rebecca Gill, "'Now I have seen evil, and I cannot be silent about it': Arnold J. Toynbee and His Encounters with Atrocity, 1915–1923," *Evil, Barbarism and Empire: Britain and Abroad, c. 1830–2000*, ed. Tom Crook, Rebecca Gill, and Bertrand Taithe, 172–200 (Houndmills: Palgrave Macmillan, 2011).

14. Homero Aridjis, *Smyrna in Flames*, trans. Lorna Scott Fox (Simsbury, CT: Mandel Vilar Press and Takoma Park, MD: Dryad Press, 2021). The title "in Flames" is arguably a mistake, given that many Turks still think of the deaths in Smyrna as the results of a fire, hence at least plausibly or partially accidental, when (as the novel is not alone in showing) so many of the casualties were the result of deliberate, face-to-face violence well before the fires were set.

15. On the Greek invasion, see Michael Llewellyn-Smith, *Ionian Vision: Greece in Asia Minor 1919–1922* (London: Allen Lane, 1973, republished in 2022 by Hurst & Company with a new introduction by the author). Citations are from the 2022 edition. Llewellyn-Smith gives less importance than Aridjis to the *chettes* or irregulars and greater importance to "the imperishable hatred between Armenian and Turk" (330) and comes close to suggesting that the willingness of the Armenians to resist "was to invite a terrible penalty," namely a slaughter that was "systematic, and involved the Turkish regular army" (331).

16. It's worth noting that the added nuance of ethnocentrism, however distressing, is there as well in García Márquez's massacre description. García Márquez pauses to mention that the troops who do the killing are from the highlands of Colombia and are visibly distinguished from the (more mixed? less indigenous?) population of the coastal region that have been brought in to subdue them.

17. I am grateful to Laura Doyle for organizing a conference called "Empires, Economy, and Culture Before and After 1500: Implications for Global and Postcolonial Studies" that was held September 20–23, 2012, at the University of Massachusetts–Amherst. That conference first forced me to think about premodern empires and how my lazy assumptions about world history might have to be adjusted to take fuller account of them. At the time, mine was one of the "expressions of concern about any widening of the decolonial focus to earlier periods and non-European empires," in Doyle's words, "for fear of taking pressure off Anglo-European responsibility for its destructive legacies" (7). As will perhaps be obvious, I continue to worry about the politics of this shift, which has been accentuated by the "world literature" formation; as Doyle puts it, "the demise of postcolonial studies and the displacement of this field by an apolitical world literature" (20–21). I'm not as sure as Doyle seems to be that the term *decolonial* applies to earlier moments or that it creates a satisfying rhyme with political movements today. When was "resistance" really resistance to the empire as such, to the conquests that form empires, as distinct from the desire not to be conquered and subjugated—and perhaps a desire to be the one doing the conquering and subjugating?

18. "The Parallax of 1922: The Greco-Turkish War in History, Memory, and International Politics," an online panel discussion organized by the Hellenic Observatory of the London School of Economics, 2022.

19. Robert Young, *Postcolonialism: An Historical Introduction* (Chichester: Wiley-Blackwell, 2016).

20. See Sven Lindqvist, *A History of Bombing,* trans. Linda Haverty Rugg (New York: New Press, 2001), 97.

21. Larry McMurtry, *Oh What a Slaughter: Massacres in the American West, 1846–1890* (New York: Simon & Schuster, 2005).

22. Mark Mazower, *The Greek Revolution: 1821 and the Making of Modern Europe* (New York: Penguin, 2021). Atrocities committed by the fighters for national liberation are amply documented in Mazower's history.

23. Ernest Hemingway, "The Quai at Smyrna," in *In Our Time* (New York: Boni and Liveright, 1925). For what it's worth, "On the Quai at Smyrna" is probably the first serious work of literature I read as a child.

24. Michael Llewellyn-Smith, *Ionian Vision: Greece in Asia Minor 1919-1922.* London: Hurst and Company, 1973.

25. See Matthew Stewart, "It Was All a Pleasant Business: The Historical Context of 'On the Quai at Smyrna,'" *Hemingway Review* 23, no. 1 (2003): 58–71; Adam Long, "Ernest Hemingway in Turkey: From *The Quai at Smyrna* to *A Farewell to Arms,*" *Hemingway Review* 38, no. 2 (Spring 2019): 75–86; David Wyatt, "Hemingway's Secret Histories," *Hopkins Review* 2, no. 4 (Fall 2009) (New Series): 485–504; Marcos Norris, "Reading 'On the Quai at Smyrna' and 'A Natural History of the Dead,'" in Consideration of Hemingway's Anti-Humanism, *Hemingway Review* 42, no. 2 (Spring 2023):

75–90; and Melissa Kalyoncu, "A Literary History of the Izmir/Smyrna Fire," MA thesis, Department of English and Comparative Literature, Columbia University, 2022.

26. The literature on Smyrna has an echo of Las Casas: shutting out "the shrieks of women and children being burned alive" by playing a phonograph record of Italian opera on the deck of a British dreadnought (104).

27. There is much evidence of screaming in Llewellyn-Smith, *Ionian Vision*, 330, 333.

28. Ernest Hemingway, A Farewell to Arms (New York: Modern Library, 1932).

29. I am grateful to Emily Chen for bringing to my attention the ambiguity of atrocity and meat-eating—which brutality is primary?—in Han Kang's *Human Acts* and *The Vegetarian*.

30. Aridjis, *Smyrna in Flames*.

31. Ishikawa Tatsuzo, *Soldiers Alive*, trans. with an introduction by Zeljko Cipris (Honolulu: University of Hawai'i Press, 1938).

32. Cipris, introduction to *Soldiers Alive*, 39.

33. The army priest, who participates in the killing, says he doesn't pray over the enemy dead. The adjutant remarks, "So religion doesn't cross frontiers, does it" (99). After this exchange, we read: "Perhaps he [the colonel] was suffering from moral anguish over his role as a leader in the great massacre" (100). He had hoped that religion can console him for the "certain sad emptiness" that comes over him when he kills Chinese captives. The problem is emotional, not moral. "Not that [his moral anguish] surfaced in his consciousness or in any way affected his conduct as an officer. War was the undertaking of a nation, and the spiritual contentment of a single man held no claim to consideration. Of course he knew that" (100).

34. With this trajectory in mind, you can look back and see other suggestions of moral scruple, however inadequate, that have been dropped along the way. The book makes the standard suggestion that though the officers disapproved, the enlisted men were uncontrollable: "With bold strides they roamed the city streets, searching for women like dogs chasing rabbits. Such unbridled conduct was strictly controlled at the North China front, but here it was difficult to restrain the men" (122). Genchō, an army priest who participates actively in the massacre of Chinese prisoners, can "think over the day's carnage not only without the slightest pangs of conscience, but even with exhilaration" (99). Here too the existence of "pangs of conscience" is posited even as those pangs are denied. Looting, which as we have seen is a universal driver of violence against civilians, is presented as an accident: "Because the supply ships had not yet landed, the soldiers were compelled to search for rice, meat, and vegetables wherever they went" (96).

35. James Wood, "Hysterical Realism," in *The Irresponsible Self* (New York: Farrar, Straus and Giroux, 2004).

36. Haruki Murakami, *Wind-Up Bird Chronicle*, New York: Knopf, 1995).

37. Kamila Shamsie, *Burnt Shadows* (New York: Picador, 2009).

38. Gabriel García Márquez, *One Hundred Years of Solitude* (New York: Harper and Row, 1967).

39. Salman Rushdie, *Midnight's Children* (New York: Avon, 1980).

40. Jeffrey Eugenides, *Middlesex* (New York: Farrar, Straus and Giroux, 2002).

41. Orhan Pamuk, *Snow* (New York: Knopf, 2002).

42. William Gardner Smith, *The Stone Face* (New York: New York Review of Books, [1963] 2021).

43. Philip Gourevitch's account of visiting the memorial to the dead in the Rwanda genocide sustains a similar ambiguity: "The more complete figures looked a lot like people, which they were once. A woman in a cloth wrap printed with flowers lay near the door. Her fleshless hip bones were high and her legs slightly spread, and a child's skeleton extended between them. Her torso was hollowed out. Her ribs and spinal column poked through the rotting cloth. Her head was tipped back and her mouth was open: a strange image—half agony, half repose." Thirteen months have gone by since the killing, as Gurevitch says. The effects of time are visible. "The dead looked like pictures of the dead. They did not smell. They did not buzz with flies. They had been killed thirteen months earlier, and they hadn't been moved. Skin stuck here and there over the bones, many of which lay scattered away from the bodies, dismembered by the killers, or by scavengers—birds, dogs, bugs." His description is his verbal memorial, his way of keeping the killings fresh in his own fashion, imperfectly and incompletely preserved, without denying the time that has passed. It's a mode of solidarity. It reminds us that, for better and for worse, time is not just decay. Philip Gourevitch, *We Wish to Inform You That Tomorrow We Will Be Killed with Our Families* (New York: Farrar, Straus and Giroux, 1998).

44. Jenny Erpenbeck, *Visitation*, trans. Susan Bernofsky (New York: New Directions, 2008).

45. Arundhati Roy, *The Ministry of Utmost Happiness* (New York: Knopf, 2017).

Chapter Five

1. Kurt Vonnegut, *Slaughter-House Five* (New York: Delacorte, 1969).

2. About the blaming, Vonnegut agrees enthusiastically; the absurdity of basing your selfhood on the desire for revenge gets called out in the novel more than once.

3. If coming unstuck in time and the visit to Tralfamadore are seen as symptoms of Billy Pilgrim's war trauma, we are obviously back in the domain of causes.

4. Roy Scranton, *Total Mobilization: World War II and American Literature* (Chicago: University of Chicago Press, 2019).

5. Primo Levi, *If This Is a Man/Survival in Auschwitz* (New York: Orion Press, 1959).

6. Claude Lanzmann, "Hier ist kein Warum," in *Au sujet de Shoah: Le film de Claude Lanzmann* (Paris: Belin, 1990), 279. Susan Neiman extracts more or less the same point from Hannah Arendt on Auschwitz: "To seek understanding, explanation,

catharsis, consolation—all goals of philosophical and literary reflection about earlier forms of evil—seems out of place" (238). "Seeking explanations" is "in this context, obscene" (286). Susan Neiman, *Evil in Modern Thought: An Alternative History of Philosophy* (Princeton, NJ: Princeton University Press, [2002] 2015).

7. Another interesting reference here is the commentary on Alcoholics Anonymous discourse in David Foster Wallace's *Infinite Jest* (New York: Little, Brown, 1996). "No whys or wherefores allowed" (374). "Do not ask WHY/If you don't want to DIE" (375).

8. This bit of classic wit is not as helpful as it seems. The catastrophe it imagines is the comprehension and forgiveness of *everything*, which is to say at a scale that few would be hubristic enough to propose. In so doing, it distracts from those more limited and contingent efforts to comprehend that are more widely practiced and, if not necessarily forgiveness, from whatever the affective, moral, and political results that greater comprehension might have.

9. "What is surprising," LaCapra says carefully, "is that Lanzmann takes up in his own voice, without adequate qualification and exegesis, the statement of an SS guard to Levi. He postulates this statement as constituting a valid law" (102). "A great deal—perhaps everything—depends not on whether one poses the *why* question but on how and why one poses it. . . . Levi himself wanted an answer, however partial and inadequate" (103, italics in original). Dominick LaCapra, *History and Memory after Auschwitz* (Ithaca, NY: Cornell University Press, 1998). In Vonnegut too, these words are repeated by a prison guard.

10. Jeremy Hawthorn, commenting on this scene, suggests "that Pannwitz's inability to see Levi as a human being is symmetrically matched by the narrating-Levi's inability to grant full humanity to Pannwitz" (151), while also noting an asymmetry: that Levi keeps thinking about Pannwitz afterwards, with curiosity. Jeremy Hawthorn, "The Face-to-Face Encounter in Holocaust Narrative," in *After Testimony: The Ethics and Aesthetics of Holocaust Narrative for the Future,* ed. Jakob Lothe, Susan Rubin Suleiman, and James Phelan (Columbus: The Ohio State University Press, 2012), 143–61.

11. Arno Mayer, *Why Did the Heavens Not Darken? The "Final Solution" in History* (New York: Pantheon, 1988).

12. Another hypothetical villain is the non-Jewish Kapo Alex, a banal thug who "displayed a lofty contempt for his ragged and starving chemists: '*Ihr Doktoren! Ihr Intelligenten*!' " (128). The proto-fascist class resentment, which does not entail membership in the Nazi party, reaches out for connections to other moments of atrocity.

13. Charlotte Delbo, *Auschwitz and After*, 2nd ed., trans. Rosette C. Lamont (New Haven, CT: Yale University Press, [1995] 2014), 91. Delbo and her fellow prisoners, starved and emaciated, have been put to work shoveling out a ditch. The work is backbreaking and seemingly meaningless, as there is a barbed wire fence just beyond it. She asks herself, "Then why the ditch?" And she replies to herself, "Why anything?" (90). On the next page, however, she discovers that there is after all a reason why, if not a satisfying one: "They want to make a garden at the camp entrance" (91). It is worth

adding that if racism is missing as a motive for the mistreatment of the French women, Delbo notes carefully that it does make a difference in the treatment of the Jewish women.

14. Götz Aly, *Hitler's Beneficiaries: Plunder, Racial War, and the Nazi Welfare State*, trans. Jefferson Chase (New York: Metropolitan Books, 2006). On the economics of Auschwitz, see also Adam Tooze, *The Wages of Destruction: The Making and Breaking of the Nazi Economy* (London: Allen Lane, 2006).

15. Inga Clendinnen, *Reading the Holocaust* (Cambridge: Cambridge University Press, 1999).

16. Sterling Michael Pavelec, *War and Warfare since 1945* (New York: Routledge, 2017).

17. It is not just Christian conservatives and militarists who are haunted by that specter. The idea of racism as original sin—the phrase has been a point of contention in the *New York Times*'s *1619 Project*—leads to much the same fatalistic view of eternally recurring atrocity. Like any other villain, racism is of course a way of making sense of atrocity. It is not intelligibility as such that is rejected here; it's history as a space of meaningful differences between less and more racism, more and less atrocity, hence also as a space in which there is room and motive for human effort.

18. Mark Levene and Penny Roberts, eds., *The Massacre in History* (New York: Berghahn, 1999).

19. The higher figure of 40,000 is given by Jörg Friedrich in *The Fire: The Bombing of Germany 1940–1945*, trans. Allison Brown (New York: Columbia University Press, 2006), 310. It is worth mentioning that Howard Zinn too cites Irving's statistics for the casualties at Dresden.

20. See Joachim Neander, "The Danzig Soap Case: Facts and Legends around 'Professor Spanner' and the Danzig Anatomic Institute 1944–1945," *German Studies Review* 29, no. 1 (February 2006): 63–86.

21. As if despite himself, however, Vonnegut does help understand the less exceptional history of which the world-historical atrocity is a meaningful part. His story about the candles and soap can also be read as a 1960s version of the commodity-origin narrative, taking in contemporary consumerism as well as the Holocaust.

22. William E. Connolly, *Capitalism and Christianity, American Style* (Durham, NC, and London: Duke University Press, 2008), 120. This line of thinking is further developed by Steven Johnston in *American Dionysia: Violence, Tragedy, and Democratic Politics* (Cambridge: Cambridge University Press, 2015).

23. "So it goes" is not restricted to atrocity, or the collective intentional killing of humans. The death by fumigation of bacteria, fleas, and body lice gets the same phrase (107), as does champagne that has gone flat, and certain other deaths also get it even if they are merely conjectural. One death that interestingly does *not* get a "so it goes" is the death of Vonnegut's father, mentioned in my first sentence above.

24. It seems worth noting that, when the COVID-19 pandemic broke out and

Camus's *The Plague* was suddenly all the rage, that novel was not a neat fit with COVID (nor for that matter a self-evident parable of French Resistance to the Nazi Occupation), and this because of its insistence on the absolute meaninglessness of the disease. It's clear that, for Camus, something can and should be done to treat the sick; there is a heroism of private citizens stepping up to serve the public welfare. But nothing is known about the causes of the plague they are called upon to fight. Camus was being programmatic: the world is incomprehensible. Yet this was not true about fascism, which had its sources within the society, French as well as German, that it attacked. Nor is it true about the COVID pandemic, one of whose sources was the destruction of the natural environment, exposing humans to the mutating viruses of undomesticated animals. For Camus, nothing can be understood or done about the plague's causes. It is immune both to history and to action.

25. John Hersey, *Hiroshima* (Stellar, 2014). Alexander Kluge cites an American visitor to Halberstadt who interviewed survivors. "The starting point of his study was the assumption that these unnecessary bombing raids created tenacious enemies, who would not stop thinking of revenge . . . The hypothesis could not be confirmed. Would he like another piece of cake?" (82). Alexander Kluge, *Air Raid* (London: Seagull, 2014).

26. The term was not respectful, but it would seem ungenerous to accuse those who used it of propagating a stereotypical association of fatalism with Muslims or non-Europeans.

27. Levi, *If This Is a Man.*

28. Nancy Fraser, "Is Capitalism Necessarily Racist?" *politicsslashletters*, May 20, 2019, http://quarterly.politicsslashletters.org/is-capitalism-necessarily-racist/.

29. In the "listless playthings of enormous forces" passage, Vonnegut adds that one effect of war is "that people are discouraged from being characters" (208–9), and the same holds for atrocity. "But old Derby was a character now" (209). The execution of a "character" after an atrocity that rules out characters gives this sequence an allegorical energy.

30. It's possible that a German taking a teapot from the ruins of Dresden would not have been shot; the Nazis certainly did their share of looting in the countries they occupied. But this was of course their own soil, and that might have made the authorities more severe. In any case, perhaps because Derby's execution occurs in the war's final days, when the Germans were about to disappear, the Russians were about to take over, and the prisoners were about to be shipped home, Vonnegut shows no interest whatsoever in anyone's nationality, including that of the Germans who presumably pull the trigger.

31. Ashik Kumar, "Fuck These Postmodern Writers: Meena Kandasamy's Depiction of Atrocity," *politicsslashletters,* August 28, 2017, http://quarterly.politicsslashletters.org/fuck-these-postmodern-writers/.

32. Meena Kandasamy, *The Gypsy Goddess* (London: Atlantic, 2014).

33. I am grateful to Ashik Kumar for bringing this passage to my attention. See Kumar, "Fuck These Postmodern Writers.

34. Julian Herbert, *The House of the Pain of Others: Chronicle of a Small Genocide,* trans. Christina McSweeney (Minneapolis, MN: Graywolf Press, [2015] 2019). Things that don't fit into the most familiar political patterns: the killing of Chinese by Mexicans. It was the revolutionary forces, fighting Porfirio Diaz, who seem to have opened up the possibility of the massacre, maybe even perpetrated it.

35. "The only atrocities associated with [the Korean war] were attributed to North Korean and Chinese troops. This is not unusual. As one expert in military law put it: 'Battlefield war crimes committed by one's own forces are almost never charged as such. Instead, they are simply alleged as the Uniform Code of Military Justice offenses of murder, rape, or aggravated assault . . . They are denominated war crimes only if committed by enemy nationals' " (244). Marilyn B. Young, "An Incident at No Gun Ri," in *Crimes of War: Guilt and Denial in the Twentieth Century*, ed. Omer Bartov, Atina Grossmann, and Mary Nolan (New York: The New Press, 2002), 244; Gary Solis and Edwin H Simmons, *Son Thang: An American War Crime* (Annapolis, MD, 1997), 108.

36. Hwang Sok-Yong, *The Guest*, trans. Kyung-Ja Chun and Maya West (New York: Seven Stories, 2005). Hwang structures his novel as twelve chapters for twelve rounds of shamanic exorcism, "designed to relieve the agony of those who survived and appease the spirits of those who were sacrificed on the altar of cultural imperialism half a century ago" (7). "During the Korean War," the author writes in a prefatory note, "the area of North Korea known as Hwanghae Province was the setting of a fifty-day nightmare during which the Christians and Communists—two groups of Korean people whose lives were shaped by two different 'guests'—committed a series of unspeakable atrocities against each other" (8).

37. The killers of El Mozote offer the same argument: "If we don't kill them now, they'll just grow up to be guerillas" (75). Mark Danner, *The Massacre at El Mozote: A Parable of the Cold War* (New York: Vintage, 1993).

38. "The atrocities that happened here weren't carried out by strangers—it was us, the people who'd lived together harmoniously in the same village . . . It was Satan who did it" (106). "We'd become the Lord's crusaders; they were the minions of Satan" (114). Hwang Sok-Yong, *The Guest.*

39. Bapsi Sidhwa, *Cracking India* (Minneapolis: Milkweed, 1991).

40. Arundhati Roy, *The God of Small Things* (New York: Harper, 1998). It is perhaps no more than coincidence that in "When Mr. Pirzada Came to Dine" Jhumpa Lahiri puts an account of the atrocities committed in the course of the further partition of Pakistan in 1971, that is to say the independence of Bangladesh, into the mouth of another child narrator, much as Salman Rushdie does in *Midnight's Children.*

41. Jhumpa Lahiri, "When Mr. Pirzada Came to Dine," in *The Interpreter of Maladies* (Boston: Houghton Mifflin Harcourt, 2000).

42. Lydia Davis, "Addie and the Chili," *Harper's*, January 2019, 69–71.

43. Peter Singer, "Famine, Affluence, and Morality," *Philosophy and Public Affairs* 1, no. 3 (Spring, 1972): 229–43.

44. "Perhaps the best argument against modern warfare," Claudia Card writes, "is that it cannot be conducted without atrocities" (12). If warfare cannot be conducted without atrocities, and if the record shows that warfare cannot not be conducted, then it follows that atrocity is, again, a form of fate. Claudia Card, *The Atrocity Paradigm* (New York: Oxford University Press, 2002).

45. Theodore Roethke, "The Waking," in *Words for the Wind* (Garden City, NY: Doubleday, 1958).

46. Gabriel García Márquez, *One Hundred Years of Solitude* (New York: Harper and Row, 1967).

47. This may be noticeable only because such a destination is lacking in the massacre scene in John Berger's *G.*, another work inspired by García Márquez. In *G.*, correspondingly, those who expose themselves to the army's guns seem to know exactly what they are doing. With the exception of the child and the Roman girl who is minding him, they do not try to escape.

48. John Berger, "Che Guevara Dead," *Aperture*, Spring 1968, https://issues.aperture.org/article/1968/1/1/che-guevara-dead.

49. John Berger, *G.* (London: Weidenfeld and Nicholson, 1972).

50. The other tenet of liberal wisdom that Berger is trying to avoid is the idea that atrocities are senseless, chaotic, incomprehensible, or (what amounts to the same thing) that atrocities are simply to be expected from time to time on the basis of what we know of human nature and the human condition, hence are to be dealt with on an ad hoc basis. Berger wrote *G.* before the current fashion for trauma theory, which generalizes the atrocity as the very paradigm of historical experience: experience as non-experience, as an event so overwhelming that it is unassimilable to conscious experience. And he was writing before the fashion for humanitarian intervention, which suggests that something can indeed be done to stop atrocity, but it must be done by ourselves, that is, by outsiders who represent a normal and orderly world, rather than by people on the ground, who are seen as morally compromised if not stereotypically and universally genocidal. I also want to give him credit for preempting both of these seemingly persuasive styles of representing atrocity.

Chapter Six

1. John Hersey, *Hiroshima* (Stellar, 2014).

2. Kenzaburo Oe, *Hiroshima Notes*, trans. David L. Swain and Toshi Yonezawa (Marian Boyars Publishers, 1995).

3. Charlotte Delbo, *Auschwitz and After*, 2nd ed., trans. Rosette C. Lamont. (New Haven, CT: Yale University Press, [1995] 2014).

4. Primo Levi, *If This Is a Man/Survival in Auschwitz* (New York: Orion Press, 1959).

5. Levi also mentions two diphtheria patients separated from their room by a wooden wall who, having heard his name by chance, "never ceased groaning and imploring" (197). Levi writes: "Naturally I would have liked to have helped them, given

the means and the strength, if for no other reason than to stop their crying" (197–98). The tense here ("would have liked to") indicates that he did *not* help them. He then proceeds to admit that he did in fact help them, bringing them some water and some soup. "The result was that from then on, through the thin wall, the whole diarrhoea ward shouted my name day and night . . . without my being able to do anything about it. I felt like crying. I could have cursed them" (198).

6. Zadie Smith, "The Embassy of Cambodia," *New Yorker*, February 11 and 18, 2013, 88–98, https://www.newyorker.com/magazine/2013/02/11/the-embassy-of-cambodia.

7. It is easier to mock the rhetoric of numerical comparison of atrocities than to decide once and for all that it should be disqualified. Consider for example an essay that starts by quoting the report of the police president of Hamburg about Operation Gomorrrah, the fire storm ignited by Allied bombing in July and August of 1943. "The scenes of terror which took place in the firestorm area are indescribable. Children were torn away from their parents' hands by the force of the hurricane and whirled into the fire. . . ." According to Overy, more than 18,000 people were killed in the raid of July 27 alone. That is a large number. But "it is certainly unimpressive," Luttwak goes on, "compared with what the police president's own men achieved: Hamburg's reserve police battalion 101, manned by 'ordinary' policemen, never numbered more than five hundred and its members were armed only with pistols and bolt-action rifles. Even so, it had killed 38,000 Jews by November 1943, when it took the lead in the Erntefest ('harvest festival') operation in the Lublin district, in which another 42,000 Jews were killed" (23). Edward Luttwak, "Opportunity Costs," his review of Overy in the *London Review of Books*, November 21, 2013, 23–24. Sven Lundqvist's *History of Bombing* also has a talent for numerical synthesis. For example: "British air attacks on Hamburg killed more people than all German air attacks against English cities put together. About 50,000 people died in a single night, the night of July 27, 1943. The majority of them were women, children, and old people" (95). Lindqvist supplies ample description of the results on the ground. One example, after Dresden: "It became harder and harder to identify the victims. Now they arrived in bathtubs or wooden tubs. On the top of one tub a note read: 'Thirty-two dead from the X bomb shelter, number X, X Street.' 'My God! Thirty-two dead! And they could all fit in a bathtub. And the tub wasn't even full'" (104). Sven Lindqvist, *A History of Bombing,* trans. Linda Haverty Rugg (New York: The New Press, 2001).

8. The Rape of Nanjing at the hands of invading Japanese troops in the winter of 1937–1938, in which more noncombatants probably died than at Hiroshima and Nagasaki combined, is not up for comparison here.

9. "The Embassy of Cambodia" has a lot of history in it—perhaps even more than shows on the surface. The Monty Python skit to which Smith alludes is from 1970. 1970 is the year the Khmer Republic was proclaimed, leading circuitously five years later (as it happens, the year of Smith's birth) to the Cambodian genocide in which some 1.7 million people died. These temporal coincidences may not be significant. It

may or may not be relevant here that Gabriel García Márquez, whose massacre description in *One Hundred Years of Solitude* is one of the most visited landmarks of this would-be literary itinerary, rearranged the date of his birth (1929) to make it coincide with the historical atrocity to which he was referring in 1928. Smith is more obviously interested in other connections between the present and the Khmer Rouge massacre, for example the fact that its target was a section of the population she calls "New People" or "city dwellers" (94). The story notes that this is a category to which Fatou and her glasses-wearing friend Andrew belong.

10. "It was Satan who did it" (106). Hwang Sok-Yong, *The Guest*, trans. Kyung-Ja Chun and Maya West (New York: Seven Stories, 2005).

11. It's much the same ambiguity—a concession that interest in strangers must be limited, and a dissatisfaction with any given set of limits—that George Eliot put into her famous lines from *Middlemarch:* "If we had a keen vision and feeling of all ordinary human life, it would be like hearing the grass grow, and the squirrel's heart beat, and we should die of that roar that lies on the other side of silence." You might say, channeling Smith, that these are the two paths that fiction has to walk, traditionally and impossibly, at the same time. Knowing you can't, and nonetheless unable not to try.

12. Claire Messud, *The Emperor's Children* (New York: Vintage, 2006).

13. William Gibson, *Pattern Recognition* (New York: Putnam, 2003).

14. Joseph O'Neill, *Netherland* (New York: Pantheon, 2008).

15. Don DeLillo, *Falling Man* (New York: Scribner, 2007).

16. Hammad is like us in his epiphany that "most countries are run by madmen" (78), and perhaps even in his doubts about the anti-Semitism of one of his friends: "Hammad wasn't sure whether this was funny, true or stupid" (79). DeLillo, *Falling Man*.

17. Roy Scranton, *Total Mobilization: World War II and American Literature* (Chicago: University of Chicago Press, 2019). Scranton quotes Paul Fussell's judgment was that World War II was "wholly meaningless." He quotes Fussell: "It takes some honesty, even if that honesty arises from despair, to perceive that some events, being inhuman, have no human meaning" (230).

18. Jonathan Franzen, *The Corrections* (New York: Farrar, Straus and Giroux, 2001).

19. Don DeLillo, *Underworld* (New York: Scribner, 1997).

20. Bharati Mukherjee, *Jasmine* (New York : Grove Weidenfeld, 1989).

21. This pattern of immigration as redemption goes back at least as far as Abraham Cahan's *The Rise of David Levinsky* (1917), where Russian anti-Semitic violence at the beginning of the novel sponsors the journey to America and motivates the protagonist's ruthless social ascent. Though recent examples sometimes involve a much fuller treatment of the relevant historical episode, they usually keep to the same rough scheme.

22. Junot Diaz, *The Brief Wondrous Life of Oscar Wao* (New York: Penguin, 2007).

23. Jeffrey Eugenides, *Middlesex* (New York: Farrar, Straus and Giroux, 2002).

24. Michael Chabon's *The Amazing Adventures of Kavalier and Clay* (New York: Random House, 2000).

25. Dave Eggers, *What Is the What: The Autobiography of Valentino Achak Deng* (San Francisco: McSweeney's, 2006).

26. Yambo Ouologuem, *Bound to Violence*, trans. Ralph Manheim (New York: Harcourt Brace Jovanovitch, 1971).

27. Amitav Ghosh, *The Hungry Tide* (London: Harper Collins, 2004).

28. Boubacar Boris Diop, *Murambi, The Book of Bones*, trans. Fiona McLaughlin (Bloomington: Indiana University Press, 2006). In much the same neighborly spirit, Edwidge Danticat's treatment of the 1937 Parsley Massacre of Haitian workers in *The Farming of Bones* (1998) indicts the government of the Dominican Republic.

29. Frederic Jameson, *Allegory and Ideology* (London: Verso, 2019).

30. Scranton, *Total Mobilization*. Scranton quotes a 1951 Robert Lowell review of Randall Jarrell: "The determined, passive, sacrificial lives of the pilots, inwardly so harmless and outwardly so destructive" (36). Scranton's subject is a "portrayal of power relations that sees agents who exercise power as first and foremost victims of that self-same power" (36).

31. This is apparently true to the historical record. According to Gerald Astor's *The Mighty Eighth: The Air War in Europe as Told by the Men Who Fought It*, which relies on the diaries of the airmen, the civilian dead were invisible to them. What the airmen saw was their own deadly struggle with fighters and flak, a struggle to hit their targets and escape with their lives. Written accounts of the air war are plentiful and relatively reliable, Astor notes, because the Army Air Corps demanded of its personnel, at least initially, two years of college. My father had not attended college, but he arrived later, when the Air Corps "ran out of qualified candidates" (xi) and instead assigned written examinations. Gerald Astor, *The Mighty Eighth: The Air War in Europe As Told by the Men Who Fought It* (New York: Berkley Caliber, 1997).

32. Pivoting on the ambiguity of the German word for victim, *Opfer*, which also means sacrifice, Fatima Naqvi argues that victimhood contributes to a sacrificial logic of democratic equality and social belonging (14). Naqvi takes off from Baudrillard's diagnosis of the West's self-perception as a "victim society," paradoxical because, as Naqvi notes, "the West is still, in economic and political terms, in a position of superior power and, if anything, victimizer rather than victim" (1). She is mainly interested in Austria, which of course had some national investment in seeing itself as victimized by rather than complicit with the Austrian Adolf Hitler. "Victim status, rather than being shunned per se, appears as a means to create a tenuous affiliation within a radically atomized society" after 1968 (3–4). Fatima Naqvi, *The Literary and Cultural Rhetoric of Victimhood: Western Europe, 1970–2005* (New York: Palgrave Macmillan 2007).

33. Daniel Swift, *Bomber Country: The Poetry of a Lost Pilot's War* (New York: Farrar, Straus and Giroux, 2010).

34. A. C. Grayling, *Among the Dead Cities: The History and Moral Legacy of the*

WWII Bombing of Civilians in Germany and Japan (New York: Walker and Company, 2006). It matters "to recognize and accept that the Allied bomber forces' area-bombing campaigns constitute moral crimes," Grayling writes, because "it is only if a civilization looks at itself frankly and accepts what it sees [that it can] hope to learn from the exercise, and progress in the right way and direction thereafter" (274). Admitting that the bombing was wrong "places on even firmer footing our just condemnation of the atrocities of Nazism in particular and Axis aggression in general, because we do not pretend to have clean hands ourselves" (280).

35. Tami Davis Biddle, *Rhetoric and Reality in Air Warfare: The Evolution of British and American Ideas about Strategic Bombing, 1914–1945* (Princeton, NJ: Princeton University Press, 2002). Richard Overy, *The Bombers and the Bombed: Allied Air War over Europe, 1940–1945* (New York: Viking Penguin, 2013).

36. Astor, *The Mighty Eighth.*

37. Precision was more of an aspiration than a reality. My father flew his missions, in early 1945, under "conditions of heavy cloud cover, which included the majority of missions for the Eighth Air Force over the winter of 1944–45." During that period, "42 per cent of bombs fell more than five miles from the target. Of those inside the five-mile radius, the average circular error was 2.48 miles." Biddle, *Rhetoric and Reality in Air Warfare,* 243. No mention is made here of what was hit by the bombs that did not hit their target.

38. Astor, *The Mighty Eighth.*

39. Overy, *The Bombers and the Bombed.* Overy writes: "All of these raids, and not just the attack on Dresden, were undertaken in full knowledge that these cities were filled with civilian refugees from farther east, and that their destruction was likely to cause not just dislocation but high casualties as well" (213). After Dresden, Overy writes, "for the first time the real nature of area and blind bombing came under public scrutiny" (215).

40. Jörg Friedrich, *The Fire: The Bombing of German 1940–1945,* trans. Allison Brown (New York: Columbia University Press, 2006). On "spontaneous violence" against downed aircrews, see also Overy, *The Bombers and the Bombed,* 310–11.

41. Overy, *The Bombers and the Bombed.*

42. Stephen E. Ambrose, *The Wild Blue: The Men and Boys Who Flew the B-24s over Germany (*New York: Simon and Schuster, 2001).

43. Ambrose then decides that Germany's economy was indeed crippled in the last ten months of the war (249), so that what the bombers did "was critical to the victory" (251). Other historians have disputed this.

44. Scranton, *Total Mobilization.*

45. Grayling, *Among the Dead Cities.*

46. The series seems on target, on the other hand, in its treatment of the risks the airmen ran. The premise of the book by Donald L. Miller that's the basis of the series is that the bombing was an experiment in waging war without the bloodshed of trench

warfare. If so, the experiment was not a success; in the first year or two, anyone who survived the flak and the fighters was lucky. "Bomber crews . . . suffered the highest casualty rates for any branch of services in the Second World War" (Patrick Deer, *Culture in Camouflage: War, Empire, and Modern British Literature* (Oxford: Oxford University Press, 2009), 63. Scranton: "One statistical study followed 2,051 American bomber crewmen through a series of twenty-five missions with the Eighth Air Force over Germany. Slightly more than a quarter of the men completed all twenty-five missions. 15.8 per cent were lost for noncombat reasons (death, disease, administrative removal), and 58.3 per cent—eleven hundred ninety-five men—were killed or lost in action." Scranton, *Total Mobilization*, 26. By early 1945, with fewer German fighters in the sky, the odds of surviving your twenty-five missions were higher.

47. Alexander Kluge, *Air Raid* (London: Seagull, 2014).

48. Primo Levi, *If This Is a Man/Survival in Auschwitz* (New York: Orion Press, 1959).

49. "We Italians had decided to meet every Sunday evening in a corner of the Lager, but we stopped it at once, because it was too sad to count our numbers and find fewer each time . . . It was better not to think" (34). Counting is on the side of thinking. Levi is wary of it, but he never stops doing it. "As will be told, the Buna factory, on which the Germans were busy for four years and for which countless of us suffered and died, never produced a pound of synthetic rubber" (82). "The result of this pitiless process of natural selection could be read in the statistic of Lager population movements. At Auschwitz in 1944, of the old Jewish prisoners (we will not speak of the others here, as their condition was different), '*kleine Nummer,*' low numbers less than 150,000, only a few hundred had survived; not one was an ordinary Häftling" (102). "We were ninety-six, when we arrived, we, the Italians of convoy 174,000; only twenty-nine of us survived until October, and of these, eight went in the selection. We are now twenty-one and the winter has hardly begun" (159). Levi, *If This Is a Man/Survival in Auschwitz.*

50. Friedrich, *The Fire.*

51. Thomas Hippler, *Governing from the Skies: A Global History of Aerial Bombing*, trans. David Fernbach (London: Verso, 2017).

52. Overy, *The Bombers and the Bombed.*

53. Hippler, *Governing from the Skies.*

54. Eric Hobsbawm, "War and Peace in the 20th Century," *London Review of Books*, February 21, 2002, 16–18.

55. Martin Puchner, *The Written World: The Power of Stories to Shape People, History, Civilization* (New York: Random House, 2017). The moral of Puchner's chapter is that Alexander's love for the *Iliad*, which inspired his conquests, led to the spread of the Greek language, alphabet, and culture, spawning cosmopolitanism and its best-known ancient institution, the library of Alexandria. Culture follows and justifies conquest: it's a moral that the epic tradition would not forget.

56. Matthew White estimates that 500,000 people died during Alexander's cam-

paigns, including 250,000 civilians. In absolute numbers, he ranks these thirteen years only 70th among the 100 worst atrocities of world history. But if there were 125 million people alive around 330 BC, those killed as a direct result of Alexander's wars would be a higher percentage of the world population than the number of Jews killed in the Holocaust. *The Great Big Book of Horrible Things: The Definitive Chronicle of History's 100 Worst Atrocities* (New York: Norton 2012).

57. Jill Lepore, *The Name of War: King Philip's War and the Origins of American Identity* (New York: Vintage, 1998).

58. "Almost without exception, the English interpreted Algonquian assaults, and the taunts that accompanied them, as expressions of mindless savagery or as divine retribution rather than as calculated assaults on the English way of life" (96). Lepore, *The Name of War.*

59. Hayden V. White, *The Greco-Roman Tradition* (New York: Harper and Row, 1973).

60. It is worth speculating that the standard anti-humanist position might hide a secret complicity with the mainstream view that there is nothing of value to get out of commentary on Alexander's bloody conquests. See for example Sayak Valencia, *Gore Capitalism*, trans. John Pluecker (South Pasadena, CA: Semiotexte, 2018). Her thesis, Sayak says, is that gore is the core. "The foundation of gore is humanism itself" (119).

61. Ari Shavit, *My Promised Land* (New York: Spiegel and Grau, 2013).

62. Overy, *The Bombers and the Bombed.*

Epilogue

1. Bret Stephens, "Israel Was Shattered on Oct. 7. Can It Recover?" *New York Times*, November 12, 2023, Opinion section, 6.

2. As of this writing, developing events, including the thousands of dead women and children whose pictures the major media have found themselves unable not to cover, seem to have had no impact on Stephens; he remains as morally tone-deaf as ever. "I blame Hamas, not Israel, for the devastation." Bret Stephens, "Israel Has No Choice But to Fight On," *New York Times*, March 13, 2024, A19.

3. Marco D'Eramo, "Mithridatisation," *New Left Review,* blog, February 21, 2022, trans. Francesco Anselmetti, https://newleftreview.org/sidecar/posts/mithridatisation.

4. Michel Foucault, *Discipline and Punish: The Birth of the Prison,* trans. Alan Sheridan (New York: Vintage/Random House, [1977] 1979).

5. Kristofer J. Petersen-Overton, "The Bull of Phalaris: Atrocity in the Canon," APSA Preprints, January 8, 2020, https://preprints.apsanet.org/engage/api-gateway/apsa/assets/orp/resource/item/5e15f685afc3ff001967352f/original/the-bull-of-phalaris-atrocity-in-the-canon.pdf.

6. Ari Shavit, *My Promised Land* (New York: Spiegel and Grau, 2013).

7. Most of Shavit's interviews are with his fellow Israelis. But there is one with a Palestinian from Lydda. "What hurts Ottman most is the humiliating way the soldiers

search the women's bodies at the checkpoint on the outskirts of Lydda. One soldier takes Ottman's cash, another takes his wristwatch. The rucksacks of the Jewish soldiers are now filling up quickly with necklaces and earrings, silver and gold" (129). To the extent that it condones the atrocity, however, Shavit's text should not be wholeheartedly congratulated for the act of national self-accusation it does nonetheless perform. See S. Yizhar's Hebrew classic *Khirbet Khizeh*, which offers further testimony to the causal link between atrocity and acquisitiveness. Trans. Nicholas de Lange and Yaacob Dweck, afterword by David Shulman (Jerusalem: Ibis, 2008).

8. Colonialism, as a structural motive for violence, is no more central to Mark Danner's account of violence in El Salvador in the 1980s than to Shavit's conception of what happened at Lydda. The guerrillas whom the army was seeking did not call themselves indigenous, nor did the villagers who were accused, falsely, of aiding the guerrillas. In retrospect, however, *The Massacre at El Mozote* can be understood as one atrocity in a colonial war, supported by the United States as an anti-Communist crusade, for which violence like this was not exceptional. The soldiers went along the lines of villagers, Danner writes, "pulling from their fingers any rings they saw, then ordering them to turn over their jewelry and crucifixes and anything else that might have some value" (64). This in addition to wanting to know "the guerrillas' means of support—how they were getting their food" (66) and "who was selling them arms" (66). Mark Danner, *The Massacre at El Mozote: A Parable of the Cold War* (New York: Vintage, 1993).

9. George Saunders, "Thursday," *New Yorker*, June 12, 2023.

10. G. W. F Hegel, *The Philosophy of History*, trans. J. Sibree (New York: Collier, 1901).

Index